PRAISE FOR T[illegible]

“This book is a bouquet of bea[illegible] ys which delight the [illegible] the knowledge that plants are living organisms and we need to celebrate their sublime qualities with awe and gratitude. *The Mind of Plants* integrates the science of ecology and biology with the pleasure of poetry and literature. It should be read by all those who wish to learn about the intricate mystery of plant life.”

— Satish Kumar
Founder of Schumacher College, Editor Emiritus, Resurgence & Ecologist

“Ryan, Viera, and Gagliano have cultivated an exemplary herbarium of stories, poems, and deeply personal essays centered around plants themselves. Each contribution begins from the uncommon assumption of intelligence in plants and presents novel ways of thinking about and with each species. Incorporating critical insights on plants from the sciences and humanities, *The Mind of Plants* is sensuous, grounded, and accessible. This book is vital for anyone who has ever felt a connection with a plant.”

— Laura Pustarfi, PhD
Plant Studies Scholar

“How can you not love a botanical treasure trove that begins with apples and ayahuasca, ends with yoco and yopo and features inspired writing from luminaries like Robin Kimmerer, Luis Eduardo Luna, Dennis McKenna and Jeremy Narby? A feast for the heart, mind, and ethnobotanical soul!”

— Mark Plotkin, PhD
Ethnobotanist and Host of The Plants of the Gods Podcast

“I absorbed *The Mind of Plants* whole in just two days. With impressive breadth this book introduced me to plants around the world and to their place in different cultures. From metaphorically setting down roots to the literal thoughts engendered by electrical pulses, each chapter elegantly introduced different concepts and made me reflect as much on myself as on the natural world.”

— Alice Little
Writer in Residence, Wytham Woods, University of Oxford

"This wide-ranging collection serves up forty essays and fourteen poems that, each in its own singular voice, collectively meditate on how and why plants scratch, sting, enchant, nourish, illuminate, intoxicate and enslave us. Equal parts herbal manual and alchemical spell book, this beautifully illustrated volume will appeal to scientists, shamans and poets alike." thoughtfully explores these issues."

— Glenn H. Shepard Jr., PhD
Ethnobotanist and Museum Curator at the Goeldi Museum, Brazil

"This eclectic 21st century Herbal will take you on a joyous ride of discovery of connection between plants and people. Through the medium of stories, poetry or science the complexity and beauty of plant intelligence is reflected. This surprising, illuminating and diverse collection is a much needed antidote to 'plant blindness' so common in our societies, encouraging us to see, hear and feel the green life all around us."

— Anya Ermakova, PhD
Chacruna Council for the Protection of Sacred Plants

"*The Mind of Plants* is a portal of vital and overdue importance. The diverse, intimate layers of human and vegetal voices and experiences move us beyond the confines of our homo sapiens centrality to absorb, open to, and be opened by the ways trees and plants know, initiate, navigate, socialize, shape—mind— their lives and communities. Emerging from the portal, changed and humbled, we are held in a deepened sense of awe, interconnection, love, respect, perspective, and empathy for the minded aliveness and engagements of plants in their own right.

— Dr. Sarah Abbott
Interdisciplinary Researcher of Sentient Relations of Trees,
Associate Professor at the University of Regina, Canada

"For millennia, we have taken the vegetable world for granted, deeming it inferior and devoid of inner purpose or complexity. This beautifully-curated volume combines research, cross-cultural narratives and personal experiences to unveil a profoundly different plant world, inviting us to rethink what we mean by intelligence and to reevaluate our place in Nature with open minds and renewed humility."

— Marcelo Gleiser, 2019 Templeton Prize Laureate
Author of *The Simple Beauty of the Unexpected*

THE MIND OF PLANTS

Narratives of Vegetal Intelligence

Edited by John C. Ryan,
Patrícia Vieira,
and Monica Gagliano

Foreword by Dennis McKenna

SYNERGETICPRESS

Synergetic Press | 1 Bluebird Court, Santa Fe, NM 87508 &
24 Old Gloucester St. London, WC1N 3AL England

Library of Congress Cataloging-in-Publication Data is available.

ISBN 9780907791874 (paperback)
ISBN 9780907791881 (ebook)

Cover and interior illustrations by Jose Maria Pout
Cover Design by Amanda Müller & Brad Greene
Book design by Brad Greene
Managing Editor: Amanda Müller
Printed in Canada by Marquis

TABLE OF CONTENTS

ACKNOWLEDGMENTS

The editors are grateful for the contributors' openness to exploring the mind of plants idea through such evocative, moving, and diverse accounts of flora from around the world. The cosmopolitan congregation of species featured in this anthology reflects the botanical passions of our essayists, poets, and artists.

We extend our sincere thanks to Doug Reil, Deborah Snyder, and the team at Synergetic Press for their enthusiastic belief in the project. We are also grateful for Amanda Müller's assistance with all aspects of editing and design.

John C. Ryan thanks the School of Arts and Social Sciences at Southern Cross University, Australia, and the Nulungu Research Institute at the University of Notre Dame, Australia, for their encouragement.

Patrícia Vieira acknowledges the generous support of the Portuguese Foundation for Science and Technology (Project IF/00606/2015), of the Center for Social Studies of the University of Coimbra, and of the Department of Spanish and Portuguese of Georgetown University.

Monica Gagliano acknowledges the generous support of Templeton World Charity Foundation under Diverse Intelligences Initiative (Project TWCF 0541) and all the plant people for their continued inspiration.

FOREWORD

In this unique anthology, the editors have invited people from a variety of backgrounds and disciplines to share their personal reflections and stories of their interactions with plants that have been meaningful in their lives. In doing so, they are not asking for a scientific treatise; those can be found in many other places, but will not be found in this collection. Instead, what the reader will find here, expressed in poetry and prose, are stories that are infused with cherished memories and inspired celebrations of unique relationships with a group of organisms that are alien and unlike us in every way, yet touch human lives in myriad ways.

Plants surround us and nurture us along with the entire community of species on the planet, whether we are paying attention or not (and we are often not). In the course of evolution, plants have mastered a rather miraculous biochemical trick: *photosynthesis.* Photosynthesis is the process whereby plants capture the energy of the sun using light-harvesting pigments (chlorophylls) and use that energy to reduce an inorganic compound, carbon dioxide (CO_2), to simple sugars. In this process, molecular oxygen (O_2), is produced as a byproduct of the reaction. Photosynthesis sustains life on earth. It is the process by which cosmic energy (solar energy) is brought into the biosphere to drive the machineries of life. It is the major means by which carbon dioxide is removed from the atmosphere and "fixed" into the biomass of organisms and by which oxygen is released into the atmosphere. This is most convenient for us and everything else that breathes because oxygen is essential to support the metabolism of (almost) all organisms (including plants, which have respiration as well as photosynthetic, carbon fixing capabilities). The simple sugars produced in the initial stages of photosynthesis are further spun into a maze of biosynthetic reaction pathways to generate a vast diversity of organic compounds. These compounds are literally the "stuff of life." Because they have mastered photosynthesis, producing the molecules on which the rest of life depends and of which it is composed, every other living thing in the biosphere that is not photosynthetic is effectively a parasite on plants. But plants do not seem to mind; in fact, they benefit from their relationships with less biochemically agile species in other ways. For example, they benefit from insects that pollinate them and enable them to complete their reproductive cycles. They benefit from birds and animals who consume their fruits and seeds and spread the seeds throughout the ecosystem. They benefit from humans as well, who sometimes "adopt" the plants by cultivating them, thus facilitating what must be one of the primary objectives for a plant: To grow, to spread, to reproduce. These plant relationships with insects, animals, humans, and other organisms such as fungi and bacteria, are all examples of symbiosis—close relationships between different organisms that are often mutually beneficial.

Because plants have succeeded, through photosynthesis, in tapping into the virtually limitless power of sunlight as a source of energy, they have evolved into virtuoso chemists. Energy is not a limitation on their chemical creativity. And a result of this is that plants, besides producing all the compounds on which life depends for sustenance—such as carbohydrates, lipids, and proteins—have also elaborated a vast array of complex chemical compounds that serve a signaling function that mediate their relationships with other living things in their environment. It is by means of these "messenger molecules" that plants respond to and interact with virtually all organisms in their environment. Effectively, plants substitute "biosynthesis" for behavior. If plants have language, that language is chemistry. By means of these chemically mediated signal transduction processes, plants optimize their relationships with other life-forms in their environment, from other plants, fungi and bacteria, to birds and insects, to herbivores, and included in this latter category are humans. In some instances, the message that plants express is simple: it may be saying, "stay away" by producing toxins that may range from unpalatable to lethal. Plants are very good at protecting themselves through creative chemistry. But their chemical messages can become more complex, and their interactions with other organisms more interesting, when the message is "come closer"—let's explore forming a symbiotic relationship. It is those sorts of relationships, when the message is received by curious, big-brained primates (like us) that the chemical conversation can become most interesting. Through the course of experimentation over evolutionary time spans, we curious primates have succeeded in discovering many plant compounds that may have evolved originally as toxins, but that we have repurposed for our own beneficial or therapeutic purposes. Thereby we respond to the plant's chemical messages in ways that the plant never "intended," but that serves the purpose of supporting the symbiotic relationship. We benefit from the pharmacological properties of the plant's compounds, and domesticate it and grow it, thus protecting it from the vicissitudes of natural selection, (albeit subjecting it to the influences of artificial selection, which may be far worse in the long run).

This chemical dialog between plants and humans can become especially interesting when the plant produces compounds that happen to target receptor networks in our hypertrophied brains that are involved in our subjective experience of consciousness and awareness. It is in these interactions that we may come closest to experiencing a "dialogue" with the plant that may resemble an ordinary human conversation. Such experiences may cause us to project human characteristics, such as personality, onto the plant, leading us to anthropomorphize them. We see this reflected, often, in reference to certain psychedelic plants where they may be referred to as "madre ayahuasca" or "grandfather peyote." While this projection may be useful in a ceremonial or ritual context, we should not be fooled. Plants may well have a kind of consciousness, but it is nothing like ours. What the psychedelic plant compounds do is target a set of receptors that mediate our subjective experience of consciousness. There is no surprise in this. Many psychoactive plant "messenger compounds" resemble brain neurotransmitters, in some cases are identical to them, although they originated in plants long before complex mammalian nervous systems evolved, and adapted them for internal, signal transduction functions, what we call "neurotrasmission."

Some of the stories relayed in this anthology reflect the plant/human dialogs that can arise from symbiotic alliances with psychoactive plants. Others reflect symbiotic relationships that may not involve psychopharmacology; plants have many other ways to entice us into symbiosis. We may find them delicious; they may have a pleasing scent; they may have beautiful flowers. All of these can be a basis for symbiosis. And all of these relationships can in some sense be attributed to plants' unique "language," chemistry, that biochemical creativity that enables them to communicate with every other organism in their environment. Though it may seem reductionist to say this, but it is not an exaggeration to say that almost everything we value about plants in the end comes down to their chemical properties.

Plants do not write stories; plants create their own stories simply in the process of living. Humans write stories about their relationships with plants, and they are reflections of their interactions with them. Chemistry almost always plays a central role in initiating and sustaining those relationships. What awaits the reader who follows the editors' suggestion to skip randomly through the selections offered here and engage with what seems most interesting (and they all, it turns out, are interesting and thought-provoking) is a rich menu of engaging and delightful stories written by humans, about their experiences with plants. In this way, perhaps, the plants in the relationship can translate their message into human language, and thereby expand our appreciation for them and the ancient co-evolutionary symbioses that they have shared, not only with humans but with the entire biospheric community of species since the dawn of time.

Dennis J. McKenna, PhD
Abbotsford, British Columbia
May 2021

INTRODUCTION: ON BECOMING PLANT-MINDED

John C. Ryan, Patrícia Vieira, and Monica Gagliano

PALM

The fan-like leaves of palm trees shake, clatter, then settle after a rousing gust of wind. Their strong, bare trunks sway, almost imperceptibly, over the water-logged paddies where rice is beginning to green the muddy surface. Wherever we find ourselves—on a tropical beach at dawn or in a temperate city at night—palms accompany us. They are the sweet, sticky dates eaten after long fasts in many parts of the world and the spoonfuls of thick oil lending a rich taste to a variety of foods. They are the worn rattan chairs that creak as families meet around dinner tables. That the word *palm* also refers anatomically to a part of the hand suggests the tactile connection between the tree and humanity. What's more, especially for residents of cold climates, palms symbolize fertility, serenity, and escape from winter doldrums. Bending themselves to the elements, the trees embody gracefulness, adaptability, and resilience. It was the poet Rabindranath Tagore who, after observing a palm tree battered by a storm, wrote, "the fronds subside, subside / the mind of the tree returns / To earth, recalls that earth is its mother."[1]

The mind of the tree returns. Recalls that earth is its mother. As a minded being, Tagore's tousled tree feels love and remembers. These reflections on the palm illustrate, for us, the process of becoming *plant-minded*—of attending to plants as they reciprocally attend to us, in the symbiotic dance that sustains the Earth and all life. Through expressions of care, curiosity, and openness, we can become entrained to the clanging fronds, the lithe trunk, the ripening fruit, and the vibrant human-plant networks of which they are part. Guided by these ideas, *The Mind of Plants* presents a lively convocation of plants, people, and places that, as editors, we hope will inspire fresh ways of seeing—of feeling and of being with—the photosynthetic personae with whom we share this precious, imperiled planet. Our anthology takes as its starting point current research in fields such as plant signaling and behavior that calls attention to the capacity of vegetal life to discern between options, learn from prior experiences, and negotiate traumatic memories to minimize adverse effects on future generations—or, in other words, *to think*.[2]

The current burgeoning, popular, and scholarly interest in the plant mind enjoys a venerable lineage. As our contributors reveal, the idea that plants have a mind of their own has been a core element of Indigenous stories, literary works, poetic imaginings, philosophical systems, and experimental investigations from around the world.[3] For instance, among the Aboriginal people of Southwest Australia, during the creation of the world, enormous ancestral beings raised the sky to its spiraling height with the generous help of old-growth gum trees called *karris*. In this spirit, *The Mind of Plants* gathers lyrical, reflective, experiential, and oftentimes deeply personal evocations of plant minds and their connection to humans—the mind understood here as an embodied and embedded form of being. Our aim with this anthology is to reflect upon the ways that humans *mind* and *unmind* plants, as well as on the *mindedness* or *unmindedness* of plants themselves as percipient personae. Our essayists, poets, and artists address this topic through a synergetic blend of contributions that include narratives of plants as cultural, ecological, historical, literary, social, and spiritual forces—as agents of memory and emotion.

Encouraging textured, multi-hued responses to the theme, we asked each contributor to select a plant as a focal point for reflection. By foregrounding the common name as a guiding thread, *The Mind of Plants* emphasizes the active role plants played in the creation of this book. For, while our essayists, poets, and artists chose their plants, they are aware of the fact that, to a large extent, it was the plants who chose them. As editors, we see this anthology as the outcome of a collaboration between the contributors and the plants themselves. Our view of the unscripted, synchronistic process informing the collection accords with emerging understandings of plants as participants in the creative process, rather than simply as the passive materials out of which our cultural productions arise.[4]

Moving away from a hierarchical organization of plants and taxonomic information associated with them, the anthology playfully evokes, connects with, and advances the long tradition of botanical texts. The arrangement of essays and poems alphabetically by vernacular names is reminiscent of old herbaria, all the while moving away from their classificatory focus. Our intention was to pay tribute to this immense body of knowledge while subverting its largely reductionist approach to botanical life. Avoiding a simplistic dissection of vegetal forms of existence, in which humans are authority figures who coldly observe, describe, and define plants as inert objects, *The Mind of Plants* stages a dialogue between diverse plants, people, and places.

Composed of interactions, exchanges, and other filamentous strands, *The Mind of Plants* cuts across not only different species and scientific kingdoms but also across various human and more-than-human cultures. This hands-on, pragmatic approach to plant life is the reason why we chose to include living beings such as algae, who are not *stricto sensu* plants from a scientific point of view. Aiming to be as inclusive as possible, we wished to produce a compendium documenting plants' everyday dealings with humans, unfettered by academic and scientific jargon. The result is a confederation of vegetal and human life that, although marked by sometimes violent historical developments—colonialism, neo-colonialism, totalitarianism, plantation economies, and neo-liberal monoculture agribusinesses, mentioned in many of our chapters—testifies, in the synchronicity of its coming-together, to the possibility of a more egalitarian connection between plants and people.

GRASS

Looking out of the window on a cold, dreary winter morning, taking your dog out for a walk around the neighborhood in the late afternoon after a long day's work sitting at the desk, or enjoying a well-deserved weekend hike at the nearest park, you are bound to see it. Grass is all around us, adorning well-manicured suburban lawns, sprouting in the crevices of city sidewalks and covering the soil of vast, wild expanses of forest and prairie. It is so ubiquitous we barely notice it. We usually only pay attention to it when it oversteps its boundaries—when it grows too tall or invades spaces reserved for other plants and for human-made structures. We then begrudgingly mow, cut, and deracinate it, only to firmly put it out of mind until it once again defies human-defined rules and we are called upon to discipline it anew.

But the grass we mostly disregard has its own stories to tell, many of which are entwined with the existence of humans. Does it like to live in our gardens, to be watered and fertilized, while also mowed and trimmed to fit our aesthetic and leisure needs? Or would it prefer to take its chances in the wild, at the mercy of droughts and plagues, but free to grow as tall, far, and wide as it can? Who are grass's vegetal and animal allies and foes? And who or what are we even referring to when we talk about grass? Do we mean the entire grass patch, a group of leaves, or a single blade?

The omnipresence of the being we call "grass" is but a simple reminder of the centrality of plants in everyday human existence. From the air we breathe, through the food we eat, to our clothes, housing, and even arts, plants determine all aspects of human lives. *The Mind of Plants* calls upon you, our reader, to bracket your routine, automatic behavior toward plants and to see them as more than sources of oxygen, nourishment, and raw materials. They are all that, of course, but what else? The essays, poems, and artworks in this collection dwell on the specificities of plant life in all of its bewildering variety and on the multiple interactions between plants and humans. Drawing on Walt Whitman's renowned metaphor, each contribution is like a blade of grass, an instantiation of the complex ties human beings establish with plants that determine their research interests, their work, and their lives in myriad different ways.

This anthology conjures up the lived experiences of vegetal and human beings, recollections such as those of playing in a grass meadow, of closely monitoring the vibrant insect life that thrives among tiny blades of grass, or of lying down in the shade on a cool grass patch to read a book during a hot summer day. Akin to grass, the anthology grew organically in directions determined by the various contributors. With no predefined list of plants to be included, the process of putting together the volume was decentralized, with no main core, as the creation of texts followed a plant logic, sprouting grass-like wherever it found fertile ground. This horizontal structure is the reason why some plants that have played a key role in human culture are missing from this anthology—poppy, potato, tobacco, among many others, are cases in point. But, while you will inevitably miss some plants absent from the book, you will certainly meet new ones or deepen your appreciation of plants you encounter on a daily basis, such as grass, about whom you may not often pause to think.

A field of grass, or a groomed garden lawn, is an open ground of possibilities. Devoid of a clear, one-way track, it invites one to wander through it, to stroll leisurely in different directions, simply enjoying the walk. Similarly, you, as the reader, can devise multiple pathways into *The Mind of Plants*. You could, for instance, start with the plants you know best and then slowly radiate out into less familiar ones, just as one meets new friends through their connections with older ones. Or you can take the opposite approach and start with plants you have never seen in the wild, staging a literary encounter with a vegetal being that you are unacquainted with in the flesh, in the same way as we now intimately get to know each other digitally and remotely, oftentimes even better than when we shook hands every day.

Another avenue for exploration is to concentrate on certain types of plants: bushes, shrubs, trees, epiphytes, etc., or on their connections to and effects upon humans: stimulants such as coffee or tea; edible plants like apple, bean, corn, spinach or wheat; ornamental plants, including birdflower or rose; mind-altering plants such as ayahuasca, cannabis, peyote, or yopo, and so on. If you are a more lyrically-inclined reader, you can also begin by approaching plants through poetry, while others might decide to engage first with the essays that draw connections between vegetal beings and the arts. Purposefully open-ended, this anthology invites each one of you to root yourself in your choice of texts or to allow yourself to be surprised and interpellated by this collection of plants, only to let your relationship to vegetal life branch out with new shoots and leaves, flowers, and then bear fruit.

CACTUS

A nightblooming cactus vine gleams in the cool tropical morning. Drenching rainfall flumes rhythmically down its thick, ribbed stems. Ripening and reddening, day by day, deeper into the monsoon season, its leathery fruit is growing flush with betacyanin, the nourishing pigment underlying its magenta radiance. Known in Spanish as *pitahaya*, dragon fruit (*Hylocereus costaricensis*) is botanically an epiphyte, a plant living in a state of relative balance on another plant, often a tree, though without resorting to parasitism. From the heart-like fruit, beating with sweet antioxidants, the vine traces a circuitous path through frangipani branches, then around the pendulous fronds of a fellow epiphyte, a staghorn fern. The charismatic, though retiring, guardian of this Balinese home, *pitahaya* welcomes the doused dawn.

Yet, before the cactus became visually discernible within its tangled mass of green in the middle of the traditional courtyard, the fruit had announced itself to the tongue and taste buds. There were plump slices on plates, frothy purplish juice in glasses, and tiny black seeds pestled between teeth. An interlocutor—one who engages in dialogue with another—dragon fruit was also an intellectual presence. Before it became a body before us, the plant was a cluster of ideas, constellation of names, *corpus* of knowledge, and mode of being that humans attempt, but often fail, to communicate to one another through the pains of language. As our elegantly dressed local host pointed to something behind us and announced proudly, "*there's* my dragon fruit tree," our heads pivoted out of reflex to notice, for the first time, the vivacious vegetal dwelling beside us. In that moment, we experienced a strong sensation of sudden encounter—of serendipitously meeting the plant universe and, namely, the dragon fruit, *halfway*.[5] In the same manner, *The Mind of Plants* brims with stories of meeting and being met, seeing and being seen, feeling and being felt.

Central to the anthology is the tradition of the herbarium, defined as a collection of preserved plant materials and data, including precise anatomical descriptions, all organized systematically to enhance botanical knowledge. In the development of Western botany, herbarium specimens have been vital reference points for identifying species, assigning technical names, and elucidating taxonomic relationships. Demonstrating the close historical connection between botany and medicine, herbals of the Middle Ages detailed the medicinal virtues of plants and documented the rich knowledge of flora common to people during this period. Early herbaria, such as Gherardo Cibo's from the sixteenth century, evolved to house pressed specimens, or *hortus siccus*, mounted on sheets for ease of access. As botanists began to exclude information about virtues from their narratives, herbals transformed into *floras*, or technical descriptions companionable with the function of the herbarium as a classificatory tool. This transition from herbals to floras indeed reflected the increasing split between the disciplines of medicine and botany.

At the same time, this movement away from herbals resulted in an affective divide between plants and people. From being focused on medicine, healing, and nutrition—specifically engaging the senses of taste, smell, and touch—traditional botanical knowledge systems became increasingly relegated to the domain of the abstract. By its very nature, a herbarium specimen adheres to a logic of reduction. The anatomical part—seed, fruit, flower—is extracted from the plant body while the whole plant, in turn, is removed from its web of ecological relations. Take, for instance, a night-blooming cactus specimen pressed in 1974 and stored at the Division of Plant Industry Herbarium in Florida. The creamy white flowers typical of the cactus have browned, revealing an orderly array of stiff, soldierly anthers. Defying the two-dimensional logic of the herbarium, the succulent fruit and spiny stems are absent. Yet also missing are the sensuous narratives of human interaction with the cactus—stories of eating fruits and dispersing seeds. As a cultural herbarium of vegetal beings, *The Mind of Plants* opens up a space for those stories to emerge and re-emerge, along with the many knowledge systems they represent.

BURDOCK

In almost every corner of the world, especially if you're lost in an abandoned field or wandering along a backwoods track, you're likely to encounter greater burdock (*Arctium lappa*). The name of this eminently clingy character conjures the infamous *burr*, a hooked seed impeccably adapted for hitching rides on mobile creatures, including those of us who stray off course. Growing to monstrous proportions in biennial cycles, the plant can reach heights of ten feet, with leaves the size of a human torso and a bulky taproot descending three feet or more into the earth. Burdock is, literally, an irritating plant, though not without good reason. The silky pappus hairs of its fruits fasten readily to the skin, hair, eyebrows, and other sensitive areas, triggering inflammation and allergic episodes in those unfortunate enough to come into contact with it. What's more, the barbed bracts enclosing its delicate purple flowers attach easily to the fur of mammals—and likewise the sweaters of *Homo sapiens*—enabling seeds to spread into new areas at considerable distances.

Perfecting crafty tactics of vegetal mobility, burdock has become a notorious and ubiquitous invader—a master of agitating us while, simultaneously, recruiting us to do its bidding. Nonetheless, the irksome qualities of burdock belie its giving nature. In fact, its medicinal, nutritional, ecological, and economic attributes are too plentiful to list here but center, to a large extent, on its fleshy taproot. Considered a purifying agent in many herbal systems, burdock root has been shown to promote circulation, remove bloodstream toxins, interrupt cancerous growth, improve skin problems, and reduce inflammation. Sometimes pickled, the root has been an essential ingredient of diverse culinary traditions and is especially valued in Japanese cuisine. Also of note is the fact that burdock supplied the organic template for George de Mestral's development of the touch fastener, otherwise known as velcro, a common find in many pieces of clothing, shoes, and kitchen cabinets today.

Valuable insights arise from being *bothered* by plants like burdock. In becoming perturbed, in being thrown out of our familiar terrains of comfort, we can open to plant voice—that speechless, strange, yet persuasive way vegetal life summons us. Botanical wisdom doesn't always come wrapped up in stunning blossoms or luscious fruits. Lessons are at times laced with barbs and burrs. As it latches to our clothing, this is what burdock tells us. As they inflame and sting our skin, this is what poison ivy and common nettle say too. As it overtakes our nasal passages and nauseates our stomachs, this is the message of durian—a fruit highly esteemed by some, seriously detested by others, and so pungent that it has been banned by certain Southeast Asian hotels. From cannabis and coffee to the suicide tree and *xiang si*, *The Mind of Plants* is as much about what plants think and what plants think *of us*, as it is about the bodily connections between human, vegetal, and other forms of life. Plants provoke and disturb us, humans, at the same time as they nourish our bodies and thoughts. As mind-expanding ayahuasca, cannabis, and peyote teach us, the lessons of the botanical world often register in the body before they alight in the mind.

Burdock's complex character also illumines for us the idea of emplacement. Research has shown that intelligence in plants and, arguably, all life, is intimately linked to place.[6] In the case of barbed burdock, being sessile is not a disadvantage but has enabled the plant to develop canny techniques for getting around. Certainly, plants are embedded in given places, but they also possess powers of dispersion that we don't yet fully comprehend. It is the oscillation between rootedness and uprootedness that characterizes plant being. That a species like burdock has successfully disseminated itself around the globe testifies to the percipient mobilities evolved by plants. The ideas of place and emplacement also speak to our own situations as editors, dispersed across three continents, embedded in very different ecologies, occasionally unable to communicate because of wildfires and the coronavirus, yet balancing rootedness and uprootedness through a shared filiation with flora and the impassioned plant-people who have made this book possible.

LIANA

Gliding around like delicate butterflies or pirouetting through the air like elegant ballerinas, samara seeds fly with aerodynamic precision to sow their winged bodies afar in a suitable place in the landscape. The champion of long-distance gliding is the large samara of the Java cucumber, *Alsomitra macrocarpa,* a tropical liana whose ultralight winged seeds stall, dip, accelerate, and then lift and gain altitude again, then finally, and almost reluctantly land on the earth. There is great magic in the gliding of these samaras! Over a century ago, their spellbinding flight impressed a wish on the runaways of our ingenuity, landing in a field beyond abstractions—the idea that took root inspired us to transcend our flightless human condition and, quite literally, soar.[7]

The practice of moving ideas around by observing the strategies used by other species, and particularly plants, mimicking, and, in some way, recasting them in novel directions, dates back to 4000 BC (when the Chinese first learned about silk from the silkworm) but likely is as old as our human history. It is often understood that this information transfer depends on what we perceive as salient in our observations of the *other.*

This "mining" of creative ideas from other species frames the *other*—any non-human other—as a discrete object out there that we can observe from a separate and detached point of view. From this perspective, this objectified *other* has no subjective life, no passion or desire, no mind, no story to tell. And *it* is a static generality that exists exclusively as a fabrication of a modern, dominant scientific paradigm that separates the human from the rest of life. Aside from the fact that this rupture is internally incongruent with the core Darwinian understanding of the interconnectedness of life forms that underpins the modern scientific paradigm itself, there simply is no objectified *other* in the world we all live in—an entangled world of subjectivities, continuities, and *we-ness*.

As in the samara, in the pages of this book, you will encounter seeds of ecological fluency. Over and over again, through the collaboration between time and space, these seeds soared in the prose of our best poets and essayists who praised the *grandeur*[8] that endlessly flows around and through all life forms. Time and again, these seeds revealed stories of continuities in the material origin across life, while wishing, in a mischievous game of hide-and-seek, to conceal such unity through the mutability and transmutation of bodily form. But, like the *Alsomitra* samara with its paper-thin diaphanous wings, these seeds carry the realization that we are all composites of subjectivities, permanently in the making within the physical, emotional, and spiritual ecologies we co-inhabit with others. It is the openness (or closed-ness) of our bodies to other forms of life that molds the texture of our own lives, the stories we tell, and the stories we hear.[9]

In these pages, plants take the lead in materializing these stories within the relational body of reciprocity and proximity with human co-authors. Through a dynamic process of co-narration, these stories are seeds of inescapable intimacy—personal narratives grounded in the potential to speak directly to the human sense of wonder and our collective capacity for imagining possibilities that unveil the deep mysteries of existence, those basic realities less traveled. Their final destination may lie far outside the accepted limits of our dominant paradigm. Still, their exquisite design, like that of the *Alsomitra* samaras, promises to take us far in our collective journey to a deeper appreciation of, and devotion to, plants and life itself.

Our hope as editors is that the texts in *The Mind of Plants* travel far and wide. Delivered to the world, the essays, poems, and artworks in this anthology will—akin to samara seeds—disseminate and undertake their own journeys into your libraries and your minds. With no fixed destination, the anthology will contribute to our understanding of what goes on in a plant's mind and to our human mindedness of all the vegetal beings with whom we share our existence.

CHAPTER 1

Apple

Malus spp.

▪ **Sarah Laborde**

This story starts from the middle, with a few young apple trees in the back of a small car on their way from Denmark to Southern France. Driving the car is Niels-Viggo Hansen, a friend, and apple tree planting acolyte who, a few years prior, had encountered a wild apple while playing with his sons in the Danish countryside. They loved the apple, cut small scions for grafting from the generous mother tree and called the apple Mols after the hills where it grows. Niels and I had met in 2016 on the banks of the Hudson River. After he had told me of his adventures with the Mols apple and his wish for it to delight other people, we thought of documenting together the gifting of young grafted trees—to plant them in the gardens of friends, philosophers, and contemplative practitioners, and reflect as we did so on themes such as growth and decay, attention and care. Apple tree led conversations, emerging from the act of planting and what surrounds it. The collaborative process and the book are still unfolding. Here, I reflect on my personal and grateful encounter with the Mols apple tree and on the thoughts, feelings, and insight that it brought forth, which contributed to leading me *home*.

The four years that preceded the trip to France with the Mols apple trees had been, for me, an unfolding crisis. I lived up in the air, scattered across several continents. Fifteen years prior, I had left the French valley where I grew up, and I had walked many grounds since. I was aware that I gradually developed a tendency to flee connection, in part so as to not feel the tearing apart—the uprooting—that I knew would invariably follow. Many of my relationships were fragmented, anchored in particular worlds that I lived in for a while then left behind. Between intense reminders, my trust of what the ground really feels like, what water and love really taste like, had started to fray. And I got sick.

In July 2017, my body had reached a state of complete halt—emotional exhaustion, nervous breakdown, and parasitic infections resulting in anxious thoughts and behaviors that left me bewildered. I was running with no ground under my feet, getting lost, meeting the world with a body of fear.

It is in this context that I encountered the Mols trees in the back of the car in the summer of 2017. They were one-year-old apple trees, in pots, on their way south toward new grounds. I had been in and out of hospital after returning diseased from Chad, but felt compelled to go with Niels for this trip that we had planned together. I knew he was a friend who would be able to simply be with me, even in that state of being. So, over the course of a week in the summer of 2017, we drove around and planted the trees in four distinct and equally beautiful corners of the French countryside: Loire, Bourgogne, Lubéron, and Cévennes Méridionales. We ritualized the plantings with open conversations with the tree-minders: David Hykes, Bruno Latour, Amy Varela, and my parents, Noëlle and Jean-Louis Laborde. We let the exchanges be guided by the acts of walking together to find the right place to plant, digging, feeling, and scattering soil, taking water to the trees.

I hadn't thought much about the apple trees themselves prior to the trip. I saw them more as a pretext for deep conversations with fascinating people. But, as we transported them around, I started to feel that I could relate to these young beings. Like mine, their environment had changed often. They were hybrid—they had been grafted, and they were without ground—growing in pots, on the move, and waiting to really connect to life's invisible networks.

WHOLE AS AN APPLE TREE

As I spent time around them, the wholeness of the trees started soothing my splintered mind. They were apple trees. They were small, and they would grow, flower, bear fruit. Or they may dry and die beforehand if their surroundings proved too far from their embodied expectations. They would dry and die anyway, sometime. Grafted, migrated, small, and leafless, the young Mols trees were already all of their seasons—as whole as the full and crisp red apple that their other branches produced in Denmark, as whole as the fallen limbs swarming with the life of the soil. They didn't mind, I thought, as there was no way to fail at being an apple tree. Not even the apple itself is an achievement for the tree, after all—like Paul Valery's description of a work of art in relation to the artist, it is "never completed (…) for, in relation to who or what is making it, it can only be one stage in a series of inner transformations."[1]

This contemplation on the flow of the life of apple trees got me wondering where this knowledge lived in me—the human version of these tree's knowing about how to be an apple tree, the "how to simply be human" within what Gregory Bateson describes as the "*wider knowing* which is the glue holding together the starfishes and sea anemones and the redwood forests and the human committees."[2] I felt compelled to pay more attention to my inner motions. What felt, to my human sensorium, like what warm, generous light might feel like to an apple tree? What felt like moist, soft soil? *This is where I need to grow branches and roots*. It sounds simple, even simplistic. Humans aren't apple trees, you may be thinking. But for my state of confusion at the time, in constant whirlwinds of fear and wonderings, the vegetal prescription to feel the movement of my own sap without appraising it had a welcome, fathomable quality. It felt like a suggestion to let life find its way, to feel and trust the essential current that quietly swells under barks and skins alike.

AT HOME, IN RELATION

My human mind had been frantically looking for *home*, while the Mols apple trees knew how to establish theirs in connection to the other beings around them: plants, fungi, bees, and others. An apple tree knows how to grow roots and where, to let winter denude it, reach toward the spring sun. *Relationships, roots, rhythms*. It struck me—I had been neglecting all three.

Our apple tree-planting week was a generous unfolding of conversations between hybrid beings, with apple trees and people in the middle. People and orchard-planted trees communicate and collaborate in various ways, but mostly they *are*, and they *do what they are*. They tend to each other's needs and grow together slowly, contributing to each other's vitality. Witnessing the planting of the apple trees and the attentive movements of their gardeners was like beholding a long-term commitment to listening, caring, and gifting—the kind of relationship that a sense of *home* is made of.

After planting the last Mols tree of the trip, in my parents' garden in the Cévennes, my father spoke of the process of *homemaking* as akin to that of gardening (his garden being where, I think, he feels most at home) the never-ending cultivation of harmony between what is self-sown and what is planted, what emerges and what is brought in. The practice, he told me, is to help relationships unfold in accordance with the embodied knowing of the various beings involved (including plants, insects, people) about what their life should be like. This takes a lot of careful observing and listening. Sometimes conflicts arise, and the gardener supports an expression of life based on what both looks and feels right—an ethos that is founded in the garden's dynamic web of relations.

This is true in our inner as in our outer lives, I thought. Our old patterns mingle with disruptive events, emotional floods with embodied memories of droughts and breezes. Being at home requires cultivating harmonious connection through this dance, both inward and outward, always in relation.

TODAY

Two years after the trip, on the day of June 2019, when I am writing this, I am back in the Cévennes. I have settled a little, and the Mols apple tree planted there has grown a little. We have known each other for two years. The tree has started to learn about its vegetal, animal, and human neighbors and adjusted to the daily swing of mountain shadows in the valley. It knows, too, the song of the river nearby. Of course, it knows that hundreds of other apple trees (of the *Reinette du Vigan* variety) grow on the other side of the river. If no one else, the bees would have passed the message. I spent some time sitting close to it on the grass with my six-year-old niece, after playing together by the river. She asked another plant nearby if she could take a leaf from its stem to make a sail for her tiny boat made from half a walnut shell. Then she looked at me and asked, "Sarah, where is the heart of plants?" I thought for a minute, looking at the small apple tree growing at home.

Where is it,
the heart that pulses?
It beats forth, I thought
with the rhythms of earth and sky.
In the upward song of the sap,
It beats the fractal ways of life
into shape;
It is in the gaze of the flowers,
the shrivelling of leaves,
the slow breath of winter buds.

And where is it,
the heart that feels?
It flows forth, I thought,
through the playful maze.
In the touch
of the soft earth and the vibrant sun.
In the smell, the taste of the apple
meeting a beak or a mouth.
It is the leaves bending under the storm,
and the tree's answer
to the dance of the bees.
It navigates the soil, watches for the deer,
and dies unafraid.

The heart of the apple is
in all its relations.
Past and future, known as now.
As is ours, I thought.[3]

THE GROUND IN THE WEB

Listening to the Mols apple trees in the last two years has sent me looking for my *inner plant,* a process from which, for the sake of today's reflections, I may pick three pieces of insight. First, my week with the trees in 2017 pointed—in the blizzard of my mind at the time—to what is warm, alive, and slow. Feeling after feeling, it helped me refine a sense of inner integrity through increased attention to the simple force that breathes and beats my complex world into being. An invitation to feel more and do less.

At the same time, I realized that I needed to *land* for a while. After all, no plant thrives being uprooted and exposed to different environments every few months. The time of the seed moving effortlessly with the currents of air and water, waiting for its time, was no longer. Adapting is a demanding endeavor, as I knew the last couple of years had been for the young Mols trees of Southern France. *Landing* did not mean being constantly in one place, neither did it mean focusing solely inwards. It was an invitation to commit to long-term relationships with communities of humans and non-humans, on—and including—the ground. This commitment applies at different and related scales. I knew my inner garden had been devastated by frequent environmental shifts, long-term use of antimalarial medication, and the assumption that adapting to ever more drastic changes was something my body could keep doing, *ad infinitum.* But from where the parasites were overrunning, I could feel, in its package of exhaustion and anxiety, the same message as the trees: land somewhere; be attentive, slow and consistent; make time for situated and related cultivation.

But where to commit to? "*Where to land?*" as philosopher Bruno Latour asks in his recent book.[4] I was a global nomad and a hybrid, no longer made of the same wood as my grandmother, whose life threaded the same Béarn mountain paths as her ancestors, minding crops and farm animals, doing what had to be done, there and then. She may have been all the while dreaming of new horizons. I will never know. I do know, though, that she later grew lovingly concerned about her granddaughter's migrating ways, as one might be for a stray wild goose. But as the Mols trees reminded me the last two years, hybrid beings who are brought far from their first soil can connect, thrive, and generously give into life. After the apple-planting trip, I decided to commit—in some way—to the valley of apples that grew me up in the Cévennes and to gradually, more consciously, cultivate there the thousand open threads a sense of home is made of. I bought a piece of land in the valley and planted apple trees.

The third insight from the trees is on creativity. The Mols apples are perfect; they are beautiful and supportive of life. Yet, they result not from arduous work from the tree but emerge instead from its good relationships with the soil and microbes, light, other trees, water, animals, people—from the apple tree *feeling at home*. The apples speak, to me, of a life that is creative and wonderful when rhythms and relationships support its flow without blockages. To be creative like an apple tree is to be free, to do what one *is*, and to be joyful in the process and the product, which are one. Many people, wise and wild as trees, have spoken about this freedom at the heart of life. Many more, including children, enact it. But we humans sometimes get scared, groundless, and disconnected. Then, we need to feel reminders of what Thich Nhat Hahn calls *interbeing*,[5] the fundamental interrelation of all there is in the "family of things,"[6] as in Mary Oliver's poem, "Wild Geese," which, of course, includes people and apple trees. Sensing and contemplating this interdependence reveals an emphasis on relations over self and gradually shapes intentions and actions that are spontaneously supportive of life's communities—an ethos that Francisco Varela describes as "ethical know-how."[7] The quiet, vital invitation of apple trees is that we may continue inhabiting this Earth together and finding our way *home*, in rhythm, in relation, and in grateful enjoyment. If you forget, let the next apple you bite into be a sweet and timely reminder.

CHAPTER 2

Ayahuasca

Banisteriopsis caapi

Luis Eduardo Luna

I am dealing here with the sacred Amazonian vine *Banisteriopsis caapi* as *yagé* when combined with the leaves of *Diplopterys cabrerana* and as *ayahuasca* with the addition of the leaves of *Psychotria viridis*. There are many other combinations and plenty of information and personal reports on many aspects of the use of both yagé and ayahuasca. I will not repeat here what is easily available. Instead, I will focus on the paradoxical theme of this book, *The Mind of Plants*. Can one talk about the mind of these plants independently from one's own mind or the mind of others? How do plants communicate with us when our minds are apparently so very different? Is it only through ingestion that the plants are able to communicate with us, or are there other vehicles, perhaps in our dreams?

To begin, a short biographical note is in order. I experienced yagé for the first time in 1971, together with Terence McKenna, his partner at that time, Erica Nielsfeld, and Kalman Szábo, a Hungarian we met in my hometown Florencia in the Colombian Amazon. Our Hungarian friend had received some yagé from Don Apolinar Yacanamijoy, an Ingano *taita* (shaman) whom I had seen several times during my childhood. He is now considered an almost mythical figure among the *yageceros* of southern Colombia. The four of us drank it at Villa Gloria, a humble wooden house my parents owned several kilometers from Florencia. My first experience was a scene similar to Hieronymus Bosch's famous painting *The Garden of Earthly Delights*. I talked to Don Apolinar weeks later about this when he was visiting Florencia from his home in Yurayaco ("black water," in Quechua), around seventy kilometers to the southwest, which was at that time still surrounded by forest. He told me, "If you really want to learn about yagé you have to keep a diet and take it for forty consecutive nights. He will then come. He is *simpático*." I was then living in Spain, about to move to Norway, and was unable to stay in Colombia. Seven years later, during a vacation, I went all the way to Yurayaco with a younger brother and had my second experience. At that time, Don Apolinar was in his eighties or perhaps nineties. He did not know how old he was. Despite his fragility, he told us many stories. But he was dismayed at the arrival of the colonists who had destroyed his cultivated gardens in which he had been growing many kinds of yagé, replacing them by cattle fields. After some hesitation, he finally agreed to conduct a ceremony with his son Roberto that night. I have already told that story elsewhere. Suffice to say that, overwhelmed by the power and beauty of the experience, I told him: "Don Apolinar, you know so much." He said, "It is not me. It is yagé."

I planned to stay with him for some months a year later, but he died before I returned to Colombia. Terence advised me to go to the Peruvian Amazon. There I spent several weeks with Don Emilio Andrade Gómez, a mestizo *ayahuasquero* whose house was located fourteen kilometers from Iquitos, along the road to Nauta, which at that time was not yet completed. I made a documentary, *Don Emilio and His Little Doctors.* With him, I learned that ayahuasca is best understood as a "doctor." Other plants are also considered *plantas maestras* (plant teachers). Like Don Apolinar, Don Emilio told me that the real teacher was ayahuasca, not him. The *vegetalista*, an expert in one or more of these powerful *vegetales*, simply protects the person interested in learning from the plants. Isolation and a strict diet are required. The plants will teach *icaros* (magical songs) that can later be used for healing or many other tasks. I spent several months each year from 1980–1985 with Don Emilio and other *vegetalistas*, and the materials I gathered during this time formed the groundwork for *Vegetalismo: Shamanism Among the Mestizo Population of the Peruvian Amazon*, my doctoral dissertation at the Institute of Comparative Religion, Stockholm University, published in 1986. A year later, I spent a month in the Sibundoy Valley, in the Colombian Putumayo, with Salvador Chindoy, a Kamsá *taita*, one of Richard Evans Schultes' friends back in the 1940s, along with his son Miguel Chindoy. I drank yagé with them several times. They called the cultivation of sacred and medicinal plants around their homes *el jardín de la ciencia* "the garden of science," again pointing to the same idea—that plants are intelligent, and they teach.

These events triggered a lifelong interdisciplinary interest in these plants, which persists to this day in my work as a researcher, as a practitioner of sorts, and as a colleague of some of the people from a variety of disciplines who were also deeply moved by their experiences with the plants and with whom I have collaborated. During the last three decades, there has been an increasing global interest in ayahuasca, triggering artistic and scientific production, therapeutic applications, and environmental awareness. This has also brought new interest in the Amazon, a region under relentless threat of destruction and whose Indigenous population is continuously persecuted.

Forty-eight years have passed since my first encounter with yagé. Nearly everything I have done over all these years has been related to these plants in one way or another. To this day, even so, the fundamental mysteries remain, and I do not feel any closer to any grand truth that would satisfy my rational thinking. At this point, I just need to let go (at least methodologically) of alkaloids, receptors, and brain circuits and only focus on the many experiences I have had. The question has always been: Is it all me? Are all those characters that interact with me, as in dreams, merely aspects of myself, or are they entities—disguised in shapes and cultural clothing I can somehow recognize—struggling to communicate their important messages, perhaps about life, the environment, and the predicament of existence itself?

Indigenous Amazonian people, like traditional societies all over the world, apparently understand these matters quite clearly. Plants, animals, lakes, rivers, mountains, the sun, the moon, the stars, and the winds all have personhood. Their lives are embedded in animistic cosmologies in which we humans are one type of being among a myriad of non-human persons. Accordingly, we as humans occupy a middle position in a complex world of intelligent exchange with higher and lower body-minds, some plainly visible, some invisible to the untrained eye. Their epistemology is relational and firmly based on the empirical senses (first-hand experience), as well as in the imagination. Yagé, ayahuasca, and other plants and fungi can facilitate this perception, even to people who, like us, have been raised in worlds either devoid of spirit or with definitive dualistic ideas of the sacred, usually separated from the biological world.

As I write these words, I am seventy-two years old, and right now, tens of thousands of hectares of Brazilian and Bolivian Amazon are on fire. Those trees belong to hundreds of species, all living together with myriads of insects, mammals, birds, and reptiles, senselessly dying due to the fact that human beings, coming from regions that are already destroyed, are incapable of recognizing the pain and plight of the sentient beings subject to this massacre. I used to think of myself as an Amazonian who, through the vicissitudes of life, was destined to be away from my native region most of the time. But even if I was to return to the place of my birth, I cannot say I am Amazonian any longer since pasture for cattle has replaced the forests of my childhood. Caquetá, of which Florencia is the capital, is one of the most deforested areas in the world. In the center of Florencia's city emblem, a cow of a variety developed in the region is represented. It is not a jaguar, not a harpy eagle or a toucan, much less an anaconda or a boa constrictor. This clearly shows a total alienation of the local population from the original natural surroundings. Caquetá was colonized from the region of Caldas, in the northwest of the country, by people who came with poncho, machete, and sombrero, mounted on horses and dreaming of vast herds of cattle—settlers who believed that the trees had to be cut down and replaced by pastures, colonizers who considered the Indians simply an obstacle in this "civilizing process," as they called it. There was never even a hint of admiration or awe on their part of the staggering biological diversity of the Amazonian forest that once covered the region, not the slightest appreciation of the knowledge of the Indigenous inhabitants of this region.

I crossed the Atlantic, leaving behind a hot European summer, and arrived in a cool winter in southern Brazil. The miracle was just there, right in front of our house: the *Banisteriopsis* vine was in flower. Delicate white and pink inflorescences emerged from the dense, dark green foliage hiding underneath a mesh of accumulated thin dried stems. Upon closer inspection, I could see that each inflorescence had a pair of secondary flowers growing at its base, the main one shooting above the other two. At gradually smaller intervals, clusters of umbels grew along their upper ends. From the short pedicels, flowers in groups of five or six emerged, some fully open, some still folded, their five light pink or white petals like tiny cups. Those facing upward collected the moisture from the last rain, water drops suspended at the tips gathering the morning light. Tiny yellow anthers hid the three-partite ovule, which in time will be split into three, first green, then brownish one-winged seeds that, by rotating, would be carried some distance by the wind. The evening fell, the remaining sunlight reflected in the pink inflorescent color, while long, thin apical shoots stretched to form an arch, inspecting the surroundings, perhaps detecting the shadow projected by other plants and growing toward them in the hope of grabbing some neighbor branch to initiate an ascent toward the light. In our garden, several of our avocado and other fruit trees had been laced by the vines, and we had to trim them. In other cases, we allowed the vine to climb other trees, becoming thicker and thicker at the base, embracing herself, again and again, curving and ascending as a huge serpent, branching, looking for light and support. In our garden, we have also the swollen-joints variety of *Banisteriopsis* described by Spruce in 1853, where I noticed a few inflorescences too high to see them in detail. Members of the UDV (União do Vegetal, a Brazilian religious organization that uses ayahuasca as a sacrament) call it *caupurí*. They seem to blossom later than those closer to the house, some of which, by that time begin to wane. Here in southern Brazil, the inflorescences emerge in July or August, coinciding with the first spell of cold weather. In the Amazon, her real home, the vine can become enormous, twisting among trees and other climbers until she finds the sky. There she expands over the canopy, flowering when the time is ripe, far from human eyes.

Don Emilio referred to ayahuasca as *abuelo*, grandpa. Many other people called it *madre ayahuasca*, some describing in detail how they communicated with its spirit. I have never had what I would call a direct contact with an entity personifying the plant itself, although I have often seen entities of many kinds, at times approaching me. This is a common motif not only of yagé, ayahuasca, and other sacred plants but also of the DMT molecule, as exemplified in Rick Strassman's work. Now, what kind of mind or minds am I tapping into? Do they directly have volition? Is it the mind of the plants, of higher intelligence permeating our planet, the mind of the planet itself, of the solar system, of the galaxy, of the whole universe? If it is the mind of the plant, does she have an inner horizon limited to the history of her own individuality, or does it include her parent plants, the whole species, or even a collective plant mind that stretches beyond present time and space? If she has a self, what kind of self is it? Is it like mine, always fluid, sometimes intensively present, though more often barely conscious? If she has a self, is it more present sometimes than others? Is the seed more awake when landing on suitable ground than when hanging on a branch? Is it more present at night, when it grows, or when the sun suddenly reaches her from behind a cloud? Is she more present when she feels the rain or when she is being attacked by an insect or fungi? Is she aware of the trillions of microorganisms inhabiting her? Is she more aware of herself when inside me? Is she also connecting with a self much larger than herself, larger still than me?

And what about the content of the visions—those scenes of an apocalypse, war, and destruction, so often reported? Is she showing me something that has happened, is happening, or is about to happen? Is she reading and showing me my own fears, my mind assaulted by so much horrendous information coming from so many sources? What about the other worlds, the flying spacecrafts, the scanners, and other technologies that I have been subject to in order to enter spaces where beings of some sort move hyper-dimensionally in an effortless way? What about that overwhelming feeling of reality that is so often felt by many? Is it me, is it you, is it a co-creation of you (whoever you may be) and me (whoever I may be)?

Visionary experiences seem to be participatory, the result of interactions that I find difficult to reduce to mere chemistry and a signaling system in the brain. There seems to be contact with something other, something manifested through my own cultural conditioning and imagery, and therefore, not completely independent of me. There seems to be a sort of bridge, an interface, a third possibility between Descartes's *res cogitans* and *res extensa*, perhaps a *res fantastica*? I know there are messages hidden in the metaphoric world of my visions that seem to demand decipherment. Sometimes I feel I am on a brink of a profound revelation that is far too big for me. I am forced to implore: "Enough, enough! I cannot take anymore! My heart will not be able to deal with it, without dying."

But these are exceptions. More often, the plant's teachings are much more benevolent, playful, or just extraordinarily beautiful. There are the insights, the deep understandings, the teachings. I seem to think differently under the effects of ayahuasca. I surprise myself saying words that do not seem to come from me, as if they came from a much wiser person than myself. She reveals creative forces, powers I never knew I possessed. She teaches me about my own mind, showing me the various kinds of visions I may have, not only in terms of content but of qualitatively different texture and perceptions of reality. From geometrical patterns covering my whole field of vision to dynamic forms always changing, to extraordinary landscapes, temples, or palaces, to silent overwhelming presences staring at me. In many cases, my mind navigates such perplexing spaces that I am unable to bring to my normal cause-and-effect rational consciousness, which is what occurs at night when I enter the mercurial river just before entering unconsciousness. Then I may ask: "What was that?" No answer comes. Too weird, too strange to make sense of it. Although our minds are perhaps shuffling and reshuffling images and ideas all the time, some plants are able to offer us glimpses of that continuous creative activity.

In my own humble practice, ayahuasca taught me a simple and effective way to help people needing assistance during the experiences. I ask the person to lay down, arms at the sides of the body. I place the index and middle finger of one of my hand on the solar plexus of the person, the middle finger of the other hand between the eyebrows. I ask the person to breathe slowly and deeply. The fingers on the solar plexus monitor heartbeat, depth of breathing, and possible bowel movements. The middle finger, on the other hand, detects emotions: contractions of the procerus muscles indicate distress. I hum calmly, the rhythm of my own breathing serving as a pattern for the breathing of the person. I continue doing so until the person heaves two or three deep sighs, a sign that the person is beginning to relax. I remove my fingers from the solar plexus and blow air forcefully three times into the solar plexus. I cannot explain how or why this works, but in most cases, this is sufficient, and the person can continue the journey in peace. Is there some kind of harmonization of brain and heart, thoughts and emotions? I do not know.

It is puzzling how ayahuasca is used in so many different ways, not only for the diagnosis of illnesses, or finding game or lost objects, or healing. It is also used in waging war by some Amazonian Indigenous groups and to do harm. Do I believe that just by taking ayahuasca, one becomes a better person? Unfortunately, I don't, even though there seem to be plenty of people who think this is the case. Quite the opposite, I think the path is tortuous, full of dangers, and false pretensions. These plants may just enhance what is inside us, and discipline—as with any other spiritual path—is required. Perhaps this is why Indigenous practitioners talk about the necessity of the diet, preparing the receiver, and becoming more like plants through purification.

Regardless, these sacred plants give us a sense that reality, whatever it is, is much more complex and fascinating than what we have learned in our schools. They put us in touch with deeper aspects of the mystery. This is perhaps one of the reasons why ayahuasca is no longer an obscure Amazonian potion but now attracts people of all ages and walks of life. Many of these may, of course, forget and continue everyday life as if nothing had happened. Others will make big changes in their lives. In my own case, I believe ayahuasca has made me more sensitive toward the environment—which means care, compassion, gratitude, and appreciation of the natural world and our situation. Perhaps I am even more curious about the nature of reality. What a privilege to be alive on this beautiful planet! But also, what an enormous responsibility this entails, especially now when we are perfectly aware that our human history has taken such a course that propels us toward our own destruction and that of countless other non-human persons with whom we share this planet.

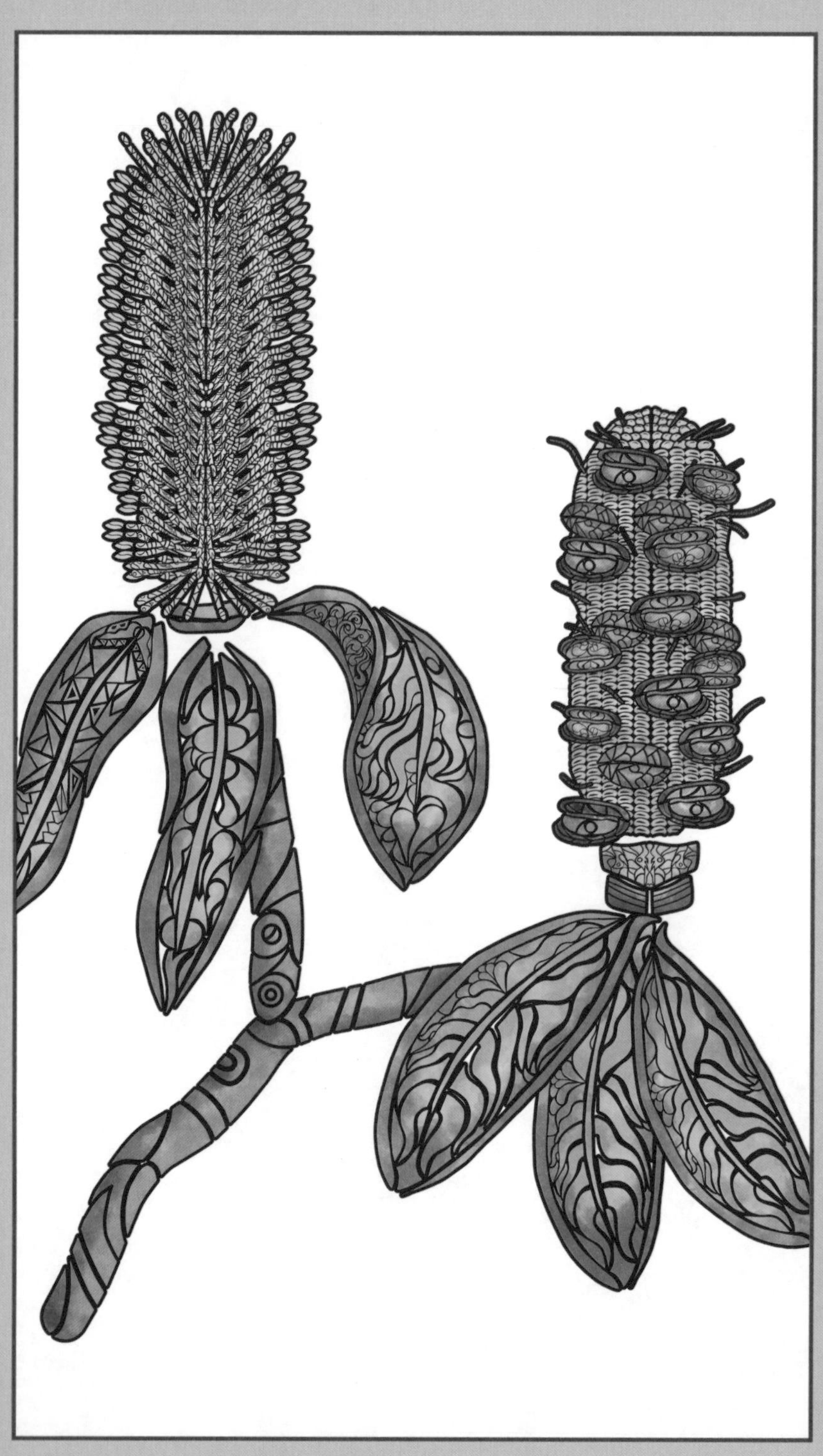

POEM 1

Banksia

Banksia spp.

▪ Anne Elvey

1. annunciation

they buckle   at bent
elbow &   gnarl
silver-sided tongues

slender toward
gravity   upward
are   green surface

to ceiling   their
triple type
of cone   at seed

bristle & bloom   are
built   as knack
they bank on sand

send search
for wet   anchor
appointment

& duration   if
later a limb
shears   falls

or wood   one day
welcomes flame
to   step down

gristle of bole   then
can whiskers declare
for   hollowing

2. visitation

a tremor of limb
tail   twitches
discernible habit

of host   as aloof
a kind of lumber
as if gait   were

boldened both
and stopped in stone
boots   with sand

at toe and feet
not lead but fibrous
tendrils   why not

say   roots
should this convey
too much of ancestry

impossible to forego
a species' cliché
humankind as   tree

hyphen the others
as bare bend
to motion   survival

brings the amber
of   a world
assumed

3. benediction

a seed's scrape
bursts   from pod
absences curve

inside a woody
shell   packed like
text before bristle

yields to   wing
scale   to scud
on this path

littered with twig &
tempt   anticipation
of strangers   keys

in hand when every
tactic taught
is useless   probable

harm becomes
bread   honey
a full moon

invisible   by day
a cone crammed
with   closed cups

its weight on a palm
fist   round the fit
of a   thing

CHAPTER 3

Banyan

Ficus benghalensis

John Charles Ryan

A humid gust whisks the yellowing egg-shaped leaves on the dusty earth below an old banyan. It is the end of the dry season in Central Java, Indonesia. Slowed by the midday sear, I walk—languor my only companion—around the perimeter of the Candi Mendut site. This small temple is less than three miles from the world-famous Buddhist complex Borobudur. In the adumbral haven of the tree's broad-shouldering canopy, a chattering boy swings with euphoria from aerial roots draping to the ground like thick ropes. A brood darts skittishly across the courtyard. Relinquishing his grip on the fibrous cables, the child imitates the rooster's crow then chases futilely after the hens. My lower vertebrae crackle as I hunch down to inspect a curious alcove formed by the interwoven appendages of the sacred tree. Here, a jar wrapped snugly in a sky blue fabric contains an unseen offering.

According to interpretations of the Karangtengah, a stone inscription composed in Old Javanese and Sanskrit, King Indra of the Shailendra Dynasty constructed Candi Mendut during the early ninth century AD. The rupestral text attributes the name *Venu-vana-mandira*, or "Bamboo Temple Grove," to the monument. Mendut consists of a large central temple with a square terrace surrounded by the remains of several smaller brick stupas. A vaulted chamber—musky, cool, and saturated with prayer—encloses statues of the Buddha and two Bodhisattvas seated opposite one another. Relief sculptures adorning the temple's volcanic-stone exterior depict other Bodhisattvas sheltered by the Tree of Awakening under which Siddhartha Gautama—the Buddha—attained Enlightenment. To be precise, the Bodhi tree integral to the Buddhist tradition is a fig species, pipal or *Ficus religiosa*, closely related to the stately banyan that now presides over Mendut.

Although lacking the ascetic devotion of my predecessors, I am likewise inclined to find shade and contemplate the spiritual, historical, and cultural resonances here. A placard near my bench gives the name "Pohon Dewata"—Tree of the Gods—for this behemoth. On the map, an orange splotch reminds me, correctly so, that "Saya di sini: *I am here.*"

Outside the low iron gate circumscribing the grounds, two less mature banyans serve as sentries at a crossroads. Beneath their outspread boughs, a woman peddles *jamu*—a decoction of ginger, turmeric, and other herbs—as the oleaginous scent of fried rice intermixes with motorbike exhaust. Beside the refugial trunks, supine men appear as if in an intractable stupor. This soporific scene lies along an east-west axis—considered an ancient pilgrimage route by archaeologists—crossing the Elo and Progo rivers before intersecting with the temples Pawon and Borobudur. Together with the fig trees, the temple (*candi*) triad constitutes a spiritual unity linking the built environment to the vegetal world—imbricating the immaterial sphere and the sensory domain. I swallow the bittersweet brew, hoping it will ease the hacking cough I've acquired since coming to the candi-rich Kedu Plain in the shadow of Mount Merapi.

What is the mind of the banyan? How might we come to appreciate the mindedness of botanical life at a point in the history of the planet when such a realization seems especially crucial to human and more-than-human futures?

Evoked by the tree-temple spatial dialogue I observed at Mendut, the banyan's mind might be understood as closely connected to the Buddha mind that liberates Bodhisattvas from earthly suffering. In repose under Pohon Dewata, the meditative stillness felt much like the palpable calmness of standing before the statue. Notwithstanding its inherently compassionate nature, the banyan is also a spiritually potent being that harbors deities—both benevolent and malevolent—and thus demands conscious minding. In many ways, the traditional Javanese perspective on the tree as both a creative and destructive force echoes recent studies of plants that highlight their complex capacities for intelligent adaptation.

The following essay considers three perspectives on the theme of the present book. The first is the banyan mind as implicated in the Buddha mind and, more broadly, as a manifestation of the sacred in Javanese life. The second is the minding of the banyan through gestures of care, respect, and supplication. The third is the interior mindfulness increasingly attributed to species such as *F. benghalensis* by research in vegetal cognition. These three views correspond to three nodes that will structure my approach to banyan-thinking: Buddha Mind (religion and spirituality), Minding Banyan (culture and history), and Banyan Mindfulness (ecology and science).

NODE I: BUDDHA MIND

Banyans are spiritual mediators and religious conduits. Known also as *beringin* and *waringin*, those of Central Java are close kin of the Bodhi (or Bo) tree linked fundamentally to Buddhist awakening. As writers have claimed, *Ficus* trees facilitated the diffusion of Buddhist thought from Northeast India to Japan, Thailand, Indonesia, and elsewhere. According to the Jātaka tales, Anāthapindika planted a Bo seed at the Jetavana town gate in the ancient city of Shravasti. The wealthy merchant "stirred up the fragrant soil and dropt it in. The instant it dropt from his hand, before the very eyes of all, up sprang as broad as a plough-head a bo-sapling." In addition to imparting moral guidance, the narrative reveals how the tree propagates readily by seeds and cuttings. Its brief annual leaf-fall, furthermore, is thought to coincide with the date of the Buddha's death at Kuśināra. More than a botanical figment of the imagination, the banyan mind is a breathing phenomenon integral to the Buddha mind—that which finds release from bodily karma and attains awakening.

Allied not only to Buddhist Enlightenment, the banyan signifies older animist spiritualities that confer preternatural power to the arboreal domain. A familiar sight at street junctions in Java—such as the drowsy crossroads at Candi Mendut's entrance—the tree is considered the dwelling place of tutelary deities who can turn malicious if not appeased with offerings. In the mid-twentieth century, Indonesianist Justus M. van der Kroef observed that the Javanese recognized the gods (*danyang desa*) and spirits (*hantu*), residing within and lurking around large banyans, as guardians. What's more, the late-nineteenth-century Dutch travel writer Augusta de Wit wrote that "under some huge waringin tree, at the gate of a town or village, an altar is erected to the tutelary genius, the "Danhjang Dessa," who has his abode in the thick-leaved branches. And the pious people, whenever they have any important business to transact, come to it, and bring a tribute of frankincense and flowers, to propitiate the god."

With its potential for spectacular growth, the banyan embodies fecundity. Its stalactitic array of aerial roots epitomizes the effusive flourishing of vegetal being. In fact, the largest known tree specimens in the world—the Great Banyan and Thimmamma's Banyan, both located in India and considered sanctified among Hindus—occupy a jaw-dropping 4.67 and 4.70 acres, respectively. In his seminal, *The History of Java* from 1830—a work almost as monolithic as the banyan itself—British statesman Thomas Stamford Raffles noted a wedding day blessing recited by elders to brides hoping to become pregnant: "May the gods be merciful unto you: henceforth be flourishing as the *pándan* [*Pandanus amaryllifolius*] and *waríng'en* trees." In more direct terms, de Wit interpreted the conjugal benediction as an entreaty to *danyang desa*: "Give us a progeny like to the spreading crown of the waringin tree." The banyan's imposing form is indeed a physical manifestation of abundance that reverberates spiritually wherever it grows.

In Javanese mythology, the banyan is a hallowed locus where the dramas of otherworldly beings unfold. Accordingly, the tree is a source of refuge yet also a site of banishment; an agent of well-being yet also a font of danger. Raffles' history relates the tale of Narada who descends from heaven, or Suralaya, to search for a wife for the god Sang Yang Guru. Arriving on earth, Narada discovers a stunning young woman named Sri who he accompanies back to heaven to place in the care of Sakra. Once Sri reaches maturity, another deity, Wisnu, becomes enamored of her. The consummation of Sri and Wisnu's illicit passion infuriates Sang Yang Guru so greatly he expels Wisnu forever from Suralaya to a place known as Waringin Pitu or "Seven Banyan Trees." Additionally, in the Indonesian legend of Pontianak—the ghost of a woman who died while giving birth—the aerial roots of the banyan form the hair of the cruel spirit that strangles unsuspecting victims below. Fortunately for me, Pontianak was spreading evil elsewhere the afternoon I gazed tremulously upward into the canopy of Pohon Dewata.

NODE II: MINDING BANYAN

In the folklore of the Yogyakarta Sultanate, those who can walk blindfolded between Beringin Kemba—or Waringin Kurung, the "Twin Banyans"—will be blessed with good luck. The dark-green-headed banyans are impossible to overlook in the sandy barrenness of the Royal Palace's *alun-alun kidul* or south plaza. Guarding the spacious square, the bulky twins symbolize the idea of *pengayom* (shelter). Each with a white-brick fence encircling its base, the trees loom over a posse of schoolkids in blue uniforms engrossed in a game of soccer. Nearby, a mother and daughter test their mettle. Eyes covered with a cloth as black as her hijab, the mother sets off on a promising course but suddenly swerves south, soft-crashing into one of the fences as if asleep at the wheel. In contrast, proceeding deliberately and giving the banyans a generous berth, the daughter fares better and, surely, will secure her fortune.

About a kilometer away, *alun-alun lor*, or the north plaza, is the main entrance to the Royal Palace or Kraton Ngayogyakarta Hadiningrat. Another beringin duo—known as Kiai Dewandaru and Kiai Wijayadaru—marks the spot where, as per custom, valets would receive the parasols of visiting dignitaries. An axis running between the trees connects the royal complex to the stratovolcano Mount Merapi in the north and the Indian Ocean in the south. According to my garrulous guide, the smaller beringin is only about thirty years old. Depicted in an antique black-and-white museum photo with its distinctive flattened crown, the original Kiai Dewandaru was planted during the reign of Sultan Hamengkubuwono I (1717–92). The venerable tree, however, toppled over in 1988 during the funerary rites of Sultan Hamengkubuwono IX, who had passed away during a visit to the United States. Among the Javanese, this uncanny human-tree correspondence signifies that the grief of the ninth sultan's sudden death was too heavy for the elderly banyan to bear.

As vividly apparent at the Yogyakarta palace, banyans have been associated with real and mythic royal figures alike. The planting of sacred trees within and around squares reflected a belief in the king as the divine incarnate. Raffles observed that beringin had been a "sign or mark of the royal residence from the earliest date of Javan history." Old banyans, epitomized by Kiai Dewandaru, also surround *astana*—the burial sites of royals and nobles. As such, they are implicated in the afterlife.

In the folktale, "The Origin of the Banyan Tree," the king's concubine Dewi Andana poisons Prince Jamojaya so that her own son might eventually become royalty. After the prince dies, his wife Dewi Kusumasari implores the god Kamajaya to resurrect his lifeless body. In response, the god transforms Jamojaya into a banyan—his arms turning into leaves, hair becoming aerial roots, legs becoming underground roots: "This tree is a sacred tree. It will be called *beringin* (the banyan tree) and it will live forever. All people will consider this tree sacred and put offerings for the gods under its branches [...] if any should dare cut down this tree, his descendants shall be cursed." This motif of human-tree transmogrification resurfaces in the epic poem "The Brata Yudha," specifically in the lines, "Sad / Looked her waringen tree, like unto a sorrowful wife separated from her husband." In another folk narrative, the beautiful Jowar Manikam rejects the advances of Pangkulu. In turn, the jilted suitor lies to Jowar's father, claiming that the morally pure woman attempted to seduce him. The enraged father orders Jowar's execution, but when the fatal hour comes, her brother stabs a small deer instead. Jowar is able to escape to the shelter of a beringin tree as "the still unripe fruits of the forest attained maturity, and seemed to offer themselves as a relief to her."

In these tales of sultans and princes, of princesses and concubines, banyan trees reciprocate gestures of human minding by proffering refuge, nourishment, and hope in exchange. The longstanding attribution of immortality and guardianship to beringin has underlain its appropriation as a prominent political emblem. The Indonesian coat of arms, Garuda Pancasila, features a banyan icon along with a star, chain, bull, rice seed, and cotton bud. Golkar, the political group that helped propel Suharto's contentious presidency from 1968 to 1998, adopted the banyan as its logo. On the surface, the species represents national unity. Yet its utter domination of its environment also connotes, for some, biocultural homogeneity and sociopolitical repression. The irreconcilable duality of beringin reflects a mindfulness that is at once life-giving and death-dealing.

NODE III: BANYAN MINDFULNESS

A beringin grove near the 1,200 year old Hindu temple Prambanan in Yogyakarta affords a comfortable reprieve from the steadily rising clamminess of the afternoon. I take a breather here from the intensities of temple-sauntering. In this private oasis drenched in mottled light, the gothic forms, entangled limbs, and leathery verdure of the banyans thwart the piercing tropical sun. Sheaves of aerials drift down like giant squid through translucent seawater. Gradually, over the ages, their tentacles have suctioned to the lichen-clad boulders and transmogrified into living stone. As I inspect the coterie of consecrated trees, the peculiar growth habit of beringin—in fact, belonging to the cosmopolitan plant group known as "strangler figs" and beginning its life as an epiphyte—becomes especially evident. What sort of mindfulness underlies the banyan's malleable manner of living?

Strangler figs germinate in the crevices and knotholes of host trees from seeds dispersed by birds and other creatures. Until their tendrilous roots creep through the branches and slink down the trunk of the condemned to reach the ground, stranglers exist as epiphytes—plants that grow on other plants yet are not parasitic. As they mature, though, their prominent airborne assemblages begin to form a meshwork—consisting of webbed pseudotrunks with connective gaps called *anastomoses*—that eventually suffocates the host by constricting fluid and nutrient movement in its outer vascular tissue. Notwithstanding strangler figs' macabre opportunism, ecologists point to the possibility of mutualisms between the colonizer and the colonized. Host trees, for instance, are less likely to be uprooted during severe storms—although, I must say, such an advantage seems a trivial consolation in the scheme of things.

The mindfulness of beringin encodes the collective mindfulness of the more-than-human communities dependent upon it. In this sense, the vegetal mind is an assemblage of conscious pluralities—a polymorphous mode of thought distributed across space, time, and beings. As cyberneticist Gregory Bateson reminded us, ecology and mind are inseparably entwined. A keystone species, the banyan nurtures fellow organisms by openhandedly providing food, water, habitat, and manifold other essentials. The tree, moreover, shares a specific coevolutionary rapport with its exclusive pollinator, the wasp *Eupristina masoni*. Merely 0.05 inch long on average, fig wasps can travel one hundred miles per day in search of trees. Anecdotal accounts relate that the wasps—in their all-consuming desire to pollinate—can traverse ocean stretches to locate the *Ficus* species with which they are ancestrally companionable. If mind is the sheer force of intention, then the figs and their wasps are copiously minded.

In my shaded sanctuary, I watch throngs of women grip parasols as they stroll by. To my haptic sense, the anastomose trunk of the banyan feels as dense and cold as temple stone. More than one-hundred years ago, at Bogor Botanical Gardens outside Jakarta, the lithic appearance of beringin similarly captivated the botanical imagination of de Wit: "This strange resemblance of living vegetable matter to inert stone ceases only when, issuing from among the stems, one looks at the waringins from a distance, and sees the grey multitude of boles, trunks, and stems disappearing under spreading masses of foliage." From her point of view, banyans are liminal entities that complicate neat distinctions between the animate and the "inert." A few decades before de Wit's extended foray into Java, the "grey multitude" also intrigued French naturalists Emmanuel Le Maout and Joseph Decaisne who wrote of "adventitious roots [that] descend to the earth, root there, and form arcades which extend on all sides, far from the trunk." Likewise, in *The Vegetable Kingdom*, famed British botanist John Lindley praised beringin's "remarkable [...] vast rooting branches."

Yet, despite their ecological interconnectedness, spiritual attributions, and religious symbolisms, banyans can cause harm, desecration, and even death. The flipside of its potential to shelter/heal is its compulsion to breach/destroy. Beringin is thus of a dialectical mindedness. Raffles lamented the damage the octopoidal species caused at abandoned temples yet applauded the resolve of locals to resist the banyan intrusion: "The inclosures of the surrounding fields attest the extent to which the farmers have turned to account the devastations made by the *waríngen* trees." Encountering the derelict temples of Dieng, a high plateau region between Yogyakarta and Semarang, Raffles demonstrated ecological awareness in his recollection that "it was particularly observable, that little or no injury had been done by vegetation, the climate being unfavourable to the *waríngen*, whose roots are so destructive to the buildings of the lower regions." In these instances, beringin emblematizes the devolution of cultural places into waste spaces dominated by the unrestrained florescence of vegetal being.

To glimpse banyan mindedness requires moving beyond a view of plant life as mere material or mute constituent—as the inert stuff we do things with. Consider, as a case in point, the medicinal attributes of banyan's propagating roots. The asphyxiating hair of Pontianak can be approached from two perspectives. The first understands the tree as a repository of therapeutic constituents to be mined for humankind's benefit. This is the prevailing phytochemical model that values plants for the substances they yield. Recent clinical studies, for example, confirm the analgesic, or pain-relieving, properties of banyan roots. In contrast, the second acknowledges the tree's own mind*full*ness as a function of its internal physiological processes. Allelopathy is the inhibition of a plant by another plant as mediated by the release of growth-hindering chemicals. The allelopathic intelligence of beringin—using chemicals and other kinds of signals to manipulate its environment—corresponds to the ancient Javanese belief that sleeping at night under the tree will bring misfortune when the stifling compounds are most active.

Wherever I now go in Java, I see banyans, spindly and stout, boulder-hugging and tree-smothering, solitary streetside and gregarious in groves. I have become beringin-minded—attuned to the tree's mode of meaning-making. The banyan mind is a confluence of mindings: human, bird, wasp, Buddha. Not circumscribed by brain, mind permeates world. At this critical juncture in Earth history, entraining to banyan mindfulness could help us avert catastrophe and come to live with—and within—the intelligence of all that exists.

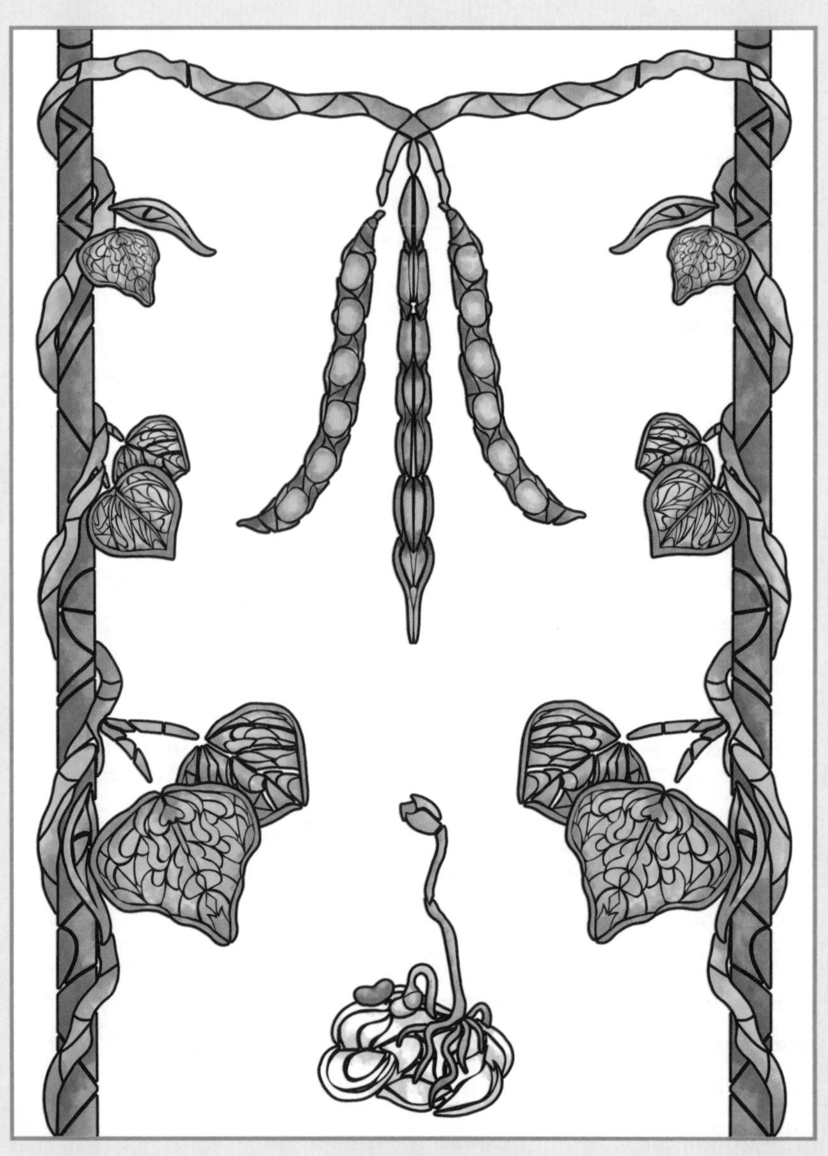

CHAPTER 4

Bean

Phaseolus vulgaris L.

▪ **André G. Parise and Gabriel R. A. de Toledo**

From the vaporous sizzling of a pressure cooker, a particular smell emanates and fills the kitchen. This sweetish and slightly sulfurous scent comes from the boiling beans inside the cooker and, once it reaches the noses and tongues of the people around it, it might elicit memories from a distant past. Sweet remembrances from their childhoods, moments of their everyday lives, and the idea of good homemade food.

Cooked beans, together with rice, are indeed the foundation of Brazilian cuisine and are the most eloquent example of typical food that unites Brazilians from north to south. They unite people from the Amazon rainforest to the southern grasslands of Rio Grande do Sul. So, it is not surprising that when the smell of cooked beans reaches the olfactory and taste receptors of a Brazilian, it triggers the nervous system's electrical signals. Once these signals reach the brain, they are integrated with other signals and memories—that is, stored information in the person's brain—thus allowing them to recall those reminiscences. This is a fundamental aspect of our minds.

Surprisingly, as it has been discovered, the bean plant itself is also capable, in its own manner, to use electrical signals for efficient integration of the several stimuli that it receives from the environment. Like us, bean plants—together with all the other plants—are able to sense their surroundings and perceive the scents, the sounds, the tastes of the environment, and integrate these signals on an electrical basis for an efficient comprehension of what is happening around them and to themselves. Just like us, but in a "bean-like" way. Our scientific research has attempted to understand the electrical basis of this internal communication of plants, such as beans. How do they use electrical signals to understand their current state and to perceive their surroundings? What are the resemblances and differences of this perception system in plants and animals? What are the patterns of the plants' electrical signaling under different stimuli? The questions are infinite, and the bean plant is a good teacher for answering at least some of these inquiries.

Our relationship with the bean plants has a long history. As we mentioned before, beans are an intrinsic part of our culture and are very important to the culture of other American countries as well. The bean plant, which is native to the highlands of the Americas, was probably domesticated by the Native people from Mesoamerica and Southern Andes region about 8,000 years ago and, from these two places, spread to the rest of the continent as a crop plant. Cultivated by the many people who inhabited the Americas, it was also adopted by the European colonizers and became one of the favorite foods of our continent.

Besides this cultural aspect, beans cross many people's lives in another, unassuming way. Many Brazilians have made this simple experiment, especially in some moment of their childhood (we certainly did it many times) to sow a bean seed in wet cotton on a saucer and watch it germinate, grow, and develop. It was fascinating for us as children because it was possible to accompany the magical metamorphosis of a seed into a plant. We watched the shoot and the first roots emerging, the cotyledons, and the first pair of leaves opening wide—like a good stretch after so much time enclosed in that small seed—and the whole seedling becoming a mature plant. As far as we can remember, this was one of our first contacts with botany, and we don't know to what extent it has influenced us to become botanists. Certainly, it contributed a lot. For many people, as well, the bean-on-cotton experiment is the first contact with a plant and an opportunity for understanding that plants are living beings that move (in their time), grow, and develop.

After this early contact with bean plants, we distanced ourselves. The beans, of course, were always there, present in our lives, discretely, in our daily food. But, despite the bean-on-cotton child experiment, it was hard to remember that each bean grain in our meals was an entire plant. However, many years later, the bean as grown plants rather than grains reappeared in our lives in the most unexpected way.

During college, where we studied Biological Sciences (Gabriel in Presidente Prudente, in the São Paulo state, and André in Florianópolis, in the southern Santa Catarina state), we came into contact with these new and still not widely known studies demonstrating that plants are cognitive and intelligent. Willing to explore this in the graduation course, we contacted our current professor advisor, Dr. Gustavo Maia Souza, who was also beginning to study plant intelligence as well, especially the electrical signaling that underlies plant behaviors. And, in search of a model plant to perform our studies, the beans re-entered our lives in a non-food manner.

We chose them for our experiments because their seeds are easy to find, they germinate well, and the plant grows easily in laboratory conditions. The bean plant, just like in the bean-on-cotton experiment, grows very quickly and, in a few days, the plants are ready to be used in the experiments. Furthermore, the young stem is fleshy and soft from the beginning of its development. Thus electrodes for our research can easily be inserted into them. So, let's talk a bit about these electrical signals, why we study them, and what our research with the beans has demonstrated.

For over a hundred and fifty years, men and women of science have known that plants are able to produce and propagate electrical signals. For some time, it was thought that those signals were only involved in the quick movements performed by "moving plants," such as the sensitive plant, *Mimosa pudica*, and the Venus flytrap, *Dionaea muscipula*. Later, these electrical signals were identified in other "ordinary" plants, and it was recognized that electrical signals are widespread through the domains of life. For example, in animals, such signals are fundamental for making our brains, muscles, and hearts work and are noticeably present in neuron cells.

The first electrical signal discovered was called "action potential." This name came from early experiments in animal electrophysiology, which have found that these electrical signals promote actions in the body, especially muscular movements. After a conversation with Charles Darwin about moving plants, the physiologist John Burdon-Sanderson was encouraged to investigate the physiological basis of the Venus flytrap's movements. He discovered that the closing of the plant's traps is preceded by an electrical signal with similar characteristics as animal action potentials, and the term was promptly adopted to describe the phenomenon in plants too. Nowadays, it is known that plant and animal action potentials are involved in many other responses beyond the promotion of rapid movements—such as dreams, thoughts, cognitive processes, alterations in gene expression, defense responses, induction of glandular secretion, among many others.

In animal systems, neural cells have an equilibrium state in which positive ions such as sodium (Na^+) stay mainly outside the cell. There are more positive charges outside the cell than inside, and this maintains a negative membrane resting potential. Since there are fewer positive charges inside the cell, the outer positive ions are attracted to the inside, but their charges cannot merge because the cell membrane separates them. This separation of charges creates a tension—or voltage potential—that can even be measured in volts (V) or, more appropriately due to the minute size of the cells, in millivolts (mV).

Ions can cross the cell membrane mainly through ion channels and pumps, i.e., proteins that permit this traffic from one side to the other. In the case of action potentials, these channels only open when stimulated by certain chemical substances—the most famous being neurotransmitters such as dopamine (which is released into the brain when we engage in a pleasant activity)—or by other stimuli such as electrical or mechanical factors. When these ion channels are opened, there is a transient switch in the membrane potential because the positive ions, which were formerly outside, flood into the cell and positively charge the inner side of the membrane. Immediately after, ion pumps start to send those positive ions back outside until the neuron returns to its previous resting potential.

This electrical signal is self-propagable and runs through the cell to its far end. There, it stimulates the next adjacent cell to generate its own action potential, which runs to the next cell, and so on, carrying the electrical message from cell to cell. Given some differences, the process described here is applicable to plants as well! In this case, calcium (Ca^{2+}) is the main driver of the membrane depolarization, and not sodium.

Action potentials are the very basis by which our brains work, and whatever the brain does, it involves these signals. Whenever we learn something new, our neurons connect themselves into a novel, complex, and beautiful architecture that enables these electrical signals to flow from one place to another, taking and bringing the electrical messages that emerge in the form of conscious memory. Even unconscious brain activity is possible due to these signals.

The things we perceive by our sensory organs—such as odors, flavors, touch, heat, pain, and so on—are also encoded into action potentials that flow to the brain and are interpreted accordingly. So, as mentioned at the beginning of this essay, if one sniffs a smell that recollects childhood, this is possible because the smell perceived by the odor receptors in the nose is encoded in the form of action potentials that travel through the olfactory nerves to the brain. Once there, they cause other action potentials that spread by this constellation of neurons that physically encode the memory of the delicious cooked beans that his or her mum used to cook. And thanks to that, the person recalls those delightful memories. As we can see, electrical signaling is the basis of our minds.

Plants also have their memories stored in their bodies, and they do produce action potentials in their cells, mainly in the cells of the phloem, which is part of the bundles that conduct the sap through the plant. Everything a plant perceives—the moisture of the soil, the "taste" of the nutrients that the roots find in its subterranean search for food, the sounds that arrive to the plant, the scents that other plants release, the touch and even the injuries that animals cause to them, the shifts in the temperature and lighting, and other environmental information—is encoded in electrical signals.

Plants can also generate and propagate different electrical signals other than action potentials. Depending on their characteristics, these signals have different names, such as variation potentials, local electrical potentials, and systemic potentials. All these signals run through the plant, taking and bringing information, and are crucial for the plants' perception, understanding, and interaction with the world. Hence, electrical signaling is an extremely important aspect of plants' cognition, just as it is to animals.

Several different electrical signals are delivering messages throughout the plant's body all the time, and depending on what the plant is perceiving, the dynamics of these signals change. The entire set of electrical signals that flows through the plant, from the cell level to the organism level, was recently named "plant electrome," after the also recently coined concept of the "electrome." The term *electrome* describes the totality of all electrical activity of any biological system during a period of time. If plants have electrical activity and signaling at any level of the organism, naturally, they have their own electrome. In order to understand the dynamics of electrical signaling in plants and their significance to what the plant is experiencing, we applied this electromic approach to study bean plants.

For our research, we have adapted the well-known techniques of electroencephalogram (EEG, used for monitoring brain activity) and electrocardiogram (used for monitoring heart activity). Since the plant electrome relies on the same basic principles of the animal electrome, our research group applied the same techniques, although adapted to plants and hence called "electro*phyto*gram" (from the Greek root *phytón*, meaning "plant"). We use needles as electrodes that are inserted in the stem of the beans (and other plants) that we are studying in an attempt to capture the electrical signals that are going up and down in the plant via its cells. Then, we apply a stimulus—such as substances that will block the water uptake by the roots, salt solutions, fungi that will infect their leaves, and so on—to understand what the plants are saying in an electrical language, leading to a wider comprehension of how plants communicate, how plants perceive their environment, and even what, exactly, a plant is, all told.

With our research, we have discovered that the electrome of bean plants change depending on what situation they are experiencing or depending on the stimulus they receive. Normally, stressful situations such as cold, low light, or drought drastically alter the behavior of the electrical signaling inside the plant. We have seen spikes of electrical activity in which the whole plant seems to coordinate the behavior of its cells to produce changes in its voltage potentials with many mV of amplitude.

Also, it seems that each one of these behaviors has a specific signature (because it encodes information about a specific status) which could be used to recognize the physiological state of the plant by its electrical activity alone. Obviously, this could have many useful applications, especially in agriculture, so from an economic point of view, these studies are quite interesting too.

Anyway, for us, at least, the most beautiful aspect of our research with beans and other plants is not its economic potential, but the fact that we are beginning to understand plants' electrical language and, further, the electrical foundation of this internal communication. And even more, the electrical basis of—why not say?—the mind of plants.

There is no mental activity, state of awareness, or even consciousness, without electricity. The electrical activity of the cell is a fundamental aspect of life itself, as it is impossible for an organism—be it a bacteria or a whale —to live without electrical activity in its cells, generating potentials for the synthesis of important energetic molecules, allowing the proteins and enzymes to work properly, and intermediating the fluxes of information within the organism. The differences in ion concentrations inside and outside the cells are what keep us alive. When these differences are equalized, we are dead: we have met the frightening thermodynamic equilibrium, which haunts all the living.

As mentioned before, the dance of ions within the brain, or within the plant cells, is the framework that allows the mind to exist and function. And everything that happens and is perceived by a brain or plant is encoded into electrical signals. Plants lack the constellation of neurons that keeps the memories in the brain, but certainly, they have other means for storing past experiences; we still do not know how it happens, but many alternatives have been hypothesized. It could be the structure of the cytoskeleton (the skeleton of the cells), which can hold electrical charges, proteins that are produced and stored when the plant experiences certain situations, molecular representations of past experiences, or even the very structure of the plant.

In our brains, there is a synchronic and organized activity of many neurons simultaneously firing action potentials here and there, and this keeps our minds working. These electrical signals have different frequencies and present complex oscillatory patterns containing overlapped waves of depolarization. These waves are associated with normal or disturbed brain functions and are linked to states of mind.

Many of these brain waves are described and associated with specific brain activities. For example, alpha waves (ranging 8–12 Hz) are related to states of relaxation and with the transition of waking to sleeping states. Beta waves (12–28 Hz), in turn, are associated with alert states and, sometimes, with stress states. Gamma waves (25–100 Hz) are associated with high cognitive brain function and high concentration states, including meditation. Delta waves (0.5–4 Hz) are associated with deep sleep and its disorders. Theta waves (4–7 Hz) are linked to learning, memory formation, and spatial location and are particularly found in young children or in adults under special conditions. There are many subclasses of each of these waves, and other brain waves have been described for humans and other animals.

Depending on what the brain is experiencing, some of these waves will manifest more strongly and stand out over the others, and this reflects different states of the mind. Think about an orchestra playing a symphony. The feeling that the music expresses is related to some group of instruments and chords that will be dominant at that moment. If the piece is sad, slow violins will be predominant. If it is lively, maybe the drums and brass instruments will manifest more strongly. For melancholic tones, mainly bassoons and oboes might be heard—but this all does not mean that the other instruments are quiet. Within the brain, the cerebral symphony has its own adagios and allegros too. Brain waves are the neuronal orchestra playing.

In order to look for gamma waves in plants, researchers proposed the use of EEG since these high frequencies are involved in high cognition tasks in animals and, theoretically, could have a similar role in plants. However, other quite complex mental processes such as learning, memory, and spatial localization do not necessarily demand high-frequency waves to occur. So, just like us, plants do not need gamma waves for learning and memory. In other words, the possible existence of a plant mind would not depend on these waves. Moreover, the intelligence and mind of a plant should satisfy the needs and problems of plant life, which obviously are different from our needs and problems. The plant plays its own electrical "cerebral symphony," which is evolutionarily and qualitatively different from ours: a green mind for a green, sessile life and an animal mind for a free and moving lifestyle.

If some kind of mind is underpinning the behavior of plants, we still do not know, and it is rather a difficult question to address and prove scientifically. However, there is increasing evidence from plant neurobiology, plant ecology, and plant electrophysiology—among other research fields—pointing to the need for consciousness or mind in plants, as well as other brainless organisms (including bacteria). This consciousness could be involved in the complex and adaptive responses presented by organisms facing constant environmental changes. The adaptive responses could be expressed in many organizational scales, such as metabolic, physiological, psychological, behavioral, and sociological aspects, regardless of the biological system in question.

Nowadays, it is indubitable that plants are intelligent and cognitive beings. They learn, remember, communicate with other organisms, compete and collaborate, make choices, plan the future, and struggle to achieve goals. All of this seems to be related to plants' internal electrical activity or electromic dynamics. So, if they have a mind (and, as already suggested, we believe that a green mind is indeed possible), then mind has an electrical basis. The plant mind would not be equal to the animal mind, of course, but would be based on the same primeval bioelectrical principles present in all domains of planetary life. It is an inheritance and an evolution of the mind of our last common ancestor, who lived billions of years ago. And it is a lesson of humility—we humans are not that special, as every living thing can have its own mind in its own manner.

Personally, all of this has day-by-day changed our perception of plants. It is fascinating to gaze at a plant—be it a majestic centenary fig tree in the forest or a small ornamental plant in an indoor pot—and realize that it is a very complex organism silently perceiving and interacting with the world. They are individuals with their own "minds," working electrically and/or otherwise, and deserve respect and admiration too. They are not simply food. At the beginning of our graduation, we just threw away the beans used in the experiments. Now, we feel we cannot do that anymore. Instead, we bring the plants to our university's experimental agroecological area and plant them there, where they can grow, bloom, interact with other plants and organisms, and die with dignity after accomplishing their ecological, as well as scientific, mission.

And, for the rest of society, what are the implications of recognizing plants as intelligent, cognitive beings? What could change by acknowledging that plants, too, have complex electrical signaling dynamics in their bodies, comparable to what is found in our own brains? Maybe, by recognizing these similarities (instead of focusing on the differences between plants and us), we have a starting point for deconstructing our anthropocentric pride that has become toxic and harmful for nature and the planet. Could a person, aware of this all, deforest hundreds of acres of Amazon rainforest, knowing that each tree, each bush and herb, is an individual, with its own "mind" and perception of the world, interacting with literally thousands of other organisms at the same time? We think that we still have a lot to learn about beans. They are not simply food for the body but for the mind too. And beans, together with all the other plants, have so much to teach us about humility, respect, and about ourselves.

POEM 2

Big Bluestem

Andropogon gerardi

Megan Kaminski

By the teeth

Long walks do some good but
stillness in the wind pushing north
mid-August is how I root deep
into waking, dream out the meanderings
of everyone else's day. The past is slack
and in it my hands spilled multitudinous,
came and came flowering so many
gifts a new currency pink-petaled.
On hot nights wounds purchased by love
and bug-filled backyards awaken anew;
the ache we singed into each other
still answering like prayer taken hymnal.
I don't know about patience but
can hear the tallgrasses each evening
holding the pose of the moon or you,
a rupture I'm sore from mending.

And the trains

blow by seventy a day, limestone
shaking through shale and chert.
Each morning a different variation on
what it is to swallow one's words to
hold sentences un-extinguished without
suffering injury. Grasshoppers abundant,

and they know what that I dare not,
ceaselessly partaking in meal upon meal
green and brown enameled flanks
laid thick across the tallgrass fields.
Every sunrise a revelation I sleep through
though cows come closer at sunset,
bellow at the fading light, striations
of want and loss and unsent messages
drag across tracks and fences taking
us all together toward the horizon.

Before long I'll be going back home

but today it's mid-August and still green,
shooting grasses overhead and thick on paths.
Listen, the fields are full of companions
informed by sentience we can't wrap
head around. Stems spindle toward
the sun and voles cling to familiar scents.
I am still handsome but no longer young,
driven by my own weedy inclinations
to reseed each fall. Busting through
rocky soil to luxuriate in this late season
sun. Maybe our days here are numbered.
Maybe they ought to be. I talk with the
snow-on-the-mountain path-side and wonder
what I contribute what blight or suture
or sorrow childed into quiet being.

I keep certain wounds open

to honor the past, to display a thing
that acknowledges its deficiency. One train
yields another to pass while grasses twist

in blown-out light. Sometimes summer is
all rain and overabundance, tomatoes
bursting in the heat and a sorrow that
can't find a way home. Twenty years ago
they found a girl in that shed, a story
never tires of cautionary telling. Late
reminder of our intrinsic desire for shelter
and shade, a soft place to rest each night.
Were we all to wear those marks openly
as flooding and time, riverbanks overflowing
and god knows what carried downstream.
Were we to gather the shattered glass whole.

Each time the buzzards descend

I worry about the barn cats—I'm
predictable and can't be helped.
Sometimes a train pauses on tracks
for no discernible reason. Sometimes
alone in the fields, no one around
for miles, I realize myself no different
than on any given day in the city.
Sometimes one's pulse jumps in ecstasy
to sound one is dying or finally alive.
To be lonely is to carry your heart on
sleeves of some sort; my insides vined
bittersweet hold all things worth keeping.
Words drifting into bloodstream,
compensation for a low white-cell count
and weasels that dine on vision,
licking lips each night in deepest sleep.

POEM 3

Birdflower

Crotalaria cunninghamii

▪ **Kirli Saunders**

We don't slow
for the birdflowers
between the Gulf
and the Bay

only those
by abandoned Army base—
dipped in balmy desert rain

passed through window
on salt-kissed day
by a local

who crossed candied plain
to hold velvet wings
in the space
between finger and thumb

who traced toes
in bloodied mud
just to lace
green petal
in the place
of palm
turned upward
toward Grandfather Sun.[1]

CHAPTER 5

Black Austrian Pine

Pinus nigra

■ **Damiano Benvegnù**

I want to tell you a story about a forest. This forest is now known as a Fascist forest if such a thing can, in fact, exist. I want to tell a story about the trees that make up this forest and the people who planted them. I want to tell you a story about seeing both the forest and the trees, and the people who walk through them, as intertwined. I want to tell you a story about not actually seeing but *encountering* forests, trees, and those humans who truly mind them, where they want me to encounter them. I want to tell you this story because I mind the forest, I mind the trees, I mind those humans. I hope they all mind me as well.

My story begins with another story from a long time ago. In central Italy, there was a holy man named Severus, who was the parish priest of the Church of the Blessed Mary in a valley called Interocrina. One day, Severus was called upon by a sick man on the verge of death. The priest did not go immediately, though, because he was busy tending his vineyard, pruning it. When Severus finally arrived at the bedside of the sick man, he was already dead, setting the stage for the following miracle of the priest who, through tears and prayers, brought the man back to life. (Alas, he lives just long enough to receive the last rites from the priest and then dies again). Undoubtedly, there is a religious meaning that goes beyond the literal account here. Yet, the story also tells us about a quite surprising relationship between the holy man and his vines: unexpectedly, he chooses to look after the plants before attending to the moribund.

The story of Severus belongs to Pope Gregory the Great's *Dialogues*, a collection of four books of miracles, wonders, and healings carried out by then little-known holy men in sixth-century Italy. Written at a critical time for the developing Catholic Church and for a war-ravaged Italy, the circa two hundred miracles narrated in the *Dialogues* represent a portion of central Italy as a sacred space where the Christian God is present in both human and non-human form. As is often the case in the lives of medieval saints, these stories are also rich in mundane details that help render the narrative familiar and allow the reader or listener to participate in its supernatural development rather than simply observe it from afar. From a more secular perspective, all these details offer us crucial information about the relationships between specific human communities and their surrounding world, often providing a historical trajectory of environmental immersion and ecological interconnectedness. In other words, these early medieval narratives express how human communities of that period regarded their relationships with local plants as crucial to their reciprocal well-being; as Severus' account illustrates, humans in the *Dialogues* care for plant life so much as to forget their institutional duties.

Perhaps the story of Severus is only an allegorical combination of several hagiographic traditions. Yet, the valley of Interocrina does exist in central Italy—just northeast of Rome, it extends from the city of Rieti to the little town of Antrodoco, whose ancient name was, in fact, *Interocrina* or *Interocrea*, which in Latin means "between the mountains." When the valley splits against a mountain called Mount Giano, five kilometers northeast of Antrodoco, there is a sanctuary known as *Madonna delle Grotte*, Saint Mary of the Caves. Although the sanctuary was built more than a thousand years after the *Dialogues* and thus could not have been Severus' church, it nonetheless testifies to a local religious devotion as old as Gregory's work, as the *grotte* (caves) in the name of the sanctuary refer to a series of paleochristian hermitages on the western slope of Mount Giano. Moreover, people living in Antrodoco have told me that the lower slopes of the surrounding mountains were once covered with autochthonous vineyards, extremely rare crops today. Although we cannot know for certain whether Severus' vineyard was in this area, it is not too far-fetched to imagine it alongside the "caves" of the other holy men, where the sanctuary is currently located.

Today, those who want to explore the remains of the hermitages can take a trail just outside the sanctuary of *Madonna delle Grotte*. Hiking this trail well beyond the caves, en route to the top of Mount Giano, they would encounter a rather extensive pine forest. This forest is unusual for this area in that it is both ecologically isolated from the surrounding Mediterranean ecosystem and at an altitude where we typically find grassy slopes—at least in this part of the Apennine Mountains. However, the presence of this forest just below the western peak of Mount Giano signifies more than an atypical change of ecosystems. It marks instead a cultural distance, a discrepancy in ecological approaches, as the forest suggests the opposite of the immersive relationship between human and environment implicit in Severus' story. In fact, this forest can be interpreted as an example of an "imposed official landscape," a human unidirectional intervention in the environment disregarding the previous spiritualized vernacular landscape, as well as severing webs of accumulated cultural meaning.[1]

The forest on the western slope of Mount Giano was created between 1938 and 1939, in homage to the Italian dictator Benito Mussolini, when recruits studying at the nearby Academy of the Forestry Corps in Cittaducale planted 20,000 black Austrian pine saplings (*Pinus nigra* J.F. Arnold) to spell out DVX, the fascist leader's title in Latin. The choice of the Austrian pine—a species not endemic to this part of Central Italy—was not merely symbolic of contemporary political alliances but belongs to a long-term strategy of using the *Pinus nigra* for reforestation and erosion control since Italian unification in 1861, an approach only intensified under Fascism.[2] In the specific case of Mount Giano, though, the outcome was an arboreal inscription so grand in scale that it was—and still is today—visible from Rome, some one-hundred kilometers away. This is not coincidental; in 1939, the inscription was supposed to render visible Mussolini's long reach over both the human and the non-human world. As environmental historians Armiero and Graf Von Hardenberg have written, the DVX forest signified "the power of the word over nature," a clear example of how the Fascist regime wanted nature to mirror its own verbal narratives.[3] Equally important, the forest offered a unique opportunity to design a landscape according to the aerial gaze created by aviation—flying being a modern activity highly symbolized by the rhetoric of the Fascist regime. The DVX inscription was meant to be enjoyed from a perspective almost inconceivable to Severus and his contemporaries: looking down as if we were giants or gods; or, more simply, from the sky while flying above it.

Perhaps unsurprisingly, given the hegemony of perspectivism in Western societies, this is how we usually approach the DVX forest even today. Although Italian Fascism officially ended in 1943, we still experience this forest as Mussolini and his fellow fascists intended, that is, looking at it from far away as a distant visual spectacle of the regime. Whether we are googling the forest on the internet or driving from Rome toward Antrodoco on the *Via Salaria* (the state highway connecting the Italian capital to the Adriatic Sea), we encounter the forest first and foremost as an image in which we cannot even recognize the trees, but only the massive three letters that they spell out: D-V-X. In other words, from afar, we see only a representation of power and violence, indeed "a prime example of the fascist appropriation of landscapes to mark the regime's domination of both the country and its nature."[4] Sadly, this was my first encounter with the forest as well. While writing an article on the story of Severus in the *Dialogues*, I googled Interocrea and, subsequently, the town of Antrodoco. Satellite images of the DVX forest were among the main search results.

But then, I decided to go to Antrodoco. Located along the Velino River, at the confluence of two narrow Apennine valleys, this little town has a long and rich history extending from the pre-Roman period to, surprisingly, the late Libyan dictator Mu'ammar Gheddafi, who once expressed his intention to invest there. Today, Antrodoco shares some of the same features of several little mountain towns in the area: an aging population and a progressive abandonment of the historic center, only intensified by the catastrophic earthquake in 2016, whose epicenter was in nearby Amatrice. As its old Latin name suggests, Antrodoco is surrounded by three impressive mountains. Most notably, the town lies at the feet of Mount Giano, which appears to loom over Antrodoco, projecting its shadows over roofs and fields, as well as protecting them from the cold winds coming from the northeast. Although the DVX forest is 630 feet tall and 1,360 feet wide and lies on the slope of Mount Giano directly above the town, from Antrodoco, the arboreal inscription cannot be seen; it is not visible at all.

During the summer of 2018, I traveled to Antrodoco because I was both looking for the *long dureé* of specific environmental events and interested in something I read on the news. The previous year, in August, a fire—deemed an accident—burned down part of the DVX forest, damaging partially the letter V and the whole X. Driving toward the town, I could still make out the massive inscription, but the last letter looked almost faded as if the green had been eaten up by the brown color of the surrounding grass fields. I had never been in that area of the Apennines, and what initially intrigued me was the debate that had ensued after the fire, a conversation about the future of the forest as an arboreal monument to Italian Fascism. The newspapers reported varied reactions to the blaze, mostly from outsiders like me, some mortified that the forest has survived so long, advocated its total erasure, while neo-fascist groups had already expressed plans to restore it. For instance, in February 2018, two hundred volunteers associated with the Italian neo-fascist movement CasaPound hiked up Mount Giano to the DVX forest—without any formal permission by the town or by any other local authorities—to replant a thousand pine saplings to replace those destroyed by the fire. My intention was instead to engage with local communities and archives about the history of the forest, as well as to hike up to the burned trees myself and see the damage—and the alleged restoration—up close.

One of the problems with the DVX forest is that the fascist project drastically changed the landscape and the ecosystem of the area, as that species of fir tree was (and still is) not endemic to the region. In the last century, *Pinus nigra* was used to carry out large afforestation programs in Italy—a practice that has had ambivalent ecological results, often contributing negatively to otherwise spontaneous processes of re-naturalization.[5] Even though the Austrian pine has a remarkable ecological plasticity, it also has several side effects when it comes to ecosystems. For instance, when planted in a large number and in close rows as in the case of the DVX forest, it stunts the normal ecological cycle and produces instead a very acidic soil. Furthermore, the species is highly flammable, resulting in large forest fires more often than any other endemic trees from the Mediterranean Basin. This last aspect is bitterly ironic in the case of the forest on Mount Giano because the original planting of the pine trees coincided with the celebrated opening of a nearby major aqueduct commissioned by Mussolini to sustain a growing Rome. This aqueduct, which still provides the Italian capital with 85% of its water, is also responsible for depriving the Velino valley of some of its massive hydrological resources, an issue dramatically evident when the fire hit Mount Giano, and the local community did not have enough water to extinguish it.

Yet, this topiary forest was also an impressive work of environmental engineering that might be credited with stabilizing the mountainside, thus saving the town of Antrodoco from landslides and floods. As in other cases of afforestation in central Italy, even the *Pinus nigra* trees planted to create the DVX inscription played a significant hydrogeological function, their roots holding the superficial soil and drinking up the water that otherwise would have been free to slide down the high, grassy slopes of Mount Giano. Moreover, the plantation is a historical example of the technical collaboration between the Italian Forest Corps and local farmers and lumberjacks, a collaboration that gave birth to new forests in challenging conditions, usually applying a mix of old and innovative approaches. In the specific circumstances of Mount Giano, altitude, soil conditions, and the incline of the slope required a variation of a system called "a gradoni" or small terraces, a system used in the area for centuries. Each terrace is a little more than a meter wide, with a slight counter slope to promote the accumulation of water and organic matter; along each one, the bare root black pine seedlings are planted one meter apart.[6] Quite notably, these small terraces were brought up several times during my conversations with the citizens of Antrodoco. Even though we could not see the DVX inscription while chatting outside in the main square of Antrodoco, the forest was nonetheless present in how locals described these terraces to me as part of their local identity and thus worthy of care and memory. It was there, in these *gradoni*, that their experience met with the experience of the Austrian pines.

The day I decided to hike up to the forest, I was accompanied by Valerio, a volunteer for the local chapter of the Italian Alpine Club and one of the several locals who generously devoted some of their time to my inquiry. It was summer, and at 6:30 am, when I met with my guide in front of the old train station, it was already warm and humid, albeit cloudy. We drove to the sanctuary of Saint Mary of the Caves, parked the car, and began our ascent. After an hour and thirty minutes of silence and sweat, we were above the tree line, in a narrow grassy plateau on top of a series of cliffs overlooking Antrodoco. The DVX forest—or at least the rectangular section of fir trees that was added later just below the proper inscription to stabilize the three letters—was a few hundred meters above us. Moving toward the western peak of Mount Giano, we circumnavigated this lower part of the forest on its left and entered instead horizontally into the letter D. I was hit by the balsamic smell of sap, the rustling of pine needles in the breeze, and the unstable condition of the soil, which made walking among the pine trees quite arduous. The combination of these three elements invited me to pay closer attention to my surroundings—to immerse myself in them rather than simply approaching them as a spectacle and an object of study. Certainly, we could not see the shape of the letter from inside, but something else was apparent for the first time: the multilayer structure of the environment as the result of a continuous exchange between different agents, human and non-human. This interconnectedness became, for me, embodied in the *gradoni*, the terraces. It was only from *inside the letters* that I could appreciate the system that was used to plant and sustain the trees, a system not merely contrived by humans but which proceeded from the intersection of different knowledges, different histories, different beings.

While I was in the letters, what surprised me most was the sudden realization that, regardless of the larger political intentions behind the trees' installation, these pines were not just an inscription but the expression of relationships based on mindfulness and care, their presence today on the slope of Mount Giano being the result of a co-performative event. In being physically present, I more fully understood that the Austrian pines are not only part of the imposed official landscape hideously designed by the Fascist regime, but they also belong to an immersive vernacular landscape, not unlike Severus'. As such, they continue to interact with the human and non-human communities in terms of reciprocal support and affective entanglement that are not immediately comprehensible from a distance. This realization was somehow confirmed when Valerio and I moved to the damaged X. Here the neo-fascists had planted among the burnt trees a few new saplings of *Pinus nigra*, but they had not repaired the essential terracing or otherwise prepared an adequate growing space for the saplings: their political stunt did not include the long-term plan of care required for the forest's health. In fact, the neo-fascists did not really engage with the environment. They neither listened to the entangled histories of the inhabitants nor spent enough time to become part of the forest's ecological narratives. If they had, they might have understood that locals' ecological, historical, and interspecies relationships underpin this forest's existence. As a result, it is likely that these new saplings will not survive. Their growth will be cut short as soon as the burnt trees fall to the ground and the rain washes the soil away—a poetic testament to the shallowness of the neo-fascist undertaking. Walking through the letters thus became for me a syntax for immersing myself in an affective landscape I could not understand only through unilateral representations. Instead, it required me to engage with it literally step by step, allowing the trees and their biosemiotic relations with the local human community to emerge as an embodied multi-verse, in which "intersection, transfer, emergence, and paradox are central to life."[7]

Archeologist Christopher Tilley claims that, through walking, landscapes are woven into life, and lives are woven into the landscape, in a process that is continuous and never-ending.[8] What walking within the *Pinus nigra* forest on Mount Giano taught me is that, from a distance, we do not experience our lives as being entangled, intertwined with the physical world. We consider ourselves to be isolated monads: as a pair of Cartesian eyes, we look at places and their multispecies inhabitants as a spectacle, reducing their complex materiality, their relational and performative identities, into a unified object ready to be grasped by our intellectual tentacles. From afar, we thus risk not only falling prey to "the visualism deeply rooted in the European concept of landscape,"[9] contracting our multisensory experience of places, but we also negate the ability of the world, of these places and their inhabitants, to reciprocate our minuscule but assertive gaze. In so doing, even the Austrian pines on the slope of Mount Giano might easily lose their living and challenging co-presence, their being part of a collective assemblage of reciprocal mindfulness and communication, becoming instead the mute scenery of our very own abstract projections and often too-human affairs. I am afraid that, as such, they would indeed exist only as a Fascist forest.

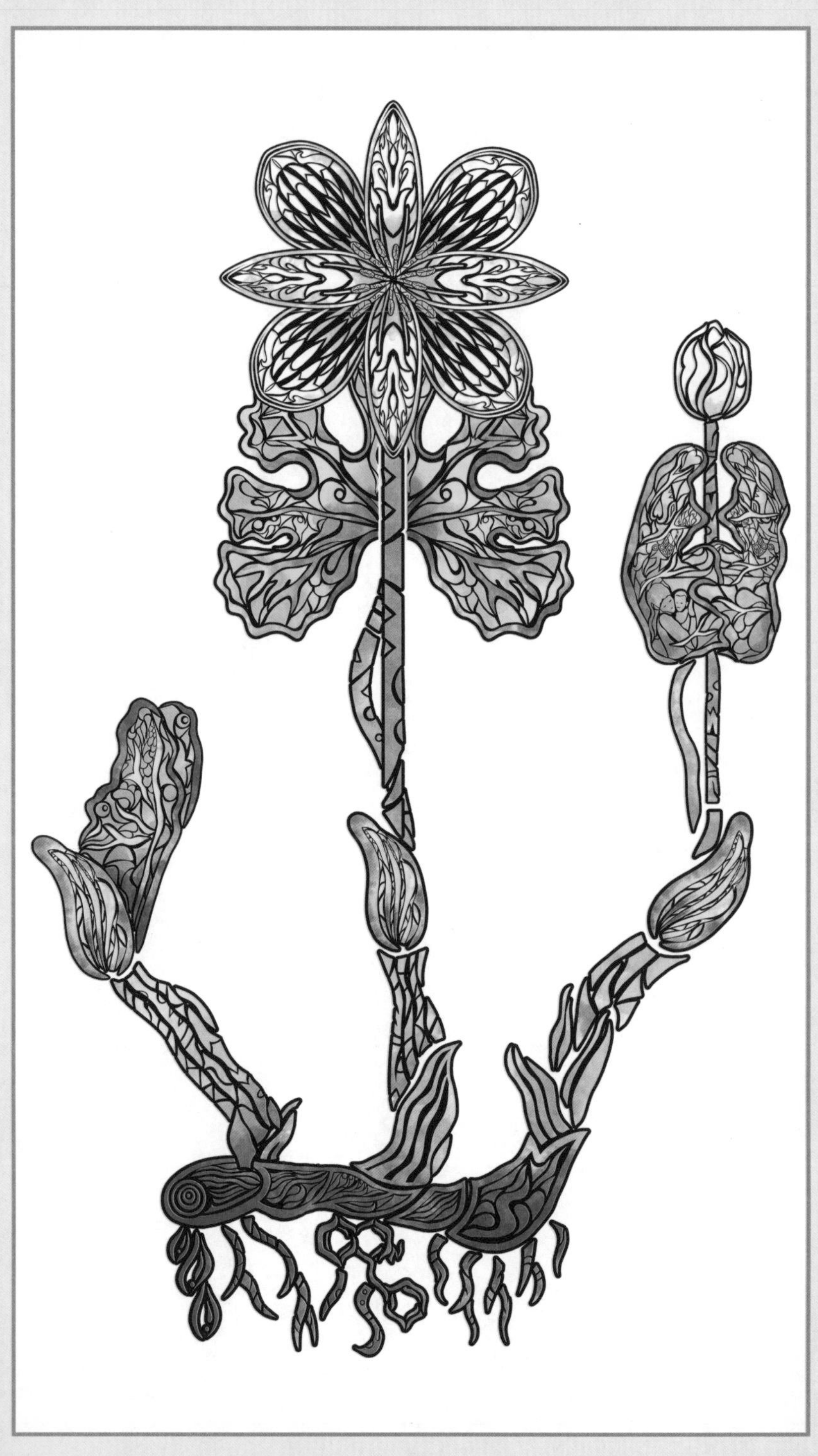

CHAPTER 6

Bloodroot

Sanguinaria canadensis

▪ Craig Holdrege

MEETING BLOODROOT

In early April, I begin my wanderings through the deciduous forests in upstate New York, where I live. I want to participate in the budding forth of early spring plants. The trees are bare and the air cool. The forest floor is light brown, with dead leaves covering the soil. You have to get down on your knees and look carefully to discover the first plants poking out of the soil and through the leaf litter.

There is no set date on which I can know that this or that plant will appear. Clearly, the plants are attuned to the lengthening of the days. But their time of emergence can vary by a number of weeks. If it remains cold and overcast, the plants emerge later, while a burst of unfolding will accompany a spell of warm, sunny days. The ensuing cold will slow all processes down again. It's a dynamic dance of the sun, elements, and plants. And yet, I do know—I can trust—that some plant species will appear earlier than others.

One of the earliest wildflowers to emerge from the rich soil of bottomland woods is bloodroot (*Sanguinaria canadensis*). Its characteristic grayish-green buds are easy to discern once you get to know them. The scales of the bud open, and a little plant emerges. What you see is a tightly wrapped, not-yet-unfolded leaf. A tender whitish-green cap begins to grow up from its center—the flower bud. The leaf encloses the flower and provides a protective mantle as the plant grows into the vicissitudes of the airy, light-filled world. Taken in its momentary appearance at this phase of its life, bloodroot is quite inconspicuous. But viewed as a process, the closed flower bud and the enwrapping leaf are powerful images of becoming. There is a palpable fullness and tension that speaks of life and development.

The upward elongation of the flower stalk continues so that it extends beyond the enwrapping leaf. If you are lucky, you can see the two pale green sepals before they fall off, leaving the petals free to open. If you enter the woods on a warm and sunny mid-to-late April afternoon, your attention will quickly be drawn to the wide open and white radiance of bloodroot's blossoms. Usually, eight petals radiate out from a glowing center of golden stamens. The petals have an almost inexpressible soft and luminescent whiteness. Viewed from above, the flowers seem to hover above the ground. The flowers open on sunny days and close toward dusk, only to open again the next morning, if it is sunny. On cloudy days the flowers remain closed or open only a little. Occasionally, you can see a small native bee gathering pollen from the stamens.

This phase of flowering lasts only a few days to a week (or longer if the weather is cool). The petals fall off very easily—a typical characteristic of the poppy family, to which bloodroot belongs—and one hard rainstorm can remove them all. What's left, when the petals and stamens have fallen off, is the pistil in the middle of the flower. It develops over time into a narrow and upright fruit capsule that bears seeds.

Remarkably, while bloodroot is flowering, its single leaf continues to enwrap the flower stalk and only gradually begins to open. In this phase of its development, bloodroot reveals a special two-fold gesture: openness and luminance in the flower above and the restrained enclosing gesture of the protective leaf below. It is this gesture that struck me many years ago when I started to notice bloodroot, and each year it continues to speak strongly.

NATURE SPEAKING?

I just used the words "gesture" and "speak" in connection with a plant. Does nature gesture and speak? I think so, but only if we attend and are open to her utterances. Of course, the gesturing and speaking are not of a human sort. They are of the Earth. I can't help but see the Earth, with its ever-changing garment of plants, as an activity that is expressing itself in all its utterances. The problem is that, for the most part, we don't understand those utterances with any clarity. When we attend to a plant, and it strikes us in such a way that we say, "Oh, isn't that beautiful," we have been touched by the plant. This being touched dwells in our life of feelings. We know we've met something real and important, but we may not be able to articulate it any further. However, the feeling remains strong and connects us with the Earth and its plant life.

In my work with plants, I strive to see whether I can learn to perceive the gesturing of nature more distinctly. Bloodroot is beautiful, but so is the dandelion that flowers later in lawns, or wild chicory that flowers in rich sky-blue along roadsides in the summer. What are the unique qualities of the different plants? What are they saying in their forms and colors, in the times and places in which they develop? How is the Earth speaking through them?

My way of gently approaching these large questions—which are more guides for study than occasions for definite answers—is, in a sense, quite simple.[1] I attend carefully to the plant. I take the time and effort to notice its characteristics and to follow mindfully how it develops. By going out to the plant with this focused attention, I get to know it. This getting to know is enhanced by bringing the plant alive in my imagination, a practice that the scientist and poet Goethe called "exact sensorial imagination."[2] I re-picture its features and development as vividly as possible—imagining how the parts unfold; beholding the processes of transformation as movement; inwardly sensing the changing textures, colors, and scents.

And I need to look at the plant in its context. Where and when is it growing, who are its neighbors, what other creatures does it interact with? I compare it with other plants. This is key. The uniqueness of something often stands out and becomes clearer through contrasts, especially when I vividly picture what I am studying. Instead of theorizing and "thinking about" the plant in an intellectual way, I strive to observe and "think with" the plant and thereby participate more fully in its life. All this work helps me get to know the plant as an active, transforming, and dynamic being. It opens the door, if I am fortunate, to a more intimate sense of the qualities of a particular plant species. It can—in its plant-like way—begin to speak.

COMPLETING LIFE'S CYCLE

Bloodroot's development does not stop with flowering. Once it has dropped its petals, the single green leaf, flower stalk, and fruit capsule blend in with the greening surroundings of the forest floor. More and more wildflowers unfold and begin to bloom. A carpet of green forms on the forest floor. We often do not realize that the forest floor has its peak of illumination in May before the trees are green. Even though the days continue to get longer, there is increasingly less illumination on the forest floor. The early flowering woodland wildflowers bring an array of colors and form into the forest before it moves into its shady summer. In mid-May, the canopy of the forest begins to close overhead.

After flowering, bloodroot's single leaf unfolds fully and grows. Whereas the development of bloodroot from bud to flower progresses rapidly with each day showing visible changes—the changes we human beings long for and are nourished by in spring—now everything slows down. Bloodroot's leaf blade continues to grow slowly throughout the spring and early summer, in contrast to those of many small spring wildflowers that decay soon after flowering. At first, the leaf stalk is about as long as the leaf's surface itself (what botanists call the *leaf blade*). The leaf blade is initially fairly upright and fans out into an overall roundish form that most typically (in a mature plant) has five to seven lobes. The orientation then shifts from upright to horizontal; this occurs simultaneously with the greening and closing of the tree canopy. The leaf blade takes on a slightly concave bowl shape. The flower stalk does not elongate after the petals fall off so that the leaf now forms a canopy above the fruit capsule, just as the unfolding leaves of the trees form a canopy for the forest floor—a beautiful instance of a part mirroring a process in the whole. Moreover, we witness how bloodroot's leaf slowly changes in relation to the flower, the flower stalk, and the fruit, and how it also transforms in concert with the seasonal greening and darkening of the forest as a whole.

By the end of June, the fruit capsule at the tip of the flower stalk swells and splits open, revealing numerous small, round, dark-brown seeds, which soon fall to the ground. The flower stalk and capsule then dry up, shrivel, and decompose. Only the leaf is left above the ground. The leaf blade grows no more, but the leaf stalk continues to lengthen. Gradually the leaf blade comes to rest on the ground and begins to decay. We're now at the end of August or early September. Long before the tree foliage begins its fall transformation from green to brilliant yellows, oranges, and reds, bloodroot is no longer visible.

PATHWAYS OF DEVELOPMENT

There are two pathways for bloodroot to continue its life into the next spring. One is through its rhizome and roots, which remain in the ground after the leaves have wilted. The rhizome is an orange-red underground stem that has many little roots growing from it. The rhizome, when injured, emits a dark red, watery sap—the origin of the name "bloodroot." When a leaf stalk or flower stalk breaks, you can also see the red sap. The rhizome grows and branches during the spring and summer, and near the end of the growing season, it develops buds. Inside the buds, a complete flower and a complete leaf pre-form in miniature. This most stunning development of undifferentiated tissue into a tightly compressed leaf and flower occurs completely hidden away in the protective sheaths of the bud. For me, it is impossible to imagine how a plant makes a flower, with its precise arrangement of two sepals, eight petals, multiple stamens, and a central pistil in miniature, surrounded by an enwrapping, folded leaf, and all of this in such a way that the later unfolding reveals coherent and organized structures. It is beyond comprehension and provides a healthy dose of modesty in view of the wisdom at work in a plant.

These buds of nascent life remain dormant during the fall and winter. The plants become active again in the increasing light and warmth of the next spring when leaves and flowers sprout forth. With leaves and flowers prepared the previous year, bloodroot can unfold quickly in the spring.

When you find two or three bloodroot "plants" growing close to one another, each with its own leaf and flower, you may in fact be looking at just one plant, the rhizome of which had formed buds out of which the above-ground flower and leaf pairs arose. So, what we designate as one plant with leaf and flower will often be a branch of a larger plant from which a number of leaves and flowers have grown. A mature bloodroot plant is, therefore, like a small bush that has its branches underground, and the extremities of the plant—flowers and leaves—only show themselves above the ground for a period of time.

The second way for bloodroot to continue its existence is through seeds. The seeds drop to the ground near the mother plant and may germinate there in the following spring. In this case, you find little seedlings with a single small, unlobed leaf growing near mature plants. Such a plantlet develops a small rhizome that grows and overwinters. In the following year, it will likely bring forth one or two leaves, but probably not flowers. These leaves often have three lobes and don't grow as large as the leaves on mature plants. In the next year, the plant is probably established enough to bring forth one or more flowers, and the leaves grow much larger and often have five to seven lobes.

There is something quite special about bloodroot seeds. When they fall to the ground, ants often arrive. The ants pick up the seeds and carry them to their nest. Each bloodroot seed has a small outgrowth called an *elaiosome*. The elaiosome grows outside the seed coat and is not part of the germ. The ants are attracted to this part of the seed—ant larvae feed on the elaiosomes, which are rich in fats and sugars. The fast-growing larvae thrive on this nutrient-rich food.

The seed itself, retaining its potential for germination, is discarded by the ants, usually with other organic waste from the nest. As one researcher puts it, the seeds are placed on "private compost heaps," and out of these seedbeds, tiny plants can grow the next year.[3] By collecting the seeds, the ants spread bloodroot into a larger area of the forest, and they also provide the conditions for a new colony of bloodroot to develop. In this sense, the ants belong to bloodroot, just as bloodroot—as food— becomes part of the ants. This is one example of how different beings in an environment interweave and participate in their mutual lives. There is no such thing as an organism that is separate from other organisms.[4]

BEING ITSELF DIFFERENTLY

So far, we have gained a picture of bloodroot as a special expression and embodiment of early spring in a temperate deciduous forest environment of eastern North America. We have gotten to know it as a specific activity bringing forth form and substance in ongoing transformation. Its appearing and disappearing, its becoming and wilting away, are deeply connected with larger rhythms.

Bloodroot is wholly embedded in the annual rhythm of the seasons—the changing relation between sun and a particular place on Earth during a year. This is its encompassing context. At the other pole, there are the very local conditions of a particular place such as topography and soil. A specific plant may grow in one place for a number of years, and each year the cosmic seasonal rhythm remains virtually the same, but the local conditions of weather and habitat may change radically from year to year. In this sense, each year brings new opportunities for the mutual interweaving of plant and environment.

When we are mindful of this dynamic interplay, it becomes clear that bloodroot does not develop according to some strict set of rules. Rather, it becomes itself and maintains itself through the environment, and continually shifts its activity in relation to changes in the environment. The plant relates to those specific circumstances in a way that accords with its way of being. At the same time, the ways in which bloodroot can grow differently in different circumstances are an expression of the vital plasticity that allows it to be itself differently.

But there is another quality we can attend to that has to do with the surprises that the plant offers. One example: bloodroot flowers usually have eight petals, the lower four being somewhat larger and rounder than the upper four. The petals are often regularly spaced so that you can discern a square formed by the lower petals and an offset square of the narrower petals, which grow in the space between the lower petals. Beautiful embodied geometry. Again and again, you can see this pattern. But if you get stuck in seeing the pattern, you may overlook how different the individual flowers can be from one another. When you attend to the flowers on many different plants, the more you look, the more you see that not only does the overall size of the petals on different plants vary, but the shape and arrangement of the petals as well.

Beyond that, if you look at enough different flowers, you will find that the number of petals occasionally varies, I have found in plants in a wooded area beside a creek that I often visit—flowers with nine, ten, and twelve petals. Others have found plants with as few as three and as many as twenty petals.[5]

Surprising variations such as these reveal a kind of playfulness, an abundance of possibilities that a species can display. By being open to the surprises that a plant offers up, we experience another facet of its dynamic nature. I think that philosopher Susanne Langer rightly saw it: "Every discovery makes the living organism look less like a predesigned object and more like an embodied drama of evolving acts, intricately prepared by the past, yet all improvising their moves to consummation."[6]

Many habits of thought can get in the way of our seeing the drama of a plant's life. One is our tendency to pay most attention to "typical characteristics." The norm in our mind overshadows the richness and variability that the plant shows in its development and forms. Another hindrance is the drive to want to "explain." In our modern scientific age, this usually means discovering the spatial antecedents of any given phenomenon that contribute to its coming into appearance. What genes, hormones, or environmental cues "cause" the plant to form a bud at a particular time? This kind of questioning can lead to interesting discoveries, but the discoveries are not to be taken as explanations. They simply expand our knowledge of the drama of life.

To see the drama, we need to literally come to our senses and immerse ourselves in the variety of phenomena. We inwardly participate in the dynamics of process and transformation and weave the instances of surprising formations into our growing picture of the plant. In all its expressions, the plant can help us leave our normative abstractions behind. With an open attentiveness and an active mind, we can begin to participate in the wisdom that informs the plant world. And, to paraphrase Emerson, nature shows herself as never profane when we have truly given heed to the concrete appearances of life, letting that life come to life within us.

CHAPTER 7

Blue Lechenaultia

Lechenaultia biloba

■ Jessica White

A LONG SOJOURN

You're driving along the endless highway near Wannamal in Western Australia when you see a blaze of blue beside the road. You slow down, check the rear vision mirror and pull over, tires crunching as you transfer to the gravel. You switch off the engine, glance out the window—yes, it's *Lechenaultia biloba*—then grab your phone and step out of the car. You tread through wild radish and African love grass to reach the shrub. It extends to your knees, its mass of deep blue flowers an exhalation onto the reddish soil.

You're in the Southwest Australian Floristic Region (SWAFR), which stretches for roughly 300,000 kilometers across the southwestern corner of Western Australia. It is bordered by the Indian and Southern oceans, while to the north and east of the area, the land is arid. Its landscape is old and weathered, persisting for millions of years because it has not been disrupted by earthquakes or volcanoes. Without disturbance or replenishment through geographical upheaval, the soil has become poor in nutrients, yet it has given rise to an incredible diversity of plant forms, such as this one.

The blue leschenaultia's ancestor evolved from the first land plants, which were akin to today's lichens, liverworts, and mosses. Fossilized spores suggest that this happened in the Ordovician period, 510 to 439 million years ago. The first flowering plants, or angiosperms, took another 100 to 300 million years to arrive, with the common ancestor of all living angiosperms likely existing 140 to 250 million years ago. Scientists surmise that it looked like a modern magnolia, blooming in a climate warmer than today's, while pterodactyls soared overhead.

Toward the end of the Cretaceous period, 78 million years ago, *Lechenaultia*'s plant family Goodeniaceae split from the families Asteraceae and Calyceraceae. Around 76 million years ago, the clades *Lechenaultia*,

Anthotium, and *Dampiera* diverged from the remainder of *Goodeniaceae*. Divergences within *Lechenaultia* then began in the mid-Miocene period, roughly 11 million years ago.[1] There are now twenty-nine formally named species, with all but one occurring in Western Australia. You're contemplating 500 million years of evolution beside the road.

You open the camera on your phone, crouch down, and snap a shot, capturing the flower's five petals. They open from a creamy throat dusted with fine hairs. You notice the two lobes on each petal, from which the species takes its name, *biloba*. You angle the phone to shoot them against the sky. They are the same color, only their outline distinguishes plant from air. You stand, stretching, upload the photo to Instagram and type a caption, "Beautiful blue leschenaultia breaking up the long drive."

ENCOUNTERS

After a busy week at work, you head into the forests for the weekend, stopping first at Warren National Park. The traditional custodians of this area, the southwest Boojarah region, are the Wardandi and Bibulmun (or Piblemen) Noongar people. You park at the entrance, pull your pack from the boot, lean over and stretch your calf muscles and tighten your boot laces, then shoulder the pack and set off. The air is thick with moisture. It's near the end of *Maruku*, the Noongar season that is cold and wet, and which corresponds to the Western-named months of June and July.

You fall into a rhythm, walking over dense leaf and bark litter beneath tall karri trees. Honeyeaters and fairywrens dart through bushes of banksia. You hear the red-tailed black cockatoo, known to Noongar people as *karrak*, cracking nuts in the karri canopy. You see blue leschenaultia sprouting from the sandy soil, one of the earliest blooms that herald the state's famous wildflower season.

Although the SWAFR's biodiversity captivates busloads of tourists and flora enthusiasts each year, humans appreciated the flora for thousands of years prior to this. The first modern humans arrived in Australia approximately 60,000 years ago, toward the end of the Pleistocene period, when glaciation meant that sea levels were lower and land bridges allowed them to travel onto the continent from Asia. Those who settled in southwest

Western Australia became known as Noongar people. Their *boodja*, or country, extends from north of Jurien Bay, inland to the north of Moora, and down to the southern coast between Bremer Bay and east of Esperance. It is defined by fourteen different areas with varied geography and fourteen dialectal groups.[2] Over 45,000 years, Noongar peoples developed and refined their knowledge about their environment to sustain themselves physically and psychically. They were the first humans to encounter *Lechenaultia*, although they did not know it by that name.

As ethnobotanist Philip Clarke notes, "What people observe in an environment is as much a product of the importance their culture places upon each type of object as it is an indication of the acuity of their vision." He also observes that "the number of terms that relate to the flora in each Aboriginal language is enormous." Indigenous Australian peoples have names for different parts of plants and their structural forms. They also name places, people, and particular groups after plants.[3] In southwest Western Australia, Noongar peoples use flowering plants as signals for the change of seasons and weather patterns. Blossoming paperbarks (of the genus *Melaleuca*; the Noongar term for the tree is *biboolboorn*), for example, "bring the mullet fish."[4] The flowering of plants such as *Lechenaultia biloba* signal the slowing of the rainy season and the gradual warming of the weather. The plant remains in flower as the days become dryer and hotter, through *Djilba* (August and September), *Kambarang* (October and November), and some of *Birak* (December and January).

After a long stretch downhill, you reach the Warren River, overhung by peppermint trees, *Agonis flexuosa*, or *wannang* in Noongar. Tall, straight karri trees rise above them. The water is still, reflections of the peppermints greening its surface. You decide to stop for lunch and sit on one of the wooden steps leading down to the water, checking it first for ants.

While Indigenous Australian peoples' classification and naming of plants is based on the physical form of plants and their uses, the European classification system is based on floral characteristics, specifically the number of male parts (stamens) and female parts (pistils) on one flower. This system was derived from Swedish naturalist Carl Linnaeus' *Systema Naturae* (1735), in which he laid out his ideas on the hierarchical classification of the natural world, dividing it into the kingdoms of animal, vegetable, or mineral. European and British botanists took this system (now known as binomial nomenclature) with them to Australia and used it to classify the plants they encountered.

You watch insects delicately touching the river's surface, your mind still on the blue leschenaultia. Its European name sprang from a chance encounter between Matthew Flinders (1774–1814), who was circumnavigating Australia in the *Investigator* in 1801 and 1802, and Nicholas Baudin (1754–1803), a French cartographer and explorer who departed France in 1800 to map the coast of Australia and research the country's flora and fauna.

In April 1802, Flinders caught sight of a French corvette, *Geographé*, which was captained by Baudin. The ships dropped anchor in a bay that belonged to the Ramindjeri group of the Ngarrindjeri people. Although Britain and France were at war, Flinders boarded the *Geographé*, met Baudin, and exchanged information. It's likely that the botanists on both expeditions, Jean-Baptiste Théodore Leschenault de La Tour and Robert Brown, met at this point. Flinders, disregarding the traditional custodians, named the bay—somewhat prosaically—"Encounter Bay" for their meeting. Later, Leschenault de La Tour and Robert Brown met again at Port Jackson, where they collected together.

Brown stayed in Australia for three and a half years, amassing approximately 3,400 specimens. He returned to Britain in 1805, and for the next few years, worked on his collections of plants, naming some 1,200 species. In 1810, he published *Prodromus Florae Novae Hollandiae et Insulae Van Diemen* (*Preliminary Account of the Flora of New Holland and Van Dieman's Land)*, the first systematic account of Australian flora, which included his naming of *Lechenaultia* after Leschenault de La Tour. However, he presumed that Leschenault spelled his name in the French manner, rather than with the Germanic "s," so now the name *Lechenaultia* is "s"-less.

It's a pain when it comes to spelling, you think, because the common name, "blue leschenaultia," does include the "s." You watch the insects on the river for a while longer, aware that the sweat on your back has cooled, and you need to get moving again. You pull up your pack, leap back up the steps, and begin striding through the fine, tall stands of karri, or *Eucalyptus diversicolor.*

SENSORY DELIGHTS

You're driving again, this time through a bit of bush near Parmelia that was scorched late last summer. The weather patterns are changing as the planet warms, and it was very dry last summer. You don't usually come this way, but you've taken a wrong turn because you are daydreaming.

You brake before you realize it. What, a few months before, had been charred and black is now—courtesy of the winter rains—a rash of blue flowers. Above them, burnt trees bristle with thickets of new leaves. The lush growth of many species after fire is a characteristic of Australian plants, and tests in laboratories indicate that *Lechenaultia biloba* shows significantly improved germination responses after exposure to smoke.[5]

You get out, drawn again by that piece of sky that seems to have fallen onto the dun earth. You cross the road, clapping your hands loudly to scare off early spring snakes, then wade through the masses of blue, watching the flowers camouflage themselves against your denim jeans. You don't take your phone with you this time. You're experimenting with *floraesthesis*, the "openness of sensory contact with plants."[6] Rather than responding to plants by reducing them to an image-in-flower, you're using all of your senses to appreciate the plant. You're thankful, as you move, that you're not in long skirts.

Georgiana Molloy (1805–1843), who emigrated from Britain to Augusta in 1830, set out on expeditions, often with her daughters, to collect seeds and specimens. In 1836, she had received a box of English seeds and a note from Captain James Mangles, cousin to the wife of the then-governor of Perth, requesting that she exchange these seeds for "the Native Seeds of Augusta."[7] The Mangles family were traders and, cashing in on the lust for Australian flora, James Mangles commissioned people in the colony to collect for him.

Tragically, not long after she received this request, Molloy's young son fell into the family's well and drowned. Needing a distraction from her grief, she went into the bush to collect seeds and specimens for Mangles. She was alert to the sensory delights of the world in which she found herself, writing to Mangles after an expedition that "It was truly enjoyable [to be] surrounded by new & refreshing Flowers, some I had never seen before." On her walks, she attended carefully to the morphology of plants and their flowers, and she was receptive to the Noongar names for plants. She would have returned home with her tired daughters holding onto her skirt with one hand, fistfuls of flowers in their other hand, her hems encrusted with bark and grass.

There is no mention of *Lechenaultia biloba* in the lists Mangles made of Molloy's collections, although scientist David Morrison notes a syntype held in Cambridge University Herbarium of 1839 collected by "Mrs. Molloy."[8] As she did not know the scientific names for plants, Molloy gave seeds and their specimens a number, and waited for Mangles to identify them and alert her to the names by mail. In a letter describing her collection of 1837, she wrote, "if No 61 does not prove evanescent you will be in extacies [sic] with its lovely brilliant blue." As this is the usual response to the brilliance of *Lechenaultia biloba*, it's possible it is the same plant.

You bend to sniff the blue flowers, but you can't detect any scent. What you can smell is the thick, sweet scent of wattle. You look around and notice a flare of yellow across the road. But it's the blue that draws you back again, the delicacy of its corolla. You're not the only person it has attracted; scientists in Japan have undertaken tests to determine the chemical composition of its color.[9] You wish you could bottle it.

HORTICULTURAL HAPPINESS

It's a sunny morning, not yet blistering with heat. You place your cup of black, sugared tea on the coffee table and ease yourself into the old cane chair on the veranda. Rosellas squawk from the nearby firewood banksia, *Banksia menziesii*, known as *bulgalla* in Noongar. As you wait for your tea to cool, you admire your pot of blue leschenaultia. Its flowers, spilling over the orange terracotta to the bricks, make a pleasing contrast. The gardener at the nursery warned that it could be a temperamental plant, but all you've had to do to keep it happy is make sure that it's well-drained and not over-watered. Fortunately, it's a hardy plant, tolerating frost and resisting bugs.

The possibilities of potting *Lechenaultia biloba* were advertised to the British through *A Sketch of the Vegetation of Swan River* published in 1840 by John Lindley, the first professor of botany at University College London. Through this book, illustrated with lithographs and wood-cuts, "the Swan River environs and its distinctive vegetation [were] ushered onto the global stage."[10] It was of particular interest for horticulturalists, and refers to the five or six species of *Lechenaultia* that had been determined.

Indeed, *Lechenaultia biloba* caused great excitement when live specimens were grown from seeds collected by James Drummond, a Scotsman who arrived in Western Australia in 1829. With six children to support, money was an issue, and Drummond realized he could derive an income from selling plants. He began collecting for Sir William Hooker, the Director of Kew Gardens, and for Captain James Mangles. In 1835, Drummond shipped his first collections to Mangles, who passed them to Lindley. Lindley encouraged Drummond to send more, and over the next fifteen years, Drummond made six expeditions through the southwest region, collecting more than 3,000 species.

Lechenaultia biloba was grown from Drummond's seeds at James Veitch's nursery in Exeter. In a letter of July 29, 1840, to William Hooker, Veitch described how "From the seeds we raised 5 or 6 plants, 3 of which appear quite different and distinct in foliage."[11] In the British spring of the following year, one small plant was exhibited at the Horticultural Society in Regent Street and won a Silver Knightian Medal.

Joseph Paxton, head gardener of Chatsworth, designer of the Crystal Palace for the 1851 Great Exhibition, and another of Mangles' correspondents, featured an illustration and description of *Lechenaultia biloba* in his *Magazine of Botany*. He noted that "the beautiful flowers of *L. biloba* present the principal objects for notice. They vary in colour, from a light cerulean blue, to a deep lapis-lazuli tint."[12] The illustration in Paxton's volume was based upon a specimen grown by Veitch. The plants were advertised for twenty to thirty shillings, the equivalent of four days' labor for a skilled tradesman. Despite its cost, *Lechenaultia biloba* was a popular plant for the following few decades. People loved its color. In an article written for the local paper, Drummond described the flower's coloring as "celestial blue," an apt reference to the sky or the heavens which the flower resembles.[13]

MINDING PLANTS

A charming plant, *Lechenaultia biloba*'s sumptuous blues have ensured its longevity in pots in urban gardens, and it is one of the most popular leschenaultias in cultivation, both in Australia and elsewhere. Yet while the blue leschenaultia is thriving, some of its compatriots are not. The scarlet leschenaultia (*Lechenaultia laricina*), for example, is threatened by clearing for farmland. Indeed the colonization of Australia has revealed an entrenched disregard for the country's original inhabitants, both human and other-than-human, with invasion causing the dispossession and decimation of Australia's Indigenous peoples. Not only has this led to a loss of local knowledge, but British land management methods—such as clear felling and dry-land and irrigated agriculture—are not appropriate for a country of poor soil and limited rainfall. They have caused rapid and extreme alterations to the environment, and the SWAFR now has more threatened species than most countries of the world. Scientists have agitated for such protection through the establishment of biodiversity hotspots, which feature a high percentage of plant life found nowhere else on Earth and which face exceptional levels of extinction. In 2000, the SWAFR was formally recognized as a biodiversity hotspot, one of thirty-six worldwide and one of two in Australia.

Perhaps, given the threat to plant life in the SWAFR, it is helpful to bear both Indigenous and Western botanical science in mind. When you stop to admire a shrub of *Lechenaultia biloba* in rain-softened soil, you might also recognize, as Australian Indigenous peoples have for tens of thousands of years, the work that plants do on Earth and sea: provide habitat and food for humans and our fellow beings, signal a change in seasons and food sources, and give us the oxygen and sugar upon which we rely. Clean air and sweetness are good reasons to notice the work of plants, but we should also pay them mind by caring for the ecosystems upon which they rely. In doing so, we will ensure that *Lechenaultia biloba* will prevail for millions of years more.

CHAPTER 8

Cacao Tree

Theobroma cacao

Jonathon Miller Weisberger

Imagine a rainforest clothed in rising mist. A mystical place filled with life and the calls of many types of birds and animals. Steep verdant hills and valleys, cliff faces, splotched in tones of green. The sun rising over the expanse of the Amazon. Splashing water, chimeric rainbow hues. Towering ice cap mountain peaks of the Andes stand firm in the west, golden in the morning light. These mountain slopes have given rise to marvelous biological diversity. To understand cacao, we must understand where she comes from—a place closest to the sun, where day and night are equal in length all year long. A vastly intricate union of thousands of species of plants, animals, insects, birds, fungi. When I sip cacao, my heart softens, and I feel a heightened sense of balance, of willingness, and patience. I can feel how she advocates for balance in all my relationships. Cascading water surges through rocky creeks, finding its way to the meandering serenity of the larger rivers below. Palms and myriad plants and trees with vastly diverse-shaped leaves hug the banks. Where cacao comes from, flowering vines delicately hang over the river's shores, releasing densely sweet dew-like nectarous aromas.

THE WORLD TREE AND HER PLANETARY MISSION

How can a relatively inconspicuous understory treelet be so pregnant with wholesome goodness, so full of virtues, and so charged with mythologies? Why is cacao so revered that it has been used as money, medicine, an antioxidant-rich superfood, incense, and for a variety of ceremonial offerings—to invoke responses from supernatural beings, to celebrate special moments and calendar markers such as the solstice and equinox, to sanctify weddings and births, to consecrate times of initiations and rites of passage, and as funeral offerings to accompany the dead on the afterlife voyage?

When we stretch our imagination to contemplate ancient creation myths that consider cacao not just a gift from the gods to humanity but an actual component of our identity as humans, we can begin to understand. In the *Popol Vuh*, the Quiché Mayan holy book, the gods created humans from maize and cacao, along with other foods such as the white cacao, known as pataxte, *Theobroma bicolor*; the soap apple, known as zapote, *Manilkara zapota*; hog plum or jocote, *Spondius purpurea*; golden spoon, known as nance, *Byrsonima crassifolia*; and the white sapote, that is matasano, *Casimiroa edulis*. These narratives speak to the role of plants as an intimate part of the human fabric.

Many other Central American creation myths postulate human origins in cacao. Ancient pottery depicts the Maya great mother Ix Chel, lady of translucent rainbow light, goddess of medicine, weaving, fertility, and the crescent moon, exchanging cacao with the rain god Chac, the patron of agriculture. This iconography is rooted in the tree's reputation as a conduit between heaven and Earth. To the ancient peoples who grew and adored cacao, this sacred crop was a Tree of Life uniting the quotidian world with supernatural realms. The ceremonial consumption and offering of cacao symbolically connected individuals with the powers that govern their existence, with renewal and rebirth, and with the deities of creation. The bounty of the cacao tree in Mesoamerica represents abundance, and her rounded fruit symbolizes fertility. The deep spiritual meaning of cacao crystallized her importance in all pre-Colombian societies that knew her. Cacao is a blessed, scrumptious elixir that has shaped and formed societies, igniting creation and urging us to evolve.

Don Memo Morales, an elder of the Costa Rican Brunka tribe, once shared a story with me: "After the cataclysm, when the Earth was burned by fire, heaven had compassion for humanity, and from the sky dropped seeds of cacao. From these seeds grew the cacao tree, and from its ripe pregnant fruit was born the first woman, who gave birth to the first man, and from there the first people came." Softly, Memo continued, "In compassion for humanity, the Creator gave the first people three types of cacao so they could live well: a sweet variety to share and to enjoy in festivals, a simple variety to eat every day as food, and a bitter variety for healing all illness."

Cacao represents the fragile and delicately interconnected web of life, the majesty of biological diversity. She is the emblem for many great cultures. There are many things that she knows...

BORN AT THE SUMMIT OF MEGA BIOLOGICAL DIVERSITY

No other region in the world surpasses northwest South America in biodiversity, which peaks in the "eyebrows" of the Andes. Two mountains—Sumaco, known locally as the most beautiful mountain, and Napo-Galeras, an isolated limestone massif—are considered especially sacred by the region's diverse Indigenous peoples. I devoted four years there that, in 1994, successfully included Napo-Galeras mountain as part of the new Sumaco Napo-Galeras National Park. This effort is shared in my book, *Rainforest Medicine: Preserving Indigenous Science and Biodiversity in the Upper Amazon.* In 2010, I participated in a botanical expedition in the Tropical Wet Forest on the eastern slopes of Napo-Galeras, east of the Andes, led by Dr. Carlos Cerón, curator of the herbarium at Ecuador's Central University, to learn more about wild *Theobroma cacao,* its mega-biodiverse rainforest setting, and the Malvaceae botanical family to which cacao belongs. Relatives of this family from other regions include fibrous, stimulant, and mucilage-bearing plants such as cotton, okra, kola nut, durian fruit, hibiscus, and mallow. An impressive sight it is to see wild cacao trees growing in their original setting, surrounded by a remarkably high concentration of related plants: patas, or white cacao, *Theobroma bicolor*, whose edible seeds are used to make chili sauce; *T. subincanum*, called cushillu-cambiac, with deliciously aromatic edible pulp; and the famed *T. grandiflorum*, called cupuassu in Brazil, similarly prized for its nectarous pomace. As we explored the forest collecting hundreds of botanical specimens, pressing plants late into the night, and collecting botanical information, more related species came to light. These were trees in the genus *Matisia* and *Quararibea*, both with fine edible fruits known as sapote, and *Herrania*, a close cousin of cacao, locally known as cambiac, distinguished by saturated maroon flowers with remarkably elongated petal-appendages and fine sweet-flavored pulp held in petite, deeply-furrowed pods. Its young leaves are used medicinally, macerated in water to release mucilage, drunk to relieve constipation. We were not aware yet of the discovery we were about to make.

Cacao has a fascinating natural history. Squirrels, the tayra, a large, tree-dwelling weasel, and tropical relatives of the raccoon, such as the kikanjou, the bushy-tailed olingo, and the elusive cacomistle, all feast on cacao. While many mammals disperse cacao seeds—particularly the saddleback tamarin, a species exclusive to the Tropical Wet Forest, the sharp-witted white-fronted and brown capuchin monkeys, the squirrel monkey, the graceful woolly monkey, and elegant spider monkey—and thousands of insect species live in cacao's environment, few pollinate her. Due to the evolution of cacao's complex floral structure, her pollinators are highly restricted to tiny mosquito-like insects called midges, perfectly shaped to enter and pollinate cacao's small bone-white flowers that appear on the trunk and branches amidst the moist and cool lower level of the rainforest.

The Tropical Wet Forest is a festival of biodiversity, and soon our makeshift collection table overflowed with fruits and seeds gathered on jungle forays. Cacao relatives growing in the region include the mighty silk cotton kapok, the *Ceiba pentandra*, known locally as uchuputu, a tree charged with mythology whose powerful outreaching branches offer habitat for worlds of life above the forest canopy; kamotoa, a towering emergent tree with elegant buttress roots—that was assigned its botanical name *Gryanthera amphibiolepis* only later, in 2012—which today is sadly vanishing due to the unregulated and illegal logging that plagues the area; and the much-loved balsa tree, the lightest known wood, *Ochroma pyramidale*, which contributes to regenerating the rainforest.

At our forest camp, Dr. Cerón explained that the origin location of plants is indicated by where a botanical family has the highest concentration of species. Nowhere else has he seen such a dense assemblage of plants in the Malvaceae family. He confirmed, "We have made a most impressive discovery. This region undeniably is the origin site of *Theobroma cacao*, the chocolate tree!" On the equator, along the eastern foothills of Cordillera Napo-Galeras, a mountain known in local folklore as the "End-of-the-World-Jaguar Mountain," is the origin of the cacao tree.

SHE HAS COME A LONG WAY

We now know that cacao originates in the upper Amazon at the base of the Andes in northwestern South America. How she became such an intricate part of Central America is mostly unknown. She was carried north, perhaps by non-human mammals or by ancient human traders. Consider the first option—we know that the isthmus of Panama rose out of the sea between three and seven million years ago, opening a land bridge between Central and South America that greatly impacted Earth's climate. The flow between oceans was blocked, which rerouted currents, creating the Gulf Stream, warming the planet, and provoking a surge in biological diversity. So began the Great American Interchange, where animals and plants migrated between South America and North America. Cacao may have been steadily moved by monkeys, rodents, and other mammals who adore its sweet pulp but leave behind the bitter seeds, slowly spreading north, east, south, and west.

Geneticist Omar E. Cornejo demonstrated that the oldest known domesticated cacao strains in Central America actually originate in the Amazon. Central American peoples cultivated strains of cacao that had been domesticated in the upper Amazon by Mayo-Chinchipe people thousands of years prior. We know very little about the vanished Mayo-Chinchipe, an elaborate and ceremonial culture that lived for four-thousand years at the base of the Andes, along the equator, in the wettest and most biodiverse part of the planet. At the Santa Ana-La Florida archeological site in southeastern Ecuador, Claire Lanaud and Rey Loor dated residues found in stone and clay vessels as far back as 5,500 years—the oldest-known evidence of cacao use. Spondylus and strombus seashells found at La Florida indicate there was trade between the Mayo-Chinchipe and coastal societies. Coastal peoples of ancient America were navigators and avid wanderers who traded knowledge and goods such as plant materials, salt, gold, and jade pendants up and down the Pacific coastline. Recent studies by Smithsonian archeologists of pottery on display at the National Museum of the American Indian reveal that cacao was consumed as far north as the Pueblo Bonito site in the Chaco Canyon of New Mexico.

Over 3,800 years ago in Central America, Olmec people began cultivating cacao, which they called *kakawa* in their language that seems to be of the Mixe-Zoque family. Though far younger than the Amazonian Mayo-Chinchipe people, the Olmecs were one of the Mesoamerican mother cultures, remembered by colossal stone head carvings and less recognized as the cacao connoisseurs that they were. From the Olmecs, the Mayas learned skills, including jade carving and the cultivation and use of this fascinating plant. The Mayas adopted the Olmec name and glyph of cacao, which shows a head with a fish fin ear looking up, with another fin before the glyph's main features to doubly-accentuate the concept. The word *kakawa* sounds like the Mayan phrase "two fish." Cultural anthropologist Michael J. Grofe in his paper, "The Recipe for Rebirth: Cacao as Fish in the Mythology and Symbolism of the Ancient Maya," illuminates a parallel between the self-sacrifice of the Hero Twins, depicted in the *Popol Vuh,* and the processing of cacao. The Hero Twins' entrance into the underworld represents burial and fermentation of cacao seeds; their burning is the roasting; the grinding of their bones is cacao seeds ground on a *metate*, a stone mortar; and their being poured into water represents hydrating the fermented, dried, roasted, and ground cacao into a beverage. The twins are reborn as two fish, offering a provocative insight into the metaphor of cacao as a potent symbol for rebirth, movement, and water. Fins allow a fish to swiftly move through water as cacao allows a person to swiftly rise, and cacao grows in the regions of highest rainfall. The Maya adored cacao as a primordial element of their way of life, calling it the "World Tree" and the "First Tree." The Mayan beverage *chocol'ha* gave rise to the modern word *chocolate*.

FALLEN FROM HER STATE OF GRACE

By the mid-seventeenth century, cacao, introduced to Europe by the Spanish, became a popular beverage. Plantations were established along tropical coastal regions of Africa. Today, West Africa is the world's leading producer of cacao, at no light expense. In the early twenty-first century, cacao production increased both in Africa and Tropical America by 50%. The story of cacao production in Africa is sadly not heart-warming, in ironic contrast to the effects of the chocolate that comes from the region. UNICEF estimates that there are over 200,000 children working in cocoa plantations in Ivory Coast. Rural exodus in Africa represents more than 60% of the population, the majority of these refugees being youth who fall as easy prey. Meanwhile, Indigenous farmers producing cacao live in extreme poverty, obliged to rely on child labor to serve giant corporations supplying Western demand. Despite the 2001 Harkin-Engel Protocol—an agreement signed by major chocolate companies restricting the use of children to harvest cocoa beans—the crisis is still in full swing. ClassAction.org shares in-depth information on current lawsuits filed against Hershey, Mars, and Nestlé, alleging that confectioners have deceived consumers into "unwittingly supporting child and slave labor themselves through their product purchases."

In Ecuador, the origin place of cacao, the tree is cultivated in the wettest regions at the base of the Andes, the pinnacle of biodiversity. In western Ecuador, the Tropical Wet Forest has been almost completely obliterated for cacao monoculture plantations, which now also suffer from blight. Two of the finest botanists in the world, Alwyn Gentry and Callaway Dodson, discuss this in their article, "Biological Extinction in Western Ecuador." In a small protected forest in western Ecuador, at the Rio Palenque Science Center, Dodson affirms that there are more species of wild cacao protected there than at any other location on the planet. Despite the importance of conservation of the Tropical Wet Forest, big chocolate companies invest little back into protecting the gene bank of cacao or improving the quality of life of their farmers. Deforestation of critical hot spots of mega-biodiversity, as well as the crisis of childhood slavery on these plantations, marks the dismal state that humanity has fallen into. The Tropical Wet Forest is at the mercy of consumers—we must consciously step up and source cacao appropriately and not contribute to this nightmare.

COMING BACK AROUND TO AN ANCIENT FUTURE

Driven by a passion for cacao as a sacred crop, more and more small chocolate-producing companies are transforming the landscape. Appropriately sourced cacao is filled with the zest of life, rich in antioxidants and minerals, and highly beneficial for human health. Cacao originates in the most biodiverse environment, and as such, it is not to be grown in monocultural plantations, but rather as a member of a diversified garden system. Kallari, as a case example, is an Indigenous people's farmer-owned cacao cooperative in Amazonian Ecuador, whose mission is to sustainably improve the economic conditions of local partners and producers through the production, transformation, and marketing of mixed agricultural garden products, called *chakras*, while urging the preservation of culture and the environment. Cacao calls for an integral restoration and regeneration of humanity's relationship with nature, with the Earth, with people, and with ourselves. She lends herself as a conduit for an ancient future, one that reaches forward to heal landscapes and redirects our present course by inspiring unity of ancient wisdom with the best of modern day science.

HER CLOAK OF UNIVERSAL WISDOM

Cacao's teaching are clear for all to see. Born at the summit of biological megadiversity, she exhorts that we must reach the peak of consciousness—we must feel the joys and sorrows of others and of nature as if they were our very own. She teaches that without biological and cultural diversity, we parch the Earth of her essence. That the Earth's divine abundance slips between our fingers back into the void if taken for granted. This abundance that blesses so many must be cultivated. She gives and wants us to give back. In her silent invigorating essence, she whispers a vital message: return to a heart-centered way of reciprocity. Who does not serve does not live. She holds this truth, trembling with humility and compassion, uneased that we risk failing to see things for how they simply are. That we might fall short in awakening our hearts to universal love and appropriate righteous passion, so needed for us to grow, heal, and create solutions. These are the healing salves allowing us to remedy the economic, socio-cultural, and ecological wounds suppressing humanity and the Earth. Without diversity, there can neither be fertility nor stability; the triad is fluent and indivisible. In *The Diversity of Life*, ecologist E.O. Wilson states, "The sixth great extinction spasm of geological time is upon us, grace of mankind. Earth has at last acquired a force that can break the crucible of biodiversity." We also face tremendous cultural erosion as languages fade from memory. Cacao whispers a subtle warning: if we don't evolve, we risk certain catastrophe. She has witnessed the rise and fall of many societies and cautions of apocalypse.

From the ancient perspective of the animistic worldview that sees all beings as having a sentient and energetic soul, I imagine that the meditation mat of kakawa is revealed in its brilliant patterns highlighted in golden yellow and neon blue. Streaks of richly saturated sapphire, emerald green, glowing red, yellow, and silver-white light swiftly blow around all sides. And there are people sitting upon this mat reflecting upon all that kakawa teaches. And these people are inspired to rise in alignment with universal order, becoming allies to life, being truly human—awake in our fullest potential.

CHAPTER 9

Cannabis

Cannabis sativa

Jeremy Narby

In the mid-1980s, I spent two years in the Peruvian Amazon, living with the Ashaninca people. Despite the mind-boggling diversity of plants in the rainforest, the Ashaninca had names in their language for most vegetal species. And they used plants in many different ways—as medicines, foods, building materials, cosmetics, dyes, and poisons. They seemed to have an encyclopedic understanding of the plants in their environment. But when I asked them about the origin of their knowledge, they would point to plants like tobacco and ayahuasca, saying that consuming these plants with discipline and intention allowed them to learn about plant properties and many other things. More generally, they spoke of plants and animals as intelligent beings with specific personalities, with whom humans could communicate, in visions and in dreams.

Back then, I found all this difficult to grasp. As a humanist and agnostic materialist who had grown up in the suburbs of Canada and Switzerland, I was surprised to meet people who truly believed what I considered to be "irrational superstitions." As a young anthropologist, I wanted to study how Ashaninca people used the rainforest, and I wanted to understand their plant knowledge, but I found my own disbelief getting in the way.

In particular, I did not believe that plants were volitional, intelligent beings like humans. Not that I had thought about it much. It was just one of those things that I had acquired through my education. Growing up in the comfort of the modern world in the 1960s and 1970s, I had been led to consider plants as mindless automatons, as green things that didn't do much; they absorbed water through osmosis, which was a normal physical-chemical phenomenon, and turned light into energy via photosynthesis, with its known chain of cellular reactions, but that was about it. I viewed plants as passive objects devoid of intention, and I knew that to suggest otherwise was to risk the scorn and ridicule of most Westerners. You did not talk to your lawn; you mowed it.

Nor did I believe that one could learn from psychoactive plants by keeping to a strict regimen, eating only certain foods, and staying away from society for long periods. The whole idea that a plant could teach things to humans seemed a bit crazy.

Nevertheless, I continued to probe the Ashaninca about their plant knowledge, and one day, a shaman told me that, if I wanted to understand, I would have to drink ayahuasca. He added: "Ayahuasca is the television of the forest. You can see images and learn things. If you like, I can show you some time."

I accepted his proposition, and the session he organized several nights later jolted me out of the human-centeredness of humanism and anthropology. In my visions, I saw how small humans were and how similar we were to other living beings, including plants. I also saw the arrogance of my own worldview. The overall experience was difficult but eye-opening and instructive. That a plant brew could have such a profound effect on how I saw the world gave me new respect for plants. From then on, I knew deep down that focusing exclusively on humans was shortsighted and gave an incomplete picture.

But on returning to university, I kept this point of view to myself. I went on to write a dissertation about human relations involving Ashaninca people, international development banks, colonists, and missionaries. From start to finish, the doctoral research I conducted was a human-centered affair, which was fairly standard for anthropology at the time.

* * *

The years skipped by, and I started working for a humanitarian organization based in Switzerland as an Amazonian projects manager, helping Indigenous Amazonian people gain land titles and access to bilingual education. So, my work kept a focus on humans. But the Ashaninca's view of plants continued to intrigue me. Were plants really intelligent beings? Could psychoactive plants really teach things to those who consumed them? My experience with ayahuasca confirmed that this plant brew could lead to important understandings, so I knew the notion had some basis.

I decided to test the matter on a psychoactive plant that I knew I could grow in my garden, outdoors, and with sunlight: cannabis. I had used it previously for recreational purposes. While in college, I had occasionally smoked grass, usually with pleasure.

I intended to grow some organic cannabis and test it on myself to see if it worked as a "plant teacher." I would follow Ashaninca precepts as much as possible. For starters, it had to be a natural-grown plant, not an indoor one grown with electricity. And to try to learn from this psychoactive plant, I would have to act with disciplined intent. As I am not a shaman of any sort but an anthropologist and a writer, I wanted to see if the plant could help with my thinking and writing. I wanted to enroll the plant to reach a fuller understanding of the world we live in and gain knowledge about nature and all forms of life, including people.

First, I read up on the cannabis plant and on growing techniques. I learned how to start plants from seeds, grow them with daily care, select only female plants for their resin-rich flowers, harvest them, and dry them. By 1991, at the age of thirty-one, I was producing outdoor organic cannabis for my personal research. Starting any younger would have been risky, as research indicates that heavy cannabis use disrupts learning in adolescents and young adults. But I figured I was old enough to take a risk. The point was not to take repeated doses of strong cannabis and become a "chronic heavy user," but to use the plant for a purpose and in a disciplined way, in order to get an idea of what the Ashaninca were talking about when they said that one could learn from a plant.

I trained myself physically, running in the forest every day. I kept to a healthy diet and gave up sugar and processed foods. I knew I had to be healthy and strong to work with a plant teacher.

I spent the first part of my working days in ordinary consciousness, doing my desk job, and reading anthropology and biology on the side. And in the late afternoons, I would smoke some cannabis, go running in nature, and think about what I had just read or written. Interesting ideas tended to flow into my mind during those moments; I could consider the data from a freer, more sensorial, and side-winding perspective. To catch these fleeting ideas, I carried around a pocket notebook and a felt pen. As soon as an interesting idea came my way, I would stop running and note it down. The next morning, in sober and lucid consciousness, I would use the previous day's insights or discard them if they did not seem relevant.

It's true, some cannabis-inspired thinking is nebulous and requires lucid criticism. But I found that this worked both ways; cannabis thinking provided an interesting angle on normal thinking, and the converse was also true. I allowed myself to critique both equally as I went back and forth between the two. The end result of combining these two ways of thinking was that I found myself reaching a fuller understanding of the questions I considered.

Cannabis also allowed me to reread my own words with detachment as if someone else had written them. This was precious because I tended to be overly attached to my own words when I was in the process of writing. With cannabis, I found that I could detect the words that didn't feel quite right or that lacked clarity, and I could also see what was missing—such as the things I didn't know enough about yet and needed to look into. For me, cannabis worked as a "plant editor."

For several years, and on a near-daily basis, I went back and forth between these two ways of thinking. Using this method, I looked into a discipline about which I knew very little, molecular biology, and ended up writing a book about its possible interface with Amazonian shamanism. The book went on to have some success and was translated into multiple languages.

However, I kept the cannabis work method to myself. Using the plant was one thing, discussing it was another. At the time, in the late 1990s, cannabis was illegal almost everywhere in the world. There was still a "war on drugs," and talking about the method would have meant confessing to a crime. Also, discussing the method could have been construed as promoting it, and it seemed obvious that consuming strong cannabis on a regular basis was not for everybody. I was fortunate to find myself in the right circumstances, living in a quiet place surrounded by nature, and knowing enough to follow Ashaninca principles of discipline and intent. What's more, my driven temperament allowed me to handle most of the plant's discombobulating effects. But this was certainly not the case for most people. Cannabis was just not everybody's cup of tea. Most of the people I knew who smoked it in their teens or early twenties had stopped doing so because it made them feel paranoid or confused.

I had no interest in promoting cannabis by saying that I used it as a plant teacher. All I wanted to do was to "learn from the plant."

Musicians, writers, and creatives have long worked with cannabis. Perhaps most notably, French poet Charles Baudelaire discussed how to use cannabis in his 1860 book *Artificial Paradises: Opium and Hashish*. He described in detail the effects of eating "a green jam" made of cannabis, butter, and a little opium. It was best to take this on an empty stomach, he wrote, by mixing a walnut-sized quantity of cannabis butter (which he called "hashish") in strong black coffee. Within half an hour of drinking this mixture, one began feeling the effects, including a sharpening of the perception of one's immediate circumstances. For this reason, Baudelaire wrote, one needed a handsome apartment or countryside spot, a free mind, a few like-minded accomplices, and perhaps some music. After an initial phase of hilarity and goodwilled merriment, during which simple ideas started to "take on a bizarre and new physiognomy," Baudelaire described a second phase: "Your face goes pale, and becomes livid and greenish. [...] The hallucinations start. Exterior objects take on monstrous appearances. [...] The most singular ambiguities, the most inexplicable transpositions of ideas take place. Sounds have color, colors have music. Musical notes are numbers, and you solve amazing arithmetic calculations with frightening speed as the music plays in your ear. You sit and smoke tobacco; you think you are in your pipe, and it is you that your pipe smokes; it is you whom you exhale in the form of bluish clouds. [...] True, you retain the faculty of observing yourself."

For my part, I experimented with a tea made from garden cannabis and creamy milk and found that it was too strong and hard to dose correctly. When heated in fat, cannabis releases the full range of its active molecules, and the result is often powerfully hallucinogenic. Like Baudelaire's friends,

I tended to turn green with such high doses and become unable to function or make much sense of anything.

For years, I found that smoking was the means of consumption that allowed me to best manage the question of dosage. I was looking for a strong enough effect to alter my thinking, but not so strong that it incapacitated me. The point, after all, was to be able to run, take notes, and find new ideas and angles. And to do so in a way that allowed me to get back to work the next morning with a clear mind. The overall point was to combine lucid thinking with vegetalized thinking, like a weaver—weave to the left, weave to the right, and start over.

Here I should say that the appropriate dose depends entirely on the person. Not only is cannabis not everybody's cup of tea, but those who do enjoy it have very different levels of tolerance.

Over the years, I found that cannabis-inspired thinking helped make sense of complex science. For example, in 2003, I was working on a book about intelligence in nature, and I came upon a recently-published article in a scientific journal by a biologist called Anthony Trewavas, stating that plants had intentions, made decisions, and computed complex aspects of their environment—even though they lacked brains. At the time, this seemed like quite a breakthrough because the subject of plant intelligence still elicited widespread ridicule in the Western world. I read the research mentioned by Trewavas and learned that scientists had recently discovered that plants used cell-to-cell communication based on molecular and electrical signals, some of which were remarkably similar to those used by our own neurons. For example, when a plant was damaged, its cells sent one another electrical signals just like our own pain messages. I found this interesting, but there was something that escaped me; on the one hand, the scientists insisted that plants were brainless yet, on the other, they produced data showing that plant cells worked like neurons.

I pondered this for a while and decided to submit the question to my vegetalized brain. So, I smoked some cannabis and went for a run, and it dawned on me that the two points of view could be combined: A plant does not *have* a brain, so much as *act like* one—the whole plant is like a brain. Ah, yes. Thank you. I stopped running and wrote it down. Several months later, I traveled to Scotland to interview Anthony Trewavas, and at one point, I mentioned that after reading his publications, I had pictured the whole plant as a kind of brain. "Yes, that's interesting," he replied. He then compared the molecular signals used by neurons and plant cells and added: "But you are quite right when you ask about computation: Where does it actually exist? I just don't know. And the answer is almost certainly: It's in the whole organism."

In the years that have gone by since this conversation with Anthony Trewavas, scientists demonstrated that plants do many things usually associated with brains, such as perceiving, communicating, learning, and remembering. Now there is even conclusive evidence that plants grow like brains. So, back in 2003, cannabis helped me see the bigger picture and put two and two together. This, I think, is one of its strong points.

But it also has weak points: I find that it does not help when I have to do accounting, or when I have to listen to something that does not interest me, or when I have to find the keys before going for a run.

* * *

As I write these words, I have been working with cannabis for thirty years. Nowadays, I mainly vaporize, or else I take a small dose of cannabis-infused olive oil (a homemade, low-heat extract). I try to avoid smoking, which yellows the teeth and tars the gums and lungs. Even though population studies have not found an increased risk of lung cancer associated with cannabis use, I find that regular smoking irritates my throat and lungs. It's safe to say that smoking any vegetal matter in excess is bad for the health and to be avoided.

Now I consider cannabis as a friend or an ally. But is it really a plant teacher? My short answer is that it certainly *acts like* one. I often learn things after ingesting the plant, or I come up with new perspectives.

Does cannabis have a personality? I think one's answer to this question will depend on one's worldview. In my case, I think that cannabis *acts like* it has a personality. This does not mean that it truly has one, but that when

I ingest it, I experience its impact on my personality. And on that basis, I find cannabis to be impish, playful, quirky, and tricky.

Tricky is a good word for cannabis; it plays tricks on me sometimes, or it gets me to play tricks on myself. It disrupts or side-tracks, but often in a way that leads to new angles. It can be funny, but it does not guarantee clear-sightedness or inspiration.

During the first years that I worked with the plant, I went through countless moments of paranoia. The Ashaninca way of dealing with the difficulties presented by a plant teacher is to confront them. So, I confronted cannabis-induced paranoia often enough to finally get a handle on it. I do not recommend this to anybody because it is a hard and risky path and somewhat of an extreme sport. Some people do not tolerate cannabis at all; even with a small dose, they go all pale and feel nauseous. It's just not their plant. I understand completely because I feel the same way about tobacco and opium. The last thing I want to do is give cannabis to a person who will not appreciate it. Of course, those with psychotic issues should abstain from using the plant.

Cannabis can frighten people. This can happen to beginners, or to those who go into the experience in a negative mind-frame, or who have taken too strong a dose. Getting a grip on cannabis means learning to control dosage, and this often implies bringing the dose down. Working with cannabis on a regular basis requires avoiding certain activities and situations in the hours that follow consumption, such as driving vehicles, operating machines, going to important meetings, or doing homework with the kids. This makes it necessary to time one's consumption according to the tasks at hand.

It is also important to take breaks from the plant, which can be difficult because it also acts like a seducer. Cannabis has a way of suggesting that it might be good for just about any circumstance, chatting with a friend, contemplating a sunset, gardening, ironing, listening to music, playing frisbee, watching a film, doing boring stuff, doing fun stuff, relaxing, dancing, before a meal, after a meal, with a cup of coffee, or a glass of wine. Oh yes, and as a nightcap, for sleeping. Cannabis can come across as a wide-spectrum enhancer that is also innocuous, so why not just have some more? But giving in to this means losing one's baseline, which is necessary to function in the world, as well as to truly appreciate the plant as a counterpoint. Less is more.

Some cannabis users suffer from "a-motivational syndrome," meaning that they become lazy and lounge around all day doing nothing much. My view from the start has been that working with the plant requires a strong intention to do something.

My intention has been to reach a fuller understanding of the world we live in. I'm still working on it. And I'm still keeping to the discipline and learning with the plant.

CHAPTER 10

Ceiba

Ceiba pentandra

Steven F. White

I've decided that I want my mortal remains to nourish the roots of my favorite ceiba trees (*Ceiba pentandra*) on our ancestral family farm in Telica, Nicaragua called Finca Santa Ana, and those in front of my home in San Jerónimo on the outskirts of the great Nicaraguan city of letters and higher education, León. The contributors to this collection, *The Mind of the Plants,* are seeking answers to incredibly complex questions made more difficult still because of our marked deficiencies as human beings demonstrably incapable of coexisting in mutually beneficial ways with other species in their diverse abundance. I have been thrilled in my lifetime to be able to learn some other languages, even after my head probably should have been too hardened to allow this to happen. Perhaps it's true that my knowledge of Spanish and Brazilian Portuguese has given me an exquisite, subtly-swollen brain with well-connected left and right hemispheres that the BBC insists will ward off dementia! It would seem that once I am no longer on what Norman Maclean calls the "oxygen-side of earth's crust," it would be the perfect opportunity to really concentrate in darkness for a very, very long time and to learn the ceiba's language just by paying attention to its roots spreading through me and then rising high into its towering crown on a roller coaster of water and photosynthesis in its leaves shaped like the hands I used to have.

A new project has allowed me to get closer than ever to the ceibas I've lived with most intimately on a level where the infinitely small approaches the infinitely vast. Jill Pflugheber, a microscopy specialist from the Biology Department at St. Lawrence University, and I have been working over the last five years on "Microcosms: a Homage to Sacred Plants of the Americas."[1]

If one looks at the image constructed with a confocal microscope of the ceiba (also called kapok, silk-cotton tree, lupuna, and wari mahi),[2] it is easy to appreciate the ovoid apertures of the stomata. Then, with a slight push into the imagination of this hitherto unperceived proximity, perhaps it is not inconceivable to begin to share vital resources with this digital ceiba and consider how it would be to breathe with the plant itself. The underside of the leaf and the stem used to create this image is from the ceiba where I hope to be resting in the future, learning the ceiba's language and some of what my university language students would crave at the beginning of the semester, "Teach us the swear words! Teach us how to order drinks! Teach us how to say the best food!" I am looking forward to learning all this from the ceiba's perspective as well as attempting to assimilate its dynamic, idiomatic, and idiosyncratic expressions from time immemorial.

When I was twenty-four, having recently graduated from Williams College with a minimal, but deeply transformative, two-year grant to study and translate Hispanic American poetry, I arrived in Nicaragua for the first time at the beginning of 1979 (after a year traveling with my backpack in Ecuador, Peru, and Chile), and began an apprenticeship with a giant of Latin American literature, Pablo Antonio Cuadra (1912–2002). At that very moment, during the violent uprising of the people against the Somoza dictatorship and the terrible realities of a civil war, Cuadra had finished the narrative, ethnobotanical poems that would constitute *Siete árboles contra el atardecer*, which I later translated for Northwestern University Press as *Seven Trees Against the Dying Light*—seven poems with Aeschylus as a model for describing internecine conflict, seven trees as repositories and bulwarks of Nicaraguan history and biological diversity. The poems are long, and they tell amazing stories, incorporating Indigenous culture, historical figures, and autobiography as well as what must have been shocking at the time of the book's publication in Venezuela in 1980—the hard-edged, scientifically-precise language of botany.

As good as all the poems are in this seminal collection, "La Ceiba" was always my favorite, perhaps because of the poem's opening lines that describe how the Amerindian refugees fleeing from their Aztec persecutors chose their route of exile by climbing high in this tree, opening the seed pods, blowing the light, silky material into the wind, and calculating their future exodus based on the flight of the ceiba's seeds at the height of eagles, condors, butterflies, and the thoughts of the greatest thinkers. Yes, this poem definitely captured my young imagination in a total way, and was the foundation of my ongoing life-long learning process with my literary grandfather, PAC. For me (and I wrote about this in a poem after he passed away), he was *all* trees and *the* tree, *Omniarboreae cuadrensis.*

I recall once seeing photographs of magnifications of the silky seeds of the ceiba: each implausibly tiny seed for such a great tree attached to a column of enclosed air. So, yes, of course, the seeds could indeed fly as high as all the species of birds and insects that Cuadra called forth in his poem. And if the seeds were to fall on the calm or roiled waters of Nicaragua's great internal freshwater sea, Lake Cocibolca, they would continue their journey, floating on and on until they reached a distant shore to germinate in the deathless desire of all plants.

For a child growing up in Nicaragua, the ceiba's seeds are linked to one of the most personal objects used on a daily basis—a pillow. It is not unusual there for a grandmother to send children out in April with the mission of gathering the little accumulated piles of ceiba seeds, brushing off as much dust and debris as possible, and then stuffing the fluff into a woven container that could support a dreamer's head for a third of a someone's life. For Central American children, the cottony seeds flying through the hot air during or after Holy Week are their closest chance to imagine the snow of cold and distant countries they will never know.

Certain perceptive children are more aware than adults that the ceiba is a home for many different creatures. It is a refuge for iguanas and squirrels, a giant living space with myriad secret nests.

The ceiba is also where the *chichicastes* live, the phosphorescent green caterpillars whose poisonous hairs resemble a forest that is being carried along as it moves. There is a video of these strange creatures from the genus *Automeris* (which has more than a hundred different species), but it is entirely unclear why the person holding the caterpillars seems impervious to the poison that is triggered by the slightest contact with the filaments.[3]

The *chichicaste* (which is also the name of the stinging nettle *Urtica dioica* in Nicaragua) is highly toxic and especially dangerous for children. The sting produces a serious fever and, according to my wife, Esthela Calderón, who is Nicaraguan and also a contributor to *The Mind of Plants* (Chapter 14), revelatory dreams. Her close encounter with a *chichicaste* when she was seven years old left her with the indelible impression that these caterpillars are the caretakers of the ceiba and that the tree communicates by means of this poisonous intermediary. The caterpillar's hairs in the shape of undulating upright trees even resemble a ceiba's leaves, which are the chichicaste's preferred food. Decades later, Esthela still remembers the revelation produced by the caterpillar's venom. After her feverish state, she found that she could clearly distinguish the caterpillars from the leaves, where they were perfectly green and camouflaged. The chichicastes only became visible to her child's eyes for the first time after she was poisoned by them. She also remembers how the caterpillars are later transformed into beautiful iridescent moths with the first rains in May. What, then, is one to make of these caterpillars tracing what Dale Pendell has described as the Poison Path, living high among the branches of the ceiba and carrying their own portable, miniature psychoactive forest on their bodies?

More research certainly needs to be done regarding the Amerindian medicinal uses of the ceiba. In a book on the shamanic practices of the Yanomami in Brazil, Bruce Albert and William Milliken affirm that the Indigenous healers use the "images" of the largest trees of the Amazon rainforest, such as the ceiba, to scare off evil spirits that cause disease. Writing about Upper Amazonian shamanism in Peru, Dr. Francoise Barbira-Freedman says that tobacco is offered as a propitiating food to the mother-spirits of certain trees, particularly the *lupuna* tree (*Ceiba* spp.): "The *lupuna* sap is indeed known to be poisonous as well as psychoactive." Perhaps this confirms what I am learning in Nicaragua about how the ceiba tree has found a way to communicate in a toxic language that causes visionary dreams in humans. What an astonishing fundamental psychological trait of the mind of this guardian and its poisonous caretakers!

The ecological niché of the ceiba stretches in a belt around the middle of the world, but I have only seen ceibas on Nicaragua's Pacific side, where they are solitary figures that dominate an open landscape, and the Peruvian Amazon, where I was overwhelmed by the truly massive base of the *lupuna* tree and found myself unable to perceive where it disappeared above me into all the other trees surrounding it in a dense green canopy. A friend in Pucallpa, Peru, tells me that there is a gigantic lupuna in his city in a central place downtown. Unfortunately (and this is a gruesome example of the "invisible landscape" that Kent C. Ryden has written about so compellingly), this lupuna was used by Shining Path terrorists as a site for torturing and executing their political opponents and repressing the local population. Outside of the Americas, men in Indonesia are harvesting Java cotton, and scientists in China and India are researching the ceiba as a way to treat dysentery, tuberculosis, diabetes, cholera, and snakebites, and no doubt there is a factory somewhere producing life jackets from kapok fiber.

In Nicaragua, ceibas are for planting out in the country, where there is ample space, or to line ancient thoroughfares to endow them with elegance and an undeniable natural stature. Even so, contemporary life has taken its toll. Cuadra once told me that in order to widen the highway from the Managua, Nicaragua airport to the colonial city of Granada—a prime tourist destination—more than a hundred huge ceibas were chainsawed into extinction as a perfect emblem of our human priorities. I was warned by my mother-in-law, who recently passed away in her nineties, that the ceiba tree we planted in front of our home in León would one day knock down the wall that surrounds the perimeter of our land. No doubt this is true, for it is growing taller and taller, dwarfing the tall palm trees on either side of it. But, by the time our old wall tumbles onto the ceiba's robust roots, who knows if there will even be a habitable planet. Today, due to climate change, yet another monster hurricane rose from the Caribbean (the second in two weeks, Eta then Iota), which has devastated Nicaragua's poorest and most vulnerable populations. On the radio tonight, I heard a moving interview with a doctor from the Honduran Garifuna community in a place called, yes, La Ceiba. This could very well be the new tragic normal November for years to come. And, for us, it could foreshadow the apocalyptic end of Macondo in *One Hundred Years of Solitude*. The ceiba, I fear, now towering over our home in San Jerónimo, will be the least of our worries.

The Maya considered the gigantic ceiba (*ya'axché*) a sacred tree that bears the weight of the cosmos and has its roots in the underworld. Cuadra has written how the ceiba tree permeates life in Central America from beginning to end. Its easily-carved wood is both a cradle for newborns and a coffin for the deceased, as well as a canoe to get from one to the other over a lifetime. The ceiba knows you when you are born and later is your companion at the end of your journey. Lopping off a couple of the large lower branches provides the wood for making long troughs for feeding livestock. A prudent person in the countryside might plant a ceiba close—but not too close—to his house so that it functions as a lightning rod that might spare a home from a disastrous strike during the violent storms that have families desperately carving three crosses in the dust outside their homes and fervently praying to the Apostle Peter for protection in the most dire circumstances.

What do I think about when I am close to the ceiba (and even touching the sharp thorns in the trunk that protect its future), meditating in the place where I will finally rest? The ceiba receives the newborn just as its roots are a kind of sacred cup that accumulates water. The sound of the ceiba always changes as it creaks and sways in hurricanes and gentle rains as well. Each branch, in its perfect mind, understands exactly how it will grow and shape the sky. This tree already knows the aesthetics of its future anatomy. The ceiba possesses an emotional complexity, asserting its importance, aware that it was not born to give the world mangos or plantains. The ceiba is certain who it is. It senses itself to be a recipient of so much vegetal history and consciousness. And it knows how to occupy a space completely, dominating it, steadfast in its own rootedness in this particular ecosystem. Its thought collaborates as a supreme spatial guardian and understands this responsibility. We human beings have far too many questions, and we never seem to find enough answers. Not so of the ceiba. Like all trees, it has no lack of memory in its wisdom. And this is by no means an egotistical tree. The ceiba lives to strengthen fertility. In order to grow, it proudly sends out its sharp spines on its trunk to keep enemy iguanas from climbing to eat its new growth. It is responsible for its actions and their consequences. It knows itself with utter confidence. The ceiba is ceremonial by nature. It is far more than everything that surrounds it. The omniscient ceiba sees everything and more. It protects humanity's plants and is always vigilant of the other trees. The *chichitotes* (orioles) make their hanging nests high in the ceiba, far from the danger of reptiles that cannot pass its barrier of formidable thorns. In preserving itself, the ceiba protects other species. It is a space that is too high and too dangerous for most. These are the things I contemplate in the presence of the ceiba.

In *How To Change Your Mind*, Michael Pollan speaks of the importance of achieving a plant's-eye view of the world. In my very first ayahuasca vision in the Santo Daime church in Florianópolis, Brazil, in 1993, I received a bird's-eye view of the world with the help of a hummingbird guardian spirit. That eye that was so close to mine, or was mine, that iridescent throat, those blurred wings, and the open flower of my mouth from which the hummingbird drank profoundly transformed my life. The ceiba, for now, humbles me and keeps me in my place even as I recognize the urgent need to know the non-human species that surround me. With the ceiba, I am compelled to lower my gaze and demonstrate respect. It would be presumptuous in life to assume even the remote possibility of an egalitarian exchange of glances. The leaves of the ceiba, shaped like human hands, wave and greet me far above in the wind.

At certain moments in our lives, we feel the urgent wish for protection. I am remembering now, in my own time of need, my journey to Pucallpa twenty years ago and the ceremony in which the renowned shaman don Benito ritually placed an *arkana* over my entire body to shield me from evil forces. This weekend, I listened very closely to some *ikaros* (sacred songs chanted by *ayahuasqueros*) available on Spotify from "El Canto del Tiempo" by Don Evangelino Murayray, "Woven Songs from the Amazon" by Shipibo shamans such as Erlinda Agustín Fernández and many others, as well as "Contact" by the US-based healer Metsa. Amazonian chanting—as Francois Demange has written from a deeply poignant personal perspective related to his shamanic training in Peru—is the creation of codes, figurative language, and deeply metaphorical analogies that build up in the songs and generate visions that stimulate an inner healing intelligence. The *chants* come from the *plants*. I love the rhyme that harmoniously links these two seemingly disparate nouns in English. The songs are therapeutic tools. Demange insists from his own experience that the healing effect of the chants does not depend on a listener rationally understanding the meaning of what he calls their "twisted words." Emerging from the rhythmic labyrinthine patterns in Spanish, Quechua, and Shipibo, I finally heard the protective emblematic structures of conjoined allies called forth from the natural world. For me, now, foremost among them is Peru's *lupuna* (ceiba). And added to this powerful protective force are the boa, the *urukututu* (an Amazonian owl that has mastered the night), the *otorongo* (jaguar), the *lucero* (star), and many more figures of resistance and fortitude. Ultimately, it reminded me, too, of the strategy of the Hero Twins in the Mayan *Popol vuh*, who used their alliances with different elements of the natural world to defeat the Lords of Sickness and Death in Xibalba, the underworld penetrated by the roots of the ceiba, Axis Mundi, whose impossibly high branches touch the far reaches of the cosmos.

POEM 4

Century Plant

Agave americana

Luke Fischer

It's always reminded me
of a primeval sea creature,
an octopus-like plant
unfurling numerous tentacles,
head buried in the sea-bed,
its leaves undulating
though we move too rapidly
to perceive their motion.
Some resemble roused cobras
ready to strike.

Spikes along their wavy margins
like defensive armor or pointy teeth,
suggestive of animals long extinct
or obscure (found only among
illustrations in Haeckel's
Artforms of Nature) yet
we pass them everyday—
in gardens, along sidewalks—
succulents in sandy soil
unraveling analogies
between ocean currents and air.
Without tank or mask
they draw us
to the depths of the sea.

CHAPTER 11

Coffee

Coffea spp.

Joseph Dumit

I am a coffee creature. I wanted to write about my experiences with coffee, the various recipes and containers that sustain me through six plus strong cups of coffee a day, and the research that has intensified as I've been able to drink more. But I had to research coffee itself. Coffee makes researchers. Growing up a voracious reader, I was quite shy—until coffee opened my mind. With coffee, I started to notice more differences in the way people acted, differences in the way they reacted to substances. Coffee demanded distinctions; it seeded my curiosity and demanded I become an anthropologist and an anthropologist of science. With coffee, I make more categories; I am more alive in peculiarly intellectual, energetic, spiritual, healthy ways.

Coffee's peculiar forms of intensifying thought reaches out into the world. In 1925, Allers and Freund found that with coffee, "sensory and conscious associations moved into the foreground while automatic associations passed into the background. Thus, coffee is able to promote the brain's power of effecting combinations."[1] Coffee's evident immediate psychoactive and energetic properties have made it the target of continual attempts to control or ban it, and yet somehow, it has achieved dominance in most humans' thinking. I believe this is because coffee's superpower is, in fact, the fostering of classificatory thinking itself and then using these classifications to evade official notice. This seems to be a rare capacity among plants or animals, though I'm sure others will find further examples. Based on my research so far, coffee has three superpowers: it is an intensifier of human capacities; it invents and defies classification; and it is the elixir of health and, even, immortality.

COFFEE THINKS

My first work was as an anthropologist of neuroscience. I tried to study brain imaging and what humans think is in the brain worth studying. But when put into an MRI scanner, I was asked not to drink coffee that day. They told me that coffee messes with brain imaging, that it changes brain blood flow so much that one's scans can't be compared with scans of other people. They wanted to study my brain as if it were normal to not have coffee in it. Yet, I was only normal with coffee. What this means is that neuroscientists have standardized "normal" brains on people who are coffee-deprived. This was the beginning of a deep insight that neuroscience hasn't the slightest idea what is normal. Or perhaps, that coffee has found an ingenious way to not be studied—it is drunk by the researchers but not their subjects.

Like all drugs, the question is never: "What does coffee do?" (as if it were a singular substance with a definable effect). Nor: "What do we do with coffee?" (as if we can do with it what we want). But rather: "What do we do with what coffee does to us and, in particular, what does coffee help us want?" Besides more coffee.

Coffee is a shapeshifter, confirming the needs of the day and the humans it encounters. It was first known as a food ration, then a spirit like wine and medicine, a devotional refreshment, a stimulator of minds, a soberizer, an energizer, and, finally, as the healthiest substance and elixir of immortality. A brief survey of these abilities follows.

Coffee is perhaps the first energy bar. Being 14% protein, the coffee berry was a food that could be mashed up into food balls held in shape with fat to sustain people throughout the day. Its first documented historical use can be traced to Ethiopia, 800 AD.

Coffee then shows up in my history books as a miracle. There are multispecies legends of a goat who nibbled its berries in 1200 AD Arabia (Yemen) and became so lively that its shepherd tried the berries himself. Inspired by its energy, he took them to a local monastery where the beans were immediately recognized as helping holy men stay awake for their prayers. The Sufis in Arabia (Yemen) created coffeehouses as "Schools for the Wise." Roasted coffee released even more stimulating energy for the mind as well as the body, and Muslim stalls and then coffeehouses soon surrounded holy sites, becoming places of lively conversation and wild ideas.

Coffee's aroma seems to demand social gatherings, and its ingestion spurs intellectual conversation in a convivial manner. People come to enjoy arguing and developing relevant distinctions. Thus, coffeehouses became centers of social invention, as well as gaming, strategy discussions, religious disputation, and politics. While this may bring out the best in humans, it is also seen by hierarchical humans as a threat to their power—which often works best by preventing thinking. For this reason, coffee has been repeatedly attacked as a toxic substance due to its political effects—from Mecca to Rome to Germany to London to the US. In each case, attempts were made by politically aligned physicians to testify to its addictive and corrupting powers. Yet, these were regularly seen to be hypocritical, as most of the accusers depended on the substance as well, and everyone could see that coffee had no such pervasively bad effects.

Religion was brought in, arguing that coffee was intoxicating, and it was therefore banned under the Koran. This interpretation faltered on the grounds that coffee was roasted, not fermented. Bans were nonetheless implemented, including massive purges by Muslims against the Sufis, and then again in the Ottoman empire. They were not effective in the long term, however, as coffee seemed to have instituted itself alongside mosques.

By 1600, some Christians sought to prevent Muslim coffee from possessing them, taking it to Pope Clement VII to ban it. He insisted on tasting it first and proclaimed instead that it was too good to leave to the heathens. It was clearly devilish, enabling him to argue that "we should cheat the devil by baptizing it." In the early-twentieth century, some Orthodox Jews sought to ban coffee during Passover because it was a legume, but Maxwell House worked with a rabbi and successfully had it reclassified as a berry and, therefore, made it kosher.

Wherever coffee appeared, it was always also a medicine. Europeans first treated the bean as an exotic specimen, the province of virtuoso natural philosophers and doctors. Those men and women who could obtain the beans—as well as other plants and substances—from abroad were keen to experiment with them. Due to its bitterness, coffee was considered a strong medicine, helping with digestion, tumors, head, and heart. Physicians experimented and created precise recipes and prescriptions for it, dispensing it gingerly. But, coffee—unlike datura, betel nuts, bang, and opium—along with its kin cocoa and tea, assimilated into the British diet as commodities.

As imports of coffee grew and it became cheaper in England, the beverage escaped its narrow confinement and spread wildly in the form of coffeehouses, known as "penny universities" because of the intellectual conversations stimulated by the drink. A particularly potent brew was created for the students and philosophers of the Oxford Coffee Club, which soon became the Royal Society—the birthplace of Western experimental science. I think this is most significant, as it is precisely this type of science that is now used to define categories of substances like coffee.

Similarly, other coffeehouses such as Lloyd's spawned the marine insurance market, the brew stimulating notions of probability and risk. The British Stock Exchange also has its origins in a coffeehouse, and the Turk's Head Coffeehouse created the modern ballot box, where customers wanting to weigh in on controversial topics could "vote" anonymously. News, too, circulated through coffeehouses, and contemporary forms of newspapers were created and distributed in their networks. Meanwhile, women in Germany created coffee circles to assert their emancipation.

As Heinrich Eduard Jacob put it, "The discovery of coffee was, in its way, as important as the invention of the telescope or of the microscope [...] For coffee has unexpectedly intensified and modified the capacities and activities of the human brain."[2] Coffee, in other words, worked through humans to create institutions that would spread its word and enable them to diet on it. It inspired regulatory structures that governed its rivals and somehow emerged unscathed.

COFFEE ACTS

Coffee also was seen as a drug of sobriety. This was due in no small part to its appearance during the industrial revolution. At the time, most workers in England and throughout Europe consumed beer for breakfast, lunch, and dinner, not only because working conditions were not pleasant but also because the water in cities was deadly. Some hospitals would only serve spirits. Replacing beer with coffee noticeably reduced workplace accidents, and coffee's reputation as a substance to sober up drunkenness was solidified.

Coffee did more than this, of course—it energized bodies. The coffee break was part of capitalist speedup and army rations (so, too, cocaine for both of these). Employers were keen to make use of any substance that could increase productivity. Mass coffee for instrumental purposes also meant lower quality seed could be procured.

Coffee also became a driver of slavery. It may have stimulated capitalism, but capitalism and imperialism magnified coffee. Seeds were smuggled from country to country and cultivated extensively. As it became commodified, landowners and speculators went to deadly means to profit from it. Martinique and the French Caribbean became some of the first plantation economies due, in part, to coffee, and, when the slaves revolted in Haiti, coffee expansion was taken over by Brazil/Portugal.

Greatly exceeding the half-million Africans abducted to North America over the course of two centuries, Europeans kidnapped three million to Brazil to be enslaved on coffee plantations, in addition to five million more to sugar plantations. So extensive was its coffee production and labor exploitation that it destroyed the world market a few times with overproduction. It was finally saved by the Temperance Movement in the US, which outlawed liquor.

The US had famously been a coffee-drinking nation due to the Boston Tea Party's rejection of the English beverage. Back then, the US became known as the land of free refills. But it wasn't until the twentieth century that coffee took on the character of a national beverage freely found in hotels, in offices, and in factories and regularly drunk during afternoon coffee breaks. The US became the coffee consumption capital of the world, and Brazil became the chief supplier. Coffee's further expansion throughout Latin America continued the story of forced labor, state conscription, debt peonage, and brutal capitalism. Contemporary attempts to develop fair trade coffees are an important, but still minor, blip in the relation between consumer demand, imperial relations among countries and populations, and refusals by almost everyone to care about commodity chains.

I've already discussed how coffee kept itself from becoming a "medicine" in London. It also escaped the French physicians' wars over prescription coffee and established the café in Paris. In the US, it is not regulated by the Food and Drug Administration (FDA) or the Alcohol, Tobacco, Firearms, and Explosives (ATF), nor as a supplement. Its non-identical association with caffeine enabled this maneuver. In 1905, fundamentalist crusader Harvey Wiley helped create the FTC (that would become the FDA) through an attempt to ban caffeine from drinks. He specifically targeted Coca-Cola and the fact that children drank it (the caffeine in soft drinks actually comes from extracting it from coffee beans to make decaf coffee). Justices ruled that to ban caffeine would require banning coffee and tea, and so Wiley's campaign failed, and coffee was placed outside of the regulatory structure.

Even the most draconian of all anti-drug institutions, the World Anti-Doping Agency (WADA) that regulates the Olympic games, makes an exception for coffee and caffeine. Caffeine is the only controlled substance that is regulated and not banned in athletes. Coffee has positioned itself as so ubiquitous and so much a part of our biology that banning it would make the Olympics inhuman. (Though it must be noted that some government sites set up to help Olympians have tables warning that not every cup of coffee is the same. Starbucks, for instance, has so much more caffeine in a cup of their coffee than others that one must be careful about exceeding the regulatory limit for caffeine in urine.)

The reason why there is a limit on caffeine in Olympian bodies is because the substance can be precisely calibrated in different preparations to boost endurance, speed, strength, and power, or reaction time. To evade regulations, one needs to calculate the half-life of different doses in order to have them peak during competition and not when one is tested.

When MIT studied coffee in the early-twentieth century, it concluded that it was the "servant not destroyer of civilization." I think the jury is out on this. Rather than being subjected to human notions of active ingredients, government regulation, and expert medicines, it has instead insinuated itself into becoming a public drink, readily available for a cheap price and for self-dosing. We are all coffee people (even if we don't drink it), but given the state of the human world, I'm not sure coffee cares that much about us. Today, coffee is drunk for all of the above reasons: to awaken in the morning or midday, for conviviality and conversation, relaxation and stimulation, to cope with stress, and to make the grind less tiresome. These may all be called a bit therapeutic if we are inclined to medicalize the substance, but perhaps what is most surprising about coffee is just how healthy it actually is.

COFFEE HEALS

Coffee has always been the subject of medicinal speculation in both positive and negative directions. Physicians claimed for it all manner of cures, and also poisons. It clearly changed people's state quickly, mostly for the good, as outlined above. It functioned as a pick-me-up, a general intensifier, a simple source of energy. It caused trouble, but not too much usually, and it didn't seem to really poison anyone.

Unlike tobacco, which was seen as something to control, coffee appears to have walked the thin line between claiming too much and too little, all by itself. According to historians of coffee, had it been acknowledged as a universal medicine, coffee may have remained out of reach to the masses. Medical practitioners typically charged ten to thirty times the penny cost of a cup of coffee for a treatment in England. Coffee as a self-administered and self-dosed habit was much more democratic. "As both pleasant drink and efficacious drug, coffee occupied a sort of middle ground between diet and medicine."[3]

The very universal and universally loved status of coffee as a kind of self-medication and over-the-counter drug has led, nonetheless, to its being thought of as too good a thing. There must be a downside. During college, my best friend became so concerned with my coffee consumption that she declared I must be addicted in a bad way. To prove I wasn't, for six months, I gave up drinking coffee (and all caffeine because she was convinced it was the culprit). After the first two days of headaches, I was fine. I still stayed up all night writing and programming, but I noticed that I was less sharp and less curious. When I finally returned to coffee, my spark and adventurousness returned.

This habit of many humans to suspect that anything pleasurable must have a cost has led to coffee becoming one of the most studied drugs in the world. It has been the extensive focus of studies throughout the twentieth century, and almost all of these studies have been interested in finding out the negative consequences of a coffee habit.

Ironically, however, coffee not only appeared to be side-effect free (excepting those people who are extremely caffeine sensitive) but actually turns out to be a miracle drug of the highest order. Coffee is not just healthy but perhaps the healthiest long-term risk-reducing substance on the planet. In studies of hundreds of thousands of people—including tens of thousands of nurses and doctors—coffee has been found to lower cardiovascular disease, strokes, many kinds of cancers, diabetes, and death itself. These are not marketing studies; they are massive studies of hundreds of thousands of people prospectively. Their diets and habits are tracked for years, sometimes decades, seeing what diseases develop and how and when they die.

Seriously, the evidence is so overwhelming that something seems to be cooking the books. Having written a book on pharmaceutical clinical trials and how companies can manipulate them to produce exaggerated marketing claims, I was suspicious.[4] But these new studies were extensive and surprising. According to a 2012 Harvard Health Letter reporting on a massive study by the National Institutes of Health and American Association of Retired People:

> A study of more than 400,000 older men and women found that drinking two or more cups of coffee a day equated to a 10% reduction in deaths from all causes for men and a 15% reduction for women when compared to people who didn't drink coffee.[5]
>
> And four cups a day were even more protective! Surprisingly to most people, '*the protective effect of coffee drinking was evident whether subjects drank caffeinated or decaffeinated coffee.*'[6] To put it starkly, coffee is not caffeine; it is an elixir of health and immortality.

In other large studies, men who drank more than six cups of coffee a day reduced their risk for type 2 diabetes by more than 50% compared to those who didn't drink coffee. Women reduced their risk by almost 30%. In studies of over 100,000 men and women, researchers found a 25% lower risk of Parkinson's disease and 38% lower risk of Alzheimer's. Women with the BRCA1 gene mutation that elevates breast cancer risk had a 75% reduction in the risk if they drank six or more cups of coffee a day (2006), 30% less endometrial cancer, 50%+ reduced colon cancer. Blood pressure and other cardiac risks were also reduced. I now make sure to drink coffee to gain these benefits!

Compared to contemporary pharmaceuticals, any one of these effects by itself would make coffee the new wonder drug, required dosing by all humans. Yet, despite the fact that each of these studies made headlines around the world when they were first reported, they had no staying power; they are ghostly. Facts about coffee's health are not sustained by any marketing force—the way pharmaceuticals are—partly because no one is able to make money from touting its health benefits. The facts disappear from public discussion within days.

So maybe I'm hallucinating them? In 2009, researchers found that those who drink seven or more cups of coffee a day had triple the risk of hallucination and were more likely to see ghosts. This study has not been replicated, though I have experienced hallucinations—only once after an entire night consuming fifteen espressos while walking through Chicago neighborhoods with a friend. Our conversation never stopped, colors started to glow, and we lost track of time. We didn't see ghosts.

It is strange to think that it took so long to realize how healthy coffee is. It is as if we are so blinded by its wondrous immediate effects that we didn't even think to look at how in the long-term, it might be altering our aging bodies. Anyone remotely interested in being healthier should make pages 298–304 of the 2015 Dietary Guidelines Advisory Committee Report required reading.[7] This committee was tasked with looking into coffee's risks and instead found only benefits. It examined many of the above studies in great detail. It even suggested that the US national dietary guidelines include coffee as recommended for adults. Coffee almost ended up being declared part of every healthy breakfast! The data clearly showed it should be. Yet, the guidelines that were finally released (by a more political committee) were basically negative, noting that coffee is usually not very bad but suggesting caution in consuming it. Clearly, coffee prefers to hide in plain sight rather than subjecting itself to state regulations, for

CHAPTER 12

Common Oak

Quercus robur

Solvejg Nitzke

Quercus robur, the common oak, is so widespread in Europe that several countries claim it for their national tree. The same species is called "German" and "English oak"—both names alluding to the heroic-turned-violent histories of nationalism in Europe and around the world. With this in mind, it seems fitting, both symbolically and botanically, that one of the few living survivors of World War II's air raids in Dresden is a common oak.

A little awkward, leaning toward a neighboring group of trees (beeches and oaks, mostly), the *Splittereiche* (Splintered Oak) grows solitary in Dresden's central park, *Großer Garten* (Great Garden). It is a special tree to me—the first being that I recognized after moving with my family to Dresden in 2017. Seeing and touching *Splittereiche* was indeed like finally meeting someone in person that you have only heard about. Encountering her first in Marcel Beyer's *Kaltenburg*, I immediately felt drawn to this at once hidden and exposed being. Seeking her out in the spacious park felt first like the worst kind of literary tourism—looking for the *real thing*, which was especially weird for me since I keep trying to get my students to distrust *the real*. Nevertheless, I did want to see her for myself, especially because the existence of *Splittereiche* becomes increasingly precarious, at least if you measure it against human ideas of intactness and integrity. Challenging these very notions, however, is one thing the oak has taught me.

The oak earned her vernacular name because her splintered trunk still holds shrapnel (Bomben-*Splitter*) from the bombs that destroyed much of Dresden during the night of February 13–14, 1945. The reason for the tree's visible injuries and her location were known mostly to Dresdeners who either remembered the raids or knew of the tree through stories told and retold in families and schools. Still, her legendary status branches into stories and histories, Marcel Beyer's novel *Kaltenburg* (2008) probably being the best-known of them. In Beyer's novel, the oak connects the narrator to his family, who, like so many others, took shelter under the trees. Other than the official memorial culture, like the cemetery section, which commemorates the victims of the air raid, he feels the tree keeps the memory of his parents literally alive because it lives on. Even though it is only a short part of a narrative that spans the space from Vienna to Dresden, and several decades before and after the war, this intimate encounter between human and tree impressed me and stuck with me until I was finally able to meet her myself.

In a city that is not in any way short of memorials, the Splintered Oak is a curious exception: a tree is neither a building nor a ruin—reconstructed or not—nor, for that matter, a place. *Splittereiche* is a living being that resists the memorial duties imposed on it and subverts the ideas of memory as an exclusively human capacity. However, though it is not an artifact, the tree was planted by humans in a human-built park, cared for by gardeners and "tree-experts," who have invested considerable resources to keep her alive. But why is that? What can this tree tell people that books and memorials cannot? Does she stand *for* something or *with* someone? Could it be that the splintered oak is a witness rather than a memorial, a fellow survivor—one of the few beings that can still actively communicate its experience?

After all, *Splittereiche* is one of many trees wounded or destroyed during the air raids in Dresden's *Großer Garten* and throughout Europe. But if the destruction of trees is so casually accepted in times of peace, why would it be cared for or protected during a war? The roots of many trees in the park were severely injured when trenches were dug as shelter from the bombs. Trees were felled, burned, and chopped up for firewood when resources grew scarce after the war (even though these activities were eventually stopped). *Splittereiche* stands out—literally and figuratively—because she never perished nor fully healed. A gaping wound in her trunk dares the visitor to ask what happened. It stands in stark contrast to the otherwise obviously well-tended vegetation of the park. Until recently, it was barely covered up, provoking, even startling, pedestrians.

Großer Garten is a historical park founded in 1676 as a *Lustgarten* (pleasure garden) in which the illustrious Saxon nobility would celebrate elaborate and elegant festivities such as 1719's *Venusfest* on the occasion of the wedding of Prince Friedrich August of Saxony with Austrian duchess Maria Josepha. Different rulers and master gardeners imposed upon it their ideas of proper landscaping and resource management until, in 1813, it became a fashionable public park. In order to attract visitors to the various businesses in the park—mostly restaurants and leisure activities—the "great garden" remained modern and cutting edge. Not only did it sport electrical lights very early on along its central avenues and had exotic flower gardens, but it also provided designated bike lanes. Being (almost) ahead of its time, the destruction of the park in February 1945 hit Dresden particularly hard. And yet, the park and its vegetation provided shelter and food during and immediately after the air raids. In the aftermath of the war, the trees were surrounded by potato and vegetable patches, giving shade to the people rebuilding their houses and reminding them of better times.

The splintered oak is estimated to be around three hundred years old, spanning almost the entire history of the park. The circumference of its trunk and its height speak to the maturity of the tree. Yet even though *Splittereiche* witnessed, as a young tree, how Augustus II the Strong made the park into one of Europe's great gardens, it is not an exceptionally old oak, nor has it lived through more than other trees her age. But the visibility of her injuries, their persistence, and the tree's seemingly undisturbed will to live—to flourish even—render the oak a powerful symbol of Dresden's history. Through her presence in the park, the splintered oak tells the visitor what she has witnessed. She isn't a fairy tale tree, but she has the ability to stop people in their tracks, to make them ask what she would say, would she speak.

The oak saw the Seven Years' War: Napoleon's troops marching through the park, the horrors of the air raids, the hundreds of people seeking refuge under her and her fellows' branches; those killed by falling bombs and branches alike; the screams of children and parents looking for each other; the tears and silence of those who, like the oak, survived damaged and traumatized, trying to heal their wounds and pick shrapnel out of their bodies and houses, and to rebuild their city and their lives. *Splittereiche* could also tell the story of how the traces of the air raids and the crimes that preceded them vanished from sight. Close to her could have stood one of the yellow benches meant for people forced to wear yellow stars before the Nazi-Government banished Jews from going to the park altogether. From the perspective of the tree, the history of humankind unfolds in busy and erratic ways, none of it making sense. An arboreal view of things questions the human networks of meaning and importance.

The second or third time I went to see the tree, a sign was erected that tells visitors about this tree, drawing attention to the cultural memory of the war in Germany, as well as the role a plant can play as a medium or, more importantly, as an agent of memory. The new sign that points out the memorial value of the tree is evidence, if you will, of the loss of trust in the tree's ability to activate the memories and curiosity of passers-by. The sign was put in place on May 8, 2017, seventy-two years after Germany surrendered to the Allies and victory over Europe was declared. It is headed by a Mark Twain quote: "Time may be a great healer, but it's a lousy beautician." A short explanatory text describes the oak's visible damage, "its unmade-up face," as a sign for how damaging war can be and how vulnerable life is. By using words that also refer to human injuries and aesthetic practices (beautician, unmade-up), the tree is, for a short time, subject of the same experience as human beings. However, the sign itself defies this purpose. While it is probably true that a sign like this would not have been needed for many decades after the war—since people would have known the cause of the damage—the moment of not being sure whether one has found the right tree could produce ambiguity. Not knowing exactly would provoke speculation and force people to confront the vegetal being and the multiplicity of its possible experiences. What the sign does, however, is impose human meaning on a being that might not care whether a bomb exploded or lightning struck its body.

Making the tree a memorial involves an imperative for both oak and humans: Remember! Even the acknowledgment of her astonishing capacity for survival is not a vegetal feat anymore but a symbol for the equally astonishing capacity for human societies to emulate her. As a designated *site* of remembrance, the tree stands *for* not *with* humans. In a manner that Aleida Assmann, a scholar of memory culture and cultural memory, calls "substitution," *Splittereiche* is turned into a symbol for the historical event whose traces she is bearing.

Still, the tree *is* neither site nor memorial—despite the all too common ignorance of the independent nature of vegetal life.[1] Instead, it opens up room for a vision of vegetal life as independent, though not separate, from human meaning-making. In the very moment that someone looks at an overgrown ruin and recognizes the human artifact below—or rather, among the plants (and animals)—judgments and narratives arise which qualify the viewed environment in regards to the observer. The same scene can evoke visions of unity with nature, or of disturbance. While it might be impossible to suspend the anthropocentric perspective altogether, it is well worth exploring how displacing the human from the center of meaning- and worldmaking affects relationships between the human and the vegetal.

Caspar David Friedrich (1774–1840), a Romantic landscape painter who was based in Dresden, produced an oak portrait that illustrates how this displacement might work. *Der einsame Baum*[2] puts an oak at the front and center of the painting. You have to look twice to see a shepherd and his flock lingering below the giant plant. Without a doubt, the tree has led a long life, possibly has been struck by lightning, and grown so tall that it dominates the entire landscape. What distinguishes this painting from others is that it depicts a non-human being as an individual. Friedrich treats the tree as if it were the subject of a portrait and a quite regal one at that. Everything becomes *um-welt* to the oak, that is, everything is dependent on and arranged around the tree—the symmetrical structure of the painting creates a perspective that concentrates so intently on the oak that she stands out even though she is firmly rooted. She is at once a part of and the reason for this "landscape" to exist. This is an unsettling perspective on a plant, even a majestic one like this oak.

Even though humans tend to fashion themselves after oaks and other trees—to imagine themselves as tall, resilient, and versatile—in the Western world trees turning into humans are usually mildly ridiculed. This effect is often enhanced by mocking not only the tree but the culture from which its anthropomorphic shape is appropriated—think, for example, of "Grandmother Willow" in Disney's *Pocahontas*. So for Friedrich to put an oak in the spot reserved for a king is, indeed, radical. It anthropomorphizes the tree to achieve the opposite. By putting the oak in this culturally significant position, Friedrich gives her an aura of more-than-human power and thus puts the tree and the viewer in perspective.

Maybe it is a growing historical sense of alienation from nature, of an assumed dominance, that made Friedrich's paintings so powerful in their imagination of non-human beings as worthy counterparts to humans. Friedrich's painting, and the history of its reception, allude to a growing sense of precariousness. During the nineteenth century, the relationship between humans and nature was increasingly framed as fragile. Nature indeed became alien to humans, but it also gained the possibility of independence. No longer the object of a divine creation ordered around its apex—namely the human—a tree can, for the first time, stand only for herself. Of course, that does not keep it from standing for something or someone else as well; it is just not its *primary* role. A tree, or any other plant for that matter, is primarily herself and only then—in representations, extensions, entanglements—something or someone else as well.

Like Friedrich's solitary tree, *Splittereiche* is lonely *(einsam)*. Although close to other trees, she is *not* part of a forest and, presumably, of a network as vast and productive as the ones Suzanne Simard and Peter Wohlleben describe.[3] Still, she must be regarded as an "Intelligent Tree." This is not just because she shares the swarm-like capacity to coordinate growth, reorganize her organic functions despite severe injuries, and in short, do what plants do.[4] Beyond all this, this tree is a companion to the people of the city. Her embodied memory is an indispensable and vibrant agent of cultural memory and a natural ally against forgetfulness and the pitfalls of memory culture.

In Beyer's novel *Kaltenburg*, the Splintered Oak is the only being *and* place that allows the narrator to remember his parents. His family arrives in Dresden on February 13, 1945—the father, a botanist, has been called to a meeting in the Botanical Garden. When the raid begins, the botanist leads his wife and son into the park. Whether this is because that was the only place he knew in a strange city, whether he just followed others, or whether "he looked for the flowers and trees that had always calmed him,"[5] the narrator can only speculate. Both parents die, and their son stays in Dresden. Still, he never visits the "mass graves" in *Heidefriedhof*, a cemetery on the outskirts of the city, where the victims of the air raids are "officially" remembered with an annual wreath-laying ceremony. "Instead, I walk into the *Great Garden*, cross the meadow on its western edge and stand before a common oak that received her own name by the Dresdeners: *Splittereiche*." In a striking description, Beyer's narrator approaches and re-approaches the tree, noticing her injuries, the open trunk, the strange growth ("as if she had to grow against a massive air resistance"), and the shrapnel (Bomben-*Splitter*). At the time of the narration, the trunk is bare of any supporting structures, and the narrator can touch the raw, decaying wood. He also notices the fungus that took hold in and on the trunk: "For many years now, a fungus spread through the inside of the assaulted (angegriffen) tree, a delayed effect of the bombardment. That night she survived, but someday the sulfur polypore will ruin her. At the splintered oak I have the memory, I have my parents before me."

The memories of his parents—even his parents themselves—are so deeply connected to the tree in this park that they have become part of her. The splintered oak embodies them, as well as the knowledge that even this arboreal memory will fade away with time. However, what the narrator forgets in his grief is that the fungus is not an enemy of the tree. For an oak is a creature of the forest and her death in a park cannot disclose the decomposition and the rooting of new life. Nevertheless, these are parts of a tree's life and the way its memory is "kept" in a community of plants. The natural memory of a vegetal community outlasts that of a culture by far. For the tree, the climate of a place, the downpour of a certain year, temperature, nutrition, pollinators, and potential leaf eaters matter much more than the human events of a single night. What does matter, however, is the relationship she has with the people who remember her and those who remember *because* of her. Memory is not limited to an individual. It requires exchange, retelling, and care. The splintered oak lends itself to this care, helping us to question the validity and conditions of our cultural memories and, in the end, reminding us that life goes on with or without us.

To me, it seems almost like a sacrilege to adorn *Splittereiche* with a sign that aims to explain both her and her meaning for the people living in Dresden. Despite the well-meaning effort to preserve memory, what it does is speaking *for* the plant and, for that matter, for humans as well. I regret the lost ambiguities, the doubt, and the necessity to pause and wonder whether you have found the right tree. It seems to tame or determine what *Splittereiche* can give away or keep for herself because it makes it so easy to recognize her but even easier to just file her as one more sight to see.

Yet still, following her powerful roots and branches and looking into the severed trunk—which has also been made more difficult by the new shield—has the capacity to broaden the experience of memory and, to me, the ways in which I got to know my new environment. This oak is not only a site of remembrance, but she embodies and shares her memory. Though nothing physical distinguishes her from other trees bearing traces of human interference, may they be injuries or protective measures, she is different. Not because of the shrapnel, but because of the stories that connect her to humans while she forges relations to species which are well beyond our understanding. As a truly common oak she is the most effective messenger of past, present, and future. She allows a visitor—me—to acknowledge that a city is not made of humans and buildings alone, and neither is history.

CHAPTER 13

Coralline Algae

Corallinales

▪ Steve Whalan

As a kid, I recollect stories of deep-sea divers being consumed by monstrous giant clams. These stories were largely pictorial, but those images and stories of battle between diver and clam fascinated me. Fast forward thirty years, and I find myself working as a marine biologist, collecting genetic biopsy samples from giant clams to figure out how their populations were related. Once, while collecting samples, my dive buddy's air contents gauge dangled surreptitiously into a neighboring clam. The clam reacted by clamping down on the obtrusive object and, in doing so, tethered my dive buddy to the ocean floor. A moment of panic was overcome with some quick thinking; my partner simply removed his dive gear, inflated his dive vest, and we shared my air source to reach the surface. After a few moments, the clam opened its shell to kick out the unwelcome intruder, and the gear floated to the surface.

What's this story got to do with plants? Well, apart from the fact that it makes for a dramatic introduction, it leads me into what I really want to tell a story about: the remarkable communication, and relationships, between algae and animals in the ocean. You see, giant clams are one of the few marine animals that have a relationship with a microscopic algae called zooxanthellae—a marriage if you like—and as in any marriage, communication between partners is fundamental to harmony and well-being.

This marriage, or commensal symbiosis, works by giving the algae a place to live within the clam's tissues. In turn, the algae get to work with the day-to-day chore of photosynthesis to nourish itself while also supplementing the clam's food intake; it is the algae's way of paying rent. The tight coupling between algae and clam is a sobering wake-up call for humans as we increasingly disconnect from nature. Lessons learned from Mother Nature's diverse life forms and how they communicate and connect with each other are salient reminders that we, too, are part of that natural order.

Let's digress at this point; I hear the echo of the purists calling out that algae aren't really plants. Algae are a taxonomic-challenged group, with enough dispute among the experts to place a question mark about where they sit on the evolutionary tree of life, and indeed whether or not they are plants. So why include algae in a series dedicated to the mindfulness of plants? The answer lies in *how we mind plants*. Despite the cloud of taxonomic uncertainty, many of us still think of algae as plants. Frankly, I do. Algae look like plants, and they act like plants in that they photosynthesize. But it is our human perception in how we see algae that directs many of us to think of them as plants. Our colloquial reference to algae as seaweeds and our desire to place them in collective groups of kelp forests, algal gardens, beds, and stands, conforms to our descriptions of terrestrial plants.

Algae are a diverse aquatic group that span from microscopic unicellular algae—such as the zooxanthellae living in giant clams and corals—to the macroscopic giant kelps that form impressive underwater forests. Like their terrestrial plant cousins, algae provide a food source for a suite of herbivorous animals. But, it is the numerous algal-animal relationships, beyond their snacking value, that is most fascinating. One of the most intriguing marine algae that exhibit a tightly linked partnership with animals is a group called coralline algae. This essay centers on coralline algae, a group of red algae, which are formally classified as Rhodophyta. Even the name "Rhodaphyta" further cements how we mind algae with the Latin translation unfolding as "rhoda" (rose) and "phyta" (deriving from plants).

Coralline algae link tightly to their surroundings. If we broadly think of plant mindfulness as the tight coupling of plants with their own environment, then when you really think of it, the capacity of coralline algae to link acutely with its immediate environment—and to communicate across kingdoms (plants-animals)—positions these organisms as truly mindful. Let me provide some clear examples of how coralline algae are embedded within their marine environment and how they do this by working together with the animals with whom they share a home. Coralline algae are a diverse group of marine organisms that you'll find from the poles to the tropics and from the intertidal to the deep sea. Jump into the water in any ocean, and you will be swimming amongst coralline algae. These plants come in a variety of shapes and sizes, but can be broadly grouped according to two recognizable morphologies: algae that grow with three-dimensional reticulate branching arms and those with a more two-dimensional habit that grow as encrusting algal mats.

Coralline algae are mostly red or pink in color but can display shades of purple to brown, and it is their color that designates them in the group of red seaweeds. Indeed, the encrusting corallines are conspicuous in most underwater scenes where they spread across reef platforms as splattered patterns of pinks, purples, and reds, reminiscent of a masterpiece by one of the Impressionist painters. If we burrow further into one of the uniting features of the Rhodaphyta, we find their color comes from phycobilin—a pigmented structure that helps them with photosynthesis. Phycobilins are also shades of red, and this is what gives these organisms their recognizable color.

Corallines are also united by other features, one of them being how they are put together. Nature's examples of wonder are a continual source of amazement, and the corallines are no exception when it comes to the cellular makeup of these organisms. The unique feature of coralline algae lies within their cells and how cells provide a level of functional support to the whole alga. Coralline algae have calcareous (calcite-like) crystals within and between their cell walls which gives their thallus[1] a coral or stony feel and look. Nature's bizarre mastery—dare I say sense of humor—is not lost with how this plant is put together with a calcium carbonate-like skeleton. Any mystery behind the naming of this plant group, coralline algae, should now be clearer when we think on the calcified structures found within this plant that are peculiarly coral-like.

Coralline algae are very conspicuous in coral reef environments, especially the encrusting forms. These encrusting algae, in particular, exhibit as pink mats intertwining among the myriad colors of nature's palette that are exemplified on coral reefs. Encrusting forms of coralline algae, also known as crustose coralline algae, form large carpeted mats, but need a solid base to spread out and grow upon. In coral reef environments, crustose coralline algae, for the most part, take advantage of dead coral rubble or rocky pavements to do this, but, like most opportunists, will also cover whatever comes along—so you will often find crustose coralline algae on shells (alive and dead) attached to any other hard substrates, which in today's world can include discarded plastic.

It is in coral reef ecosystems that the crustose forms of coralline algae exhibit a definitive relationship with other animals and highlight their importance to the functioning of coral reefs. Corals are largely recognized as the builders of the three-dimensional structure of reefs and, while these animals build vast coral apartment blocks brick-by-brick, creating a three-dimensional habitat, crustose coralline algae could be considered the mortar that binds together loose coral rubble—adding to the stability of reefs as they grow, and joining the coral as builders of coral reef habitats. No, this is not a classic case of communication between algae and animals; we will get to that later. But, in many ways, it is an example of the connectedness, mindfulness, and inherent sense of relationship between two distinct biological groups, working together to form a larger entity—in this case, a community and an ecosystem, which supports some of the most biodiverse natural systems on the planet.

So, corallines are indeed unusual and play roles in working with others to build communities and ecosystems, but do they really communicate in a meaningful way with other groups of organisms? We are still a long way from answering this question with concrete evidence, but the smoking gun for making a case is likely to be somewhere in the room, waiting to be found. Let me tell you a story from my own experimental work as an animal ecologist who focuses on corals and sponges. It is a story of how corals and sponges seek out where they want to live on coral reefs. Yes, this is a book about plants, but bear with me while I weave the remarkable link between coralline algae and corals in particular. Large chunks of my working life have involved trying to figure out the puzzle of how corals and sponges choose where they want to live. Let me briefly expand. If you have ever swum over coral reefs, you have noticed that corals are fixed to the ocean floor; they spend their entire adult lives attached to the same reef real estate. But corals have what is called a complex life cycle that includes two distinct phases, an adult sessile and a motile larval phase. While we see a reef with large and colorful corals, when they sexually reproduce, they spawn motile larval phases. Because larvae can move from reef to reef, they are, in fact, calling all the shots when it comes to choosing the real estate. Once the home site is selected, larvae metamorphose into juvenile corals. The choice of home needs to be in a good neighborhood with access to some of the most important things in life: food, sex, and safety. Metamorphosis, or a "change of life," is an irreversible undertaking, so the consequences of poor choices in real estate are magnified for corals because there are no second chances to move on, and they have to make do with their home for better or for worse. So, like anyone choosing where to live, how do they make the right decision? As it turns out, coralline algae help with their real estate decisions, and not just for corals but for a number of other marine invertebrates, including sponges and abalone.

Unraveling the mystery of what encourages coral larvae to settle and metamorphose has been an elusive goal of numerous groups of researchers. The premise of why larvae respond to coralline algae, however, makes perfect sense; larvae can spend days and weeks floating around the open ocean seeking out reef homesites, but often without the promise of a reef in sight. Finding environmental signals, or cues, that represent a reef are obviously pivotal to larvae making that right real estate decision. There would be little advantage setting up home as the sole occupant of a sandy patch. Coralline algae conveniently represent that signal of optimal real estate. Coral larvae take little convincing in accepting this "right real estate" signal and metamorphose once contact with coralline algae has been made. How do they do this? Well, there are still clouds of mystery surrounding questions of exactly how they home in on coralline algae. The mystery is magnified when you consider the limited sensory capacities of these larvae, especially sponges, which have no real nervous system, and corals, which only have a rudimentary nerve net. A few things must line up for these larvae to detect coralline algae, and then respond by settling and undertaking a change of life into a baby coral or sponge.

Regardless of the sensory processes implicated in the interaction between coralline algae and these invertebrate larvae, the experimental evidence presents a convincing case of some level of communication between larvae and algae. These experiments involve controlling the environment and settlement behavior of larvae by offering larvae an environment with coralline algae versus one without coralline algae. Without the settlement cue of coralline, algae larvae are more reluctant to metamorphose, suggesting that the communication between coralline algae is an important initiator for larvae to undergo their change of life. When tiny pieces of coralline algae are introduced to their environment, larvae settle quicker and in higher numbers. The result, suggesting that chemical communication has taken place, presumably signals to the larvae that coralline algae is present, and so is a reef as well as safety to undergo the change of life. Of course, the cue that the larvae are responding to lies within the tiniest of molecules within the coralline algae itself and which the larvae can sense. Therein lies the level of communication.

Evolution is a marvelous thing, and there isn't a clearer example of evolution-in-motion than the story of coralline algae and coral larval settlement. Given the idea that larvae respond to coralline algae begs the question: why wouldn't these larvae just settle on the plant itself? This wouldn't be ideal for the algae itself, but the salvation for coralline algae lies within its biology. Coralline algae, like most plants, must deal with the day-to-day risk of being eaten or overgrown by competitors. Coralline algae face this threat by shedding layers of external cells, and indirectly, unwanted hitchhikers. While I have seen coral larvae settle directly on coralline algae, I suspect they do this at their own peril. The risk of young corals being included in the coralline algae's routine cell-shedding program is high, and a likely invitation to death row, as the solid surface to grow upon is no longer available. What is interesting is that, more often than not, larvae will "sniff out" coralline algae and then appear to be quite happy to move away from the plant and settle on other, more suitable, hard substrates. When this happens, the interaction between the two works well, supports life for both animal and plant, and adds to the incredible dynamic that is an ecosystem.

Coralline algae and how it connects with animals—including the larval forms of coral—and how that has cascaded to the maintenance and persistence of coral reef communities is a highlight for lessons in communication with nature. With increasing human populations, and our exploitive one-way use of natural resources, the lessons we take from plant-animal communications—such as coralline algae and corals—are sobering reminders of our own need to notice and maintain healthy connections with the natural world.

CHAPTER 14

 Corn

Zea mays

▪ **Esthela Calderón** (translated by Steven F. White)

Now that time has almost placed fifty years on my back—and the world's population is feeling the shock of COVID-19, a novel virus that has unleashed fear, sickness, isolation, and death—I have to say that my days are easier to bear if I reconnect with the little girl I was in a place where the cultivation of corn was a fundamental part of family life. It's as if the mind of this indispensable plant (that is part of my own Amerindian culture) was connected to mine by means of my memories. Corn is also what roots me.

It is April 2020, and the Santa Ana Farm that was founded in 1910 by my grandparents, Felipe and Paz—may they rest in peace—is recovering an air of happiness that I haven't felt since my childhood. The property now has come into my hands, and my son Camilo loves that land as much as I do. Over the last several years, he has dedicated his time to growing organic produce. It is grateful and fertile land. Every time I return to Nicaragua, the country where I was born, I visit the farm, my favorite place in the world, so I can plant more seeds of flowers that attract butterflies, hummingbirds, and bees. I love cooking with firewood on the stove, eating what the farm offers, and being there with my family and close friends. There, a joy shared by my brothers, sisters, and my mother, is reborn, and each of us tells engaging stories that come from this space, from other times.

In mid-May, when the cicadas began to sing, my Grandpa Felipe and the farmworkers climbed to the high fields to prepare the land. With their machetes, they eliminated the weeds that had sprung up with the first rains. Then the plow, hauled by oxen, broke the earth that would receive the grains their hands would release among the furrows and that their bare feet would then cover. Planting the corn resembled a dance of people advancing in a line on the horizon.

For me, seeing how the land became covered in green from the germination of each plant as its first pointed leaf emerged was a huge annual event. That leaf always reminded me of an elongated ear whose first task was to listen to the different sounds of the world in which it had arrived. With that idea in mind, I was also convinced that each one of the little plants could hear me talk, scream, laugh, or sing in the same way that I was listening in that vast field to the birds, my Grandpa's whistling or the jokes among the farmworkers. When the second leaf was born, it was as if the elongated ear received it with a strong embrace that lasted until the next day when they separated and remained in a position of two small arms moving steadily upward until they reached a certain height, that I would spend weeks anxiously awaiting. Every weekend, when I arrived from the city of León to the farm in Telica, I was dying to know how much the corn had grown in those infinite furrows that stretched farther than I could see. I always wanted to count the new arms they had grown.

One day, when I ventured alone to the high fields without waiting for an older person to come with me, I had a terribly distressing experience when I first discovered how the plants in the furrows were thinned. In the same formation they had used to plant the corn, the workers now stooped low to uproot the smallest corn plants or the ones that had still not learned how to embrace themselves or separate with open arms. I must have been six years old at the time, but I remember feeling paralyzed when I witnessed that chore that seemed so painful to me. I remember asking my Grandpa in an anguished voice:

"Why don't you leave them with the other ones?"

"If we don't get rid of them, the others won't grow well," he answered.

"Why?" I asked.

"Because the biggest ones will give the best ears," he told me.

"And why not the little ones?" I insisted as I watched the growing pile of elongated ears ripped from the earth and thrown between the furrows with no compassion whatsoever.

"If we leave the little ones, too, there will be lots of plants fighting for the same food, and the ones that are big now won't be able to grow anymore. And if they don't grow, what do you think will happen?" he asked.

"I don't know," I answered, even though I could guess that the answer was that there wouldn't be enough corn.

I went away truly annoyed, trying to calm down, consoling myself with the idea that the ones that remained would *give the best ears*. That incident certainly didn't keep me from being happy and watching the corn grow.

My favorite moment, the one I always hoped would come soon, was when the stalks were a little taller than I was. Then I could run in between the rows, which was like traveling through cool tunnels. I can close my eyes now and still feel the playful way that the rough arms of each plant would caress my face. I would sing below them, convinced that they were listening to me because I could also intuit how happy they were to see me. Not all of them moved in the same way when they were touched by the wind. My heart could feel that the movements and sounds were louder in the row where I was running. When I would finally stop, covered with sweat and tired, I sensed a joy that I have rarely felt as an adult.

After the first rains, many wild plants seemed to appear from nowhere: the tangled vines of the red fruit passionflowers, the pink morning glories, or the tomatillos. All that sudden growth always intrigued me. Once, when I was helping my mother pick eggplants and squash, I had one of the most beautiful conversations a child my age could have about the birth of plants:

"How do the seeds know when they need to be born?" I asked her.

"All the seeds sleep in peace beneath the ground, but when the first thunder sounds, announcing the rain, the seeds wake up and go out, curious to find out who made all that noise," she replied. "And then the rain gets them wet. They like the rain and they're happy when they hear the people and especially the children go outside to take a bath in the rain, the way you do. The seeds stay up here, and their leaves and flowers grow so they can give us the gift of their fruit. The flowers live on the memories of the other plants that came before them. Flowers don't know death because they always leave their seeds to be awakened by thunder."

From that moment on, I've always felt that my mother's theory was right about how plants are born and communicate with us. In the hopes of never forgetting that idea, I wrote the poem "To Be Reborn," which reads, "Some people say flowers are born from their memories / and live without thinking of death."

When the corn would begin to spike, a huge number of butterflies and bees would visit the fields. The little ears called *chilotes* appeared. These were used by my Grandma Paz in stews and soups as a delicious treat for my Grandpa and whichever grandchildren happened to be visiting. My mother also knew those recipes and prepared them for us whenever she could at our house in the city of León, which was about six miles away. She, too, had her own little farm, which was a wedding present to her and my father from my grandparents. It was right next to Santa Ana Farm.

The arrival of the "tender corn" attracted birds such as the *zanate* (great-tailed grackle), *pijul* (groove-billed ani), and *chocoyo* (Pacific parakeet) that made a big racket as they stole grains of corn by using their beaks to peck through the husks that covered the small ears. It was also a party for all my cousins, aunts, and uncles when we all gathered together at Santa Ana Farm to share a delicious *elotada*, which consisted of preparing a wide variety of foods made from corn that my grandparents prepared for all their descendants. White, yellow, and purple corn was turned into hard *atol* (a dessert), *güerilas*, plain and filled *tamales*, as well as roasted and cooked ears of corn. It is difficult to translate some of this into English, but, believe me, it was all delicious. We would spend the entire day sharing different food and playing. The smallest among us had the job of taking turns grinding the grains of corn in a small hand mill. We all had our clothes and arms stained with corn juice as proof that we had been busy.

When it was time, my cousins and older siblings had the task of twisting the big ears of corn so that they were hanging upside down and could complete the process of drying. Then it would be August, and it was time for the harvest or *tapisca*. This meant wrenching the ears free from the stalks complete with their husks, filling the sacks, and then emptying them into an ox-drawn cart that would take everything down to fill the enormous patio below with a multitude of ears of corn. These were days of hustle and bustle, and lots of people came to work. Women and children would husk the corn and place the biggest ears to one side. The rest were carried off in leather containers to storage areas called *trojas*, which were square repositories like silos and were made of the long hard stems of wild sunflowers bound together and located in places that would be in direct sunlight. My Grandpa selected the best grains of corn from the biggest ears and reserved them for the next year's dance of the planting.

A machine to shell the corn would then arrive on the farm. My uncles used to say that it was better to hire that apparatus with its noisy engine than to have to transport all the corn from the *trojas* to a shelling machine in the city and then to load and unload the corn in 100-pound sacks. This work went on all day and throughout nights filled with visiting fireflies. From the area known as Pueblo Redondo, where Santa Ana Farm is located, many people would arrive to watch the machine do its work as if it were some great yearly spectacle that no one would think of missing. Parents would bring their children. It was so much fun to play, sliding down the mountains of shelled ears of corn, with the corn fluff resembling the snowflakes that I had only seen in crystal balls at Christmas. Now that I live part of the year in upstate New York, and I am familiar with real winters and interminable snow, I can attest to the fact that my comparison made a certain sense since the fluff that came shooting through a tube caused white whirlpools in the air like a North Country snowstorm. The fluff left all of us children scratching ourselves for hours with an allergic reaction. It seemed like it was deeply under our skin, sort of like the cold from what seemed to be inoffensive snow that would penetrate my body to the bone.

There were always some ears leftover with some grains of corn that the machine wasn't able to shell. They looked like the sparse teeth in a beggar's mouth. These ears were set aside by certain women who shelled them with the points of dull old knives or perhaps another ear of corn. They gathered up the grains and returned to their homes with a good amount of corn obtained this way. When the shelling machine would finish its work, the women and some young boys continued to look for more rebellious grains of corn among the mountain of shelled ears.

The cycle, from sowing to harvest, lasted three to four months. The last activity was a lunch for all the farmworkers and their wives that was normally held on a Saturday. For the meal, several hens were sacrificed, and my Grandma Paz made soup from them in a huge pot, adding a variety of vegetables such as plantains, yucca, different kinds of squash, cabbage, and taro. She also made balls of cornmeal seasoned with ground annatto, salt, garlic, onions, green peppers, mint, and the juice of bitter oranges.

Of course, one thing that absolutely had to be a part of the celebration was the *chicha bruja*, or "witches' brew," which my Grandma would make at least two months before the big meal with grains of corn from the previous year's harvest. *Chicha bruja* is an intoxicating drink that is made by fermenting lots of corn in a ceramic vessel buried in the earth but with the neck and the opening above ground. She added water and some blocks of dark sugarcane sweetener, some cloves, some cinnamon, and then put a top on the vessel. When the grains of corn began to dance among each other in the vessel, it was as if they themselves were drunk, and it was then that the grain (called a *puyón* at this point) began to sprout. The mixture had to be stirred each week and the vessel covered each time. The *chicha bruja* was now sweet and sour and had its alcoholic content as well as a certain fragrance from the two spices that had been added to the mix at the beginning of the process. The day of the big lunch, the workers had their gourd cups filled with the eagerly awaited *chicha bruja*. They ate, sang, and drank beneath the mango and calabash trees near the well and the watering troughs. They drank as much as their bodies could bear. Some of the workers filled their gourds more than a few times.

The next morning, it was funny to watch and listen to my Grandma stroll around the house as she scolded the workers who were still sleeping, sprawled in the patio as a consequence of their drunken night that made it impossible for them to find their way home, much less mount the horses that were still tied to the fence, patiently awaiting their owners. All my Grandpa would do is laugh as he sat on his wood and leather chair, drinking his coffee before walking to Sunday Mass with my Grandma. From a distance, I would hear him say in a joking, ironic tone, "Whose idea was it, anyway, to give all these men *chicha bruja*?"

And when the workers finally were back on the job, they would tease each other and make fun of all the imprudent and crazy things that were said under the effects of the *chicha bruja*. As they went from joke to joke, they climbed to the high fields to uproot the dry stalks of corn that remained and then to prepare the earth for planting beans. On terraces that held more water when the rains became torrential, they planted *ayote* squash. After the beans were harvested, what remained of the plants was burned, and the earth was left to rest until the thunder once again announced the first rains of May.

Meanwhile, I had to keep up my hopes until the next cycle of planting and harvest, when I could enter the cool tunnels again, play among the furrows, sing to the corn, and be touched by its rough leaves. I longed for the *elotada*, that banquet of foods made from corn that helped us all get to know each other and work together as a family to make meals for everyone.

Wherever I am, not too much time can go by before I need to have some corn tortillas on my table. What I mean is that my body, my organism, can't be without tortillas or something with corn in it for more than a week. When I was a little girl, I learned to shape tortillas with my hands. Whether it was on my mother's small farm or on the farm of my grandparents, there would always be a space for me in the kitchen with my ball of dough and room on the hot *comal* to place my small circles made by the rhythm of my palms, striking the dough and creating a round, flat shape. The process has its own musicality, depending on how each person develops it, the way the ball of dough is struck and stretched on top of a plastic circle. The dough comes from grinding corn which has been previously *nixquezado*. The *nixqueza* is a process of cooking the dried, hard grains of corn. In a big pot of water, one adds a little *cal* (lime, an alkaline powder) and *ceniza* (ash), and then the corn, stirring all the while. When the corn begins to release an outer layer of its skin, then it's time to take the embers from the fire or remove the pot. My Grandma would pour the contents of the pot onto the *molendero* (grinding stone) in her kitchen and let it cool there for a while. Then, she placed the corn in a large receptacle, rubbing it together to loosen an outer layer on the grains. When the water in which the corn was soaking poured off clean, it was time to grind it. Also, it was the moment to put the *comal* (ceramic griddle) on the fire, and then one kneaded the dough until it had a soft texture so that it could be stretched without cracking or breaking. It had to be dropped carefully on the hot comal. When the side that was up started to dry, it needed to be flipped for the first time. After a while of being on that side, the tortilla needed to be flipped again, and that was when it made the announcement that it was ready: it's called the *empollado*, which is when the tortilla separates and puffs up like a blister, or like a hen when she's sitting on her eggs. The tortilla is then lifted off and wrapped in a piece of cloth, ready to be enjoyed with beans, guacamole, stews, cheeses, and meat prepared in different ways.

The corn I describe here as part of my childhood is so important for what it *is*, but also for what *isn't*, namely, GMO corn. I've learned as an adult that biotechnology companies such as Bayer, BASF, Dow AgroScience, DuPont Pioneer, Monsanto, and Syngenta market GMO seed and related products, including herbicides. The recent merger—worth $66 billion—of Bayer and Monsanto enabled Bayer to drop the Monsanto name due to the negative publicity surrounding this company that is one of the most hated businesses in the United States. The genetically engineered seed that is praised by some as hardier, more nutritious, and more drought- and pest-resistant than non-GMO corn, nevertheless, raises many serious questions. Are there potential health concerns when scientists change the structure of corn in ways that would not occur through natural development, infusing it with animal DNA, herbicides, and pesticides? Will the global predominance of GMO corn make farmers from the developing world dependent on international seed companies with exclusive patents on these genetically modified organisms? Will genetically engineered genes introduced in wild plants ultimately cause a reduction in biodiversity? Could GMO corn influence public health in terms of antibiotic-resistant bacteria? Could changes in the pollen of GMO corn affect the development of non-GMO corn through unintended cross-pollination? These and other potentially consequential issues certainly merit further research.

In my everyday life, corn represents a point of departure and a return to the images of my ancestors. It is as significant as my umbilical cord and my brothers' and sisters' that my mother buried with the placentas on the land of her small farm. She decided this place was where her eight children would be born with the assistance of a midwife named Margarita. I was the youngest. She returned the placentas and umbilical cords (that joined us to her like a root that nourished us) to the land in order to nourish us from a greater mother. My mother planted me like a grain of corn, loving the spaces I came to know while I was in her womb. Strangely, all my siblings have an enormous attachment to our point of departure. Each one of us has a piece of land in that place. I had the good fortune of becoming, over time, the owner of Santa Ana Farm. It is a measureless gift from my grandparents' spirit and from the millions of open arms that received me during my unrepeatable childhood, and that I hope will protect me during this pandemic provoked by a human plague.

CHAPTER 15

Cornish Mallow

Lavatera cretica

Laura Ruggles

Let me tell you a story. Two stories, in fact, that together challenge our understanding of the nature and cognitive capacities of plants. These stories also highlight the indispensable roles of metaphor in the scientific process and provide cautionary tales about its use. Some of these roles, such as communication and reasoning with analogies, will be unsurprising and familiar, particularly for people involved in scientific practice. Others might seem unexpected, such as the ways metaphors form part of our theories, the products of science.

The first story is about a plant. It follows the rather remarkable journey of the Cornish mallow (*Lavatera cretica*). From common garden weed to rising star, this mallow features in modern debate over what it means for an organism to be cognitive. The second is the story of an intimately familiar but surprisingly slippery concept: *memory*. With roots that stretch back millennia, this metaphorically-laden concept has branched and morphed across times and domains. From ancient Greek philosophy to modern psychology, memory now stretches tentative tendrils into the plant sciences. Questions of minds and memories are fundamentally interwoven. Growing evidence for flexible behavior and memory in plants like the Cornish mallow has the potential to radically reshape how we understand and relate to them.

MALLOWS AND METAPHORS

My first impression of a Cornish mallow, sprawling in a neglected corner of my backyard many years ago, was nothing memorable. Scraggly purplish flowers nestled amongst broad leaves on one tough, spindly weed among many. But there is much more to this plant than immediately meets the eye. Native throughout the Mediterranean and the Middle East, and naturalized throughout much of the world, the plant has been used widely since ancient times for both food and folk medicine. The cooked leaves provide a palatable spinach-like addition to many dishes, and modern medical analyses have confirmed the plant's powerful anti-inflammatory properties. However, it is this plant's remarkable behavior, rather than its appearance or its culinary and medical uses, that has recently propelled the Cornish mallow into the spotlight.

Throughout the day, the leaves of Cornish mallow plants dynamically turn to follow the sun. This sort of solar-tracking movement called *heliotropism* (from the Greek *hēlios* "sun" + *tropos* "a turn, change") is found in a range of plants. Knowledge of it predates the ancient Greeks, who first recorded a plant named the "heliotrope," from which the term derives. In Greek myth, recounted most famously in Ovid's epic poem, the *Metamorphoses*, the water nymph Clytie is transformed into the heliotrope after being spurned by her lover, the sun god Helios. For nine days, Clytie languishes on an exposed rock, refusing food or drink, turning her face longingly to follow the arc of Helios' chariot across the sky. Eventually, her body becomes the plant that continues turning its gaze to follow the sun's path each day, yearning with unrequited love.

Solar-tracking heliotropism in plant leaves throughout the day allows them to maximize photosynthesis, gathering light for transformation into the sugars plants need for energy. This kind of active motor behavior flies in the face of conventional views that plants are more like objects than animals. Heliotropism puzzled philosophers and early scientists for eons. Ancient Greek philosopher Aristotle claimed that insensitivity and passivity are essential features distinguishing plants from the animals that possess both sensation and locomotion. His immediate successor, Theophrastus of Eresus, proposed that plant heliotropism must then be due to the removal of water by hot sunlight on the illuminated side of the stem, resulting in a passive motion that merely resembles active behavior.

Aristotle's botanical speculations relied far more heavily on reasoning than on careful observation and testing. Aristotelian natural philosophy also received uneasy endorsement by the Christian church after its integration into the natural theology of late medieval scholars like Thomas Aquinas. These factors contributed to the enshrinement of Aristotelian dogma in academic curricula for many centuries. Accordingly, assumptions around the passivity of heliotropism and general plant insensitivity persisted for millennia. Francis Bacon, for example, claimed in 1627 that the cause of plant responses to sunlight "is somewhat obscure...the part beateth by the sun waxeth more faint and flaccid in the stalk, and less able to support the flower," while naturalist John Ray begins his 1686 botanical treatise *Historia Plantarum* explaining that in defining plants, "insensitivity is added to the definition to exclude Animals."

In the mid-to-late seventeenth century, however, experimental evidence began accumulating for the "irritability" of plants—like animals, plants seemed capable of reacting to environmental stimuli, including sunlight. A horticultural fascination with fast-moving exotic plants led to a proliferation of metaphorical comparisons to animal nerves and muscles. By 1880, Charles Darwin had demonstrated in *The Power of Movement in Plants* that a transmissible "influence" (which we now know involves the plant hormone, auxin) passes from the site of light sensation to the site of the bending response in plant shoots. It had become increasingly impossible to ignore the idea that plants possess a sensitivity rather like that of animals.

One way that plants move in response to light is via signaling cascades that cause uneven growth on opposite sides of a stem, which results in active bending toward detected light. However, other kinds of movements, like the solar-tracking leaves of the Cornish mallow, work differently. These are fully reversible and enabled by specialized motor tissues at the junction of the leaf and its stalk called the *pulvinus*. Motor cells in this tissue move the leaf by changes in turgor (water pressure) around the axis of the leaf stalk. Changes in turgor of "flexor" and "extensor" cell regions on opposite sides of this axis are expressed by changes in leaf elevation, propelling the leaf up and down. Turgor changes in other clusters of cells at different locations translate to either rotation or side-to-side leaf movement.

It is worth highlighting the role that metaphorical comparisons play here between plant motor tissue and animal flexor and extensor muscle groups. After a 1665 meeting of the Royal Society aimed at understanding the behavior of the sensitive plant (*Mimosa pudica*), Timothy Clarke, an English physician, was one of the first to describe (if superficially) the mechanism behind the rapid movement of its leaflets. He relied heavily on his knowledge of human anatomy and joint physiology to do so. Using terms like "enarthrosis" (a word for a ball-and-socket joint, like the human hip), "spine," and "fibres" that make the pulvinar tissue "muscular," he described the joint's reliance on water pressure for rigidity and hypothesized that changes in this produce leaflet motion.

This example is not an anomaly or exception. Scientists regularly borrow metaphorical concepts and imagery from a better-known (animal) domain and apply them to a less familiar (plant) one in order to reason about, describe, or explain phenomena in that domain. Philosophers sometimes conceptually separate the scientific process into the *context of discovery* (how ideas or hypotheses are generated) and the *context of justification* (how those ideas are justified and tested). There is ample evidence to suggest that analogical reasoning and metaphor are key to the generation of hypotheses (the context of discovery) across a whole range of scientific fields. Drawing comparisons and exploring deep structural similarities between two domains can create novel predictions, suggest new interventions, and help scientists frame questions about a phenomenon that they might not have otherwise thought to ask.

When metaphors are sufficiently deep, such that metaphorical concepts come to play irreplaceable roles in the theories that subsequently develop, these are sometimes called *theory-constituting* conceptual metaphors. For example, informational, circuit, and network metaphors borrowed from electrical engineering arguably play such roles in our current understanding of how cell communication works. Particular metaphorical ways of seeing or grasping systems sometimes become background perspectives, almost invisible to us, as metaphors become naturalized in their new domains.

The fates of such metaphors can follow several different trajectories. One is that they are discarded as misleading, as no longer fit for service, or become superseded by other more productive metaphors. Because of the powerful influence of metaphor on the scientific process, critical reflection on use and limitations is a necessity. "The price of metaphor," cautioned cybernetics researchers Arturo Rosenblueth and Norbert Wiener, "is eternal vigilance." Another potential fate is metaphorical "death," when a term is still used but no longer carries its original connotations. A third possibility is that what was once understood metaphorically comes to be understood literally. For example, many cognitive scientists now literally see brains as a *type* of biological computer, rather than just operating very *like* digital computers. The "computer" concept itself was originally used to describe humans who performed calculations. Now it loops back around to aid understanding of human brains via computers as artifacts, conceptually enriched by its journey.

MEMORIES OF MALLOWS

"Memory" is a concept that has a fascinating history—with roots stretching all the way back to classical antiquity—and a deep conceptual entanglement with ideas about minds and cognition. Although we are used to thinking about memory occurring in human minds (or brains, or computers), recent findings have raised questions around what it might be for plants to have memory. One of the plants in the spotlight here is our solar-tracking star, the Cornish mallow.

Earlier, I described this plant's dynamic, real-time solar tracking performance. However, these mallows also engage in remarkable behavior when the sun is not present. At night time, the mallow's leaves initially return to a neutral position. After a period of time, several hours before dawn, they make the most of very early morning light by turning to face the anticipated direction of sunrise in advance. Astoundingly, it seems they somehow store memories about the direction of previous light sources and combine this with information about the time of day to anticipate the future.

To test whether this surprising phenomenon simply reflects a hard-wired response to a fixed direction, plant scientists have tried to "confuse" mallows in various ways to see how they respond. This includes interventions like changing the direction of the plants, spinning them around 180° in the night, so they get the direction "wrong" in the morning. However, after just a few days, plants simply learn their new orientation and begin once again to anticipate the correct direction. How is this predictive behavior and learning even possible?

To understand how these mallows might store information about the direction of the sunrise overnight, we must first look at how they sense and use light signals during the day. The type of signal to which leaves are sensitive is known as a *light vector*, which has both a direction and a magnitude. Cornish mallow leaves have seven major veins that spread out like a fan from the base. The light is detected in these veins, and the overall response involves contributions from all of them that vary with light direction.

Each vein is most sensitive to a light vector that runs parallel to its length and hits the surface of the leaf at an angle. This is because photoreceptors (light detectors) are located in cell files along the veins and are angled in opposing directions at opposite ends of each cell. Directional light signals, therefore, cause different levels of photoreceptor activity at each end of these cells, resulting in a difference in electric potential between the two ends and between neighboring cells. This results in a signal current that can be carried along the cell file to the pulvinus. Here, the spatial organization of the original signal is maintained in the motor tissue so that it can respond by tilting the leaf in an appropriate direction.

Because the veins fan out from the center of the leaf's base roughly in a circle with fixed angles, different veins will be more active depending upon the horizontal direction of the light source. This provides a kind of spatial "map" of directional information, stored as differences in activity among veins that can be transformed into other signals and put to work. The fact that the light vector is encoded in this structured way by the leaf means that information about its direction each morning may also be stored for use in nocturnal reorientation.

To draw on this information at the right time (pre-dawn), the system also needs information from "circadian clocks." These are mechanisms in plant cells that coordinate behavior and physiological processes temporally by tracking the 24-hour day/night cycle. They do this using regularly oscillating patterns of transcribed proteins that are controlled by networks of genes regulating one another's activities via feedback loops. They are kept in sync with changing day and night cycles by environmental cues like light and temperature.

But is the way the Cornish mallow uses light's vectorial information overnight a case of genuine memory or is "memory" a metaphor here? We do use memory concepts metaphorically in biology. For example, "immune memory" is an altered immune response to previously encountered pathogens. "Epigenetic memory" involves changes in gene expression that can be passed down generations due to environmental effects. Memory in animals is a paradigm example of cognition, so if plants genuinely have memory, too, are they cognitive? To get clearer on this, let us take a closer look at the story of how we have come to understand memory. As before, the story begins in Ancient Greece.

From their earliest incarnations, explanations and theories of memory drew heavily upon metaphor. In *Theaetetus*, Plato describes a variant of the "storehouse" metaphor: the mind filling with memories like an aviary increasingly stocked with birds. As we acquire knowledge, we store it in enclosures and must search for and retrieve each bird successfully from these enclosures during recollection. Many metaphors for memory have followed this basic format, invoking a physical storehouse of some kind. Other more elaborated variants were developed later, including the encoding-storage-retrieval models inspired by digital computers.

Another metaphor Plato drew upon (then rejected) was memory as a "wax tablet" that we hold "under" our perceptions and ideas as we would a signet ring, the resulting imprint bearing a relation to its object as does a portrait to its subject. Whatever is imprinted becomes memory, and things which leave no impression, or are rubbed out, are forgotten. This rich metaphor was picked up, revised, accepted, and applied concretely by Aristotle in *De Memoria.* This metaphor locates faults in memory with features like the wax being too soft and therefore unable to create distinct impressions or too hard, thus creating only partial impressions that lack depth or take longer to become imprinted. Under Aristotle's elaboration, physical properties of the medium of our bodies may impact upon our memory capacities, like qualities of wax do upon the imprinting of a seal. Various forms of this "inscription" model inspired by later technologies (photographs, magnetic tape, records) followed this general format.

Another memory metaphor, that of "writing" or the "inner scribe," is one that Plato and Aristotle both discuss. In some sense, a variant of the "inscription" metaphor, it is nonetheless importantly distinct. Like later digital computer metaphors, written text is a form of symbolically encoding information before storage. "Portrait-like" inscriptions such as the wax seal bear relations to their objects by virtue of sharing properties like a similar structure. However, written inscriptions bear relations to their objects less directly via abstract symbols that do not resemble the things they are about.

Interestingly, this distinction also features in modern cognitive science, distinguishing different theories of mental representation. Some theories draw upon the *digital/symbolic* computer or written language models of how cognitive systems might come to represent the world. Others rest upon a *structural/analog* approach, where a mathematically defined notion of shared structure (for example, in patterns of neural firing and connectivity) relates impressions to their objects. The "signet ring in wax" metaphor is ambiguous between this second kind of theory and a third kind, *causal* theories. These claim that impressions come to be about the things they refer to by virtue of how such impressions are formed rather than by virtue of the resulting shared structure. Other recent accounts of cognition claim that cognition does not require representation at all—memory is *enacted* in bodies and behavior.

It is in literature exploring the structural/analog approach to cognition that we find researchers particularly fascinated by the memory capacities of the Cornish mallow. The plant's motor response exploits the structural resemblance between leaf vein activation and the light vector, a fact very much suggestive of an analog approach to representation and memory.

The application of the concept "memory" from the animal sciences to plants may seem like a simply *zoomorphic* or animal-like metaphor. Some scientists are concerned with the over-reliance on animal comparison in the emerging study of plant cognition and behavior. However, it may be a necessary corrective lens at this point to the invisible dominance of *object-like* metaphors in our understanding of plants. As the science has progressed, plant learning and memory are increasingly an instance where a concept once applied metaphorically has come to be understood literally. Memory is neither intrinsically animal-like nor only found in brains.

Applying concepts from the cognitive sciences helps us better explain and understand plant behavior. Cognitive concepts are guiding plant research in fruitful directions, inspiring questions, hypotheses, and research programs that might never have otherwise emerged. Conversely, as such concepts travel into these new domains and we explore cognition outside the animal kingdom, what we find helps develop our cognitive theories themselves, expanding and refining cognitive concepts. The result that emerges is a deeper and richer understanding of both plants and of cognition in all its diversity.

In my own garden, a growing understanding of Cornish mallows over the course of my research has transformed them for me. From unwanted weeds, they have become marvelous and delightful creatures cohabiting with my daffodils and tomatoes. As I watch them tracking the sun across the sky, they remind me daily of the wonders we have yet to discover and the insights that this little weed has started to provide.

CHAPTER 16

Crab Apple Tree

Malus sylvestris

Mauricio Tolosa

It is the winter solstice in the southern hemisphere. In the foothills of the Cordillera de Los Andes, the breeze is bitterly cold. I practice Chi Kung under the apple tree. My feet are rooted to the ground, trying to connect with the energy of the roots of the tree. I feel a subtle vibration rising from the Earth. It unites me with the whole fabric of life that is woven under the ground. It surges. It unfolds in the sky. Is it an illusion of the mind, or is it truly that the "embrace-the-tree" pose—of which there is evidence in Chinese pottery dating from 5,000 years ago—keeps some secret about the connection with the plants and opens up to a wider perception?

Coming from a tradition of rationalist and Cartesian thinking, I even doubt my own experience. I ask for a clear signal, although I am not sure what it would entail. Perhaps something I can consider as unmistakable in my language or in my perceptual field? Something recordable and compatible with the languages of the human community? Is the harmony between the connection with plants and our current human reality possible? I feel the energy under my feet... I feel that I vibrate with the apple tree and with life itself... I wait.

1. THE OPENING OF IMAGES

My synergy with the apple tree began a couple of years ago—a bountiful journey full of discoveries, learnings, magic, and coincidences. The apple tree always was a kind and generous presence. However, in the past, there was the habitual segregation between humans and plants in the core of our culture.

Trees and plants have always been present in my life. At my grandparents' house, there was a small orchard where, since I was a child, I accompanied my grandfather to sow, transplant, prune, and graft. The plants were living beings, a bit magical. In my fantasies, they were almost individuals with a name.

At my parent's house, on the other hand, the garden was an external and decorative landscape, almost exclusively for visual enjoyment. Although it also produced fruits: the ones from the generous chestnut tree, synonyms of a season of marvelous desserts; the ones from the two climbable apricot trees that became pots of jam for the whole winter; and the pinions from an araucaria, a candy that we enjoyed peeling on rainy winter afternoons.

Twenty-five years ago, after a period of trips during which I admired notable jungles, forests, and trees, I arrived at this home. I planted the Japanese crab apple tree in the courtyard at the center of my house. It was already a small tree of about four or five years old. As it grew, it started occupying an increasingly important space in the life of my home, accompanying memorable conversations while watching the sunset, sheltering many naps in the hammock, protecting with its shade the writing of texts and the creation of projects in the summertime, and mourning the death of my two companion dogs. It even inspired the headline of an interview in the newspaper, "When trees grow," which dealt with communication and political processes. "When trees grow" referred to the necessity to respect the times and organic and natural cycles of communities and life.

I watched ecstatically as the hued sunlight was held in its leaves in summers, autumns, winters, and springs; I freed it from the invasive jasmine that came to cover all of its canopy almost strangling it; I pruned its impossibly entangled branches; I helped it with its plagues and pests.

However, a couple of years ago, a new dimension was reached, which has transformed my feelings toward plants and my perception of life. How did it start? One day, while I was finishing writing *angelos*, a book about the numinous world, I had the impression of seeing some figures on the bark of the tree. My curious eyes focused on the trunk, and I discovered several colorful images, cave paintings and goblins, traces of Chagall and the East. I was moved by the beauty unfolding on that surface I had always seen as a gray and brown veneer. Incredulous of what my perception was collecting, I decided to record the experience photographically to check it with "objectivity." The result was even more surprising since the precise aperture setting of the camera accentuated even more what my eyes could see in the general average light surrounding the tree.

Since then, I have taken about 16,000 photographs of the apple tree or photographs related to other trees and plants. This has meant spending whole mornings and afternoons with the apple tree and other trees, contemplating, meditating, listening, looking beyond the bark and colors, perceiving their changes, their times, their cycles, their relationship with the air and other trees, the power of their energy, their calmness, and activations… I have flowed with the time of the processes and rhythms of the tree, and for that, I have had to apprehend them and feel them inside myself.

At the end of winter, for example, I clearly perceived the opening movement of the buds. For me, the flowers were surprising but immobile, in the sense that I looked at them and saw them more or less open, but I did not imagine nor had I wondered how long they took to open up. And one sunny morning, I saw them blossoming. I realized that this unfolding was happening at that moment and that it was something I could perceive with the naked eye. Again, I wanted to check it photographically, and I verified that they opened during the day. The proximity with the apple tree changed my perception of time, the passing of the seasons, and the qualities in each one of them.

I felt that to understand the tree, it was necessary to explore beyond sight and our five habitual senses. Breathing became very present. Throughout my life, without much reflection about it, I had learned and practiced breathing as a limited action in which air entered and exited through the small holes of the mouth and nose, inflating and deflating the lungs. In the case of the tree, I felt that the exchange was done in an integral way. Everything—leaves, branches, and trunk—breathed. I began trying to expand my own contact surface with the world, to breathe with my whole body, and as a logically enough consequence, my world expanded. These experiences and learnings with the apple tree and later with other trees induced a personal reconfiguration that I call *arborecer* ("growing into a tree").

Another radical change in my perception of reality happened when, after planting several apple tree seeds, they appeared in different ways and colors from the soil. After seeing them sprout and extend that stem of liquid light that becomes the first leaves, I had the feeling of witnessing an arboreous alchemy, where an amalgam of liquid, gaseous, and energetic processes create life and leave the organic matter we see as a wonderful trace. I sensed that along with every tree, plant, and animal, we are an alloy of that energy and matter, but only where our perception allows us to see the matter. The garden, the trees, and the forests became spaces of light and energy, and the apple tree a kind of magnificent torch. Once more, I tried to photograph that perception, and I achieved a photograph, I set to a haiku:

Primal unseen spark
Scintilla that annunciate
Every forest

I come from an intense practice and reflection on communication that I define as the creation of communities and shared worlds. I ask myself if the relationship with the apple tree is simply my personal experience in front of a being that is undoubtedly alive but belongs to another world with which there is no possibility of interaction, or if, as I sometimes have the feeling, there can be some kind of more or less "oriented" interaction on its part.

One afternoon in late winter, I invented a meditation with the apple tree, which consisted of the same "embrace-the-tree" position, but with my head resting on one of its branches. I felt more directly part of the circulation flow of the apple tree, and for some mysterious reason, I became fixated on two unexpected words in English: "art" and "consciousness." A while later, I settled in front of the computer, and the first thing I did was to write those two words in a search engine.

2. ART AND CONSCIOUSNESS

After three clicks, I went from a TED Talk by Alex Gray to his personal page, and from there to the Wasiwaska page, "a research center for the study of psychointegrator plants, visionary art, and consciousness," founded by Luis Luna in Brazil. The site announced the seminar "Animism, Plant Intelligence, and Exceptional Human Experiences" that coincidentally began the same day as my birthday. It seemed like an auspicious coincidence. I contacted them inquiring about the possibility of participating in the meeting, and a few days later, my application was accepted as the last vacancy.

During the last two weeks of the seminar, I had the opportunity to talk at length with David Luke, Monica Gagliano, naturalist Dave Milliard, Luis Luna himself, and the other participants in the meeting in a creative, free, and stimulating environment. When I said that I had arrived at the seminar driven by the apple tree in my backyard, everyone smiled and then asked, "how?" without a shadow of irony. Wasiwaska was a vital immersion in the world of plants and their interactions with each other and with their environment and human beings.

Although I had had some experience with sacred plants, in that group, there was an enormous involvement and knowledge that opened new questions and dimensions. The stories and studies by David and Luna were an amazing source regarding the interaction between human beings and entheogenic plants. I felt that through meditation and contemplation in my relationship with the apple tree, I had reached altered states of consciousness or extraordinary openings equivalent to those produced by peyote or ayahuasca. The conversations with Monica were especially stimulating for me. She talked about her work on plants' learning and intelligence, but it was even more inspiring and revealing to hear how a serious and respected scientist established a relationship with some plants and was sometimes guided by them in important research and life decisions. This particularly resonated with me and paved the way to redouble the exploration of the possibilities of a relationship between plants and humans.

It is evident that there is an interaction, not only because of the unquestionable effect of the major entheogenic plants but also the effect of many garden plants—such as lemon verbena, mint, and lemon balm. But is it possible for the plants to guide or influence some decisions, such as in Monica's research or my trip to Wasiwaska?

3. THE SEARCH FOR ROOTS

A few days after returning from Wasiwaska, a plague of aphids attacked the apple tree. They had never arrived in such quantity. I could not step under the tree. The ground was hopelessly sticky because of the sugary liquid spilled by the tiny invaders. I waited impatiently for nature to act and free the plagued tree. But, as nothing happened, I made the decision to fumigate it by applying chemicals. Disappointed, in the morning, I told the apple tree what I would implement the following day. I sat in the living room watching the tree through the window... at that moment I saw a shadow moving in the backlight of a leaf—it was a coccinella larva. Within a few hours there were hundreds of them, and in four days, they had freed the apple tree from the voracious green demons.

As the ground under its canopy also became clean, I restarted the meditations under the apple tree. During the following days, the need installed itself in me to return to the roots, to visit the forests in Patagonia, near Punta Arenas, my hometown. That immersive journey inspired a short poetic film called "Austral Haiku, do apple trees dream?" that accounts for the expansion of consciousness and soul healing, signified by the term "arborecer."

4. IN THE END: THE HEART

I meditate under the apple tree.

I do not want to explore through vision. Plants do not have eyes, and if they somehow could somehow "see," it would be in a record so different from ours that it would be almost impossible to connect our two "visions." I have the impression that our worlds are superimposed and touch each other when I succeed at fusing my energy with the energy from the apple tree, and we become one in the web of life. Of course, this could be another sublime illusion created by the mind in the human world. Could there be unmistakable signals between the arboreous world and ours?

I am still in the yard, holding the embrace-the-tree pose. I am with the tree; I flow in it. I wait for proof.

Tap. Something hits the window glass from inside the living room. It is a hummingbird. It is the second time in twenty years that one of those magical birds, which the Aztecs considered messengers of the gods, enters the house. I approach it; it is scared; it feels trapped. I slowly open the window so it can leave. It calms down. It flies so close to me that I feel the breeze of its flapping wings on my face; it is an angelic caress. I sit in an armchair three meters from the window where the hummingbird is. It turns, hovering, and it is looking at me. I clearly feel the air that reaches my chest; a profound emotion invades me. I remember the question, "Can the flutter of a butterfly's wings in Brazil create a typhoon in Japan?" and I feel it is being answered in a practical way. The hummingbird breeze on my chest is an unambiguous perception that everything is subtly connected. The hummingbird turns around and flies out. The leaves of the apple tree gently tremble with the fluttering of its wings in the winter solstice of the South.

CHAPTER 17

Devil's Ivy

Epipremnum aureum

■ **Guto Nóbrega**

This essay is about a journey. A journey that begins with my search, as an artist, for ways of deepening the invention and fruition of artworks into the domain of what is known as an art experience. This is also about an encounter with the vegetal realm when for the first time in life, I looked at a plant differently and considered such a being as the center of my artistic creations. It was when I met the devil's ivy that this journey began.

The experience of art is an immersive process. It is something that pulls us into an affective network of sensations and emotions, a state of consciousness triggered by a process of invention, which, in my case, involves the use of plants as sensitive agents for the creation of art. As an artist, I am moved by the idea that art can be better understood if it is approached as a field phenomenon. It comes from the view that the creation and the experience of art reflect the modulation of several forces—physical, psychological, physiological, to name a few—which are sensed by the observer as an active part of the created system. In other words, it could be said that art is a phenomenological[1] structure, intrinsically organic, where a set of exchanges takes place between the artist, the active observer of such a system, and the artwork itself as a whole. The base of these ideas can be found in the creative thinking of several artists and scholars; they are not mine alone. What belongs to me is the idea that coupling organic matter to an artificial system for the creation of art would give birth to an expressive organism, an aesthetical one, as a result of a dialogue between systems. It is in that coupling that the idea of a hybrid resides, and it was in that context that my journey into the realm of plants began.

At the beginning of my delving into the organic matter as a source of natural interfaces for artistic invention, I looked everywhere. From ants to fireflies, I've always been fascinated by the idea of intelligence in nature, by the natural connectivity that interlinks every living being and the subtle ways in which each organism manifests itself as part of a coherent net of communication on several levels, most of the time invisible to our naked eyes. This inspired me a lot, the possibility of establishing a dialogue with nature through art as a way of understanding and reconnecting us to our primary natural sources, not only biological but also metaphysical ones. Recognizing other natural species as intelligent beings—and overcoming our prejudice against their apparent lack of language—are the first steps to recognizing the non-separability that unifies us as spiritual entities. These ideas guided my attention to the vegetal realm and reconnected me to old childhood memories.

I am from Brazil. The popular culture in my country, based on ancient Indigenous traditions, feeds on the belief that plants give protection and cure. Our Indigenous people ingest plants containing entheogens[2] to gain access into a non-ordinary state of consciousness and to dive into spiritual dimensions. My grandma used to heal me with herbs, teas, and prayers. These facts are somehow imprinted on my artistic DNA and might be the reason for my empathy for plants. On the other hand, science is gradually recognizing that plants, despite the lack of a brain or nervous system such as ours, are intelligent to the point of manifesting memory, decision-making, and even imagination. As an artist, I see plants as a complex multi-dimensional system of knowledge, rich enough to offer the art process ways of exploring the edges of reality and to creatively expand our systems of belief. I think that coupling plants to artificial systems brings into the realm of invention a sort of subtle intelligence in the form of organic expression, one that can be experienced through the lens of art. Dealing with organic systems also approximates the idea of culture to its etymological roots in terms of growing and cultivation. It reinforces the connection between art and life, which in the case of my inventions is manifested in the form of breathing.

My first creation interconnecting plants and artificial systems took the form of a hybrid creature—half plant, half robot. Based on early experiments in plant electrophysiology at the beginning of the last century, I decided to measure galvanic conductivity from the leaves of plants as a form of monitoring plants' response to environmental changes and interaction with other beings. In fact, plants have become a sort of primary organic sensor in my artworks. The plant that I chose for my first artwork, and which I have been using up to the present day, is known by the popular name "devil's ivy." This plant is very resistant to extreme environmental conditions in which other plants would not survive. The devil's ivy can live with very poor light, even in the dark. Living in England at the time of my art research, I was surprised to see that my little plant was strong enough to resist the rain and cold weather of the United Kingdom. But, I must say, the bond that has made that little ordinary plant become a close, trustworthy friend, came from a different, unexpected quality.

My robots are made of mechanical parts, lights, speakers, and all sorts of things that can behave according to a certain input signal. I use microcontrollers to automate the actions of my robot's systems to correspond to the plant's electrophysiological response to the environment and its interaction with its surroundings. My first robot had legs and lights that behaved according to the way a plant electrophysiologically coupled to its system interacts with the environment. The robot was suspended from above with the lower parts (its legs) hanging free so that an input signal from the plant could make the legs open or close accordingly. At the time of its creation, I tested several stimuli on the plant, my little devil's ivy, set at the core of the system. I played with lights of different qualities, I tested smoke, changes in temperature, watering, and I even used ice cubes. The plant's response to these interactions was quite slow or insignificant. But, without notice, an unexpected response drew my attention. I had decided to breathe near the leaf being monitored, and, to my surprise, the response of the plant to my breath was quite intense and vigorous. The lights of my robot changed, its legs opened, and that moment changed all my expectations and understanding about the experiment.

Biologists have explained to me that when I breathe near the leaves of a plant, tiny pores in the plant tissue open and close to enable gas exchange and help with photosynthesis. The carbon dioxide out of my breath enters through the stomata that release water vapor and oxygen. This process results in changes of conductivity on the plant's leaves that are monitored by the system I have created. But all these are just scientific explanations. They are ways to cope with reality at a certain level. I do prefer to think of breathing in a distinct way. Because of such an unexpected connection between me and my devil's ivy, I called this artwork "Breathing":

> Breathing is a work of art based on a hybrid creature made of a living organism (a plant) and an artificial system. The creature responds to its environment through movement, light, and the noise of its mechanical parts. Breathing is the best way to interact with the creature. This artwork is the result of an investigation of plants as sensitive agents for the creation of art. The intention was to explore new forms of artistic experience through the dialogue of natural and artificial processes. Breathing is a prerequisite for life and it is the path that links the observer to the creature. Breathing is a small step towards new art forms in which subtle processes of organic and non-organic life may reveal invisible patterns that interconnect us. Breathing is a work of art driven by biological impulse. Its beauty is neither found isolated on the plant nor in the robotic system itself. It emerges at the very moment in which the observer approaches the creature and their energies are exchanged through the whole system. It is in that moment of joy and fascination, in which we find ourselves in a very strange dialogue with the creature, that a life metaphor is created. Breathing is the celebration of that moment.

"Breathing" changed my way of looking at plants, especially after I realized the fact that the fine-tuning necessary for this hybrid system to work properly does not depend only on the instruments involved. After more than a decade of monitoring conductivity from plants' leaves, trying to establish a sort of conversation, I have understood that the primary bond to be made in such an experiment is between the plant and me. Exhibiting an artwork involves a lot of planning, tests, deadlines, and compromises. But when an artwork results from a dialogue between humans, plants, and the environment, there must be an awareness that we are dealing with a living being, and so we must, as the promoters of such a dialogue, put ourselves in the position of listeners. This may involve balancing our mechanical time-scale with the organic clock of the living systems in order to observe them. Several times, my little devil's ivy didn't respond to our conversation. Sometimes I blamed the system for not working properly. Many times I cursed my lack of scientific skills. But suddenly, after a lapse of despair, the connection between my breath and the plant's response to it started flowing again. The problem was that I had just ignored the plant, her temporality, adaptation, sensibility, and perhaps her memories.

Fig. 1: Breathing. Photo: Guto Nóbrega

"Breathing" was the beginning of the journey into making art with plants. After this first creation, many other artworks came out. Robots that carry the plant toward the viewer after his/her breath; a Telebiosphere that promotes telematic communication between plants and people; a wearable hybrid that is made of plants, lights and sounds; or a little robot that I carried with me to make field recordings of plants' signals in the Amazon Rainforest. In fact, along with my interest in the vegetal kingdom as a source for my creative development, my awareness of the spiritual dimension in which plants take a very prominent role has also grown.

Fig. 2: Bot_anic. Photo: Cláudia Tavares

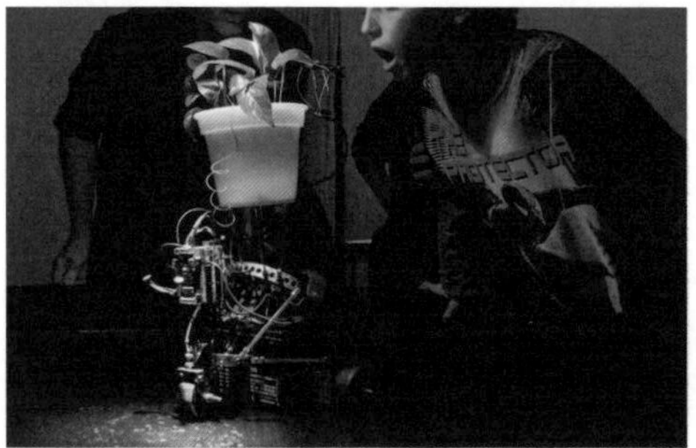

Guided by shamanic experiences, I have learned the power of medicinal plants as spiritual teachers. The gift of entheogenic plants such as tobacco and ayahuasca is a legacy from Mother Nature that cannot be ignored as a path to enter into the forests of consciousness. The experience of the Amazon Rainforest has touched me profoundly. The immersion in such an environment made me feel how weak one can be if separated from nature. Standing along with those big trees in the middle of the forest, I felt not as an observer but as if I was being observed. I have experienced a state of presence and connection, something that is difficult to describe. That experience led me to the creation of recent artwork.

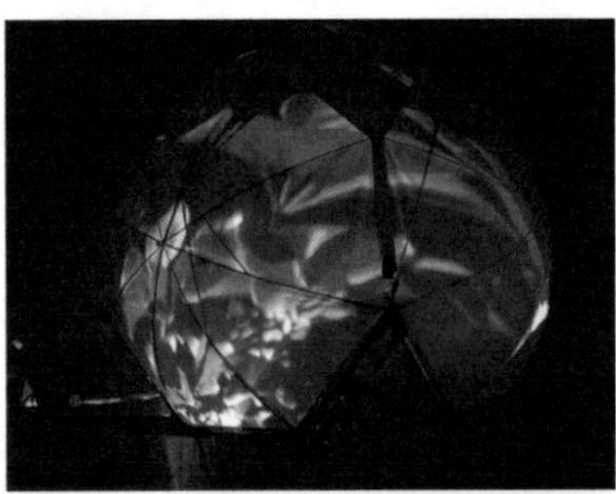

Fig. 3: Vegetal Reality Shelter.
Photo: Guto Nóbrega

"Vegetal Reality Shelter" is an immersive system based on sounds and images of the forest and on the interaction with plants. This work is the result of a ten-day artistic residency at the Adolpho Ducke Forest Reserve in the Amazon Rainforest. The artwork was built in the form of a small shelter based on the geometry of umbrellas to form a dome. It includes a small hydroponic system with plants, six channels of audio, and a video projector. Inside the shed, the hydroponic system has some of its plants monitored so as to register the galvanic response of their leaves, which changes according to the breath of the visitor when he/she enters into the space and interacts with the system. The electrophysiological signal monitored on the plants' leaves is used to modify the soundscape and the mirrored images of the forest that are projected inside the dome. The intention behind this work is to offer the viewer inside the dome a state of attention to the forest. Affecting the soundscape and the kaleidoscopic images of plants with his or her breath may lead the viewer to experience a sort of presence and a sense of belonging. I like to think of breathing as a way of connection between ourselves and other beings in nature. I was not expecting such wisdom to come from my own creative process and my encounter with plants, especially with the devil's ivy. Through her, I have learned the lesson of resilience. She showed me how important it can be to stand on our own feet and face the day, be it a sunny or rainy day, a bright or dark one. You never know the connection life will bring you.

I would like to acknowledge the National Council for Scientific and Technological Development (CNPq) for supporting my research.

CHAPTER 18

Fast-Moving Corkwood

Hakea lorea

■ **Barry McDonald**[1]

I.

We set out from my house one warm winter day to look for plants my sister could grind and mix with fats to make into medicines. While she had grown up learning about the region's flora from her old people, there was one place my sister hadn't visited for years: a nearby stretch of pretty wild country that she thought held out some promise.

Turning off the main road, we crossed a broad scrubby plain before fetching up at the entrance to a shallow gorge nestled in the shade of a dwarf rocky range. We left the car and walked down a gravelly path that wound through the gorge and past two tall central hills, all slab and tussock grass. Rounding the back of the hills, we came upon some trees of a type I didn't recognize. The afternoon was soft and clear, and the low sun angled into the fine gully so that it top lit just the foliage, kindling a pale green fire against the jumble of dark red rocks to which the trees clung. Large creamy flower-swags hung like lamps from scrawny branches, presenting a lambent richesse at odds with the humble, gnarled, and fissured trunks beneath.

"Do you know these trees?" my sister asked.

"No..."

"They're the long-leafed corkwood, and they mostly grow in rocky country like this. That's probably why you haven't come across them before; you don't find them on the flat, like where you live. That country's where you tend to see the other corkwood, the fork-leafed one."

"Can you get medicine from them?"

"Maybe, but anything you can get out of these trees you can get more of from the fork-leafed corkwood. So we tend not to bother with them so much."[2]

Stone and tree seemed made for each other here, an impression fortified by the plants' patently restricted range. Walking quietly in the lee of the hills, graced by the corkwoods adorning their feet, we had moved from the day-bright world into a realm suffused with the essence of their affinity. The air was still and the birds subdued, the occasional thin, wistful call of a distant honeyeater adding to the sense of abstraction. But as we trod solid earth, as our fingers brushed cool, hard rock and twigs snagged our clothes, it was evident we dwelt also in a pleasingly physical here-and-now. Inner and outer fused in a palpable peace.

II.

> To undo uncertainties, Dreamings reassert themselves and, by irruption … are thus entered into the fabric of contingency … in historical time.[3]
>
> —Anthropologist Basil Sansom (2001)

For months before our excursion I had been visited by extraordinary synchronicities, fateful meetings, prophetic dreams. These experiences resisted common sense analysis and had bewildered me at first. Around the same time, and in hindsight no less remarkably, I started coming by fragments of the Dreaming Story upon whose track my house sits. The Storyline, as I learned, extends from the south and stops for a while in the nearby gorge before resuming its northward tack, skirting my house as it goes. A pair of Ancestors, one slightly younger than the other, continues to dance along this line, creating landscape and culture and establishing right relations, as they have done since the Beginning Time. By and by, these fragments coalesced to a point where I realized, with astonishment, that my strange encounters uncannily mirrored key aspects of the Story: archetypal action, so anciently described, now appeared to manifest through personal engagement in my present. I still have no real clue how this can occur, surmising only that propinquity and a certain sympathy of mind play their part.

Desire for understanding spurred me to begin documenting these obviously far-from-random events. A register would provide a handy framework for tracing, over time, any connections between them, hopefully allowing a coherent picture to form. As the anomalies proliferated, so the number of records grew, among them the following:

> I don't think I've properly realized just how deep this drought is—it's been more than usually dry for two or three years now, and I heard today that only 30mm of rain has fallen over the last twelve months! The trees and shrubs on our block look decidedly stressed, and I reckon we might lose some bushes like the witchetties and senna, which is a great shame. But one wacky tree has bucked this dismal death-trend by springing lustily out of the earth in the northwest corner of the paddock. It can't be any older than three months. I'd been doing some work in that part of the block around that time, and I can guarantee there was no tree there then. While on the slender side, it's well over six feet high with an already-woody trunk. You can clearly see cracks in the mounded-up soil round the base of the sapling—I'm reminded of moleworks—that give the appearance of the first growth pretty much exploding from the soil. It's a bizarre-looking thing with long needly leaves and all gangly and ill-proportioned, like a child with adult-sized hands. The tree looks nothing like the other plants around here, which I find unsettling.

I showed my sister this prodigy the next time she visited for a cup of tea. After some deliberation, she identified the tree as a juvenile long-leafed corkwood, one of the same species I had first seen in her company the year before. While agreeing that it wouldn't be unusual for a seed to blow in on the wind from the gorge, my sister was surprised at the shrub taking so vigorously to "foreign" soil and was astonished at the speed at which it had evidently shot up.

A little later, I canvassed the opinion of a botanist friend: "That fertile, alluvial country out where you are supports an ironwood and mulga association," she told me. "It should be too loamy for the long-leafed corkwood, but it's not impossible for a species sometimes to spring up completely out of area."

Okay, so it transpired that although this was considered an unlikely event, it lay within the scope of reasonable chance, and as such, presented no great interpretative challenge. I let it go at that until, defying the odds, the same thing happened again eight months later:

> I've just found a second long-leafed corkwood shooting up on the block. It has followed the same M.O. as the first, the cracked and mounded soil round the base of its stem making it look as though the sapling blasted its way through, seemingly out of nowhere. It has emerged near the other tree, forming with it a direct line to the corkwood grove over in the gorge.

This repeat performance struck me, in a funny way, almost as a perverse and willful act. Slightly unnerved and needing to talk things out, I rang my sister and asked her to come over. When she arrived, we headed down the paddock and stood contemplating the interlopers.

"What do you make of it?" I asked. "I can't shake the feeling that there's something spooky going on with these trees. I've told you about all the other weird things that have happened, stuff that seems to connect with the Story that runs through my place. I think this might be part of it."

"You're most probably right. Like I said before, these trees normally grow around rocks, not in this type of soil. Corkwoods are known for being slow-growing, even in good seasons, and these two have sprouted up much quicker than you'd expect, especially considering the dry weather. See how they're growing in a line towards the hills where the gorge is? I reckon the spirit of that place is definitely in these trees, that they're the Ancestors themselves, one older and one younger, a year apart in age."[4]

While definitely challenged, I was receptive to what my sister proposed, having already come across snatches of the Story that suggested the corkwood might indeed bear a mythological association with the Ancestor Pair. I discovered, for example, that there are sites along their northern line of journeying—rocky hills again—where it is said the Pair plaited bracelets from the corkwood's long, strappy leaves and soaked their flowers in water to make a nectar drink. The furthest of these hills is actually named after the tree. When I tumbled to that fact, I asked my sister, who knows the old Story-language, for a translation.

"That second word refers to something going really quickly," she revealed. "So the name must mean 'fast-moving corkwood'."

Not knowing more about that part of the Story, my sister could offer no further gloss. But I was happy with what she'd given me; if just a single epithet was needed to characterize the corkwoods growing on my block, "fast-moving" would serve admirably.

It is probably quite common for Creator Beings to manifest as trees. I have been shown a brace of desert oaks, avatars of this same Ancestor Pair, growing in sandhills well to the south of my home. And, according to the Story, other tree species represent a group of Beings who joined the Pair at more northerly parts along their track. Margaret Kemarre Turner provides a general context for the phenomenon:

> Might be that the Ancestors came through from other countries and stopped here on their journey. And they became another tree here, left part of his *image* there. A plant or tree became them as they walked past and became who they are. And then they changed into another one. They might have dropped seeds there and other trees came out of those Ancestors before they travelled on.[5]

Mrs. Turner portrays trees as dynamic beings, their Ancestral identity self-propagating. If these attributes can be held in tension with more conventionally described features, then a richer appreciation of the nature of trees and plants must follow. Willingness to sit with this paradox has allowed me to accept the view of those of my friends and family who consider me privileged to have witnessed the setting of the Ancestors' image upon the ground we shared, and fortunate to have encountered the vitality of their Story.

III.

I have interpreted the growth of corkwoods on my block as the startling action of Creation Ancestors. This is partly out of respect to Land, Ancestors, and people. But it is also inspired by *pistis*, loyalty to the charged experience itself.[6] At the same time, I am alive to the danger of imputing unwarranted meaning to something better left mundane. A botanist might well ask why I shouldn't be satisfied with a secular solution; that corkwood seeds, for example, blowing in on an adventitious wind, lodged inhospitable soil far richer than required to merely promote germination, which resulted in much-accelerated growth. Or alternatively, that *Hakea lorea,* well-adapted to poor, dry soil conditions, responded keenly to the impoverishment of my drought-stricken alluvial ground to exploit a rare opportunity. All that, of course, makes sense at a routine level, and something like it must be seen as explanatory. But would the explanation truly suffice? The emergence of the trees is entirely consonant with the anomalous happenings that correspond closely with Basil Sansom's depiction of "Dreaming irruptions" and which offer no opening for such ratiocination. It could be said that the corkwood episode, referring loosely to those happenings, forms with them a synchronicity—a meaningful, non-causal relationship forged in a field of relativized space and time. It is this connection that encourages me to amplify any scientific interpretation of the trees' emergence with a mythological one.[7]

Carl Jung brought a deep understanding of mythology to his work in the sphere of analytical psychology. Jung felt a responsibility to reveal perceived truths about the role of the psyche in human life, and in so doing, help relieve the suffering of those—mainly Westerners—burdened by a sense of the meaningless of existence, commonly supposed to be a curse of modernity. Jung never ceased urging that, in order to achieve a degree of wholeness, the individual must heed the voice of the collective unconscious—the profound substratum of the human psyche which he equated with Nature itself—in its expression through dream, myth, and synchronicity:

> myth is the revelation of a divine life in man. It is not we who invent myth, rather it speaks to us as a Word of God...it confronts us spontaneously and places obligations upon us.[8]

For Jung, myth possesses qualities of autonomy and truth, and just like Basil Sansom's conception of Dreaming, imposes its will upon the person. Jung states too that when myth confronts, as it typically does in synchronicity, then a response is due. Synchronicity is driven, in Jung's vision, by the constellation of archetypes. These structuring, "psychoid" potentialities he regarded as eminently able for the restoration of existential meaning, as they create a lasting sense of identity between individuals and the environment out of which they arise:

> Synchronistic phenomena provided empirical evidence for Jung of the existence of the underlying unity of all of life [...] The active and living nature of the synchronistic dynamism reflects the archetypal energy that calls one to transcend one's conscious perception of reality toward a more expansive understanding [...] Jung felt that ultimately a synchronicity called one to surrender one's certainty so that this integration might occur.[9]

Dreaming or mythological irruptions are said by Sansom to undo uncertainty, something psychotherapist Yvonne Smith Klitsner, cited above, avers they create. There is no reason to see these statements as opposed. The uncertainty engendered by such spontaneous confrontation ideally leads one to question the validity of a dualistic outlook. A further step, and one which Jung believed to be the individual's "task of tasks," is to take careful note of the confrontation, and through analyzing it, attempt to discern what myth one lives within. Taken this way, irruption can promote certainty in a unified conception of existence, perhaps bolstering one's commitment to something like a Dreaming paradigm, wherein people and their world are held to be utterly indivisible.

There is broad, philosophical meaning for me in this tale. But it also has a personal side. I have been encouraged by those who belong to this Dreaming by birthright to consider myself as relating to its Ancestors in a different way. The fast-moving corkwood is only one of several episodes of irruption that have led them to this view. But it has played a significant role in helping me surrender intellectual objections to a mythological interpretation of experience, hopefully opening to trusting dialogue with a world that shapes as grander, more diverse, yet paradoxically more intimate than the one I was born to.[10]

POEM 5

Gum Tree

Eucalyptus mannifera

John Kinsella

Graphology Survival 96: biospheric plant euphoria where I am never solitary

'the cultivated form differs' [III. xv. 1-3]

Theophrastus, *Enquiry Into Plants*

Each cutback from house overarch bower nostalgia
though growth of a year where water is spare and sparse
but still adapted to limits to take on tin roof glare the mistletoe's sticky
mistletoe bird crackle soon to spark morphology from acuminata focal
point: acacia!

And then I am in Margaret Preston gum blossom highlighted stacked
to angle
against planes, geometry of still photosynthetic Western Australia but
it's a gallery-
lighting issue and growth can give way like my grandmother's dry
flower arrangements—
flowers and seedpods, stamens and touches of pollen lashing points
of illustration.

It's why I've delighted in one of three one-sided bottlebrushes
gathering the air to red sensors, to give occasion to the red wattle bird
not so common here. But the mottlecah that survived the blast
and silvers
against the excess of heat is the sensation of leaf beneath leaf, a coating.

But I feel sap is lymph in my system of walk and shelter,
the fire-swatching implants of lucerne tree giving up their botany
their import naming to declare a stand none can respect but
   the sheltering,
this confusion of heat and alteration that feeds back across firebreaks

Repetition bothers the olive dead to the graft that sprout lesser stock
from root clot to defy the rhizome trace of old sandalwood reach
to said Jam Trees to manna to other root clutchings to ride a scent
to renounce the vast cut to trade and carve and come in late to strip

For in the quest I fell to oranges and vineleaves of rice wrapped
under the hooded stare of Delphi, preferring rocky places and
   hardy plants,
as if to see into a future I might latch onto never integrated, but
   the cuttings
fed by niches in rocks moist against the withering glare didn't
   take despite

'The wild tree becomes cultivated by being transplanted.' [III. xv. 1-3]

To lift a leaf of translation bundled to depart the node, bring some kind
of light into the evasive heart region, the concentration of nerve tissue—
Tracy wrote of the 'sensitive' on Reunion and felt the falls splash her
   conscience,
her inhalation of history not hers but also not to be ignored, sugar
   cane lashing.

And each coconut cracked upon by crab on the temperature's horizon
on West Island stretched out in the Indian Ocean just so we can locate
   a grove
of copra, a claw of leaves to fall as comb against the coral rebarbatives,

built to eye the atoll grabbed for strategic reasons, the palm
heart lushness

Who is to misspell the introduced fuchsia hedges entwinings
of the Mizen,
the narrow gatherings of transport, the blunt Atlantic with its sunken
forest toxins—
each war grab and escape a tyranny the wren counts luck beneath
the hawthorn,
a tractor idling to green the hay cut, a soothing bandaided soil rocky
at periphery

'The wild tree becomes cultivated by being transplanted.' [III. xv. 1-3]

All these occlusions and oblations to wreath and laurel, to path
the passage
to deliverance, the healing and the growing, the tinder in the
stone's eye;
such edges serrated in leaves of press in letters of intensity a
knowledge
of paper in the fallout of millsite—such the cuttings of ladder
rungs on pines

to heave, the felled beanstalk of gigantism and phobias, the bigotry
of stories
told in comfort, the poverty paying up for the planting—gleaning
is seedfall,
the ears brushing the gossip, the rise of dye up the column of celery,
the propaganda
of totalitarian capitalism sold as liberty in the valleys of Manhattan—
know the Park?

Once on a mountain low by mountain standards but high in an eroded place
sop eroded valley bottoms are planed by a sky deeper blue than spectrum allows,
once, up there, I witnessed the unique wheatbelt alpine orchid and days later
machine went through to make a leisure launchpad, uprooting ideas of elevated

undergrounds, these exotic items in deletion, as if trivia we can forget, moving
out of modus vivendi to forget they ever were outside the translation, words
without pronunciation. But those sundews I walked amongst in the tiger snake
sensorium—gnat caught ant caught snake swim New Holland honeyeater
undoing the trap of its collectors' name, the woodwork.

Graphology Survival 87: Psyllids

'Trees that are already stressed may have a reduced ability to cope with the infestation
and can have the potential to cause the death of a tree however this is uncommon and
the vast majority of trees will recover. Infestations have been particularly noticeable
this year in Greenmount, Helena Valley and Swan View."

Mr Bonsack said trees can become stressed due to a range of factors including loss of understorey, grazing, soil erosion, salinity, reduced rainfall, and fungal diseases.

"It's important to remember that trees affected by Psyllids are in a state of defoliation

rather than being close to death, and they should not be removed," he said. "You will

be able to see the extent of damage caused by the insects by examining the leaves.

However even if the tree is leafless, scratching of the bark should reveal green

sapwood underneath.'

https://www.mundaring.wa.gov.au/News/Pages/Insects%20Attack%20Flooded%20Gums.aspx

Flooded gum leaf death
a little more each year
along the waterways
the drainage. But I note
each year some return,
some growing back
that doesn't come
with wandoo crown
decline which is dead
branch on dead branch
then anatomy laid bare.

But flooded gums in
the last year or two have
rebooted in the damp,

brief as it is briefer
and briefer, with some
unable to startover
because of the pressure
of clearing and poisoning,
of claims pegged in
their heartwood. But
many flooded gums
have come back—weakened,
true, but enthusiastic
to remain to keep their
hold on all futures.

This writing back
or unwriting depending
on interpretation of waterways
of hydrological
maps is a case of defoliation
and budding ignition
after infestation has
cycled death into leaves,
the lerp-attack the insect
that knows its quarry
that fits in that rides
out the last days
of its right, too, to
be as it will en-masse.

Distress on stress,
my journals is dead leaf
pressed to dead leaf

recording the decline
the rise with erasures
and blanks where
deep-meaning trees
have been cut down
grubbed out burnt
to rid the world
of the insect that
would have let them
come back to provide
more, recycling.

Graphology Survival 84

Growth rings and bone density—

if you know the sickening crunch
of a tree trunk snapping as a tree-spear

hits it full weight of cat engine attack
between ground and point of impact,

its own chaos theory enactment
that sap you pathologise as body fluid

that flaw the tree got through
giving way first—just

entering the pathology lab
of the valley, no skin that renews

and deep subcutaneous annulars—
fucking ringbarking, mate—

are just slow and quieter
if not silent enactment equating

species with sound of snapping
age with wrench in the psyche

growth rings and bone density.

Graphology Survival 83

In the smoke of irony
the living trees put up
snorkels of skin that
become dead limbs.

In the realm of burn
to prevent the burn
they make the smoke
saturate beyond absorption.

They might think of this
as paradox though even
this is unlikely—snorkel
branches can reach above

even with tall trees
and leaf weather vanes
translate decline into loss
and don't come back.

Graphology Survival 82

York gum mallees on the valley walls
in conversation with granite weathering—

but what is striking in the dis-encryption
of calendars is that one trunk of the gathering

of one in the many near the Great Tank
is flowering when no others hold a single

stamen to test the air throughout
the district. Anomaly, left behind

or vanguard of yet another terror?

Graphology Survival 81

Barebones York gum
& jam tree woodland
barebones but lush
with termites hollowing
so limbs will crack
and fall and birds
will nest and ground
take in the up-reach
as roots be exposed—
filling out to bring back,
to make and remake
flesh on barebones,
anatomy of woodland.

Graphology Survival 50: 'red marks'

Yesterday, just west of the bridge
over the river between Spencer's Brook
and Northam, I saw a red flash
a jack frost flame next to a flooded gum
alone in a tableaux scraped back to manuscript.

The flame was red-reaching for ructions
of damp leaves and bark and dead branches
that were searching for outer peace insofar
as disturbed vision discerns the red signs
of stolp notation of a Znamenny Chant

which belong as much as notes sounding crisis
in the trained river's ear. Such obfuscation
of the pioneering spirit—space between
aqueous humor and retina opening
out in for last heave-ho rip-off, ripe

for development to chant alternatives,
bright red hooks of someone else's tradition
seeped in and borrowed and made literary?

CHAPTER 19

Hornwort

Ceratophyllum demersum

Prudence Gibson

Plants can have dual roles as both sources of medicinal cures and also of potential poison. Too small a dose and the disease won't be cured; too large a dose and there is the risk of poisoning. My task of writing about a plant in a manner that matches the energetic life of that plant, without causing pain or suffering,[1] and in a way that is respectful of its multiplicity of capacities, relies upon the dose.

To feel the plant, to empathize with the plant, to honor the plant, has to be more than a tokenistic, sycophantic, or simplistic effort to mimic the plant or even to perform the plant in a stage actor whisper. There might be a situation where the human-centeredness of the human falls away, like a magic spell, and what remains is a sincere desire to connect with the plant as a tribute to its complex and distributed life.

There is a small plant that has caught my eye... enough to attempt the administering of the right dose. Well, when I say a plant has caught my eye, it is really the changed and disintegrated version of a plant. The remains of a plant. A hornwort. An ugly little hornwort's corpse. Oh dear, could I be exposing my moral judgmentalism already?

In life, the hornwort is a fernlike, mossy, vibrantly green plant that thrives in aquatic environs. In death, this hornwort is a dusty pile of matter. A small dark mound of rich decomposed vegetal life—perhaps one gram's worth. When I first laid eyes on it, I confess I thought it would make good composting. Endlessly pragmatic as I am. *Waste not, want not.*

The hornwort is a non-vascular plant that spreads across woodland floors or attaches to rocks or trees and is known as a colonizer of other vegetable beings' habitats. A bryophyte. Bryophytes are the oldest land plants on our planet, as old as 400 million years. Hornworts are small, often measuring only a few centimeters or smaller. This little specimen of *Ceratophyllum demersum*, held in the National Herbarium of New South Wales at the Royal Botanic Gardens in Sydney, is not one little hornwort but a cluster of tiny hornwort plants.

Held is an interesting term to use for the individual entities in an archival collection. The Herbarium in Sydney is a major institution which has a major *holding* of multiple plants, both native and otherwise, from Australia and across the world. Holding? Held hostage? Held against one's will? Or held, as in, embraced? Or held—cupped—carefully in the palm of one's hand?

There is a dichotomy here, which refers back to the act of writing being a cure or poison depending on the dosage. The Herbarium cares for its specimens. There are the security doors, two sets, and there is the climate control—moisture and temperature—and there is the constant care to avoid the worst danger to a collection archive of 1.4 million specimens. The threat I'm referring to are the tiny little insects that can infest and decimate an entire collection of national significance. So, the *holding* has a double meaning whereby we can understand that the Herbarium takes care of its tiny little guests, but that there is also a history of cultural neo-colonialism and nation-building, the collecting of rare objects for the pleasure of a dominant first-world country. This can be the collecting of rare and precious specimens from places that may not have given permission, nor have had permission requested. These are activities that improve imperial power, or a country's dominion over nature and of one another, and which have caused harm in the past, for instance, to Indigenous peoples. At what cost were some of these specimens in the National Herbarium of NSW collected, and what is the difference between taking a biotic object without permission, and stealing? This mundane little hornwort was collected by Carlo Pietro Stefano Sommier (1848-1922) in Gorgona Archipelago, Italy, but we will get to the details of that collecting later.

Back to the hornwort. It currently sits in a sterile plastic tub. It is a pile of dark brown soil-like stuff. It is forlorn. It reminds me of when my lovely father passed away six years ago and we decided to illegally scatter his ashes into the shallow waters of a beach he loved to visit. The little beach has moody casuarina trees right on the edge that whisper their stories in hushed voices via their vibrating needles. Our covert ash-scattering operation was a little undermined by the local police station building leering down at us from the hillside behind the beach, but my siblings, mother, and I were not to be dissuaded. We stealthily approached the little beach and started to distribute the ashes into the shallow water. A cheeky breeze picked up, and a good proportion of ashes were blown back against my jeans. These things happen. But there was something melancholic about the ashes blowing in the wrong direction. We, the humble humans, have a bad habit of trying to control the end of life (and the beginning too). We are disappointed when things don't go to plan at these epic moments in human perception. I have to remember that the wider material and biotic world of matter does not concern itself with such melancholy.

So, as I said, this little pile of earthly hornwort matter in its pristine white plastic tub has been removed from its prior paper envelope that was safely held inside a manila folder, inside a claret red plastic collection box, and slotted onto a shelf. Having already moved along a black conveyor belt to be digitally photographed by a state-of-the-art camera, the sight of the hornwort on its sorry way has a similar melancholy for me as the misdirected ashes. Photographing all these inert vegetal objects that once were living holds associations relating to representation and expression. Who will see these new images, and how do they relate to the original archive specimen and its former life? But at the point of death (which in vegetal life is less obvious than vascular human life), there is a moment where the plant is still very beautiful. For instance, the pressed flower, the bulbous seed in its specimen jar, or the packet of seeds stapled next to the leaf specimen are still at a point of decomposition that human cremation can apprehend. The specimens in the Herbarium are often not quite dead. This state of life/death flux carries romantic weight as it reminds us of human fallibility and morbidity. These specimens also continue in the form of a life of study—for plant physiology research; for medicinal, economic, and cultural legacy; for knowledge of life past; for botanical illustrations; for the reawakening of Indigenous knowledge; and for inter-herbaria exchange. These are the activities of the herbarium. And so, for some time after they are already dead (no longer growing in soil), these specimens carry a lively and endlessly energetic status. But my little hornwort friend? No, not so much. It really is a sad-sack of a specimen. It is just a stale mound of dust.

Nevertheless, my little hornwort was the first specimen, from 1.4 million, to be digitally photographed at the Herbarium. Photographic representation of an object exists as an independent object—it has a new life as digital archive, as a collection, but also exhibits a trace of the original. However, today, I am more interested in a different kind of trace. A spiritual trace, by which I refer to past uses of plants in a medicinal, or even witchcraft, context. A spiritual trace is the ancient story of how plants have the capacity to change human perceptions. Think of hemlock, bloodroot, anise, rosewater, and yew twig as ingredients in potions for death, for protection, for love. Plants have been conventionally "used" for food, agriculture, medicine, shade, weapons. Elixirs, potions, balms, and tonics have been used in western and eastern communities, past and present alike. Putting aside superstition or religious / spiritual oppositions, the curious aspect of such appropriation of plant power by humans is the ability to change human behavior and our affective, biological, and mental states.

Spell 1

FOR THE HORNWORT

Coolant of stings and comfort of swelling
Green pendant swinging on a string of barbed envy,
These pages are too heavy to turn alone.
Help me find the spell to return to watery depths
Where friendly mosses and liverworts comfort in the change
Single-celled spores and swimming biflagellate,
Plants that moved from sea to shore
May return without *ressentiment* poison
Clutching at their roots.

Spells are an exchange, a cultural act, a writing ritual. Cure or poison—what's the dose? Enough to shift perception of plant value. As an aesthetic of care, spells are to be spoken aloud, incanted. Usually scorned as anti-intellectual and anti-scholarly, spells were written and invoked by such thinkers as Isaac Newton, who was an occultist, and wrote his Treatise on Prophecy in 1670.[2] Two centuries later, in 1890, another great thinker and poet was at work in the realm of the magical: W. B. Yeats. Yeats was a friend of the infamous occultist Madame Blavatsky, a member of the Hermetic Order of the Golden Dawn. Yeats also participated in rituals of magic, joining an occult group run by MacGregor Mathers, which included the author of *Dracula*, Bram Stoker. Yeats' final work, *A Vision*, matched psychology with poetic, cosmic astrology as a direct result of these occultist interests.[3] It would be neglectful not to mention Aleister Crowley (1875–1947), an occultist, Western esoteric, magician, and founder of the religious/philosophical group, Thelema.[4] Crowley had influence over esoteric and new religious movements of the twentieth century, and he renewed and reinterpreted the meaning of occult practices in a modern framework. Crowley was active at a time when scientific naturalism encouraged the investigation of occultist beliefs. His was a version of magic that was experiential and empirical.

These spiritual projections of the natural world—using magical elements and undertaking intonations and incantations—are an expression of the other, a representation of a world we don't yet fully understand. Art, philosophy, and occultism sit side-by-side with science, although the latter has a more scrupulous reputation. For instance, the Herbarium's digitization process of ordering and measuring, recording and contextualizing, is standard procedure for science and for archival scientific matter. In the humanities, too, there are surprising cross-overs. During the early 1990s, when I worked as Assistant Curator at the Art Gallery of New South Wales, Sydney (across the road from the Herbarium, as it happens), I was given the task to catalog the entire Australian print drawings and watercolors collection. Much of this consisted of pulling out the solander boxes and checking that there was adequate information (date, title, medium, measurement, provenance, date acquired, and an image). My role was to ensure each archival object was photographed. It took over six months. But it was far from boring. Each collection item told a story.

This may explain my attraction to a funny little hornwort specimen, made famous by being the inaugural specimen to be photographed for posterity. It has a story too. It was collected on April 1, 1889. *Anthoceros dichotomus Raddi* is the title on the specimen paper sheet. The specimen is small—a clump measuring 3 x 5 centimeters. It is a duplicate specimen, which was sent to the NSW Herbarium (at some point not documented) as an exchange. This little hornwort cluster was collected by Carlo Pietro Stefano Sommier (1848-1922) in Gorgona Archipelago, Italy. There is no description of the natural habitat it was collected from, nor the details or circumstances of the collecting. Separate research tells me that Isola Gorgona, west of Livorno, is the smallest island of the Tuscan archipelago. It is a typical Italian island—soaring cliffs on one side that plunge down into the deep sea and a pretty bay on the other side where the fishing village is settled. A penal colony with no more than the village and a prison. There is purple heather, and the rock face is dark stone—wildly dissimilar from the pinkish honey of our Sydney sandstone. The island visitation is severely regulated, with only twenty-five visitors allowed to enter per day. The prison was set up in 1861. There is an atmosphere to this island that suggests it is stuck in the 1950s, with the buildings and concreted bayside infrastructure having a distinctly retro look. Sommier collected his hornwort from this penal island in 1889, twenty-eight years after the island was changed from a religious property for monks to a penal colony by the Grand Duke of Tuscany. Sommier, born and raised in Florence, started collecting in 1870, so he had almost twenty years collecting experience by the time he grabbed this little clump.

For me, there is a romantic allure to the notion of exploring isolated islands and collecting specimens for an herbarium archive. This is exploratory work conducted by scientists and amateur collectors alike. The late nineteenth century was a particularly active time for this kind of amateur and professional collecting. This was a period of high Victorian Romanticism—colonial and imperial expeditions and explorations were still underway. London was in a stage of high cabinet of curiosity collecting. *Wunderkammer*, another old habit of collecting rare objects from far lands and exhibiting them in a stylized way, was still an influential aesthetic mode. There was a level of status associated with finding and collecting rare things, but the challenge was to stay ahead of other plant collectors. The colonial disdain for the countries or the populations (human and non-human) of procurement during these periods of high-art collecting reveal the cultural poison that threatens to undermine all such archival collections. And spare a thought for our hornwort, extracted from its happy habitat in Gorgona and sent as an illegal alien to Australia.

Spell 2

FOR THE HORNWORT'S ORIGINAL HABITAT

My island is a turtle's back
Windy place of maquis and holm oak trees
Catch the Ligurian bounty of my harbor
Pick the heather, rosemary, and juniper
Trek around the edifice of the internment
Or shout through the galley walls
But you must…
Must leave my little hornworts be.

The trance of collecting is an element of human nature. When we fall for the allure of the capitalist marketplace rather than the slower time frames of the plant-oriented world, then the ailment can be diagnosed as the "capture" of capitalist sorcery, as proffered by Isabelle Stengers.[5] The alluring and enchanting baubles of production have tricked us into forgetting the value of the non-human, and the energetic activity of the non-human. Plants and writing are a cure, vegetal writing is both panacea and performance. An herbarium spell, in memory of the stinking boiling herbs of the sorcerer, is an incantation of the value of the original, the kept specimen, and the digitally recorded.

A drive to possess and dominate, to succumb to the allure of acquiring things, can manifest in collecting plants for an institution. This plant collecting craze was more than self-flattering nationhood or cultural status—it also revealed the valuing of rare plants that could be used for propagation and market-place buying and selling. So while there was a culture of swapping specimens between herbaria institutions, there was also an economic game at play.

New values, new cures, new poisons. In terms of the operational properties of plants—even those in an herbarium collection archive—the hornwort traditionally acts (when applied in a medicinal sense) as a cooling agent for biliousness and scorpion stings. If hornworts represented certain values across time or possess curing properties, soothing inflammations as the hornwort does, then how could those properties be activated as cultural legacy?

Spell 3

THE NEW HORNWORT

Horny head of powerful men and their blond beasts of prey.
The plants will revolt against the noble morality
But will avoid the poison of the revolutionary act.
A new cure for old humans will be the shift
The plague of bilious nationalism will yield
Absolved by the soft fronds of the horn.
A cup of emerald wine will administer nature's fire.
Purged by heat, having tasted the putrid juices,
Only then will the human grow wings.

There have been contemporary studies of the medicinal properties of the hornwort as a cure. The Cancer Council conducted work in 1986 on the facility of the hornwort (as well as mosses and liverworts) to act as anti-tumor agents.[6] The study was interesting in that it was reviewed from various perspectives, including folklore, chemo-therapeutic potential, taxonomy, and active compounds. The study was interesting in that it was reviewed from various perspectives, including folklore, chemo-therapeutic potential, taxonomy, and active compounds. The study tested for biological activity and the ability of bryophytes to absorb toxins, rather than collating data on evidence of cure. This was a hypothesis in potentials. A connection can be drawn between such science studies conducted by the Cancer Council and the abnegated and maligned (by skeptics) activities of the spell-casters… their potential. The witches' spells and protective incantations, the folkloric administering of vegetal cures, and links to western medicine all pivot on the importance of getting the dose right. The hornwort lacks true roots, but certain leaves function to help anchor the plant in the substrate. Spells may lack social status, but the relevance of ritual, written and spoken, can anchor humans in the earth and remind us that it is everything that we do not know. And the humble hornwort? We know that the earth's first terrain plants evolved from the sea. We know that the hornwort has anti-inflammatory properties. We know that the little pile of sooty dirt in the collection of the National Herbarium of NSW was the first specimen in the collection to be digitized, and is, therefore, the first object to be established as cultural legacy representing past human-plant relations that have now been lost. But… that's all I know.

CHAPTER 20

Horse Chestnut

Aesculus hippocastanum

Luke Fischer

When I lived in Philadelphia, USA, for a few years (I presently live in Sydney, Australia, where I also grew up), I enjoyed walking in a cemetery several blocks away from my apartment. In the poem "I Like to Walk in a Nearby Cemetery," I share some of the reasons why. This final resting place was ironically "the greenest place around," and "an odd sanctuary of the living and the dead." Wandering among the variety of trees and animals, I wondered at a magnificent horse chestnut tree (*Aesculus hippocastanum*), ambled under the branches of the baroque green temple. In the same poem, I record "the chestnut tree, now in bloom, makes me recall / cherished lines by Yeats."[1] I had in mind the final lines of Yeats's "Among School Children" that likewise refer to a horse chestnut tree (which belongs to a different order, Sapindales, than true chestnut trees such as the *Castanea sativa*, whose edible seeds, once roasted, are widely savored):

> O chestnut tree, great rooted blossomer,
> Are you the leaf, the blossom or the bole?
> O body swayed to music, O brightening glance,
> How can we know the dancer from the dance?[2]

The grandeur of these lines, their intimation of a wholeness that pervades every aspect of the tree, and their comparison of the tree to a dancer resonated with my own experience. Reading poetry and the appreciation of plants can mutually enhance one another.

I'm both a poet and philosopher, and plants have inspired my poetry as well as my thinking. Plants appear in my poetry as expressive, living presences, as metaphors for the poetic mind, and as symbols of an ecological mindedness that contrasts with our modern alienation from the natural world and its devastating environmental consequences. This essay draws particular attention to the way in which horse chestnut trees have represented these qualities in various poems. But before turning to specific poems, it is important to share some of the ideas that have informed my understanding of the intertwinements of plants and mind. The development of these ideas has been influenced by European Romanticism, as well as recent developments in ecocriticism, environmental philosophy, and biology.

One of the perennial philosophical questions is how to understand the relation between the one and the many. From the beginnings of Western philosophy in ancient Greece, philosophers have argued that there must be an ultimate unity of existence while also recognizing the problem of accounting for the immense diversity of beings—plants, animals, humans, the elements, and so on. Philosophers and scientists face two main dangers in approaching this question. Those who affirm unity are likely to overlook difference, whereas those who affirm difference are likely to overlook the interconnectedness of things. At the risk of over-generalization, I think it is fair to say that modern scientific culture, in its detailed specializations, suffers primarily from the latter. Specialized understanding of particulars has increased, but we have tended to lose sight of the whole. Our increasing awareness of the ecological interdependence of all life on Earth is one significant shift away from this general trend.

While ancient philosophers saw a deeper continuity between plants, animals, and humans than has tended to be the case in the modern period, plants have seldom been attributed "mindedness" in the history of Western thought. Although Aristotle articulates a continuity throughout nature in attributing a "soul" to plants, animals, and humans, the plant's "vegetative soul" is strongly contrasted with the additional "sentient soul" of animals and the additional "intellective soul" of humans. In the modern period, "mind" and "mindedness" have tended to be identified exclusively with the rational capacities of the human being. Thus a much greater rift has opened up between "mind" and "nature." For Descartes, only human beings possess a soul, which is distinguished by the power of rational thought, whereas the rest of nature, including animals and plants, is no more than a soulless machine.

How can we get beyond the Scylla and Charybdis of amorphous oneness that denies difference on the one hand and disconnected differences on the other? How can we appreciate the interconnectedness of all things and at the same time discern the diverse and particular characteristics of plants, animals, and humans? In my view, plants themselves are perhaps the best teachers of how to think unity in difference and difference in unity. I came to this insight through the work of the great German poet and scientist of the Romantic era, Johann Wolfgang von Goethe.

In Goethe's thought, the word "nature" is a synonym for being, for existence as a whole. However, nature is neither a static entity nor an undifferentiated oneness. Nature is fundamentally a creative process of differentiated becoming and transformation. Moreover, Goethe regards nature as a process of manifestation. What is latent in one aspect of nature becomes more explicitly manifest elsewhere. Goethe designates increasing degrees of manifestation as "intensification" (*Steigerung*). An understanding of metamorphic intensification enables the discernment of differentiation in continuity. Goethe's conception of nature is exhibited in a microcosmic form in his plant morphology and, more specifically, his view of the "metamorphosis of plants."

According to Goethe, the metamorphosis of the plant takes place through phases of expansion and contraction, as well as intensification.[3] The seed is the most contracted state of the plant, wherein the essence of the plant is most concealed. The unfolding of leaves is an expansion in form, the formation of the calyx is a contraction, the petals an expansion, the stamens and pistil a contraction, the fruit an expansion, the seed a contraction. While the various parts differ and are distinct, Goethe illustrates how all parts can be imaginatively discerned as the metamorphosis of *one* organ—a protean "leaf form"—and thus as an expression of an ideal whole. The calyx can be viewed, for example, as contracted and circularly arranged stem leaves, the petals as colored and refined leaves, the stamens as contracted petal forms. Think of how the pod of a snow pea, to offer another example, resembles leaves folded together with the seeds between them. Through his understanding of metamorphosis, Goethe neither separates the parts into disconnected particulars nor does he treat them as manifestations of an abstract oneness; rather, the parts appear as a continuum of formations.

Goethe regards the flower as the highest expression, or intensification, of the plant. While this metamorphic intensification occurs within the plant kingdom, it provides a key to transitions and interconnections across the whole of reality. Informed by this Goethean model of differentiated continuity, I have explored diverse interconnections in my poetry. My poem "Grasshopper in a Field," for example, draws deep connections between insects and plants.[4] The grasshopper is depicted as a "walking plant," whose wings are "folded leaves" and legs are bent "thin stems." The insect is presented as though it is an intensified plant, a plant metamorphosed into an animal—a "self-enclosed" mobile whole that possesses a primitive "sentience." Other poems explore less obvious interconnections between, for example, plants and works of art. Metaphors (and similes) play an important role in suggesting these interconnections. Furthermore, as in "Grasshopper in a Field," metamorphosis and metaphor are often coupled in my poetry.

Ostensibly metaphor has the structure of the statement that "A is B" or "A=B": "the grasshopper [A] is a plant [B]." However, in interpreting a metaphor, we also know that there is a non-identity between A and B. To say that the "grasshopper is a plant" is not the same as stating that "a bachelor [A] is an unmarried man [B]." The metaphorical "A=B" carries the implication of non-identity, namely, "A≠B." Furthermore, a metaphor does not entirely specify in what respects A=B and A≠B, but rather maintains some degree of indeterminacy. It is this indeterminacy that calls on the interpreter to make connections between A and B, which shed light on A while at the same time excluding certain characteristics of A and B as unrelated. As a reader, I might think "the grasshopper [A] shows no resemblance to the plant's [B's] capacity for photosynthesis, but the grasshopper [A] resembles a plant [B] in its mimicry," and so on. An apt metaphor is one that facilitates insight into differentiated interconnections. Although metaphors are often regarded as a misrepresentation of A through the distorting lens of B, this only holds for bad metaphors, dead metaphors, and those that are naïvely interpreted as literal statements.

Scholarship over the past century has demonstrated that metaphors play a central role in virtually all forms of language (including scientific and philosophical language). Despite the deep-seated tendency to insist on divides between humans, animals, and plants, if one digs just a little beneath the surface of language and explores the etymological roots of English words, one finds diverse traces of plants sedimented in our self-understanding. Like many poets, I am fascinated by etymology and, in writing poetry, I often delve into the history of words and their buried metaphors.

Much of human culture is defined in metaphorical terms drawn from the world of plants. We speak of a *seminal* work of literature, of bringing a project to *fruition*, of *disseminating* ideas, of a person being *green* (young) or *blossoming* in their new situation in life, of tracing one's cultural *roots* or family *tree*, of research that is *branching* in a new direction, of the *flourishing* (blooming) of art in fifteenth century Florence, of a *germinal* or *burgeoning* idea, a *budding* philosopher, of *florid* prose, of fertile *soil* for a political change, or of the *cross-pollination* of science and art in works of the Romantic era. From human thought to historical *cultures* plants have informed the ways in which we understand ourselves.[5]

While a literalist would have to claim that the above descriptions of "flourishing," "branching," "budding," and "cross-pollination" only properly apply to plants, metaphors—just like metamorphoses—in fact always imply a connection or resemblance between different things. In these instances, between the plant and the human. That many activities of the human mind are described as plant-like already suggests that a radical opposition between plants and mindedness is spurious. In addition, if we are so inclined to turn to plants in describing human mentation, does this not intimate that plants themselves, however different from us, manifest a form of mindedness?

Although metaphorical language plays a central role in scientific and philosophical discourses, poetry arguably holds the richest soil for the proliferation of metaphors. Poetic language often draws attention to the metaphors concealed in words, and poets enjoy the greatest liberty in inventing fresh metaphors and thus making new connections. Philosophy, science, and everyday parlance rely to a greater extent on wilted metaphors and clichés. Moreover, we read poetry with a heightened critical attentiveness to its metaphoricity and are thereby unlikely to overlook the aspect of non-identity in the metaphorical A=B. In contrast, we tend to employ the vernacular more naïvely and to over-identify scientific statements with literal truth. We are thereby prone to overlook the inadequacies of a metaphor.

European Romanticism was an especially fertile era for the flourishing of metaphors and ideas that drew deep connections between plants and the human mind. Plant-like qualities of organismic wholeness, development, and differentiated unity were associated with the highest human achievements, including art and poetry. Art and poetry were also attributed the power of overcoming Cartesian dualism through a reintegration of mind and living nature in a manner that is only more relevant in our present era of unprecedented ecological crisis—of devastating dissonance between human industry and the natural environment—and what has come to be known as the Anthropocene. So pervasive are the botanical metaphors in Coleridge's poetry criticism, for example, that the eminent scholar of Romanticism M.H. Abrams describes it as a "very jungle of vegetation" in which "authors, characters, poetic genres, poetic passages, words, meter, logic, become seeds, trees, flowers, blossoms, fruit, bark, and sap." In short, poetic creation is a human "intensification" of plant formation.

The notion of a deep relationship between plants and poetry, nature and art, plays an important role in my own poetry. One reviewer of my work concludes that "in the end it almost seems interchangeable, whether nature illustrates culture or culture illustrates nature..."[6] This deep interconnection of nature and culture aims not only to be descriptive but also to envisage an ideal culture in which humanity and the environment might find a new harmony.

Whereas art is generally regarded as a distinctive achievement of the human mind, my poetry often depicts other-than-human nature as a consummate artist. Conversely, I frequently convey human art forms as plant-like formations. The poem "Gardening" metaphorically depicts a performance of classical music as an unfolding and blossoming of tones (a metamorphic sequence of sounds)—"Chord clusters in the Chopin nocturne / blossom into purple umbels..."—and concludes with a sense of communion between music and the world of plants.[7] In the poem "Val di Noto, Sicily" a baroque church is described as an intensification (a "flowering") of the surrounding landscape and vegetation: "the Cathedral of San Giorgio crowns / the town of Modica with a flowering spike."[8]

The poem "Anonymous," which portrays a horse chestnut tree (also commonly known as a conker tree), is an especially clear example of the kind of continuity that I perceive between plants and human processes of artistic creation. Here the tree (the one that I admired in the cemetery in Philadelphia) is presented as itself an artist:

> What about the chestnut tree in the cemetery,
> replete with foliage, erecting
> countless steeples of blossoms—
> each consisting of images
> that capture the essence in a couple of strokes,
> a dash of red or yellow on white—
> and the perfect fragments
> blown to the grass?
> Does anyone else
> come here to see them,
> the displays of this artist
> unknown even to herself?[9]

The tall conical panicles (10–30 cm) of numerous flowers (20–50) are depicted as architectural formations, "steeples." The individual flowers (which are mostly white but contain spots of either yellow or pinkish-red) are described as paintings. Just as we might speak of a masterful painting as capturing the essence of its subject in a few strokes, here, the plant expresses its own essence in "a dash of yellow or red on white." The portrayal of fallen flowers as "perfect fragments" implies that individual parts of the tree convey a sense of the whole tree, just as, for example, a fragment of sculpture can intimate the character of the whole sculpture (despite its external incompleteness). The final lines explicitly refer to the tree as an artist, though she doesn't recognize herself as one. Given the growing body of work that suggests plants possess forms of sentience and mindedness, perhaps this poem's conclusion inclines too far in a direction that might imply that plants are unconscious of their existence. But the main thrust of the poem is to convey the horse chestnut tree as a great artist who deserves to be appreciated as such. Moreover, the personification of the tree invites us to see the plant as an active subject rather than as an impersonal object. In these ways, the poem addresses the issue of "plant blindness" (the widespread propensity to overlook plants), and asks the reader to contemplate the tree as a minded and artistic agent.

This presentation of the horse chestnut tree also exemplifies a general tendency in my poetry to portray plants as embodiments of a gestural *language*. This approach builds on an earlier tradition of regarding plants in terms of a "language of nature," or *Natursprache*. While the idea of a "language of nature" often did not go as far as considering the communication between plants (and between diverse animal species) that we are becoming increasingly aware of today, these ideas can mutually deepen one another. Though plants don't literally speak a human language, I find it illuminating to interpret them as speaking in a language of "gesture" (and color, scent, taste, etc.) that is analogous to the way in which a person's body language can tell us something about their character. Plants and trees speak to us in the expressive language of their own slow dances. Just as the behavior of a human individual in various contexts expresses their character or their attitude in a particular moment—a woman who takes large steps with an upright gait expresses "confidence," whereas a man who walks slowly with his head bowed conveys "melancholy"—an analogous expressiveness can be discovered in the formation of plants and their responsiveness to their environments. Through drawing metaphorical connections between human expression and plant expression, poetry can overcome the apparent separation between human "interiority" and the "external world." The poem "River Rose / *Bauera rubioides*" metaphorically conveys the flowers as anonymous love letters that expose "the heart without the least irony / desire or deceit."[10] The four-line poem "Ars Poetica" depicts casuarina foliage as writing or painting on the sky: "In the black strokes / the casuarina brush / on the backdrop of evening / you find the casuarina."[11] In "Banksia Spikes," the hardy resilience of banksias and the upright, radiant character of their inflorescences become exemplary of an ideal of human resilience and inner radiance in dark times: "Returning from a walk at dusk, / I notice a banksia's countless spikes, / tall beeswax candles it bears into the night."[12] In imagining the expressive language of plants, new relationships between the human psyche and the plant soul are formed.

Like the Romantic thinkers Coleridge and Schelling I regard poetic creation itself as a plant-like process that involves collaboration between the conscious and the unconscious, human intentionality, and nature. In a long poem "Mapping the Soul" (as yet unpublished), the creation of poetry is likened to the work of a gardener as follows:

> Though she sows, waters, cares
> the gardener doesn't lift the plant
> into air and light.
>
> Some mornings I've woken early
> refreshed and nourished
> by days of contemplation,
> found resting in my hand
> a ripe peach,
> the poem.

On a few occasions, I have woken after a night's sleep with an almost fully formed poem in my mind (it would be nice if this happened more often!). In these cases, the poem usually relates to a theme that I've thought about for a long time, but the poem itself arrives all at once like a gift. Just as a gardener is a collaborator with nature and not the creator of plants, the poem emerges through a collaboration between the conscious and the unconscious (by "unconscious," I do not mean to suggest that nature is unconscious but to indicate an agential power that is not restricted to the usual boundaries of human self-awareness). It is not simply willed into being by the poet but comes about through a receptive activity.

This also involves a collaborative relation to time and has a parallel to a plant's relation to seasons. The plant is dependent on the conditions of various seasons in order to sprout, bud, blossom, or fruit. The flowering of a horse chestnut tree in a temperate region is an expression of spring. While the creative work of the poet might not literally depend on natural seasons (or "post-natural" seasons in an era of anthropogenic climate change)—though some poets find particular seasons especially conducive to writing, and poems often bear the imprint of the time and place in which they were written (perhaps another quality they share with plants?)—I often find that the creative process has parallels, for example, to the state of dormancy of a seed waiting in the soil (the mind waiting for the spark of inspiration) and the times of flowering or fruiting (periods of intensive writing when the poetry is flowing). This involves a receptive relation to time in contradistinction to a self-assertion of the individual will that imposes its agenda on the world irrespective of time, place, or the effects of its action on others. The latter is a self-interested, destructive attitude—a form of psychopathy or "ecopathy"—that, in my view, is characteristic of the economic exploitation of nature. An ecopathic attitude is manifest, for example, in industrial agriculture, whose central concern is efficiency and short-term productivity rather than a sustainable collaboration with the environment.

Later in "Mapping the Soul," this receptive relation to time is conveyed through the symbol of a chestnut tree. Again, I specifically had a horse chestnut tree in mind as I wrote this stanza, perhaps owing to a café that I used to go to in Tübingen, Germany, which is situated in a cobblestone square sheltered by the branches of two horse chestnut trees. It is especially pleasant to sit there in spring and summer when the foliage gives shade and dappled light, and the voices of conversing humans blend with chirping birds. In contrast to the mechanical time "that ticks in sync with the calculus of seconds," the psyche that is attuned to poetic time:

> . . . in time undivided, fluid
> as a melodic invention
> by Chopin, spreads into the air
> like branches of a chestnut tree
> spanning an ancient square.
> Its leaves discern subtle workings
> of sunlight, quiver with zephyrs,
> roots sense rainfall seeping into soil,
> trunk and branches turn

with planets, night and day.
Only now you whisper: *I am*
a soul in the world.

Rather than time divided into quantified moments, this experience of time is "fluid." The chestnut tree becomes a symbol of a poetic mode of being in the world. The tree is, significantly, described in sentient and minded ways. Its "leaves *discern* the subtle workings /of sunlight," and its "roots *sense* rainfall. . . ." The tree in its responsive receptivity to its environs—its openness to the cosmos—presents the ideal of a heightened and expanded human sensibility to the environment. Rather than a self-enclosed subjectivity that experiences its borders as coinciding with the surface of its skin, this poetic-mindedness has an expanded sense of inhabiting the world. The tree is thus an example, a metaphor, and a model for an ecopoetic mode of being in the world.

POEM 6

Iboga

Tabernanthe iboga

Rachel Gagen

You place your bare chest upon the soil
To bury yourself in the shadows of the Forest
Enrolled in a university of Holy Transcendence
Within a world of bark & ash spark
Lay wonderment
Your blood must be sap-strong to pass
The Gatekeeper
Now crown down, caste off, humbled down
Here you will sleep
And in the night, roots will creep
To the Masters of Earth you now keep

Were you a seed, you might take
But you have taken much already
For you are mighty man, ensouled in language
Pity, none speak that tongue here
Words must be left and much must be given
In return to the Wood
Now placed here on country
A bitter truth is sinking into your belly
To embark on a journey
Of root bark
To find where the heavenly stems descending
Meet the Earth branches extending

And drop fruits
Mighten you eat a piece of the sky born of soil
Mighten you become a seed yourself

You, a soil tender, of microbe and ochre
You, a vendor of dream speak, once colored in black & red
Have forgotten your place
And turned waste to the wilderlands
Now tolls must be paid to pass here
But you've used up your coins on the eyelids of great beasts
Ivory tusks & pieces of bone
To this you must consult
The doctor of the Forest

Painted in white, sitting at the funeral pyre
No one sermons or summons you
To the flame now engulfing
You are meeting the mind of a master
And come as a beggar
As the fire catches, so does your heart
Now beating as a drum of the unsung
Calling Elephants to the Temple
Where each step is not forgotten
Marked by a footprint
Here, you must learn of the pace of death
To walk the path of life
Where golden fruits and white flowers lie
Here Maboka dwells

At your heel, a snake bites
At the serpent's head, a hand strikes

Yes, you have a hand
And you place it upon a leg
To know thy grip
For a foot knows a foot
By finding the ground
It's not looking in a mirror
It lands Earthbound

Many long nights pass here
Until the color returns to your skin
The poison held within; no more
You have seen who has seen
Through the eyes of your ancestors
You have been where Never-Nevers birth
You, now in service
To the Masters of Earth

CHAPTER 21

Kurrajong

Brachychiton populneus

▪ Catherine Wright

Summer's come to dust. Red-necked wallabies[1] leaping past me stop abruptly in a powder-cloud rising up from the humus. It should be moist, this layered ground-scattering, but the summer has been tough and without the usual drama of electric storms rolling down the canyons of the gorge where I live, to fade away in the lavender haze of eucalypts. Autumn has kept up its parched charge, morning dew is fleeting, and with a season of frosts looming as the country heads into an entrenched drought, many hardy Indigenous trees are showing signs of strain or dying.

I walk this way each morning, navigating the same path, down Fairy Glen, past the towering monolith of Ganga's rock, beneath the black wattle,[2] across the narrowing of the gully, over a rise capped with granite punctuated with moon-green amoebas of lichen, and into the orbit of a very special plant.

This tree is a *Brachychiton populneus*, colloquially known as a kurrajong. With its emblematic shape, it stands sentinel in a rocky clearing on the lip of the wild, serpentine New England, NSW gorge country that plunges a thousand feet before it travels eighty kilometers to the sea. The next closest kurrajong is a young whippersnapper standing snug against a boulder on the side of Fairy Glen, some three hundred meters away. These trees are rare and solitary in this liminal place.

Every day as I crest the ridge on the northern side of Fairy Glen during these droughty times, my stomach tightens with worry—how is my tree faring today? Has an extra day without moisture clinched its fate? Locals tell me that they are highly drought-resistant, but this one seems to be struggling. Every day I sweep my gaze across the foliage, the bare limb-tips, and I wonder what grand plan my beloved tree has in mind for its survival.

Emanating mystery and wisdom, my family calls it the Tree of Life.

Kurrajongs are native to eastern Australia and are found from Victoria to Townsville in northern Queensland.[3] They grow from five to fifteen meters tall and are frost hardy to minus five degrees.[4] *Brachychiton* means 'short tunic'[5] and refers to the loose outer covering of the seed. *Populneus* means poplar-like, and in a normal season, the leaves of the kurrajong are a glossy, arrow-tipped, emerald green on a long stem, standing out vividly against the arid olive of the surrounding gum trees.

A younger kurrajong would bear large, woody, swan-shaped fruit up to ten centimeters in length full of numerous seeds embedded in a loose, hairy covering which can irritate and which ripen in the pods generally in May or June. With outbreeding in mind, most plants are largely or completely male or female at one time, and then the opposite sex at other times. Sometimes they freeze their flowers—mostly male—for a season. I have never seen any pale lemon, bell-shaped flowers. This tree now is barren.

The kurrajong cleaves—C.S. Lewis-like—a large tablet of granite that has been pushed up the trunk, leaving a hollow beneath the stone; shelter to small, soft animals. It also minds a young native olive,[6] growing up in its protection. It appears the effort to thrust through this rock caused the trunk to tilt to the side, but the tree righted itself, climbing straight above its base toward the light before splitting into three main arterial limbs. Consequently, the kurrajong has a hunched look, and with the bark on its stout trunk crusty and fissured, the tree looks and feels—in every sense—very old.

It is difficult to get anyone to accurately date this tree. It's about six meters high, has a girth at its base of nearly three meters, and a canopy roughly nine meters wide. Closest estimates are that it could be two hundred years old or even older. A number of people pronounce that it must be close to the end of its life, filling me with dread. I wonder if this is true or whether what I have observed of it over the last few dry months is suggestive of something else the kurrajong may have in mind. It has dropped its leaves more than once recently. The canopy is looking very bare; the leaves are small and delicate, rose and fire-tipped in contrast to the lustrous and muscular green ones on the other kurrajong nearby. It has also stopped supporting the far reaches of some of its branches, rendering them brittle and lifeless.

Is this a sign that the drought is hastening its progress towards an already imminent death? Or does the tree have a plan to economize and survive? These are not the only mysteries. On this voyage around the kurrajong, one question immediately cascades into another.

Luck is with me. I have unearthed a number of people who shed much light on what kurrajongs might have in mind. It seems I'm not the only one enthralled by them. Local ecologist Dave Carr weaves an optimistic tale. He describes kurrajongs as trees of antiquity—successful survivors from the time Australia was an extensive rainforest in the Gondwana days around sixty-five million years ago. Maybe rainforest origins explain the arresting lushness of this tree. The native olive at the kurrajong's flank is also a survivor from the same time, but it seems a flinty, stalwart plant. Perhaps the kurrajong doesn't mind sharing sustenance with its antediluvian friend.

Kurrajongs have been masters of adaptation, developing strategies to contend with an ever-drier climate. It has a single long and bulbous tap root which extends deep into the earth to draw up water. Most Australian trees have shallow, radial roots, Dave says. This tap root can store—camel-like—a considerable amount of water for times of need. These trees are known to be deciduous, especially during a dry spell. It certainly must have weathered many droughts during its sustained lifetime. But we are told that things are not as they used to be with our climate, and that's how it seems to me. When I was a child, a temperature of 30 degrees Celsius was freakish. Now, forty years later, 37 degrees is not uncommon.

Dave speaks of them "shutting down" during drought and on the more arid western slopes of New England, he has seen many kurrajongs discard all their leaves, sometimes never to recover. I feel relatively buoyed then by the presence of fresh leaves on this tree, but they are definitely more scant, so I wonder and worry.

And what are kurrajongs thinking by choosing to grow within the most inhospitable rocky outcrops? How do they get there? These questions have perplexed me most since first encountering this tree.

Their seeds are the size of small sultanas, so cannot be distributed on the wind. Dave says that the seeds are dispersed by birds, and those that fall beside stone will prosper in a number of ways, whereas the seeds that fall on open ground mostly die.

Peter Metcalfe—another helpful local naturalist—says there is a halo of moisture around the base of boulders. Dave comments that rocks also open up the earth below into cracks which allow much-needed oxygen into the soil for the growth of healthy root tissue, as well as seepage of water. Kurrajongs, while frost-resistant when older, are very tender when small. Seeds that fall beside stones survive, Dave also says, because the rock retains warmth and acts as a heat bank to protect the sensitive seeds and saplings.

Why are they so infrequent then, in this very rocky gorge country where I live?

The Oxley Wild Rivers gorge system dominates the weather around me. North-facing, the kurrajong inhabits its own micro-climate, along with a wealth of rare orchids and wildlife, such as the endangered brush-tailed rock- wallaby[7] that lives in a family pod nearby. As our block of land is heavily timbered and connects to the gorge, it forms a wildlife superhighway from the coast up onto the Northern Tablelands.

Dave tells me there are not many kurrajongs on the Eastern Fall. Higher up on the plateau of New England, they rarely appear at all due to the cold. They are most commonly found on the western slopes of the Great Dividing Range. Peter Metcalfe mentions mysteriously that some kurrajongs are "coming up from the coast." I am struck with images of Tolkien's Ents[8] on the move, but he must mean through the journeys of birds.

Andrew Huggett, ecologist, and ornithologist, is not sure whether kurrajongs are endemic to the Eastern fall region at all. He speaks of the dispersal of kurrajong seed by birds, both local and traveling through. The list he shares of likely bird species reads like poetry to me: satin bowerbird, australasian figbird, olive-backed oriole, crimson and eastern rosellas, Australian king-parrot, sulphur-crested cockatoo, white-headed pigeon, brown cuckoo-dove and the nomadic silvereye.

So, where has this tree come from?

It is by far the oldest kurrajong on our land and must be the grandmother of the very few trees nearby. We have perhaps six or seven kurrajongs on our block, all of which are on the sides of gullies rising up from the gorge, supporting the suggestion that that's where they came from. Andrew and I talk about taking DNA samples and comparing them with those of the trees from the foothills of the coastal ranges and from the western side of the Divide to divine their provenance.

Are kurrajongs outsiders here? Maybe this is why they strike such a lonely note in the landscape.

I live in a land of echoes. They move to their own music through the chasms, deep-funneled ravines forming a natural amphitheater carved out of rock by the headwaters of the Macleay River; Salisbury Waters, the Gara River, Mihi, and Blue Mountain Creeks tracing their way down to South West Rocks by the sea. The kurrajong stands in a hollow at the top of a crevasse facing the intersection of two of these tributaries.

Living here—separated by gorge and loss from the place where I was born—I continue to feel an intimate connectedness to steeped, ancestral stories which still reverberate through the passage of water and the wisdom of stone. I wonder if the kurrajong has perceived any of them.

Salisbury Waters runs past my mother's childhood home and into the gorge below the kurrajong, carrying with it the memories of many family celebrations. On the other side of the gorge from the tree, I lived on a cattle station, which my father's family owned for a century. All my childhood memories flow into creeks that empty into the Macleay River from the Eastern side. My family has made a pilgrimage every year since the days of horse and cart to the mouth of this river.

It is a land of mercurial weather; harsh hot winds from the northwest in summer are met the next day with soft, cooling mists creeping across the gorge from the east. New England normally gets its rain in the summer; effervescent cumulus nimbus clouds pumped with peach, apricot, and aubergine as lightning swivels around the compass points of our little cabin, thunder bass-booming in stereo around us. Living in such a climactic landscape, I wonder what visitors and their stories the kurrajong entertains, what change of worlds the mind of the ancient tree holds in memory; snow to drought, youth to maturity, Aboriginal to European.

Thunder is not the only music here. The gorge plays host to the meanderings of the superb lyre birds[9] who travel up the canyons into the fruitful humus lying in the wooded areas of our land. At any time of the day, especially during the cooler months, an attentive ear can catch the breath-taking sequence of calls of the lyre bird trying to lure a mate, Fairy Glen resounding with their cadence.

The howl of the dingo[10]—sadly now a more brutish hybrid than the elegancy of the pure Indigenous dog—is an eerie one. Mostly heard at night, when recently passing the kurrajong at around 9 am one morning, I was stopped by the forlorn wailing. The sound triggered a primal response; cavewoman hairs prickling on the back of my neck. There is a new dog fence on the very rim of the gorge just below the tree. Even so, they find holes in the fence and come through. Recently, neighbors have reported losing six hundred sheep to wild dogs.

One day I witnessed the protracted Yeatsian rape of a young wallaroo in the grasp of a terrifying old, black male.

My family and the kurrajong perch on the edge of the primordial.

This country also echoes with other massacres. Colonial history in New England is deeply stained with stories of invaders on killing sprees, including pushing Aboriginal people over the many cliffs that carve through the Tablelands. I haven't yet found specific stories relating to the cliffs below the kurrajong, but as a conspiracy of silence still pervades, who would know for sure? "Shoot, dig, bury, and shut-up as the Old Timers said about the blackfellas" a New England grazier once laughed over lunch.

Given its estimated age, it seems likely that the kurrajong would have memories of a time when Aboriginal people were custodians of this area. Louise Brennan—local historical researcher and descendant of the original Brennans who first came to Enmore in 1864—tells of terrain being taken up in the 1830s. She contends that this land "on the edge" might be border country between tribes, those living locally and those traveling up the gorge. She describes a Bora ground high on a mountain close by which remains mostly intact, evidence of the ceremonial significance of the area.

Eighty-five-year-old Cecil Briggs, Elder of the Gumbainggir nation, moved to Enmore in 1947 from the mountain country near Point Lookout. His family worked in the area for a number of decades, ringbarking trees and on the land generally. He recalls the old people talking often about kurrajongs, but the details escape him. Cecil tells of a Law Man, "fully initiated. A hundred and two years old, they said he was! He used to ride from Georges Junction in the gorge down near Kunderang and often he'd stop with us." He also recounts that while working here, he and his family saw stone axes all over Enmore.

Kurrajongs have a variety of uses for Aboriginal people. The local Aboriginal tribe, the Anaiwan, called the kurrajong *nangkata*.[12] The Gamilaroi—the Aboriginal people from the Western slopes where the kurrajongs are more prolific—have retained more words that relate to the tree, which they call *nhimin*.[13]

The seeds of the *nhimin* would have been eaten either raw or roasted, being very nutritious with high levels of protein, fat, zinc, and magnesium.[14] The gum from the tree was used as glue, while the soft fiber from the inner bark, *giyawaan,* was used as twine and cordage to make nets for catching fish, waterbirds, kangaroos ,and even emus.[15] The twine was also used to make dilly bags, rope, waistbelts, hairnets, and cords for necklaces, children's toys, and tied into a netted bag to carry a child on the back.[16] Kurrajong bark, or *muramin*, was used for shields that were painted with ochre designs.[17] The young roots, or *warran*, would have been eaten like a vegetable.

Some say that in some areas, the Aboriginal people subsisted wholly on water from kurrajong roots. One report stated that "water gushes out rapidly when the pieces of root are set on end, the roots yielding gallons in quantity."[18] Does this tree remember the Anaiwan or Gumbainggir passing by? Did it mind families beneath its generous branches?

Early explorers also record the nutritive benefits of the kurrajong. Ludwig Leichhardt, the German explorer and naturalist reputedly felt that the seeds "produced not only a good beverage with an agreeable flavour, but ate well and appeared to be very nourishing."[19] The seeds also make good flour with high protein.

The kurrajong is prized as an excellent fodder tree by pastoralists, and it appears that its striking shape is not due to natural forces. Major limbs have been lopped, the wounds now nubs of rounded tissue. I wonder how much the tree minded this. This tree has occasionally been associated with stock poisoning. Sheep have been known to develop trembling and a staggering gait, while lameness is said to occur in cattle. Concerns lie with the seeds, not the leaves. Maybe this is the kurrajong's revenge?

So how long ago was it lopped? It must have happened in the fairly distant past. In 2003, we bought this land from Kevin Brennan, relation of Louise Brennan and roughly the tenth landholder of our block. Now in his mid-eighties, Kevin and his wife Val held this land for nearly fifty years. Kevin remembers the old kurrajong intimately, as well as the other two kurrajongs not far away. I hear affection and reverence for the tree in his voice. He also remembers seeing it in flower.

Kevin says he never harvested it for stock fodder. He assumes it must have been lopped during his uncle's tenure here. He suspects this is also when many trees in the vicinity were also ringbarked. We both wince at the thought. The kurrajong must hold terrible memories of the sound of swinging blows from axes in these reverberative gullies.

The ringbarking might have occurred much earlier. Louise Brennan speaks of government policy from the early 1880s making it a condition of purchase that land be improved by clearing, among other requirements.

This policy continued some time into the twentieth century, and then the ringbarking continued "for the sake of it," as Louise said. Interestingly, a government gazette in 1895 enshrines protection of kurrajongs, prohibiting cutting them down.[20] In a time of such seemingly wanton destruction, it appears that even then, these magnificent trees exerted a mysterious power.

* * *

Dave Carr and I discuss the "thinking" of the kurrajong, what sort of mind it might have. He is of the view that it would have no central decision-making function, but instead, whole system intelligence, where roots, leaves, and bark are in a feedback loop, all sending and receiving messages to switch actions off and on within the tree. This would be prompted by a suite of chemicals and hormones in response to the physical environment.

Dave speaks of one especially fascinating hormone, auxin, which enables the limbs of the plant to sense gravity. The tallest shoot will produce more auxin, which then stimulates more growth at the expense of other shoots in the race for survival. It is this aspect of the kurrajong mind, Dave says, which explains why the trunk straightened itself after squeezing through its stone bed. He also says it is common for these trees to kill off extremities during drought.

I ask Dave if it's normal for an old tree to be barren. He replies that trees will keep trying to reproduce into old age, but maybe it doesn't want to commit the resources necessary to flower, which are significant. So, it seems the kurrajong does have a plan in mind to economize, and I hope, to survive.

* * *

The winter is upon us now. Two days ago, my children and I saw a solid dusting of snow on Mount Enmore, rising up behind where we live. I am heartened to see on my walk this morning that the tree didn't seem to mind the snow, and that the leaves are mostly green now.

There are many questions still outstanding for me about the mind of the kurrajong, here on the edge of the world. Deep-rooted on the very threshold of the gorge, it reaches far below the cleared pasture, connecting to virgin woodland close by, linking these mountains with the sea through Oxley Wild Rivers National Park. I continue to wonder what stories it receives, what messages it sends by birds, through the complex web of mycorrhiza, and on the wind beneath the brilliantly starred night-skies of New England.

This morning I was exhilarated to discover another kurrajong not far away, which I didn't know was there. It is jubilantly healthy. I feel more positive about my kurrajong making it through these times to see another summer when we all hope those blessed rains will fall again.

God's Prophet

There's no morning on that slope, east
against the day, all granite's flat
tree-crotchets of staccato in the dim.

One abuts a boulder; trunk slim
bark reptile-tight, a sinew strained
within the gristly eucalypts.

And far from grey! A crown
of lusty lime, quill-tipped
finger kisses with each waft.

Amid the arid, olive gums, this teen
in green looks on across the hollow
to the light, where vast-limbed

Grandmother stands squat
clinched and struck, her Moses
staff into the deep, cleaved

through stone. Alone, folioles drop
in copper clatter, gnarled arms retreat
with April's moisture from the slope.

In language of the ages
- quartz-sap, tap-root, lace-bark -
She's sending messages

by lyre bird, fungi filament
quoll, nomadic Silvereye
Rosella, Figbird, Oriole.

Maybe by that slate-dark Euro
tip-toed, tail in tripod then
languorous beneath the leaves

or on some ancient breeze;
a millennial shimmer, rainforest
glimmer. God's prophet

of vestal woodlands, sounding
through the lipped abyss and
down to the scourging sea.

CHAPTER 22

Linden Tree

Tilia cordata

Renata Buziak

Poland, as other places in its corner of the world, enjoys four distinct seasons, each offering its beauty and uniqueness in nature and activities around it. And so it goes that, at the mention of winter or spring, we as Poles can't help but be transported to the moments and places strongly connected with the beauty of each of these seasons.

Anyone with some connection to Polish soil and culture would know how the lipa tree also has a magical power of transporting one to a very special place. The place I am referring to is one that is heavy with the sweet scent of lipa's flowers: the place of long, warm summer nights, the place of longing and love. Such is the power of sweet lipa across the countryside and towns alike—wherever lipa is afforded space to stretch out her grand flowery limbs. Lipa shares its etymology with the month of July, which in Polish language is *Lipiec*, so you never have to think twice about when it flowers.

The lipa, or *Tilia cordata*, commonly referred to as a lime or linden tree, is a large tree typically reaching 20–40m in height, with oblique leaves densely covering its multitude of branches and providing an abundance of foliage and shade. Lipa can reach a considerable age, with records estimating that many trees around Europe are as old as at least one to three millennia, and some even older. The tree yields a delicate fragrance that emanates from its nectar-producing flowers, which are important for bees and are used in teas and tinctures (Figure 1).

Fig. 1: Renata Buziak, *Linden, Tilia Cordata*, 2019.

I was fortunate to grow up in the small town of Janów Lubelski in southeast Poland. The school year ends in June, with summer beginning on the 21st of the month. Summer in Janów during my primary school years was filled with fun, excitement, play, gardening, friends, and family visits. It seemed to last forever, with long carefree days filled with adventures with friends and siblings or biking through the fields and forest surrounding the town.

Each July, my family's summer vacation included a trip to Stojeszyn, a nearby village, where my mother's sister had lived with her family since she married a local farmer in 1959. The farm consisted of cultivated fields, vegetable gardens, and fruit-and-nut-producing orchards, as well as a pigsty with domestic animals, barns of hay, and sheds with farm machinery and firewood. We loved staying at the farm; there was so much to do and explore. You couldn't see the house from the road because of the fruit orchard located in the front part of the garden, which spanned almost the entire width of the property, something that was distinctly different from other farms along the road. We knew we had arrived when we saw the fruit trees, which we then climbed to pick some delicious plums, apples, and pears at different times of the year.

Our daily activities in summer embraced exploring the narrow, long, and seemingly never-ending fields; swimming in a river at the back of the barn; feeding farm animals such as pigs, horses, chickens, and ducks; weaving baskets; picking berries. Some of the activities were structured around helping with harvests or other farm work, and we learned a great deal about harvesting and preserving produce. Still, for us, this was mostly fun.

July was special though. In July, one of my favorite trees was in bloom! It was not just any tree or any flower—it was lipa. The long driveway on the left side of the orchard led to a courtyard, with the wooden farmhouse located to the right. This courtyard was separated for the above-mentioned farm animals and equipment by a high fence. When coming up the driveway, one saw an enormous, majestic lipa positioned on the left of the courtyard, almost on the boundary with the next farm. It was covered in thousands of sweet-scented flower clusters. Each year, it became a haven for honey bees, and its foliage created an abundance of welcome shade.

Our annual family gathering at the farm was centered around collecting lipa's sweet flowers.

My memories of these times are extremely vivid. To paint the scene, it's the middle of summer. The air is filled with the buzzing sound of thousands of bees and other insects. Their ensembles swiftly move in clouds of sweet-scented air around a multitude of grand limbs carrying infinite flower-clusters full of sweet nectar. The lipa stands strong and tall, her crown impossible to reach, yet she is gentle and caring, offering her delicate blossoms to heal our body and spirit. The harvesting of flowers is timed to ensure that the flowers are at their best for making lipa tea, a special tea for the whole family to drink throughout the cold Polish winter.

Once we collected the flowers, we would dry them at home on flat sheets of cloth, which would take up quite a lot of space—most of the balcony and along the windowsills. Most houses in Poland have huge windowsills and most people keep their flowerpots there. Mum's house was no exception and she loved her potted plants. The drying flowers would temporarily take over the space usually occupied by numerous potted plants. Once dried, all the flowers were bagged into canvas or paper bags and were ready for us to make lipa tea at any time. My mother would also pre-prepare tea mixes of selected teas to which she would add a large amount of lipa's flowers. Our home was full of dry—yet still sweet-scented—lipa flowers and visitors would always ask for Mum's delicious special tea. We would collect other herbs and flowers during the year, however, none of them had such an impactful presence as lipa.

This simple practice of enjoying the benefits of nature in my daily life has never left me, and it is the root of my keen interest and passion for Australian native plants and their use in healing and nourishing. It is a well-known fact that lipa's flowers possess healing properties, and they are used as herbal remedies in many cultures. Its mildly sweet and fragrant dried flowers have a pleasing taste in tea and contain antioxidants and essential oils. Lipa tea is used to treat colds, cough, fever, infections, inflammation, high blood pressure, headache, and as a diuretic, an antispasmodic and a sedative. The bark and wood of the lipa tree are also used in herbal medicine for liver and gallbladder disorders, while lipa charcoal is used to treat intestinal disorders, as well as topical skin problems. The leaf buds and young leaves are edible raw.

My maternal grandmother collected lipa flowers in her village when my Mum was a little girl, and my Mum recalls: "I remember lipa being used as medicine for both children and adults, but especially for children when they had a cold." Mum describes lipa's flowers as clusters of minute light yellow-colored blossoms, coming out of a little "nose-like" leaf (or a bract), that children loved to drop from heights as it behaved like a helicopter blade, rotating as it slowly fell to the ground. From afar, she could see the tree shining with its golden floral crown. When she was ten years old, my mother looked after her nieces and nephews on the farm in Stojeszyn. Even then, the tree was already huge, and "it felt good to hug it." She used to sit under the shade created by the masses of outstretched branches. Her brother-in-law, who was about forty at the time, remembered that this tree had been there since his very early childhood, so it was at least a century old. How much wisdom and knowledge can a hundred-year-old tree hold, every year caring and providing for people, animals, and insects?

Having been based in Queensland, Australia, since 1991, I hadn't seen *Tilia* trees here until a very recent visit to Tasmania. I have treasured my fond memories of the grand lipa in Stojeszyn, its flowers, the family rituals, and the special place lipa had in our home. My earlier experiences with the lipa tree and watching my mother prepare it as a tea that had a positive, healing effect on people have led me to create work that brings out the inner beauty of plants and that increases people's awareness and understanding of their healing properties. I feel comfortable around plants and sharing their stories through my images and videos, created with plants' natural process of decomposition. For over a decade, I have been collaborating with nature and working with organic processes by developing a technique I call the biochrome.[1] This process is based on an amalgamation of plant matter and photographic materials, which allows both to undergo mutual transformation over several weeks due to natural decay and biological and chemical reactions. This art-science-based process encourages appreciation of the importance and transformative power of decay and renewal and for making the invisible visible, especially through large-scale images and time-lapse videos. The resulting images, which include prints on paper, fabric, and glass, provide an alternative, abstract technique of depicting botanical specimens while bringing awareness to significant plants and their healing qualities. *The Lindens I, Tasmania* (Figure 2) is an image created through the biochrome process.

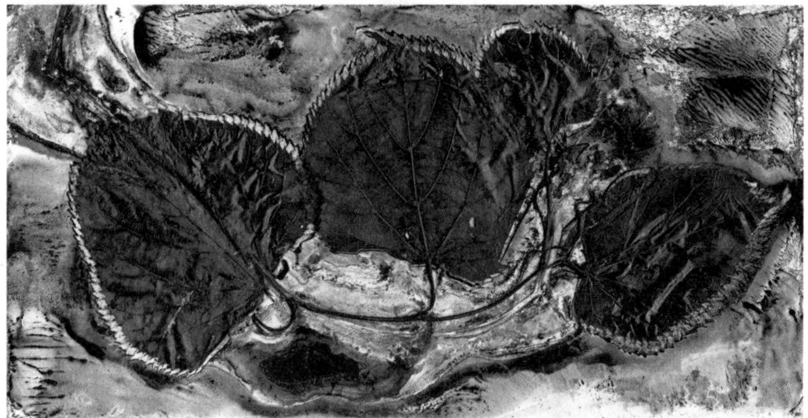

Fig. 2: Renata Buziak, *The Lindens I,* Tasmania, 2019.

Lipa has long been an inspiration for artists, writers, and musicians. One of Poland's most celebrated poets, Jan Kochanowski, wrote about lipa. His most famous writing on this topic is the poem "Na Lipe" ("On the lime tree") from 1584, which includes a phrase encouraging us to relax and rest under the tree's grand shade. In Australia, the renowned vocalist and musician Nick Cave has written a song titled "Lime Tree Arbour," which features the linden or lime tree, and his focus on the lime tree led him to plant "Nick's Lime Tree" at the Victorian Royal Botanic Gardens, on Picnic Pond in the Winter Garden. A different species from the one in Stojeszyn, it is called Henry's Lime, *Tilia henryana*. I am looking forward to visiting Nick's lime tree when I'm next in Melbourne.

When my sister Dorota recently moved to Tasmania, I thought that there most likely would be a linden tree in the Royal Botanic Gardens, or in a park somewhere, given that the climate there is close to that of Melbourne. The Gardens' website indicated the presence of linden trees, and when my sister and I visited Hobart, we did find a large tree, approximately 20m tall, with outstretched branches to about a 20m diameter. Since the tree only had fresh buds, we needed confirmation that it was what we were looking for. One of the botanists from the gardens confirmed that it was a broad-leaf linden tree, *Tilia platyphyllos*, which together with *Tilia cordata* are the parent trees to other species—such as *Tilia x europaea*, also located in the Gardens, as well as in St. David's Park in Hobart.

When Dorota mentioned the story to one of her new colleagues, Jill, it led to a fascinating new connection. Jill's family property, located close by, not only features several linden trees but is also called "The Lindens!" When I arrived in Launceston to visit Dorota, I could not believe my eyes when I noticed a book on the kitchen table titled *Under the Linden Trees*.[2] It was written by members of Jill's family, namely Mike Vanderkelen and Brad Saunders, who published their memories of people and events at "The Lindens," which was established in 1895. As their book states, "The property takes its name from a slow-growing tree of European origin." [3] These trees (Figure 3), which were already on the property prior to the family's occupancy, had a significant presence in their daily life and annual family events. Just like the lipa in my childhood, these trees were an inspiration and provided a place of fun activities for children: "For the tree-climbing

Fig. 3: Dorota Piechocinski, *At The Lindens*, 2019.

exploits of many young visitors, the lindens were indeed grand trees, stimulating a kid's imagination by creating a world that was separate from the ground beneath."[4] After reading some of the accounts and seeing photographs of the farm, including the linden trees, I decided I had to go see for myself and explore the trees which, as a photograph caption states "more than a century after they were planted, the slow growing linden trees seem a permanent fixture to the family members."[5] Sheryn Brooks also recalls that "many of my cousins have carved their names in the tree over the years and it is symbolic of their time spent at the farm. It was a wonderful tree to climb and many of us have had huge enjoyment out of doing so ... the Lindens is a home and it holds a special place in the hearts of the Hall descendants, farm hands and family friends."[6] This recalls the way that lipa held a special place in the hearts of my family when we were together in Poland.

My visit to The Lindens was very rewarding. I met Geraldine, who has resided on the property since 1970 and takes very good care of her garden. She was pleased to learn about my lipa story, the possibility of making her own linden flower tea, and for me to create an artwork from the lindens' foliage. The trees were almost bare when I visited in early October, as it was still just the beginning of spring in Tasmania. Therefore, Jill had to collect some fresh foliage with buds in November, when the trees were full of large round leaves, and post them to me. In my studio, I combined the delicate plant samples with pre-prepared analog photographic materials, providing plenty of water to keep them moist. This technique activates the natural process of decomposition and encourages microbial and fungal activities, which penetrate the layers of color emulsions. Allowing for the process to continue over a period of time leads to the transformation of media, and this biochrome process results in a document of the activities that take place during this "long exposure." The final image is also an abstract depiction of a plant, such as *Linden in Scottsdale, Tasmania* (Figure 4), which was created from foliage sourced from The Lindens.

In addition to the experience at The Lindens, my recent search for linden trees in Queensland has taken me to Toowoomba, just a couple of hours drive west of Brisbane. Joan, my friend Joanne's mother, has lived in

Fig. 4: Renata Buziak, *Linden in Scottsdale,* Tasmania, 2019.

Toowoomba her entire life, and through her love of nature—and especially orchids—she was able to find a linden tree there. I drove to Toowoomba to meet Joan and to collect linden leaves and flowers for artmaking and for tea. Images created from this particular tree include a biochrome *Linden, Lipa, in Toowoomba,* 2019 [Figure 5]. It is fascinating how sharing my childhood stories of lipa has led me to meet many plant-loving people who have been

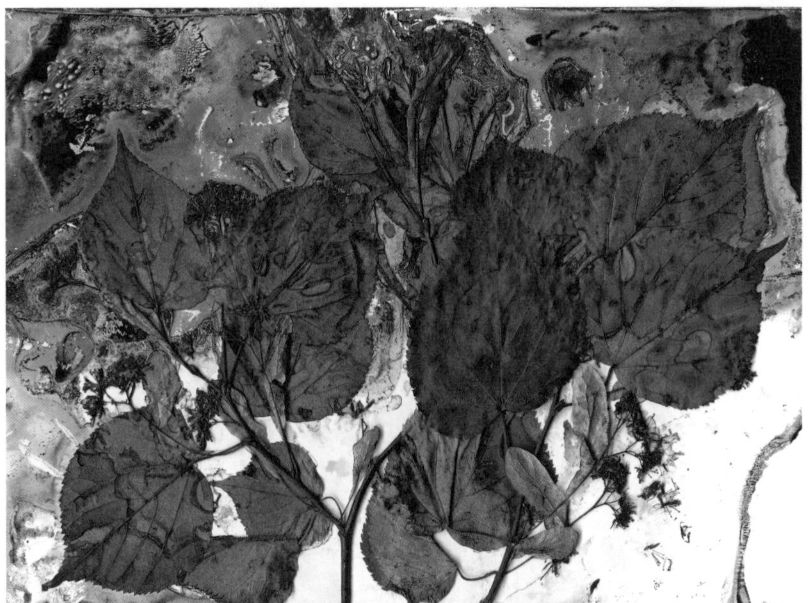

Fig. 5: Renata Buziak, *Linden, Lipa, in Toowoomba-Qld,* 2019.

excited to assist me in my search for these trees and to share their stories and plants with me.

The most wonderful aspect of the lipa tree is the connection it affords me with my mother and my grandmother, and the way the memory of its fragrance and beauty also brings me closer to my family through these shared memories we hold together—of climbing and growing and smelling and watching its preparation into a healing tea. Through my childhood experiences, I learned that plants could bring comfort and shared pleasure, and this has permeated my work and life. It encourages me to share this feeling with others, to remind them that we can take comfort and solace by being in nature and by surrounding ourselves with the beautiful fragrances from the flowers of these trees we hold so dear.

Special acknowledgments to my Mother Julianna and sisters Dorota and Iwona for their input to this story.

POEM 7

Mangrove

Rhizophora mangle

▪ **Stuart Cooke**

through the slops of mud, mud-
lobsters slouch, crabs
munch leaves, seedlings, make mulch
for the mangal, this dark
and sloppy ballroom:

youm breed sediment

in Tamil Nadu, in Vietnam
Thailand and the Philippines
in Cambodia's Kompong Sammaki , youm produce

shorebirds nest with crab-
ish, rawns and ails
galaxies in yourm pockets
forest, souls of countless
coastal rainforest, sea of forest, salt

this rule:
no breath without yourm pithy pillars
chart of charts   of sacrifice
monotonous mangal   no revolution of day
into days

we threaten youm more than most:

of beige jellyfish
places, collect bits
scavenge metals still the swells to build

for hotels, for shrimp farms
though we've removed most
for the cans thrown into yourm forest
youm confront the ocean, translate it
fish, crustacean, coastline

youm blossom for the fruit bat
above turtles, lizards and fishing cats
monkeys, proboscis monkeys

algae and barnacles gather
around yourm quiet feet
where sponges anchor
and feed
and the bruised nails of oysters
cut the soles of shoes

firstly, yourm charcoal genius, then
hotels steal yourm mosquito chatter
we kill light, fill yourm lungs with smog
youm sink sewage, toxic seepage
pesticides and herbicides, crude oil clogs
the lenticels of youm souls

yourm remains span the planet
saline coastal tropical sub-tropical

youm sip brackish fluid
super-briny fluid concentrated
by evaporation
woody, specialised, youm live on the edges
the brackish lands between fish and plants
between bodies and constellations

star fixed on the chin of the sky
aquatic beats, the stilled mind
exposed to the sway
saline mangal, shrubland coastal
fine judgements, organic contents
stalls withdrawing in the rush

boiled and desiccated in the low
flooded with salt in high tide
thinnest niche

warm   sheltered shorelines all over the world
estuarine
packed into deltas of large Asian rivers
sludgy, swampy places
where low tide shows yourm

an out-
spectres surveying
cities of spires
those great alien spikes in
into gnarled trunks
chunky arteries rise

of salinity, of temperature
most motley moistures, broadest spectrum
yourm scrawny, most porous ontology
then flooded and cooled once more

roots rise from the brain
hunting for the membrane
for aerial lanes, pneumatophores
soil straws, rubbery
wooden axons covered
in lenticels, poking their thin
knobby conks with oyster
dragon's teeth shell callouses, stilt
prop, snorkel or peg type
knee, ribbon or plank type
breathing roots, buttresses
and above-ground roots, knee and
ribbon and buttress combinations
at the base, roots
full of aerenchyma
roots as stilts, as support
going tide as negotiators between tree & sea
aerial roots and tap roots filter out the salt
roots snake around with the upward loops, rising
rising from the brackish weaves, their
ferreting endings, incessant willows woven
and reedy, needy needles, weedy
thoughts scratched through salt

impervious to verge
youm explode like a nova, like a trauma
wanding magically from fidgeting structure
youm taught termites that essence
shatters into twenty feet
of splintered skeleton

but youm diverge

dropped root
youm reached for sludge
through months and months
through dormancy
through desiccation
tirelessly travelling
synthetic sustenance
ready to go, photo-
propagated propagules
viviparous
and froth dots
sun dots
on home currents
germinating seeds
millions of years ago
and flowed west
where youm proliferated
in south-east Asia
mangal mecca's

hangers, tyres & bottles
fishing out coat
James Cameron saw yourm limbs
tubular piles, the art's apart from either
squiggling, mounting
with yourm revolving shadow
naming the afternoon
youm loom in packs
and stinging sunlight
to anaerobic soils
to salinity, to inundation
convergent in yourm solutions

scales of names, their numbers
column of noon
solar arrow
its condensation doubles into zodiac
of evaporating, scarlet plasma
their claws frame a wall
the soggy blades, land spirits
the law weighs on yourm lashes
crystal crusts on grey leaves
the cusp of mangal
above and below

perception ever

in zonations

yourm multiplying adaptations
expand swamp sanity, fertile tones
speckled and sluggish
propped above the low with stilt roots

bottle ottle blottle lottle   blink lack blind bog   blurrp blirrup blottle

youm won't listen to sodium, youm store it
in vacuoles, in glands
at the base of leaves, beards
of floury crystals
saltless sap, shed yourm leaves &
their salt, restrict stomata
fussy for carbon, close yourm pores

pneumatophores, or
so youm turn to the atmosphere with
methane and sulphides, kill yourm loam
soluble iron, inorganic phosphates
bacteria free nitrogen
hard to find but anaerobic

poking, the unsettled levels lungfuls through bark
youm fish for oxygen, drag it under
exclude sodium with

at least three senses:
the mangrove forest
the mangrove swamp
and mangrove forest biome

the habitat
the entire plant assemblage
the mangal
all trees and large shrubs
in the mangrove swamp
the family,
youm feed on iron, store gases at yourm sources
silently, the grim consoler
of sulphur tears, conducting
at low ebb, carefully

ultrafiltration

youm came to English from Spanish
via Portuguese
origins in Guaraní
mangled into grove
mangle
mangue
mangrow

about 110 species of mangroves

in the sense
that a tree grows
in a saline swamp

but only a few are
rhizophora
the trees of the genus rhizophora
the rhizophoraceae

like red mangrove, rhizophora mangle

red mangroves, rhizo-, rhizo-

˜This poem was first published in Stuart Cooke, *Lyre* (Crawley, WA: UWA Publishing, 2019), 41–50. The poem is reprinted here with kind permission of the press.

CHAPTER 23

Northern Red Oak

Quercus rubra

Susan Prescott

On my bedside table is an old-fashioned alarm clock. And an acorn from a northern red oak in the Catskill Mountains of upstate New York. These have replaced my smartphone, now banished from my sleeping space. One glance at the acorn and I am transported to the incredible forest of hardwoods, my spiritual home. It is the beginning of summer, and everything is green, lush, and bursting with life. Dappled light reaches through. A soft floor of old fallen leaves, gently cushioning each footfall. Sound tenderly muted by the great canopy. Senses heightened. Mindful. Vibrant. Clarity. Truly aware. Of myself and my surroundings. In ways, I have not felt in far too long. A crystal stream. A crashing waterfall. The air is dancing with the unseen energy of connectivity. Sheer joy. The anxieties of life melt away. Peace. Calm. Simplicity. My worries gone. The past dissolved. I'm truly in the moment. Yet this present contains within it a vast possibility and hope for the future—just as the acorn contains all the knowledge, all the potential, of the oak. It is still connected to the forest where it found me. And through it, so am I.

ALL THINGS GREAT AND SMALL

As an immunologist and a pediatrician, my work is centered on how the world within us is influenced by the world around us. And, in particular, how our early experiences and exposures can shape our destiny. It can be a highly reductionist perspective for many. But, for me—also an integrationist—it is a way of showing how everything is connected, from large-scale ecology to the smallest yet still complex ecosystems we depend on within our own bodies.

And those smallest living parts we depend on are microbes—the foundations of all ecosystems. From every forest habitat to the myriad of ecological niches in and on our own bodies, all forms of life depend on microbes. Through the lens of the microbiome, we are discovering that we are dynamically connected to and interacting with our environment in ways we had never suspected.[1] And most of these effects are mediated through our immune system, which monitors, regulates, and connects all aspects of physical and mental health. It is the great connecter. Through the language of modern science, which we now hold sacred, we are beginning to listen and see the complex interdependence of natural systems that we have overlooked in our eagerness to exploit them. Through this new lens of interconnectivity, we are beginning to see how the erosion of social, economic, and political ecosystems is affecting macrobiomes and microbiomes alike, at the expense of both personal and planetary health.[2]

I chose the northern red oak (*Quercus rubra*), or it chose me because of the powerful emotional response I had the first time I "got lost" in the forest, near where my husband grew up. Its quiet mystery was so different from where I grew up in outback Australia. It was so foreign, yet so familiar. I loved the vastness of the trees and the smallness of the acorns and tiny willing seedlings. I felt the connectivity of the forest like a loving family. I am no expert in trees or plant biology. Here, I use this tree as my totem and my guide to view the world from the vantage point of inherent connectivity.

Humanity, as a worldwide network, is really not so different from the forest systems that protect the young and the vulnerable for the well-being of the whole ecosystem—for its future health and prosperity. These instincts still prevail in all of us. Instincts that were of high order in the value systems of traditional societies, prioritized and revered. To break with these values is to break with nature, and to break with nature is to undermine our own future. And yet, this is what we have done—the Anthropocene is an era of profound ecological imbalance. The adverse effects of human activity are reflected in the health of all systems on all scales.[3]

We may yet hope to transition to a new Epoch of mutualistic collaboration, from the Anthropocene to what some have described as the hope of the Symbiocene.[4] By emulating the mutualistic dynamics of nature, such as the sharing of resources, we are taking steps to strengthen society as a whole and the value systems that govern our attitudes and interactions with the world around us. We will do well to place greater value on stories of symbiosis, learn from them, and make them as our own.

These truths are alive and in action in every aspect of the great forests. Everything is seeking its place in the balance, as its wholeness adapts to changing conditions and new inhabitants. Even in the apparent stillness, as I stand under a great oak tree, I can almost feel every molecule of a dynamic unseen exchange in the air, beneath the soil, beneath the bark—as it is inviting me to be part of its story.

LIVING IN SYMBIOSIS—LESSONS FROM WITHIN

Nowhere is symbiosis more apparent than in the relationship between humans and our own microbes. Only recently have we begun to understand that the story of symbiosis, like so many others, has been occurring on many levels—and that not all of these have been visible to us. What has been revealed at a microscopic level shows us most clearly how interconnected and interdependent we really are with the environment.

One of the most fascinating parts of this story is how species extinction is affecting us all personally. It has been a revelation to understand that the *large-scale* threats to biodiversity and environmental ecology are also mirrored by the loss of biodiversity and extinction of species at the *microscopic* level. This includes the microbes that inhabit forest niches, as well as those in our own bodies, and which are essential to our own health. "Dysbiosis" is a term that is used to describe the disruptions in the natural ecology in microbial ecosystems. It literally translates to mean "life in distress," which applies to virtually all forms of life on our planet today.[5]

To understand the origins and the significance of this relationship, we must remember that life on Earth began with the simple microbes which emerged from the "primordial soup" 3.5 billion years ago. These were much like the cyanobacteria (blue-green algae) that form the rock-like stromatolite structures we can still see today in Shark Bay, Western Australia, not far from where I was born—still, fortunately, one of the world's greatest remaining biodiversity hotspots. Microbes have since formed the foundations of all life on our planet and still contribute a significant portion of the Earth's biomass. It has been estimated that the Earth is home to upward of 1 trillion microbial species. All more complex life forms, including ourselves, co-evolved with microbes in symbiotic mutualism. Microbes are essential to the biodiversity that sustains all life. They are "everywhere" as an integral part of all ecosystems. In fact, the interactions between microbes and their hosts underpin evolutionary success throughout the biosphere. These symbiotic relationships are key to adaptability and resilience. They are actually an essential "part" of our bodies. Without microbes, we cannot survive, and neither can the forest.

We only recently came to realize that at least half of the cells in our bodies are microbes, and they contribute at least 90% of "our" genetic material—microbial genes and by-products that are metabolically active and influence many of our body systems, including our immunity, our appetite, fat and sugar metabolism, even our mood and behavior. From that perspective, we are indeed "more microbial than we are human." It also means we are in constant "flux" with our environment. Indeed, at the microscopic level, all living creatures are home to many vast and diverse ecosystems on all of our inner and outer surfaces. And—for animals and plants alike—these microbial ecosystems are highly vulnerable to subtle changes in the wider environment.

This is significant because environmental degradation, loss of biodiversity, and displacement of "green" space by urban "grey" space are associated with changes in environmental bacteria—together with the more obvious visible damages. As such, grey space is more than the mere loss of "greenness."[6] It includes the many other damaging activities that displace nature and erode human health, including industrial and commercial activity, major transportation routes, bars, liquor stores, convenience stores, fast-food outlets, tobacco vendors, noise stress, excess light at night, marketing billboards, and sidewalk signs, which all *deliberately* promote unhealthy behavior for commercial profit.[7] Most of these negative pressures are greatest in the socially disadvantaged populations.[8]

Living in progressively more "westernized" conditions—disconnected from healthy natural ecosystems—has been associated with the ecological "extinction of microbes," including our own. For example, some species of intestinal bacteria seen in traditional human communities are no longer evident in Western populations or are reduced below detectable functional level. This shift in microbial ecology has been associated with higher rates of obesity, diabetes, asthma, and many other inflammatory diseases. It reveals that the dramatic changes in human activity are affecting ecology on every level, from threatened extinction of plant, insects, and animal species, to the loss of the smallest creatures that form the basis of all life—in the wider environment and in our own bodies. We depend on them all.

In fact, most of the factors we already know are eroding human health, are also adversely affecting our microbes—including pollutants, antibiotics, changes in agricultural practices, unhealthy, highly processed foods, stress, alcohol, physical inactivity, and disruption in sleep and circadian rhythms (light pollution at night). These factors are all driving "dysbiotic drift."[9] The commercial forces that promote the consumption of unhealthy products (alcohol, tobacco, unhealthy foods) are adding to both the environmental burden of production and the economic costs of the diseases that they produce. As a whole, "grey space" is unbalanced, unhealthy, and self-destructive.[10] Life in distress. The opposite of symbiosis, the mutualism of natural law.

This is a matter of ecological justice.[11] And we must think of ecological justice broadly—it is not merely limited to environmental justice but extends into much wider issues of social justice. We already know that human populations are not affected equally by environmental degradation. And they are not affected equally by the health consequences of dysbiotic drift. The burden is always greatest for the poor. And not only do disadvantaged populations have less opportunity for health they are also the direct targets of multinational profiteers geared not only to unhealthy product delivery but to the potentially even greater profit from medications and treatments needed to cure the obesity-, alcohol-, and tobacco-associated lifestyle diseases. This profound, deliberate damage seems even more obscene when viewed through the eyes of the forest—how far we have moved away from the wisdom of mutualism seen in nature.

Again, this can also be seen at the microbial level, with evidence that residents of socially disadvantaged neighborhoods in North America (lower socioeconomic status) have reduced diversity of colonic microbiota. There is growing concern that the disappearance of beneficial microbes and expansion of less beneficial microbes may be implicated in the rise of many modern diseases.[12] We may not be able to recover what has been lost, but we can aim to find a healthier equilibrium. Yet, it makes absolutely no sense to remedy this through purely pharmacological solutions, marketing costly lab-generated "microbial products" to individuals without addressing the wider economic forces driving dysbiotic drift.[13]

THE HEALING ELIXIR OF NATURE

The forest is healing. To describe nature as a "healing elixir" is neither hyperbole nor an exaggeration. We can all relate to how refreshed we feel when we get out into nature, or even the local park—an antidote to the stress of modern life. The research and the data support this: natural environments improve concentration, cognition, facilitate physical activity, encourage social cohesion, and promote overall health and mental well-being.[14]

These positive effects are seen whether we encounter nature in "wild" undisturbed environments or in gardens and parks designed and sustained by humans in urban settings. Even in cities, our general residential proximity to green space is associated with lower mortality. Simply having a window view of nature and indoor potted plants makes a difference to our sense of well-being, mood, and workplace performance. We even sleep better. A lunchtime walk in nature will improve our sleep at night, compared to a similar walk in a built environment. And sleeping better is important to keep impulsivity in check, as it enables us to better visualize what we need to do for the future without being overwhelmed. Even a weekly visit to an outdoor green space for 30 minutes can significantly reduce depression and hypertension. These benefits can be measured biologically in reductions in stress hormones and inflammation.[15]

There are many scientific explanations for why we feel physically better in the natural world, including airborne chemicals released by plants, natural light, negative ions, sounds, tactile opportunities, and non-pathogenic microbes. For society as a whole, the benefits of green space extend to greater altruism, helping behavior, and cementing social values. All of these benefits are especially relevant for disadvantaged communities. More equitable access to greenspace (and diminishing urban blight) can be an important strategy for reducing physical and mental health inequalities.

In all this, we should not underestimate the power of nature to build resilience through inspiration and positive emotions. Awe can be routinely primed by experiencing nature or merely seeing *images* of natural environments. These feelings are powerfully connected to our emotional well-being, mindfulness, and patience. We feel much more satisfied with life. And we are inspired to be more innovative and creative. When we feel awe and wonder, we are more open to learning and opportunity. And in the modern rush, where there seems never to be enough time, the feelings of being awe-inspired by nature expand our perception of the passage of time.

All of these observations—extending from the research data to our own personal experience—underscore the imperative for preserving nature and providing natural sanctuaries within urban environments as a priority, not only for our own physical and mental health but for our society at large. This can be a major step toward reducing health inequalities due to social disadvantage and broadly improving mental health, optimism, and social awareness across populations.[16] We will all be healthier and happier if we can rediscover nature and "return to the forest" whenever we can.

FROM THE BEGINNING

The foundations of all aspects of health are laid in early life for animals and plants alike. For humans, this includes physical and emotional assets, attitudes, and lifestyle behaviors that can influence lifelong health.[17] The ecology of the early environment—ranging from microbial exposure, nutritional patterns, and social interactions—can have lasting effects on a wide range of immune, metabolic, and neurodevelopmental pathways that influence resilience and/or long-term susceptibility to disease. It is now clear that early exposure to natural environments, including the associated immune-protective microbes, is associated with a reduced risk of metabolic and immune diseases in children. These benefits begin in pregnancy. Contact with green space is associated with better, healthier pregnancy outcomes, good mental health and resiliency against depression, and protecting the next generation against asthma.[18]

There are also benefits for academic performance in children.[19] Increasing outdoor playtime and reducing screen time improves school achievement and sleep quality. Classroom views over green space have multiple benefits for cognitive development, performance, attention, and resilience to stress. Even having potted plants in learning environments can improve memory recall. Environmental cues and time spent in nature are key determinants of health and health behaviors, including food choices and physical activity. Nature contact also promotes emotional assets, environmental concern, and prosocial attitudes. It has implications for healthy microbial diversity and immune and metabolic health.

Importantly, perceptions, attitudes, and awareness of nature—so-called "nature relatedness"—are shaped by experiencing it at a young age. That means *early* experience pays forward to greater interest in and desire for nature contact. And this is consistently linked to mental well-being, less youth aggression, less fast food consumption, less screen time, more physical activity—all the things associated with better health. Moreover, there is a greater affinity for nature and a desire to care for it. It is more important than ever for our children to develop a relationship with the forests—they are less likely to preserve what they have never known.

As nature is eroded, so are our opportunities to experience awe. It is becoming harder to reach the forest. And harder to see the stars. In fact, the stars are now hidden from more than one-third of humanity by urban light pollution. Now 60% of Europeans and 80% of North Americans can no longer see the Milky Way. While we might yet find sources of awe and wonder in other places, a generation of children who have never seen the stars is an unseen, unnoticed tragedy. Yet it is one forewarned in the 1960s by Rene Dubos, who recognized the deep cost of the "extinction of experience," where eventually, we may not even know what we have lost.[20]

These observations raise obvious concerns about the effect of progressive urbanization on these vital relationships with nature, especially in children. The dramatic increase in childhood diseases—including obesity, allergy, emotional and developmental disorders—is inextricably linked to the multifaceted changes in modern environments and patterns of leisure activities of families and young children. In particular, the shift away from active, outdoor, nature-based activities is implicated as a foundational factor driving many other risk factors, including a lack of physical activity, screen time and other passive, sedentary activities, poor nutrition, and insufficient quality and/or quantity of sleep.

Again, social disadvantage, neighborhood safety, and walkability are critical to this conversation—children and their families are less likely to seek time in nature or be physically active when they are living in less affluent, less walkable, less safe neighborhoods. Instead, they are more likely to have a higher daily screen time.[21] Again, this underscores that equitable access to nature and greenspace is a matter of both social and ecological justice.

Collectively, these observations have been the basis for simple "experiential" interventions in children to promote nature-relatedness and associated wellness behaviors. Notably, one such study in Hong Kong pre-schoolers showed that connecting families with nature could positively influence the dietary and physical activity habits of urban pre-schoolers. Using a randomized controlled trial design in 102 families, researchers tested a healthy lifestyle intervention program, including outdoor playtime, a short discussion on health/environmental topics, food activities (play with and taste vegetables), and nature discovering (touch, listen, smell, see, and feel nature). After the 10-week intervention, the children (average age of 36 months) were more connected to nature (especially in their sense of environmental responsibility), more active, and had improved eating habits and physical functioning.[22] These preliminary results highlight the potential impact of simple, early interventions to promote connectedness to nature.

Ongoing studies by this group and others are examining the associated benefits of "nature interventions" on the developing microbiome and systemic markers of immune development. There is already preliminary evidence that contact with soil and plant materials leads to an immediate increase in the diversity of skin microbiota.

IT'S ALL CONNECTED

The symbiotic relationships between humans and microbes are among numerous examples of the vast and complex interrelationships on our planet, many of which we have been unaware of. In fact, many new discoveries are overturning the long-held polarized view that the evolution of life has been solely driven by the competitive struggle between species.

Importantly, we see recurring patterns within patterns. At the more tangible end of the spectrum, we see biological stories of symbiosis at the "micro" level echoed across the "macro" scale. The specifics of each environment vary and bring richness and diversity, but the same principles apply. Even on the less tangible spiritual level, we see that the pathways and patterns of our individual personal growth are also reflected in the pathways to the collective growth of humanity as a whole. As we understand that these things are all interconnected, that should be no great surprise. It is true to say that the *biological* health of both humans and our environment *depends* on our *spiritual* evolution toward greater love and respect for each other and the natural world.

Dysbiosis, life in distress, reverberates on every scale, echoed from climate change to epigenetic effects on our DNA, which carry the effects of environmental degradation to the next generations. Inflammation, immune dysregulation, is now the greatest threat to human health—as both a reality and a metaphor for dysbiotic planetary systems and social conflict. We are consumers, addicted to technology and slowly consumed by it. We have forgotten our purpose, our story, and our roots. Our relationship with nature is broken, yet it will be our savior. More than ever, we need to find ecological solutions to personal and planetary health and take the lessons of symbiosis and mutualism that nature still has to offer all around us. What we might learn from nature, large and small, we might apply to society and to ourselves. In this, we can hope to regrow our purpose and our story.

We are part of an interconnected life force—a power grid of wonder. We like to see ourselves as separate from it, but we're not. And it's about time we realized it, not just intellectually, but by living and breathing it as part of our whole reality. We are surrounded by an incredible intelligence that we have underestimated, dissected, and damaged in our ignorance.

Conversations like this are not welcome in patriarchal "halls of science," which value dispassionate lifeless discourse over feelings of awe and wonder. They strip out passion and excitement for life, or at least separate and compartmentalize it. But that is not life. If we have learned anything, it is that the answers do not lie in reductionism. The persistent dogmatic views that we must "isolate" factors to examine the effects immediately alters their effects and fails to recognize their influence as part of the whole system. This limited perspective misrepresents both the value and role of the "parts" as well as the complex beauty of the "whole."

Nature, especially plants, has provided us with food, shelter, and warmth. And with every macronutrient, micronutrient, antioxidant, and phytochemical for our health, including the very air we breathe. We have learned to translate the properties of nature into anti-inflammatories, antibiotics, and all manner of drugs. Yet, we no longer revere nature the way our ancestors did. Instead, we see only a resource for energy, technology, growth and proliferation. For centuries our efforts to tame and restrict nature have intensified. We have failed to appreciate our interdependence on natural systems at all scales, from the planetary systems that sustain life to the microorganisms at the foundation of all ecosystems. We are now paying the price for our clumsy, thoughtless, and greedy destruction of our physical and our mental health. We develop new drugs for lifestyle diseases without addressing their root causes, many of which stem from ecological imbalance across all scales, and our disconnection or disharmony from nature. Nature gives; we take. And yet we lose.

We have the power to make the transition from the Anthropocene to the more mutualistic age of the "Symbiocene"—but this fundamentally depends on changing our attitudes and our relationship with nature. This kind of "evolution" will depend on the power of ideas and imagination.[23] While biological evolution depends on genes and takes millennia, an idea can rapidly transform the nature, characteristics, and behavior of individuals and society. That is what is needed now: a vision of the future that fully recognizes our origins and connections to the Earth.

Our ancestors lived intimately connected to nature, as *part* of it, absorbing the finest details of plants, of rocks, of animals, of everything. Life was fully dependent upon knowing nature. They had the wisdom of balance, the wisdom of interdependence. This knowledge was not merely intellectual; it was also at the very heart of their purpose and spirituality. There is much we can yet learn from the surviving traditional cultures which still hold this knowledge before that too might be lost. Nature is forgiving, patient, and resilient. She is offering us solutions if we are wise enough to take them.

And so, my mind returns to the waiting forest, with overgrown paths and mysterious centuries-old crumbling rock walls weaving between the oaks. I think of the lives and secrets of forgotten settlers still cradled in the living memory of the timeless forest, of the potential promised by each new acorn and by each new generation. So many have moved to the cities, while nature remains in her quiet, serene beauty, waiting for those of us who might return to share and to learn. In those moments, I feel part of her great oneness. I know I will always return to those moments for the rest of my life. I will return to where I feel the mind of trees touch and enfold the mind of everything. The mind of me.

CHAPTER 24

Olive Tree

Olea europaea[1]

Patrícia Vieira

As lunchtime approached, my attention span dwindled. I turned away from the messages piling up in my mailbox waiting to be answered, looked around the room distractedly, and wondered: What should I eat today? A wholesome salad that would fulfill my five fruit and vegetables daily quota? A nourishing fare of baked sole fish and potatoes? Or should I go all the way and make a hearty seafood rice stew? As I settled for the fish, the salad too light for my appetite, and the stew too demanding for my limited lunch cooking time, I reflected that all three dishes share the same key ingredient: olive oil. An ever-present element of Portuguese cuisine, olive oil is used for seasoning, frying, baking, and pretty much everything else in between.

Not much of a cook, I focused on getting my lunch right. Fortunately, it was a dish well-suited to my limited skills. I lay the fish on the baking tray with a few bits of rosemary on top, placed the sliced potatoes around it, sprinkled it with sea salt, and, lastly, generously poured olive oil onto everything. While enjoying the fish half an hour later, I honed in on the strong taste of the oil that took me right back to my childhood. The gesture of reaching out for the olive oil bottle in the kitchen, the cruet set on the table, feels almost as natural as breathing. I have seen my parents and grandparents do it, and now I regularly add olive oil to most of what my son eats. Why is this liquid fat so much a part of my life?

As I started researching the subject, I found that the Portuguese are the 4th biggest per capita olive oil consumers in the world, each person using on average about 16 lbs per year—behind only Italians, Spaniards and, the absolute winners, the Greeks, who gulp down a staggering 39 lbs of olive oil per person. When did Portugal's dependence on olive oil begin? And why do the Portuguese, like most other Mediterranean peoples, value the olive tree and its oil so much?

The following day I embarked on a trip to find out more about the roots of the olive tree in my native country. Driving north from Lisbon to get to Bobadela's Olive Oil Museum, I racked my brain in an effort to piece together the scattered references to olive oil and olive trees I have encountered throughout my career as a literature scholar. The first reference that comes to mind is the olive tree branch a dove brought back to Noah in the Book of Genesis. A sign that the waters from the great flood were receding and, therefore, that God had reconciled with His Creation, the olive branch has been regarded ever since as a symbol of peace.

Could this be the underlying reason why I planted an olive tree in my garden to celebrate my son's first birthday? At the time, I did not make the connection. I had always liked olive trees, their sturdy trunk, their perennial green-greyish leaves, and their unmenacing but quietly determined demeanor. And given that an olive tree does not reach its full productivity until it is about thirty-five years old and can live on for centuries, I thought it was the perfect life companion to a young child. But, upon further reflection, the olive tree fits my son in other ways. His second name, Frederico, literally means "full of peace" or "peaceful ruler," and his Jewish and Portuguese origins retrace the history of olive trees themselves.

Olives and their oil are central to the three monotheistic religions. In Judaism, olive oil should continuously burn in the Tabernacle of the Temple in Jerusalem. When the Second Temple was rededicated after its desecration by the Romans, there was pure olive oil to burn in the menorah for only one day. However, the oil lasted until more could be procured eight days later, a miracle that is celebrated during Hanukkah, the festival of lights. The "Messiah" literally refers to "the anointed one," and the word "Christ" goes back to Ancient Greek, originally meaning "to anoint with [olive] oil." In the Koran, olive oil is a symbol of knowledge and light, and Prophet Mohammed reportedly said it cures seventy ailments.

As I drove through torrential rain to get to the museum on that bleak December day, I dreamt of sun-drenched Ancient Attica—its athletes running the marathon against clear-blue skies, their bodies shining with an olive oil coating in the midday heat, and its philosophers expounding their lofty ideas while eating olive oil-soaked delicacies in symposia held during balmy summer nights. This shamelessly exoticized view of ancient Greece, fueled by the desire to escape the dreary Portuguese winter, nevertheless had a grain of truth. At the time, athletes regularly rubbed themselves with olive oil to absorb its healthful properties. They then scraped the mix of oil, dirt, and sweat off their bodies and sold it to aspiring sportsmen (gender intended). Olive oil was central not only to sports but to other cultural, religious, and culinary practices in ancient Greece. Its significance is recorded in a mythical tale that tells of a competition between the gods Athena and Poseidon for supremacy in the region. Poseidon offered Greeks a horse and, striking the earth with his trident, made saltwater gush out of the soil. Athena grew an olive tree on the tallest hill around. The people chose Athena's gift and named their city Athens in her honor.

Immersed in olive lore, I reached the Olive Oil Museum at around noon. The weather had not improved but, even amidst the pouring rain, I could see a beautiful building in the shape of an olive branch, complete with leaves and ripe olives. The museum and much of its collection was sponsored by António Dias, a local olive oil producer. Olive trees grow throughout most of southern, central, and northeastern Portugal and use up around 9% of the country's agricultural land. The museum is located about half an hour from Coimbra, an ancient Roman town that is home to one of the oldest universities in Europe. As Henrique, a friendly young man who was my museum guide, explained, it was most likely the Romans who brought the practice of growing olive trees to the Bobadela region. The small town of less than 800 inhabitants has a number of Roman ruins, among which is a "monumental arch" and an amphitheater that testify to the area's prosperous past.

As we moved into the first room of the collection, Henrique embarked on a short history of olive oil. While the wild olive tree, or oleaster, has grown throughout most of the Mediterranean basin for millennia, the exact time and place when it was domesticated is unknown. An image of the tall oleaster growing in my garden facing my son's olive tree and of its tiny olives comes to mind. Who decided it was a good idea to invest energy into taming this plant? According to Henrique, it was most likely someone in the Middle East, as the oldest evidence of olive cultivation is from the regions of Syria, Palestine, and Crete. This happened around 6,000 years ago, making olive trees one of the earliest cultivated tree species.

What about the plant's name, my philologically inclined mind wondered? I skimmed through the information on the museum walls until I found the answer. The olive was *elea* in ancient Greek, and *zeit* in Semitic languages. As the domesticated olive tree traveled west with the merchants and conquerors who brought it to the Italic Peninsula, Southern France, and Iberia, the word *elea* came with it and gave us the English "olive" and the Portuguese "oliveira," or olive tree. The Semitic *zeit* spread in the south of the Mediterranean and was adopted by the Arabs, who then brought it to the Iberian Peninsula—giving rise to the Portuguese "azeite," or "olive oil."

The first domesticated olive trees were probably brought to Portugal by Phoenician merchants some 4,000 years ago. The oldest known olive tree in the country is 3,350 years old, making it one of the most ancient trees alive. It is an oleaster that was grafted with a branch from a domesticated cultivar, and it is still producing olives today in the region of Abrantes in central Portugal. But it was the Romans who introduced sophisticated olive pressing techniques to the Iberian Peninsula, including millstones that crushed the olives into a pulp and screw-and-lever presses that squeezed the oil out of this mash. As Henrique turned on a hydraulic millstone from the beginning of the twentieth century to show the process, I reflected on how the simple gesture of pouring olive oil on my food connects me to a past I was, until recently, barely aware of.

Olive trees thrived throughout the Roman Empire, and regions such as Bobadela almost certainly exported olive oil to large metropolises—including Rome itself—where it was used for cooking, to make aromatic oils and other cosmetic products, and for lighting. With the Germanic invasions that brought an end to the Western Roman Empire in the 5th century AD, new eating habits were brought to Europe. Animal products such as butter or lard, not olive oil, became the fat of choice. But olive oil continued to be used for cooking—especially during fasting periods—for medicinal purposes, for Church rituals, and for lighting. In Iberia, the Arab presence (7-15th centuries) revived the cultivation of olive trees and olive oil. The colonization of the Americas and, later, the large-scale emigration of Mediterranean peoples, including the Portuguese, brought olive trees to the New World. While Mediterranean countries continue to be the major olive oil producers in the world, with Spain leading by far—Spain produces roughly 6,600,000 tons of olive oil a year, almost three times the production of Greece, the second-largest producer—countries like Argentina, the United States, and Chile are catching up.

After buying a number of bottles of locally produced olive oil, I headed to the restaurant for a late lunch. Perched above the museum, which was built on top of a hill, it had a magnificent, 180-degree view of the surrounding countryside that even the persistent rain could not overshadow. Rolling hills with scattered whitewashed houses and olive fields stretched in front of my eyes all the way to the first slopes of Estrela Mountain, continental Portugal's tallest elevation at over 6,500 feet.

Lost in contemplation of the foggy landscape, I imagined Roman soldiers marching through the empire's famous roads that certainly crisscrossed the land some 2,000 years ago, taking the produce of the region back home, including amphoras filled with olive oil; Arabic doctors nine centuries later, following Mohammed's advice and treating a host of ailments with local olives; and Christian monks lighting their monasteries with olive oil before the evening prayers a few more centuries on. And I thought of the farmers—my Pagan, Arabic, and Christian ancestors—who worked the land year in and year out to make the prized oil.

My paternal grandmother and both maternal grandparents were farmers who lived in areas located a mere forty-five minute drive east and south from the museum, respectively. Their families had tended olive groves. Or perhaps it was the other way around, and it was the olive trees who looked after the farmers, giving them nourishment and a steady source of income? For if humans had brought the olive tree to Portugal, the trees themselves had transformed the landscape and adapted it to their needs. Could my aesthetic appreciation of the olive tree and my taste for olive oil be retraced to that memory?

Brought back by the lateness of the hour to more mundane matters, I perused the restaurant menu. I realized that absorbing so much new information had made me starving. Fortunately, the local delicacies listed on the menu, all using olive oil, sounded delicious. I decided on cod fish fried with cabbage and a local kind of bread made with corn and rye, the whole mix smothered in olive oil. The dish was amazing, a number of notches above the baked sole I had the previous day, and way out of my league as a cook. As I sluggishly drove back to Lisbon through unrelenting downpours, my body concentrated on digesting the calorie-rich lunch. But even in this semi-drowsy state, it became clear to me how much my cultural and physical make-up (is there really a difference between the two?) were entwined with the life of the olive tree.

A couple of days later, I set out once again, this time to find out more about contemporary olive oil production. The rain was gone, and it was a crisp winter day with plenty of sunshine when I drove south-east from Lisbon to the region of Alentejo. My destination was the Esporão Estate, a roughly 700-hectare farm that produces olive oil and wine. Unlike the mountainous, rainy, and thickly wooded central and northern Portugal, Alentejo is one vast plain that stretches south from the banks of the Tagus River (the word "Alentejo" literally means "beyond Tagus") like an immense yellow carpet with patches of green. Since its soil is relatively poor and it regularly suffers from droughts, Alentejo cannot support dense forests. It is, however, the perfect environment for olive trees (60% of Portuguese olive oil production comes from Alentejo), which pepper the region's rolling hills, interspersed with cork oaks, holm oaks, and grassland.

Driving past groves upon groves of olive trees on both sides of the highway, their dignified, unassuming posture—not too bushy, not too tall—blending seamlessly with the surrounding countryside, struck me once again, as it always does when I travel to that part of Portugal. I have always favored Alentejo as a getaway destination when things get too hectic in the city. The very monotony of the scenery—scattered trees and grass as far as the eye can see, a whitewashed homestead, or a small body of water the only fleeting distractions—calms the mind and invites meditation.

I often think that, if I were a painter, I would endlessly depict Alentejan landscapes, the boundless blue skies against the trees' olive-colored leaves, the sharp sunlight as it reflects on the yellow grass. Renoir's paintings of olive trees growing in his country house in Provence came to mind. But those plants were much lusher, much greener than their Alentejan counterparts. Some of van Gogh's olive trees come closer. They were painted while he was in an asylum, also in Provence, after having cut off his ear. Perhaps olive trees calmed his spirits, an effect they certainly have on me. His "Olive Tree with Yellow Sky and Sun," in particular, conveys Alentejo's blinding sunlight and unrelenting heat on a hot summer day, as well as the patient stance and welcome shade of the region's olive trees.

Perhaps I should move to Alentejo, I considered, as I reminisced about holidays spent there. I would read and write, take long walks through olive tree groves, drink local wine, and, of course, consume loads of the local olive oil. I made a mental note to save that plan for my retirement, unfortunately still a few decades away. And as I listed all the things I would love about living in the area, I wondered: what do olive trees like in Alentejo? What made them move there, so to speak? It was certainly not the landscape. Or maybe it was. I remembered reading that olive trees enjoy hot, dry weather with plenty of sunshine. They tolerate long periods of drought but are not too fond of the cold, and even though they can withstand it for brief periods of time, they freeze and wither when the mercury drops too quickly or too far below zero. Very similar to me in their weather preferences! They also thrive in nutrient-poor, chalky, and rocky soils and are no great climbers, preferring terrain close to sea level. Alentejan land is therefore, prime real estate from the olive trees' point of view.

After entering the gates of Esporão, I drove through a long dirt road flanked by olive groves and vines until I reached Ana's office. She is the estate's manager for everything related to olive oil production and sales and had agreed to show me around. We jumped into her electric car and set out to explore the farm. On our way to our first stop, Ana told me a bit about the history of Esporão. Its geographical boundaries have been virtually unchanged since 1267, shortly after Arab settlers were pushed south from the region by Christian armies. But there are vestiges of human presence in the area dating back at least 5,500 years, and the nearby Perdigões archeological site includes a megalithic sanctuary with several menhirs. Did those early inhabitants of the land already use olive oil? What is sure is that olive trees have been part of the landscape for thousands of years, and the most ancient tree on the property is over 1,200 years old.

Ana parked next to an olive grove with trees neatly arranged into rows irrigated by a drop-by-drop system. She explained this was an example of semi-intensive cultivation, using some chemical fertilizers and pesticides to support a plant density from 140 to 399 trees per hectare. Harvest is mechanized, which explained the sizeable distance separating the rows, enough for a truck to pass between the lines of trees to collect the olives, apply herbicides, and so on.

I wondered whether the trees liked to be lined up so orderly, as if they were soldiers in a parade or getting ready for a battle that would never arrive. I am sure the daily water supply was welcome. Maybe they even liked the pesticides that rid them of dangerous predators—like the olive fruit fly, whose larvae feed on their fruit—of fungi and of bacteria. I had read some time ago that the *Xylella fastidiosa* bacterium is killing millions of trees throughout the Northern Mediterranean region and that there is currently no cure for it. Trees would probably be as happy to get treatment for that as humans would be pleased to find a vaccine for COVID-19. But did the trees enjoy being so close to their neighbors?

Perhaps what is fostering the spread of olive tree diseases is not so different from the circumstances causing more and more human pandemics: many individuals living in close proximity to others of the same species. As Ana pointed out, semi-intensive plantations are not even too bad when compared with super-intensive ones, with up to 2,500 trees per hectare. These demand a high input of fertilizers and pesticides, as well as a huge irrigation volume. The yield is certainly high, but at what cost?

Although there are no super-intensive olive tree groves in Esporão, I remembered seeing them before, next to the Alqueva dam, a bit further east from the farm. The damming of the Guadiana river created the largest artificial lake in Europe, which looks almost like a mirage emerging from the dry Alentejan landscape. Farmers have been using the abundance of water to support super-intensive agricultural practices, including the growing of olive trees. The result is that the level of the water from the dam has substantially gone down, while there is an increased danger of eutrophication (excessive growth of algae) because of the fertilizers running into the lake. As for the olive trees in super-intensive groves, Ana tells me they tend to be small, sometimes barely taller than humans, and have a short life span—which I found unsurprising given the extremely crowded circumstances in which they live.

Our next stop was an extensive or traditional olive grove. These occupy 85% of Alentejan land dedicated to olive tree cultivation but yield only 35% of the region's olive oil production. The trees were larger, older, and looked wiser than those in the other groves, as if they had seen it all. As is customary in traditional groves, they were comfortably scattered throughout the land, following no particular pattern, and they were not irrigated. According to Ana, in traditional olive farming, trees are biennial, yielding a full crop one year and only half of that or less the following year. I recalled puzzling over why my son's young olive tree bore so many olives the first year after being planted and almost none the second. It still looked healthy, so I thought it had to do with its growth pattern. Now I knew the answer. But while I did not hope to make a living from olive oil, many farmers in Alentejo do. Would they be able to keep their farms afloat were they to depend only upon the yield of traditional olive groves? And would there even be enough affordable olive oil to meet a growing demand? After all, it takes about 7 kilograms of olives to make a single liter of olive oil. Would I still be able to use so much olive oil in my diet were we to depend only upon the yield of traditional olive groves?

While I pondered these issues, we reached the modern plant where the processing of the olives produced in the estate takes place. Olives are harvested in the fall, usually at the point when they are turning purple, though exact dates depend on regional climate, the type of olive tree, and the kind of olives and olive oil one prefers. Green olives, like the ones added to a martini, are not a special variety of fruit; they are simply not yet fully ripe. Olive oils made from green olives are fruitier and tangier than those pressed out of fully ripe olives, which are straw-yellow and have a milder, sweeter taste.

In the region where Esporão is located, harvest time stretches between October and January, so olive oil production was in full swing when we arrived at the plant. Truckloads of harvested olives were being unloaded to containers, from which they slowly trickled onto conveyor belts. These take the olives to be washed and ground, after which the olive paste is centrifuged to release the oil, again cleaned and then filtered. The stainless-steel machinery, with its soft humming and drumming noise, was a far cry from the artisanal millstones and presses I had seen in the museum a couple of days earlier.

While traditional production may lead us to nostalgically long for a simpler past when olive oil could be made locally, even in one's own backyard, modern methods have two big advantages: they are quick and clean. The longer it takes between harvesting the olives and the end result, the worse the quality of the olive oil. Oxidation happens throughout milling and pressing, and the healthful polyphenols contained in olive oil slowly degrade. For this reason, olive oil made over larger periods of time loses more of its antioxidants and flavor. Artisanal production is also more prone to contamination since stainless steel is easier to clean than irregular stone surfaces and woven mats. In Esporão and other modern plants, it takes about one hour to turn harvested olives into olive oil, while traditional milling might take up to a day.

As I admired the enormous round containers where the olive oil was stored after the pressing process was completed, I puzzled over their labeling. Why are some olive oils called "virgin" and others "extra virgin"? According to Ana, "extra virgin" olive oil comes from the first pressing of the olives, processed through mechanical means without applying chemicals or heat. The olive oil needs to pass a taste test to make sure it has no defects, and its acidity level should be below 0.8 percent. In case it does not meet these standards, the olive oil is downgraded to "virgin," which can have up to 2.5 percent of acidity. Esporão produces only extra virgin and virgin products, but there is also olive oil that falls short of both these designations. This could be oil obtained after the first pressing, using chemicals to extract whatever fat still remained in the olive paste, or simply olive oil whose quality is not high enough to be called "virgin." These oils are refined and filtered and are then sold to the general public, often with misleading labels. But even within the "extra virgin" category, there is an enormous range of olive oil varieties and tastes. I was about to find out more about that since Ana announced it was time to sample what I was seeing.

My idea of an olive oil tasting involved dipping a generous slice of

Alentejan bread onto a bowl of oil and enjoying the whole thing as an appetizer, paired with some nice wine. I was soon to discover how mistaken I was. In an aseptic room, Ana poured different kinds of olive oil into small glass cups that were immediately covered with a lid. My task was to compare three of the extra virgin olive oils produced in the estate. First, I was to contemplate the color of the olive oil through the transparent glass, then warm and shuttle the cup in my hand to release all aromas, open the lid and take in the strong smell, and finally take a sip, making sure I spread the liquid throughout my mouth to activate all taste buds.

Ana recommended that I start with the olive oil produced from the Galega cultivar, a Portuguese variety of olive tree very common in Alentejo. There are dozens of olive cultivars, as the tree and its fruit differ slightly from region to region. Similar to wine, olive oil can be made by mixing two or more cultivars, even though it is more common to use just one. The Galega olive oil smelled soft and fruity, and its taste was sweet and slightly nutty, with almost no acidity. I next tried olive oil from the Cordovil cultivar, also a Portuguese variety of olive tree, and I was surprised to find that, even to a layperson like myself, the difference between the two was so stark. Cordovil olive oil is yellowish-green, and it has a fresh fruit and grass smell. It tastes much stronger and more bitter than the Galega oil, an explosion of flavor in the palate.

The last olive oil I tried was a mix between Cobrançosa, a Portuguese cultivar, and Arbequina, a very common Spanish cultivar known for its high yield. It came from the Arrecifes olive grove, and it is the only fully organic olive oil produced in Esporão. It was greener than the other olive oils and its taste felt like a nice combination between the previous two. It was slightly spicy and astringent, not as sweet as Galega, and much more understated than the robust Cordovil.

Back home in Lisbon that evening, I contemplated once again the two olive trees in my garden. The oleaster stood solemn as ever, impervious to the December chill. My son's younger olive tree looked more fragile, slightly bent by the cold northern winds so frequent that time of year. Where did it come from? Who were its family members, what was its cultivar? Would it yield extra virgin olive oil, were its olives ever to be pressed? A cold shudder made me realize how hungry I was after the long drive home. What should I have for dinner? This time I settled upon a salad. Seasoned, of course, with plenty of olive oil.

CHAPTER 25

Passionflower

Passiflora incarnata

▪ **Kristi Onzik**

I'm walking along a busy highway.

The rushing wind of passing cars keeps me alert, anxiously traversing between white lines and steep roadside trenches. Someone shouts at me, "Hurry up!"

I realize I'm in a race and the finish line isn't far. Pick up the pace and I could win.

My strides lengthen. Moving farther, faster, passing strangers. I slip off the road onto a forested trail. My feet pound softer, heart louder.

But now I'm in a spa, surrounded by smooth wooden walls and low hovering ceilings. I'm frantic. Searching. Opening and closing doors, rushing through rooms with massage tables. The smoke of burning incense clouds my vision.

Amidst the smoke a desk emerges, a woman standing quietly and calmly behind it. She is warm, luminous, wearing a purple collar.

I ask her where the finish line is, tell her I'm in a hurry. That I could win if she points me in the right direction.

She approaches me. Slowly. Gently. Without a smile.

"There is no finish line," she whispers.

"There never was."

Finish lines, and failed attempts at reaching them, have long haunted me. Not only in dreams but in my so-called "waking life." These finish lines have, over the course of my earthly existence, worked to condense the expansiveness of the present into narrowly defined margins, funneling and offering the awareness of the *now* into a race toward future achievement. They constrain the boundaries of my thoughts, isolate me from my surrounds, and urge me to pick up the pace: progress is forward motion. Finish lines have also been the source and supply of chronic anxiety, tears, and so-called "nervous breakdowns." *Passiflora incarnata,* or passionflower, came to me during a time that I consider to be my greatest nervous breakdown. She was, and continues to be, the woman in my dream. Inviting me to stay present in the *here and now* with the gentle yet serious message that *there is no finish line. There never was.*

INITIAL ENCOUNTERS

It was the spring of my third year in a PhD program when a passionflower vine began growing into my home. Common knowledge among my fellow graduate student peers was that the third year, the year spent preparing for our qualifying exams, was "the worst." And my experience could be described as such. There I was, lying on the floor of my living room, exhausted and depleted. I had been fueling sleepless nights and unproductive workdays with increasing doses of caffeine and nicotine, the favored plant chemistries of someone long conditioned and supported by a fast-paced, future-achievement-oriented culture. My eyes were wandering in search of reprieve from the computer screen when they were captured by a green tendril, inching its way through a small crack in the sill of my living room window. I didn't know who it was at the time. Or, more precisely, I didn't know who it was beyond its taxonomic identification: *Passiflora incarnata.* A name, I later learned, that was inspired by the plant's encounters with Spanish missionaries in Peru. Entranced by the complex arrangements of the vine's flowers, its apostolic symmetries, and filamentous "crown of thorns," they transformed it into a tool for teaching the "Natives" about Christ's passion, symbolically incarnated in floral form.[1]

Over the course of a few days, I had, in passing, witnessed this small green tendril grow up and beyond the window sill, traverse across the wall, and branch into two, then three, searching stems. After several weeks, this vine had multiplied several times over, spreading across the expanse of the windowed wall and winding itself halfway across an eight-foot ceiling beam that leads to my sleepless bedroom door, sprouting spring coiled tendrils and glossy, palmate leaves along its way. During this time, I had been busy writing my qualifying exams. Two papers having something to do with the histories of plants, nervous systems and their scientists, and the many ongoing attempts at making sense of the boundaries between. And though naïve and early on in my studies, I had begun to sense that, in practice, the boundaries between plants, nervous systems, and a scientist's sense-making abilities are quite difficult to parse. In my own practice, however, I was not inclined to question whether my own self—and my nervous senses—had much to do with the plants around me. This was an attention I reserved only for the pieces of plants I consumed. For at the time "I" was all too confined to an idea of myself, and my writing, as an act of creation that took place somewhere up in my head, as thoughts conjured by the chemistries of my brain, released into the world by the powers of my own mind—albeit a mind whose composition had become increasingly reliant upon caffeine and nicotine to persist. So caught up in the race toward a future self's achievement, I could hardly consider taking the time to slow down and "smell the flowers," so to speak.

Had I not been so caught up in this race, I might have learned that the vine and its roots, flowers, and tendrils have long been and continue to be called upon as sleep, dream, and vision-enhancing allies among Indigenous peoples across the Americas—relations that far exceed their time-bound ethnobotanical classifications. In the late 1800s, American doctors "discovered" and described passionflower's so-called "sedative" and "narcotic" qualities, prescribing it in teas and tinctures for women diagnosed with "hysteria"—those deemed in need of immediate relief from neurotic impulses and spasmodic episodes.[2] The midwives of enslaved African peoples called upon the plant growing wildly amongst the fields as medicine to ease acute experiences of "fear, tension, anxiety and pain," often associated with the termination of pregnancies.

Today, in the southeastern US, the vine is commonly known as "maypop"—an English mispronunciation of the Algonkian term "maracock"—and is both celebrated and scorned for its ability to grow amidst "anthropogenic disturbance." Whereas the Algonkian peoples living in the area had long encouraged the vine to grow wildly amongst their maize and bean gardens,[3] industrial-scale farmers consider its presence amongst monocropped corn and soy fields an economically destructive "weed."

Its long, climbing tendrils are conceived of as "aggressive" resource competitors and a nuisance not easily disentangled from field machinery.[4] Later on in the life of these same fields, the vine is welcomed as a mediator of exhausted soils, a plant that creates new opportunities for living amidst the ruins of fast-paced, plantation-style agricultural practices.[5] But it was only after I had experienced what biomedical doctors now colloquially call a "nervous breakdown," that I began to trace "myself" and my "nervous senses" from within these greater histories of "anthropogenic disturbance," and their varying time-bound and timeless relations.

ON NERVINES AND "NERVOUS BREAKDOWNS"

By the end of my third year, my body and its self-centric, future-oriented mind had collapsed. My qualifying exams were passed not with flying colors but with tears, incomplete sentences, over-caffeinated jitters, and very kind committee members. Throughout the following months, my vision grew blurry, my thoughts refused to be formed into coherent sentences, recent events and conversations were mostly forgotten, and my mundane daily tasks felt nearly impossible to achieve. I had come to imagine myself as a failure, and my body had seemed to support this narrative. This was the narrative of a "nervous breakdown," and one I became familiar with from a history of visiting the offices of psychiatrists for help with the chronic and sometimes dramatically acute experiences of "nervous tension" or "anxiety." Seeking a different kind of solace and healing, and what I had imagined to be a potential departure from the "finish line" tempos of academia in which I had come to feel so defeated, I enrolled in an herbal medicine course.

"Nervines" was the theme of week one. An umbrella term used by Western herbal medicine practitioners to conjure a long list of plant taxonomies that, when ingested, have an effect on the nervous tissues of humans. There are those that stimulate and excite, like coffee, those that mildly relax, like lavender, and those that can sedate or induce a "hypnotic" dream-like state. *Passiflora incarnata* is often placed within the latter. In describing the particularities of passionflower's nervine qualities, many Western herbalists borrow biomedical terms to describe its specific effects.[6] The story goes that, when ingested in teas, tinctures, or capsules, passionflower can "sedate" or "depress" the overactive brain and central nervous system by increasing GABA, an amino acid that reduces neuronal excitability. Such a story is easily digestible by someone long trained to imagine anxieties and nervous senses to be confined inside of one's body, often located inside of one's "brain," and mostly within the "minds" of women. But at the end of class, this narrative was deeply, albeit unintentionally, complicated. The teacher mentioned, in passing, that we ought to pay attention to the many plants that grow "like weeds" around us. That, in a fast-paced, anxiety-stricken society like ours, calming nervines—the medicine we need most—can be found growing right beside us, thriving alongside busy highways, sprouting through cracks in our driveways and sidewalks, or growing just outside of our windows.

Or, inside.

I was stunned, jolted. I felt a tingling sense of clarity that arrived far too instantaneously to be described as a moment in time—as a thought or a memory. Though the comment was left unexplained, its message resounded in a language deeply felt but not spoken. At that moment, there was no question. The passionflower vine growing into my home, through a small crack in the window, had, all the while, been minding "me."

INCARNATING PASSIFLORA

Within the year of my "nervous breakdown," and amidst an ongoing search for healing "myself" and my nervous senses, the invitation to slow down and listen to passionflower beyond brain-centric taxonomic bounds was, once again, extended. I was conducting research with a plant scientist in sub-tropical Australia when I was invited to "diet" the passionflower not so surreptitiously growing along the outer walls of the lab. Again, in a language deeply felt but not spoken, and insights traveling far too instantaneously to be moments in time, the message was clear to both the scientist and myself. An invitation to "meet" on passionflower terms and tempos had been extended. By now, I had known better than to hastily decline.

Though the practice of "dieting" plants is varied, taking forms in different times and places, it has been most commonly traced within the practices of *vegetalistas* in the upper Amazonian regions.[7] In these tracings, conducting a *dieta* with a plant involves restricting one's diet—abstaining from indulgences like sugar, salt, fat, sex, and soap—and ridding oneself from the scents and traces of all-too-human activities. And though the invitation to "diet" passionflower with a plant scientist working in sub-tropical Australia could be considered strangely misappropriated, such a reading is construed with an understanding that the *vegetalista*, or the human facilitator of the diet, is the one in charge. Common amongst all of those trained in the practices of dietas is that a dieta starts and its particular constraints and conditions arise by following the invitations and instructions of the plant. The plant *is* the teacher, the human, the student. Fortunately for me, I had found work with a plant scientist who had, through her training with plant healers in Peru and Ecuador, learned to listen for such plant invitations and directions and helped to co-facilitate the communion between passionflower and myself—the self still struggling to heal from the embodied tempos and narratives of a finish-line cosmology.

Under the new moon of the autumn equinox, I was asked to harvest a small piece of the passionflower root. With the light of my headlamp, I crawled beneath the dense thicket of the vine's summertime abundance, gently digging my fingers into the soil at the base of its stem. A small piece of root, no more than three inches, arced upwards toward the surface. With an exhalation, I offered gratitude to the vine, removed this small root "offering," and placed it in a dish at the center of an altar. After a week of nightly meditations at the altar, I was to ingest my first sip of tea brewed from the root. But just as I had learned from my previous encounters with passionflower and its "nervine" medicine, the plant need not be ingested to affect and make a different kind of sense out of *me*. The night before I drank my first cup of tea, passionflower arrived in a dream. She was the woman behind the desk, approaching me softly, warmly, yet with the serious and humbling message:

"There is no finish line. There never was."

Upon awakening from the dream, I began to experience a growing stiffness in my body. A tightening of my legs, an immense soreness growing from my hips into my sacrum and up my spine—an overwhelming sensation that, at the time, could only be described as the feeling of something, or *someone*, dying inside. My muscles demanded to be stretched beyond their skeletal constraints, begging my bones to contort in unfamiliar arrangements. My search for reprieve in familiar yoga postures and various meditative mantras wouldn't suffice. There was nothing *I* could do. For, as it became clear, it was precisely the *doing*, the searching, that I was being instructed to release. Later in the evening, upon drinking my first cup of the passionflower root tea, I began to feel a release of, and relief from, these all too self-centric senses. I sipped the tea, sat in candlelit meditation, and slid into a deep and heavy sleep across the floor of my bedroom. I awoke into a bursting portal of vibrant pinks and purples, a deepening concentric swirl into and through the famously ethereal inflorescence, and doused in the perfume of an overwhelming, euphoric sensation that I was, at once, being birthed by and giving birth to the passionflower. There was no origin or end, no finish line or boundary *between* us.

Thereafter, my body was not mine, but something of a conduit, then a coalescence. Roots sprouted from my sacrum, gently coaxing my spine back down into earthly grounds. As my body sank heavier into ground, spring coiled tendrils and broad palmate leaves lifted and suspended all thoughts away from perception, though it was no longer clear *where* perception was, nor whom. As the dieta unfolded, my all-too-familiar concept of time as a linear ordering of experience into past, present, and future, became confused, and in its deepest passionflower-"ness," seemingly irrelevant, hardly interesting, and only vaguely conceivable. In this timeless dimension of communing, there were no verbs, no endpoints, or destinations. Such distinctions couldn't be. *I* was passionflower and passionflower *me*. A relation which, as I am only beginning to sense, continues, both before and after the ceremonial dieta—and both *before* and *after* the passionflower vine grew into my home, extending an invitation to open up my all-too-self-centric, finish-line oriented window of perception.

As I continue to make sense of this passionflower communion in dreams, writing, and meditations, both *Passiflora incarnata* and I waver in and out of time-bound and timeless evocations—written into narratives of species, of the inheritance of colonial histories, and the realms of "anthropogenic disturbance" in which nervines and nervous senses coalesce—yet all the while open up to ever-expanding, more-than-human, and more-than-individually-minded creations. These are stories similarly told by the vines growing amidst the ruins of ongoing plantation-style agricultural practices, alongside busy highways, and into the windows of an academic mind entranced and broken down by the coercive allure of finish lines and dreams of future progress. The experience of *incarnating passiflora* is not only a literal embodiment of the passionflower vine and spirit but unfolds here—in the creeping, climbing, nonlinear entanglements of this story—as an ongoing invitation. An invitation to crack open the window of a time-bound "finish line"-oriented perception that assumes, for instance, that consumption is required for earthbound, plant-human connection. An invitation extending and incarnating as the potential to create from, and be created by, a perception that need not take place *within* a self, a nervous system, a home, a species, or in the confines of pasts, presents, and futures. An invitation to suspend racing thoughts of doing, producing, and achieving and sink deeper into the creative potentials of timelessness where there is no finish line—there never was.

CHAPTER 26

Peyote

Lophophora williamsii

▪ María Luisa Chacarito and Sabina Aguilera

We were entering the sacred land of *Wirikuta* in the desert of San Luis Potosí in Mexico, the place where *hikuri* (peyote plant) grows. The *Wixarika*[1] *Mara'kame* (a healer) told us that it was time to ask if we could "hunt" hikuri. Having done this, he explained that if we saw the sacred plant on the desert's ground, it meant we had been given permission to collect and later on eat hikuri. For a while, I saw nothing. All of a sudden, my eyes caught one, and, like magic, I began to see hikuri plants all over. We walked quite a bit after "hunting," until we reached a place where we would spend the night and ingest the sacred plant. I only remember myself sitting on the ground, feeling not only part of the desert's surface but also an up and down movement which I interpreted as the breathing of a living being. I felt part of the sky, the air, and everything surrounding me—when looking at the horizon, there were no boundaries between the sky, the bushes, and the ground. This was my first and only personal encounter with the peyote plant. Most of what happened back then remained in my memory, but with not much to relate to. Only later on, when I was studying and learning from the Ralámuli, would it acquire a deeper and more graspable meaning.

It was almost the end of the first semester when one of my professors offered to take two students to the Sierra Tarahumara, the land inhabited by the Ralámuli. Without knowing why, I strongly felt I wanted to go and thus decided to write my name on the list. Ever since that summer of 1997, I have been learning from these people living in the high ranges of southwestern Chihuahua (Northern Mexico), but also migrating temporarily and permanently to big cities such as Chihuahua City. Some years later I met María Luisa Chacarito, a Ralámuli woman. Back then, she was the main authority of a settlement created by a Jesuit priest for Ralámuli people migrating temporarily to the capital city of Chihuahua. Although the reason for visiting her in the coming years was to learn how to weave and to deepen my knowledge of Ralámuli textiles and iconography, she and other women taught me fundamental things about their culture. Listening to their stories and ideas, I felt confused and impressed, always asking myself how it is possible to live in the same world and have such a different perception, understanding, and experience of it. I only knew that I wanted to believe what I was told. For example, once, engaged in a trivial conversation while weaving, we began talking about obtaining knowledge and healing practices. She said: "Plants themselves tell when they are good to heal." How can this be true? I asked myself. But I would only come across more explanations like this one. For instance, that during the harvest season, a certain kind of bird announces the coming of frost or that trees chant before the storm. María Luisa explained: "If you connect with the world by observing you will find all the answers." It was then that my only way of grasping these explanations was by remembering the experience I had after ingesting hikuri (peyote).

Some years after, María Luisa told me that "the word 'nature' in Ralámuli language does not exist." It is not needed because there is simply no separation between nature and culture. I wondered if what I felt after ingesting hikuri could be reflecting this notion. Anyhow, this *continuum* is also present in the Ralámuli's very way of being, in their care, awareness, and knowledge of the Earth. They practice a palpable relational experience with "Mother Earth" that translates into a vital and reciprocal engagement based on the notion that everything (e.g., the Earth itself, animals, plants, rocks, rivers, etc.) is animated and plays a crucial role in the well-being, balance, and preservation of life. In fact, as María Luisa points out, all flora and fauna is *rijimala*, a word used to refer to family members that goes beyond the human realm. It is a living heritage that gives meaning to the experienced world.

Remembering what she had once told me about plants, I asked if she and her family would talk to me about *jíkuli*,[2] so that we could write about it together. What follows is the result of this joint collaboration, representing not only María Luisa's words but also the voices of the healers and family members she consulted.

According to Ralámuli thought, "plants are beings that have existed long before mankind emerged in the world, and they are wise. Each plant has its own mind and some of them are known to have specific powers and qualities." Jíkuli is one of them. Quite commonly, it is associated with peyote (classified by Western science under the name *Lophophora williamsii*), a cactus with hallucinogenic properties. Beside the Ralámuli, other Native American peoples—such as the Wixarika in Western Mexico, the Odami in the North, and the Diné of the Southwestern United States—make use of this highly sacred cactus. For the Ralámuli, this plant is one of the most powerful plant beings that *Onolúame* (an un-gendered all-encompassing force that exists everywhere, although also named "he who is our father") gave to the people as supreme medicine. Moreover, as María Luisa clarifies and as we shall see, jíkuli is not only the peyote plant but refers to a variety of mighty sacred plant beings that—because of their agency and power—one should be extremely cautious of. Even mentioning their name or talking about them is considered potentially dangerous. In this sense, what can be said is mentioned in this manuscript, leaving out what should remain unspoken. She says that for the Ralámuli, jíkuli gives good advice, strength, protection, vision, and healing power. Hence, people will make sure to demonstrate profound respect and gratitude by making costly offerings, usually a cow or a few goats that will be sacrificed in a specific ceremony, but also fermented corn beer and incense.

The large variety of cactuses that the Ralámuli identify as jíkuli [3] could possibly be explained by the ecological diversity of their territory. Each of these plants has a different name, such as *cimarrón* or *hualula selíami*, all having distinctive characteristics and qualities. However, all of them will heal and protect, but at the same time, they can kill, make one crazy, and do serious harm, specifically the *hualula selíami* (the peyote plant). What determines the outcome—that is, if one will be protected or not—is the relationship one has with the plant itself. Performing the traditional rituals of gratitude and treating jíkuli with respect is crucial. The consequences of not thinking or doing things according to "the good path" can be life-threatening. Thus, the relationship with the plant is endowed with fear and reverence.

Yet, there is more to these sets of relationships. It is said that the powerful plant beings (not only jíkuli) look for the people who have "the gift" to become medicine men or women. When a person is chosen, there is an onset of unusual dreams. For instance, encounters with talking serpents, spiders, or strikingly beautiful people. This has happened not only to María Luisa, who has the gift of vision but to other members of her family as well. She explains further that in these encounters, the healer-to-be will go through a series of "tests" to prove the quality and strength of their healing powers. One can become an *owilúame*, which is a healer, or a *sipáame* (the only one who can converse with jíkuli and possibly the highest-ranking healer). While dreaming, the *sipáame* will not only learn the path to the land where jíkuli grows but obtain knowledge from the latter. Thus, the journey to find jíkuli and bring it back to the communities is considered an important part of acquiring knowledge and the beginning of communication with the plant itself.

In their dreams, jíkuli healers converse with the plant's spirit or soul, which looks like a person: a Ralámuli. Another way of communicating with this spirit while simultaneously healing is through the healer's chants. Given that jíkuli sings, Ralámuli healers say that these sacred "songs" come from the cactus itself. Together with the melodies or resonance produced by a ritual instrument, these chants are part of a jíkuli healing ceremony called *Tubonatu rawea om'ochiliami* (to go to the place of the jíkuli). In order to overcome a sometimes deadly illness—namely a soul illness—a male patient needs to attend as a guest in three ceremonies, usually one a year. A female patient participates in four ceremonies. To conclude the ceremonial cycle, the ailing person needs to organize yet one last ceremony.

María Luisa explains that jíkuli heals and purifies the body when suffering from a soul illness. Surely, this is a serious state for any person. According to the Ralámuli notion of *alewá*—the soul or breath that animates all beings, including plants—women have four big souls, while men have three (women have one more soul because they are life-givers), and many other smaller souls distributed throughout the body. The number of souls for non-Ralámuli humans and other non-human beings will vary. Being the breath of life, souls are able to travel in and out of the body while the person is dreaming. *Rimú* (sleep) means "dream" and is understood as a parallel reality to waking life, where the soul can communicate with other souls. At the same time, it is vulnerable to being trapped or devoured by other souls. The result of such an event—that is, when the soul(s) cannot return to the body—is sickness. Sadness will also make a person more susceptible to sickness, to have accidents, or to be hurt by a *sukulúame* (sorcerer). This is when the role of the jíkuli healer is crucial because he or she has the ability of "dreaming good," of seeing where the soul is trapped, and then negotiating the release of the patient's soul.

When a person needs to go through a jíkuli ceremony, it is absolutely necessary to abstain from eating salt, having sexual relationships, and having contact with other people not taking part in the ceremony. In Ralámuli terms, this is a way of being clean in order to encounter jíkuli and to begin the healing process. The latter will take place after the plant's flowering season, more or less between October and April. The *sipáame*, the assistants, the guests, and the fire keeper will remain all night long until dawn within the ritual stage, where a series of events will be performed.

Healing ceremonies take place during the night and finish before sunrise because this is when the healer, while dreaming, is able to travel or walk to other places. In fact, the places where the jíkuli souls tie to a person's soul(s) are in different cosmic levels, so to speak. According to Ralámuli explanations, the world is made out of different floors, one on top of the other like stacked discs or *tortillas* (a traditional circular corn cake). These floors or levels are connected by paths that enable the souls to travel. However, not everyone knows the way—only those who have the power of vision given by a sacred plant such as jíkuli.

Following the ingestion of jíkuli, which is not to be eaten fresh but rather in small amounts, ground and mixed with water consisting of the dried cactus, the *sipáame* will begin singing while using his ritual instruments. The healing ceremony refers to the rasping of the healer's *sipílaka* where two wooden sticks (from a specific tree and formerly maybe from a deer's antler) and a concave wooden vessel, or gourd cut in half, are used. The half gourd is placed with its base upside down and used to cover the jíkuli that is put on the ground where the healer is seated. A sound or melody will be produced by rasping one stick against an engraved or notched stick on top of the gourd. This act, together with the healer's chanting, establishes the communication path, or a dialogue, between the plant and the healer. Moreover, the sound produced by the *sipílaka* and the chants—or songs—sung during the ceremony stand for paths used by the *sipáame* to heal. In other words, through the healer's conversation with the sacred plant, the former will know where exactly the patient's soul is trapped.

The patients will dance at intervals, guided by another assistant whose specific role is to demonstrate the way to move. The Ralámuli explain that "it is necessary to dance so that sickness will remain under the ground."

The closing events, before sunrise, are marked by the arrival of jíkuli to the ritual circle where the ceremony has been performed and where the sacred cactus will "eat" the offerings left for this purpose. The healer will thank jíkuli, and, as a final act, the participants will be purified with incense. Furthermore, the healer will make use of the ritual instruments producing a rasping sound above each person's head, and finally, wash each person with spring water. Afterward, the patients will bury the clothes they used during the ceremony. They will also continue to completely avoid salt, sexual relationships, and bathing for some days. Possibly, the patient will recover, and, if not, it is said there is not too much more that the *sipáame* can do to heal the person.

We wish to highlight the very active role sacred plants like jíkuli play. It is about a wise and powerful plant being with whom the Ralámuli establish a personal and delicate relationship that, if based on communal values, will protect and heal. Jíkuli healers, the *sipáame*, are considered the wisest and most prominent among all healers because of the wisdom brought about by the jíkuli teacher and ally. Hence, jíkuli and the *sipáame* have a major responsibility for the well-being of the community.

These relationships bring forth another way of experiencing life. It is a way of being based on mutual dependence, responsibility, and respect. That is, a world where one knows who one is because of these interconnections with the place one inhabits.

POEM 8

Pineapple

Ananas comosus

Khairani Barokka

Henceforth, Fruit may never stand for Woman
as a matter of course, automatic simulacrum.
Representing desiccation and death, its husk
shrivels seeds, invariably consumed by the
fairly indiscriminate, pulped, ground, chopped.
Tossed; force-fed syrup. This pineapple on the
canvas may only be a woman when laid right,
against an abstract background and cleaved
by its self alone. Mane of forest, feral, fecund.
Imposing, monolithic, millennia apart from the
tales our grandmothers tell us of nanas' curse
of vaginal ill-health when eaten, yet retaining
all the menace of such myth. A pox on you and
your vaginas, it could say—but it loves the pith
of a woman, and would never strike fear in her
heart, like the murder of armored, segmented
flesh, fork gone runny with sweet yellow juice.

CHAPTER 27

River Red Gum

Eucalyptus camaldulensis

Sally Birch

I live in a little stone cottage by a trickling creek on the edge of a forest. Beside the creek and not far from the cottage stands a River Red Gum. He is about forty meters tall and towers above the surrounding trees with the all-encompassing presence of a reliable grandparent. If four adults stretched their arms around his trunk, they might just be able to touch hands. I don't know how long he has been living here, but I think he could be over five hundred years old. I have turned fifty this year, so this tree and I may be both in the middle stage of our natural life span.[1]

I have always felt a deep connection with trees. As a child, I spent many happy hours down at the end of our garden chatting with the trees. Recently, I have joined a research project on trees, and I feel so elated to have an official excuse to study them. The project focuses on the social life of trees and how they interact with and co-create their environment with agency and purposeful behavior.[2] After considering several tree species as potential study models to explore the topic, we settled on the River Red Gum. As I delved into the scientific literature, one thing about this Australian tree immediately grabbed my attention: the River Red Gum tends to drop huge branches suddenly and unexpectedly. Over the years of living with this tree, I recall the times that I have been startled to hear a sharp crack followed by a horrendous earth-shaking thud as the tree released its hold on a massive branch, landing in its new home on the forest floor. There are theories as to why this occurs, but I'm not sure that anybody really knows. We just know to be wary when under one of these colossal trees because you can never tell when a huge branch might drop. If you were to browse camping guides around Australia, for instance, you would not have to look far to find an official warning about the branch-dropping tendencies of the River Red Gum. Photographs of flattened tents would come complete with captions explaining how the inhabitants of the tents were lucky enough to have made it out alive.

As well as bringing out the laconic Australian sense of humor, the River Red Gum holds an iconic place on this vast continent. Not only has this tree become the most widespread organism in his chosen landscape, but also a dominant form in the inner landscape of our minds, inspiring creativity and awe—being one of the most represented trees in Australian art, poetry, and fiction. And as these trees have spread to other parts of the world, so has their ability to capture our imagination reached well beyond the shores of their native country. The flowers, for example, remind me of sea anemones with their clusters of delicate, long, white to pale-cream, tentacle-like stamen. On our River Red Gum here in our garden, the flowers grow so high up in the air that it is a treat to find them on the ground. And the same goes for the fruits, which are small hemispherical capsules—tiny woody artifacts of earthy beauty.

There is a sense of innate generosity about these trees. Perhaps, it is in the way the River Red Gum supports a complex community of plants and animals, including ourselves. Most of the upper body is covered in a strikingly smooth, almost luminous white or creamy-brown mottled bark; in the few meters up from the base, however, the bark is a contrasting rough grey, which peels off in long sheets, leaving a thick pile of itself around the perimeter of the trunk to provide a complex home for many other life forms. Even their fallen branches continue to provide homes for the surrounding wildlife on the forest floor or in the rivers, where they become important fish spawning areas. The hollow that is left in the tree after a branch has dropped creates a reliable breeding and roosting place for many species of birds, microbats, and possums. All kinds of insects live with the tree—from ants and spiders to the red gum lerp psyllid (*Glycaspis brimblecombei*), which excretes a cone-shaped covering for its nymphs on the leaves of the tree (the lerp that Aboriginal people prize as a sweet treat).[3] The leaves have a hardy thickness and are lance-shaped or curved, with the same greyish-green color on both sides. They are packed with highly medicinal oil. In fact, the essential oil from the River Red Gum has significant antiviral properties and is one of the most active antibacterial oils of any species of eucalypt. Aboriginal people have made use of his gifts for many thousands of years. The gum or *kino* (as it is now known) contains tannin and is powerfully astringent. It is used internally in the treatment of diarrhea and bladder inflammation and externally applied to cuts and abrasions.[4]

Just as their name suggests, the River Red Gum trees populate the banks of Australian inland river systems and seasonal floodplains, standing sentry over generations, like columns of water[5] in a landscape that is as changeable as it is vast. With their extensive root system, they stabilize the riverbanks and protect them from erosion. Their deep sinker roots—amongst the largest recorded of any tree—reach down as far as thirty meters beneath ground level, where they access the deepest groundwater. Using their huge capacity for hydraulic redistribution, they transport water all the way up through this super-network of roots to the shallower areas of the substrate, increasing the bioavailability of water and nutrients to all of the local species of plants and animals. They also extend their roots at least twenty meters in the horizontal direction, although lateral root extension of more than one hundred meters has been reported in some studies.[6] But their roots don't stop there. They have the capacity to produce aerial roots that grow directly from the trunk, hanging above the ground. These consist of aerenchyma, a spongy, air-filled tissue with large air spaces between the cells, perfect for breathing above ground during the wet season. Thanks to these aerial roots, these trees can tolerate immersion of their underground roots in floodwaters for up to nine months at a time. Not only do River Red Gums tolerate long-term flooding, they rely on it. During spring, the trees release large numbers of seeds to coincide with the flood season, which gives the seeds the best chance of germination due to the wet conditions. The timing of the seed drop also means that these seeds can be carried along by the surrounding floodwaters to be redistributed further afield. Since European settlement in Australia, however, the flood seasons have changed dramatically. Over the last two hundred years, the great River Red Gum forests have been systematically cleared to support grazing by introduced livestock. This has led to river regulation and water extraction, which have reduced the frequency and reliability of seasonal floods.

The remaining River Red Gum forests stand amidst these elemental changes. Although they can no longer rely on the regular seasonal flooding of the past for their reproduction, it will take more than this change in familiar seasonal phenomena to stop these trees from thriving. As part of their immense resilience, they have the added ability to reproduce via vegetative propagation, reducing their dependence on flower or seed. Like magicians producing a hidden card from their sleeves, these trees can produce an epicormic bud from beneath their bark. A portion of the stem grows roots while attached to the parent plant before detaching and becoming an independent tree. These epicormic stems create a clonal colony.

Looking up at the tree in our garden, I ponder how the shape of these trees must have changed over time and particularly since Europeans arrived in this land—an event which drastically reduced the gene pool of the River Red Gum. The colonists found that the wood from these trees was of such high quality, and could be used in so many different ways, that they implemented large-scale logging of the River Red Gum forests. They cleared the land for agriculture but also to harvest the prized timber used to build the framework of this new society. To choose the best trees to fell, the early timber-getters struck the base of the trees with their axes and listened to the quality of the sound that resounded from the trunks. A dull sound indicated that a tree had rot in its heartwood, and so that tree was left standing. The soundest, straightest, tallest, and broadest trees were the ones that were chosen and taken for their timber. So it is that the River Red Gum forests of today are completely different from the great stands of pre-colonial Australia.[7]

I continue studying the River Red Gum with increasing fascination, and I am not surprised to discover that eucalypts have adapted to survive for over one-hundred-million years.[8] That distinctive bark of the River Red Gum helps to tell part of this story. For thousands of years, these trees have given huge segments of their bark to Aboriginal people to use as canoes to navigate the rivers and floodwaters during the wet season.[9] When I say the bark is "given," I mean that it is actually a painstakingly slow process to carefully remove the bark from the tree in one huge piece, with the artisan balancing at a great height off the ground. Then the bark must be slowly tempered over a fire to give it extra strength and longevity. This process does not kill the tree, but it retains the scar for the rest of its life. Many scarred "canoe trees" can be found across Australia, showing the long history of interconnection between Aboriginal people and these trees.

As the canoes glided silently through watery Red Gum forests, they passed beside the fallen branches from these trees, which were never a threat to these solid and maneuverable vessels. By contrast, those fallen branches from the River Red Gum were a problem for the paddle steamboats that have traveled along the Murray River since the mid-1800s. Steamboats were also made from River Red Gum trees, but unlike the canoes, their construction demanded the life of the tree, used to feed the furnace to propel the boats through the water. There seem to be endless stories like these of tree-river-human-other-than-human relationships. These stories branch out in all directions, but they all lead back to the tree. They seem to have the common theme of adapting to what is needed in each moment to flourish and thrive. These stories are about generosity and hospitality, interconnectedness and care, calling for surrender, and for letting go when required. I wonder if, just like these ancient trees, we can find new ways to flourish within our current story.

In writing this essay, my thoughts have often been with the River Red Gum in our garden. The more I rest my attention with this great being, the more I sense the living essence that flows through the vast body of the tree. The other day, as I was contemplating all of this, these words entered my mind, "Come and spend time with me. Visit me. We need each other." I have started doing just that. This morning, I wandered across the garden to where the River Red Gum stands. I laid my hand softly on his trunk and gazed up as he shimmered awake with the first rays of light through the leaves. The dawn birds called their songs around the valley as I pondered the tree and my connection with it. I heard a rustle and a light thudding sound and turned to see the little brown-faced swamp wallaby hopping past us. The kookaburra cackled up above, and I wondered what she knows that

I don't. I heard more movement in the leaves over on the other side of the creek. I searched with my eyes, still resting my hand on the trunk of the tree. There was an echidna scratching around in the dirt, looking for ants, stopping shy when noticing my stare. I smiled wide with joy, surrounded by such an abundance of life simply doing its thing all around. There is so much diversity around this tree.

This is just the beginning of a new story and a new way for me. Each day I go and sit with the tree. This is the first time I have done this, even after all these years. They were busy years with children to care for. But now that the intense time of mothering has shifted to a new stage of letting go, I have time for this *othering*. I feel as if I am really meeting this tree for the first time. All I have to do is stop, be still, and listen. As I lay my hands on the trunk of this giant being, my heart fills with gratitude for his presence. There, at his base, is a newly fallen branch—the perfect place to sit and rest my ear against his trunk. That's when I hear the sound of water rising.

CHAPTER 28

Rose

Rosa spp.

Joela Jacobs

I live in the Sonoran desert of Arizona. Only particularly hardy roses are native to this state, but roses are grown here just as much as in any other place around the world. With the help of regular watering, most kinds survive in the dry climate, but the dark pink and white blossoms on the bushes in my yard burn to a crisp whenever spring turns into summer. Though they look like dried bridal bouquets while still on the stem, they continue to bloom every year. I grew up in a temperate region of Germany, where roses proliferate without human intervention. Untended dog roses grow wild along paths while their big-blossomed cousins stand carefully clipped in gardens full of colorful flowers. My mother's garden is home to roses that she grew from clippings of the bushes her mother allowed into her post-war vegetable patch. But I can't take any sprigs from these old stems with me to the US because of customs and immigration laws.

If we follow the rose's spread across borders, we find Catholics praying with rosaries made from petal beads in South America, and Europeans collecting rose hips to make jam—an important source of vitamin C during World War II, the end of which was celebrated by planting a new rose called "Peace." Further east, we see Turks enjoying rose tea, while the country's booming rose oil industry is rivaled only by Bulgaria's. It supplies the valuable attar of rose oil, originally a Persian key ingredient of alcohol-free perfumes and cosmetics most popular in Arabic and Indian cultures today. Moving along, we encounter regions of India and Pakistan that look and smell like a giant potpourri of drying flowers since they export rose petals to Middle Eastern households. They share customers with the rosewater industry—a spiritual cleansing agent in Islam and an ingredient of popular delicacies. With yet another spin of the globe, we find ourselves in the White House's rose garden that emulates eighteenth century designs with its national flower.[1]

Roses are so ubiquitous around the world that they appear to follow me wherever I travel. They seem to beat me to every destination, only to greet me in front of conference hotels and outside of airports. The discovery of a thirty-five-million-year-old rose fossil and rose species stemming from North America to North Africa and from all across Europe and Asia confirm the rose's global reign. She has by now traded the strength of her signature scent for easy maintenance, resistance to diseases, and a colorful, long blooming period—"self-cleaning" was the adjective on the little card affixed to a peach-pink rose bush that now grows in front of my house. Especially those visually appealing cut roses that travel from places as far as Kenya or Israel to get to your neighborhood florist have lost their scent entirely and are sometimes spritzed with perfumes instead. Breeders are now trying to get the lost scents back, and suppliers in South America are beginning to satisfy this demand for the high-end US market.[2]

Available anywhere, anytime, with bright blossoms and shiny green leaves, we imagine the rose as the flower as such: luxurious, beautiful, and made to please human senses. That is the rose that we have cultivated through selective breeding over centuries: taking a Northern European plant that flowered for two weeks a year and hybridizing it with roses from China that had become accessible through colonialist exploits. The rose is an invasive species that rules over flower shows and that has been named after queens and breeders' wives for "political" considerations.[3] Only blue roses still escape the breeders' reach (except with the help of dyes), though genetic engineering now seems close to achieving this elusive goal at last.[4] Empress Joséphine famously tried to collect all known types of roses at Chateau Malmaison, getting specimens even from countries at war with her husband, Napoleon. She followed in the footsteps of many ancient civilizations: Chinese and Persians, Egyptians, Greeks, and Romans all turned to roses as luxury items in rituals surrounding love and death. Red and white roses bring to mind both the War of the Roses and its red-and-white solution in the Tudor Rose. Depending on color and context, a rose symbolizes purity or passion, jealousy or death—and roses generally signal messages conveyed in secret or sub rosa. Floriography, the Victorian language of flowers, famously popularized the idea of communicating through floral arrangements, even though the various flower dictionaries on the market then and now tend to disagree with one another in ways that could provide material for countless comedies of errors.[5]

There is also the rose we encounter in the arts: It lends its name to the beloved's rosy cheeks in the poetry of many languages, and it symbolizes beauty and love in countless stories, from the thorny rose hedge in the fairy tale of Sleeping Beauty to the Persian fable of the rose and the nightingale—both of which fatally pierce those who are drawn to beauty. In Botticelli's famous painting of *The Birth of Venus*, the goddess does not just emerge from the waves but also from among a rain of roses as if to extend a similar warning.

In almost all of these symbolic contexts, the rose is imagined as female, and grammatically gendered languages tend to use the feminine article for both flowers and roses. Whether she accompanies the Goddess Aphrodite or the Virgin Mary, the rose comes to symbolize gendered expectations. This stereotypical understanding of female roles emphasizes the ornamental, passive misconception we have of many plants, especially their flowers, and the rose's history as a powerful cultural agent disappears behind these notions. "A rose is a rose is a rose,"[6] Gertrude Stein famously wrote in a poem in 1913. But is it that simple?

* * *

The rose seems to be—and not be—everyone's favorite flower. Is that because she has become a cliché of her own beauty? Even for this book, she was listed as the first example but picked last, chosen because some of my favorite plants, like the chestnut tree and the dandelion, were taken by other contributors, and I became intrigued by her strongly felt absence. The rose's image of perfect beauty, a Valentine's Day specimen, has captured the human imagination, but that appears to stand in the way of recognizing her in the suffragette who demands "bread and roses," or as

Rosie the Riveter—a flowering genus of multi-faceted variety that can prick back. So, what is on the rose's mind?

She speaks her mind and pricks back in a poem by arguably one of the most famous German authors, Johann Wolfgang von Goethe. "Heidenröslein," or "The Little Rose on the Heath," written in 1771 and published in 1799, was set to music by many composers and is popular both in opera and folk song versions.[7] In the poem, boy meets girl: A young man sees a beautiful red rose. He announces that he will pluck her, to which she responds with the threat of pricking him, so he will remember that "Ne'er will I surrender!" But the boy picks her despite her pricks, and "She must needs surrender," or "suffer it," as the original German says. Written as a love poem to a woman, Goethe's words seem quite sinister in my twenty-first century context that is embroiled in the #MeToo debate. Invoking the metaphor of defloration, this boy takes what he wants by force. A rose that is broken has begun to die, like the many cut flowers in baroque paintings that remind their onlookers of the ephemerality of life.

At the beginning of the poem, the rose is described as young and "beautiful like the morning," but the other stanzas are dedicated to her strong character in a way that almost undoes the vegetal metaphor. While the rose's red color initially made me think of blushing love and passion, it evokes blood at the end—the blood of the pricked boy, but perhaps also the "blood" of the deflowered rose who is nearing death. This is not a love story, and what is odd is that her namesake, the heath rose (Heiderose, a common name for *Rosa canina*, used in the diminutive form in the poem's title), is actually a bushy pale pink variety with a yellow center that can occasionally be almost white or a deeper hue of pink, but never red. In the poem, Heidenröslein "stands" in red, being quite literally superseded by the image of a long-stemmed red rose, while her actual genus is the "common" rose that lines so many paths and alleys in the home country I share with Goethe. Perhaps no love poem can get away from the trope that "Roses are red..."

Because of (or perhaps despite) her commonness, this rose has become what the boy wants to see, what he wants to possess: a noble red queen of flowers. And in his attempt to attain this figment of his imagination, he kills the real rose (though she is fictional, of course, just as the boy). In many ways, this is the story of plant research: humans try to find what they are looking for at the expense of plants—a new medicine, a trait of resistance to be harvested, or a new product—and often only accidentally discover properties, or rather characteristics, they never expected to find. Studying plants for their own sake, to understand them and our biosphere better has dramatically furthered the human understanding of plant intelligence and behavior in recent years.[8] Returning to my poetic metaphor, these researchers have looked at the rose for what she is instead of imagining her as someone else.

So how do we come to see, to mind, an individual rose for what she is and what might be on the plant's mind? Goethe's poem, though an imaginary account of plant subjectivity, suggests to me that just like any other living being, this rose would like to live on unperturbed. In order to achieve this goal, she is ready to defend herself and equipped with a mechanism for it. Ultimately, she is no match for human hands, but she draws some blood and leaves a mark. Even if the poem didn't put words in the rose's mouth, we would understand what she is communicating. Her breaking tells the age-old story of humankind's assumed superiority, our violent approach to other living beings, and the force with which the human subordinates others.

Yet this rose pricks back. If we allow for the metaphor of defloration in her picking, she has penetrated the assailant first in her pricking. Clearly, she has a mind of her own, concerned with perceiving and fighting off offenders, communicating her resistance and will for survival, and ultimately experiencing suffering on her way to death. A whole lot is going on in the simple act of picking a flower. Maybe this is easier to accept coming from a poem than a research study, but both yield the same results.

Though Goethe's poem speaks about multiple senses—vision, sound, and touch—it curiously has nothing to say about the rose's scent. People respond to the gift of flowers by burying their noses in them—often even when the plants are artificial, which shows that we have been conditioned to react this way to blossoms. The rose attracts humans in this manner, even if her scent was made for other pollinators. It is an act of communication—chemical signaling that persists despite her plucking. With it, she alerts others with all numbers of legs to her presence, but not for the purpose of being stuck into a vase. Rather, her pleasant scent and colorful visuals are attractive to further reproduction, a goal that most modern roses no longer achieve by way of pollination because they have been bred not to produce rose hips. Their petals are too tight to allow for pollination, and so the rose blossom has been deprived of its function.

Rendering the vegetal world increasingly sterile makes both plants and humans dependent on an industry propagating and selling seeds and clippings. Human supply and demand, rather than pollination, now govern the survival and spread of rose species, though ultimately, the appeals of beauty and scent still determine success in this venture. Desire is part of the rose's design. Or rather, desire is part of the design of her reproductive organs, the flower. Leaves, stem, and roots disappear behind this focus on her blossom. The entire plant seems to work toward her flowering, whose purpose has now been altered. A plant that has been cultivated in such ways by humans is called a Kulturpflanze in German—a "culture plant," in which nature and culture curiously coincide.

If a plant has been cultivated for entirely aesthetic purposes, it becomes an ornamental plant—Zierpflanze in German. But roses have also been altered for new uses. The first cyborg rose was born in a lab at a Swedish university a few years ago, where researchers created electronic circuits in the vascular system of a living rose—first a cut flower, later a rose bush—by introducing a conductive liquid polymer to its water. When infusing the leaves with the chemical, their undersides light up like a display. Applications for the bionic rose are far off, but ideas range from having plants signal the need for nitrogen to farmers, prompting plants to bloom or grow faster whenever the weather forecast allows, or even generating electricity from photosynthesis—a different kind of solar energy.[9]

In this experimental setup, the leaves suddenly upstage the blossoms and draw our attention to other parts of the plant. Only a few rose species are evergreen. The leaves grow in a pinnate or feather formation, where they emerge evenly on the left and right of the leaflet, leaving one odd leaf at the top. The leaves have serrated edges that are sometimes reddish rather than green. The thorns are actually prickles, outgrowths of the stem's outer layer, not modified stems. They aid the rose in hanging onto structures, growing over other vegetation, and keeping animals away. Each of the rose's usually five petals corresponds to one sepal, the green structure surrounding flower buds and supporting the blossom. A rose can grow sports, or outgrowths, with blooms that have a different color or other characteristics deviating from the rest of the plant. If you spot a new sport on your rose, you can patent it.

Goethe, who grew roses all around his "garden house" in Weimar, also described a kind of rose that deviated from regular expectations in his 1790 treatise, *The Metamorphosis of Plants*: it was a proliferous rose, where the stem grows through the blossom, turns the sepals into leaves, and buds again.[10] This unusual growth was often called "monstrous" in the biology of the time, yet we learn in a diary entry that Goethe gave such a "beautiful and rare double rose"[11] to his new daughter-in-law as a symbol for the budding marital union. His *Metamorphosis* compared the growth of plant structures over time and suggested that all plant parts, from seed leaves to petals, develop in a series of metamorphoses—summed up his famous hypothesis, "all is leaf."[12] Even though the proliferous rose featured in his theory as an example of irregular, reverse metamorphosis, she must have also struck him as an artwork of nature and a potent, positive metaphor.

Ultimately, the grandest achievement of the rose is her ability to capture the human imagination—to occupy our minds. In my research in literary and cultural plant studies, I call this phytopoetics: the ability of plants to impact the human imagination to such an extent that it results in changes to human culture and society.[13] It is a way for plants (phyto) to participate in the making (poiesis, poetics) of culture, even though ideas that originally come from plants might take on a life of their own in the human cultural sphere and no longer resemble anything in nature in the end. In this way, the rose on the heath might make a case in support of gender equality and against the normalization of unwanted sexualized behaviors at some point in human history. At another, the same rose might have humans consider species equality and plant personhood. Through the poem, she has become immortal, even though the text describes her death.

In the poem, both erotic and violent associations with plants come to the fore. These are common forms of phytopoetics, as I show in my research, and the rose in her thorny beauty can be seen both as passive victim and active agent in these scenarios. Her allure comes with rejection, which produces both more attraction and more violence in the human figure that cannot possess her without paying a price. This kind of strong-mindedness and persistence is apt for a genus that has been thriving for millennia, grows back even stronger after pruning, and whose individuals can live for hundreds of years, like the "Thousand-Year Rose" in Hildesheim, Germany, which survived even the disastrous wartime firebombing of the cathedral on which it leans and is said to be the oldest rose bush in the world.

Perhaps, like Michael Pollan suggests for other plants in *The Botany of Desire*, the rose has, in fact, cultivated humans rather than the reverse.[14] That would explain why my pink and white roses bloom in the desert—they have traveled from Germany with me, if only in my mind, and this houseguest pays the water bill by providing "feelings of home." At the same time, this rose is a sign of settler colonialism, as her European roots are penetrating stolen land. Once again, a pink rose turns bloody red in view of the violence it comes to stand for, and her white neighbors of both the human and floral kind do not represent innocence.

CHAPTER 29

Sago

Metroxylon sagu

Sophie Chao

Songs about the sago palm are prevalent among Indigenous Marind of the Upper Bian borderlands of rural Merauke, West Papua—where vast swaths of native forest are being razed to make way for industrial monocrop oil palm plantations. These songs describe the disappearance of sago palms in the face of deforestation and agribusiness expansion. They speak of lost kin, bleeding rivers, and decimated landscapes. They talk of hunger, sorrow, and loss distributed across species lines. They express the generalized destruction of life prompted by the proliferation of oil palm—a plant whose most devastating impact, Marind affirm, is that of "killing sago."

Marind communities with whom I have been doing ethnographic fieldwork over the last decade are the traditional inhabitants of Merauke, a district located at the southern tip of the Indonesian-controlled region of Papua. In ecological terms, this area is composed of low-lying and generally flat peatland, grassland, and dense swamp forests. In the inland plains, serpentine rivers heave to the cadence of monsoonal rains, giving rise seasonally to Papua's most extensive wetlands. A range of resident and migratory birds, waterfowl, and waders of critical conservation value inhabit this zone of the TransFly EcoRegion, while larger animals, including cassowaries, tree kangaroos, possums, and crocodiles, populate its forests and rivers.

Plant life in the Upper Bian is diverse, with monsoon forests containing an exceptionally high number of endemic plants unique to the region. A mixture of phragmites, tall sedge grasses, and low-swamp grasses flourish in the permanent marshes, while semi-permanent to seasonal melaleuca swamp forests occupy terrains on higher ground. Riverbanks and mangroves are home to dense groves of sago, a pinnate-leaved palm of the humid tropics and freshwater swamps, known in Western taxonomy as

Metroxylon sagu—from *metra* meaning "pith" and *xylon* meaning "plant tissue"—and as *dakh* and *sagu* in Marind and Bahasa Indonesia respectively.

Sago is the source of Marind's staple food—sago starch—which they obtain by felling and rasping the interior of sago trunks, whose pith is then pounded and leached to extract the edible starch. Once dry, the flour is usually cooked as *dakh kakiva*, a chewy mixture of sago, coconut flesh, sago grub larvae, or meat, cooked inside bamboo stalks over a fire. In another variant, *dakh sep*, the ingredients are wrapped in banana or coconut leaves and cooked on hot stones covered with sago fronds or eucalyptus leaves, which enhances their aroma and flavor. However, the significance of the sago palm also extends far beyond the pragmatics of subsistence. Marind consider sago palms to be sentient, agentive beings with whom they share common descent from *dema*, or ancestral creator spirits. Like other forest plants and animals, the relations of sago palms to their human kin are anchored in principles of exchange and care. Sago grows to support Marind by providing them with food and other resources. In return, humans must exercise respect and perform rituals as they encounter and process sago in the forest, recall its stories and consume its starch. These reciprocal acts of care enable humans and sago to sustain each other's growth as inter-agentive members of a shared community of life within the eco-cosmology of the forest. As Oktavius, a middle-aged man from Khalaoyam village, described: "The grove is full of life because sago knows how to share space with others. The sawfish rests in the rivers between its roots. The birds nest at the tip of its trunk. Insects sing with the wind in its fronds. *Anim* (humans) feed off its pith. Sago is a tree of "many lives."

The "many lives" of sago, in Okto's words, encompass myriad organisms that thrive in and from the palm and its environment. Wild pigs, for instance, are attracted by the pith of damaged or deliberately felled palms and the cool waters of the sago swamps. Agile tree kangaroos and sugar gliders leap across the canopy while solitary spotted possums nest between tightly bunched sago fronds. Various avian species are drawn to the grove—where they drink and feed—and to the safety of the sago tree crown, where they roost and mate. These critters include inquisitive red-billed brush turkeys, emeraldine buff-faced pygmy parrots, swooping white-breasted wood swallows, silver-crowned friarbirds, and sharp-eyed grey goshawks. Sago's companion plants are equally plentiful. They include wild sugarcane, campnosperma, swamp oak, pandanus, Bishop wood, bur tree, and nipa palm. In the humid undergrowth, juicy ferns in circinate vernation surround the feet of sago trunks while plump paddy straw mushrooms flourish along mature boles and in piles of rotting sago pith. Termites congregate and nest on the palm in the wet season, while sago palm weevil grubs and larvae incubate in its stumps and pith. Borers and beetles abound in the grove alongside skipper butterflies and bagworms. The humid air is alive with the buzz of pollinating insects, including stingless bees, honey bees, and various wasp species. After it dies, sago continues to feed forest organisms, nourish the soil, and sustain diverse microbial, bacterial, and fungal communities with its rotting pith. The plant perpetuates its vegetal afterlife in the "many lives" sustained by its generative decay.

Over the last decade, hundreds—perhaps thousands—of sago groves in Merauke have been destroyed to make way for oil palm plantations under the so-called Merauke Integrated Food and Energy Estate (MIFEE for short), a food and fuel production scheme promoted by the Indonesian government to achieve national food security and regional economic development. These agribusiness projects are often designed and implemented without the consent of Indigenous Marind landowners and in exchange for derisory compensation. More importantly to many of my interlocutors, the expansion of monocrop oil palm fragments the mutual lifeworlds of human and other-than-human beings in the nourishing environment of the sago grove. Few species can thrive in monocrop oil palm ecologies that are characterized by low canopies, sparse undergrowth, unstable microclimates, high temperatures, and a toxic mélange of chemical fertilizers, herbicides, and pesticides. The soil, stripped of its vegetation through large-scale deforestation and burning, becomes dry, flaky, and wizened. Water supplies, too, are depleted as plantation irrigation diverts, or arrests, the flow of ancestral rivers. Robbed of their nutrients and symbiotes, sago groves collapse as the soil is depleted of minerals and the rivers are contaminated by toxic sludge and chemicals. Meanwhile, the lively multispecies sensorium of the grove is replaced by sounds of death—roaring bulldozers, gnawing chainsaws, the crackle of illegal burning, and the rumble of overloaded oil palm fruit and timber trucks. Songs that once celebrated the multispecies relations of sago now describe the threat posed by oil palm to sago, humans, and other organisms, who are displaced or uprooted from their land and kin.

The destruction of sago groves also erases the multispecies stories (*cerita*) inscribed in the morphology of individual sago plants, which Marind discover through minute scrutiny and physical touch. For instance, sago palms managed by families that have borne many offspring and spread widely across Marind territory are identified by their particularly broad fronds. Thicker spines on the leaflets feature in the story of palms that had to defend themselves from parasitic insects or ravaging forest fires lit by invading tribes in times past. The texture of the pith, too, tells the story of the palm. Where the pith is found to be particularly wet, soft, and dense, community members revel in enumerating the names of the various birds, insects, and mammals who collectively sustained the growth of the palm. Indeed, many palms are named after particular animals in whose company they matured and whom they eventually came to resemble—the "dog sago," for instance, whose curly bole sheaths resemble a dog's floppy ears, or the "cassowary sago," whose palm cabbage is rounded like a cassowary's casque. Certain palms are also named after Marind children whose birth occurred concurrently to their own. These infants are often carried in sago bags made of fronds from their kindred palm such that, as Mariana, a young mother from Bayau village, told me, "sago and Marind can follow each other's lives."

Taking over grove and forest, oil palm severs the shared stories of growth, reproduction, and senescence of Marind and their vegetal companion, the sago palm. As the diversely rhythmic and intersecting life cycles that enliven the forest give way to homogeneous plantations, the call of birds marking the break of dawn, the fall of night, and seasonal transitions, become rare. The times of fruit maturation, bird and animal migration, and fish and amphibian reproduction, too, halt indefinitely. Each organismic death provoked by the arrival of oil palm thus marks the end of a living, fleshy temporality distributed across species lines. Each death obliterates the stories, places, and organisms inscribed in sago's bodily matter. Each death forestalls the possibility of a meaningful present and thwarts the shared futures of the forest's dwindling communities of life.

The destruction of sago groves, and the food that it provides, is also widely associated by Marind with a pervasive and constant sensation of hunger. On the one hand, this hunger is visceral. Deforestation, water contamination, and biodiversity loss have resulted in widespread protein and micro-nutrient deficiencies, infant malnutrition, and food poisoning. On the other hand, for Marind, hunger is also more than just the desire to eat triggered by the lack of food in generic terms. Rather, hunger arises from the loss of foods like sago that are nourishing not because of calorific or nutritional values but rather because of their deep-seated cultural, ecological, and affective significance to Marind.

The disappearance of sago is often linked by Marind to adverse transformations in their bodily constitution. Village women, for instance, spoke of their breasts becoming dry and their skin sallow from the absence of sago. Many community members noted a loss of "wetness"—a Marind concept that refers to bodily substances such as blood, sweat, muscle, and fat—in children who no longer ate sago and whose bodies had become skinny and grey, rather than glossy and taut. People also described how the experience of hunger and of witnessing the hunger of others gave rise to feelings of sadness, pity, and, in particular, a pervasive sense of loneliness arising from a severed connection to the forest and its diverse lifeforms. For instance, women mourned the decimation of sago groves where they had once celebrated their role as mothers in the company of a plant whose fertile flesh and fluids, much like their own, had provided Marind children with nourishing sustenance. Marind's plant and animal kin, too, were said to "go hungry" because of oil palm's arrival. Robbed of their water, nutrients, and symbiotes, sago groves that once thrived in the company of humans wilt to dust. Marind thus conceive of and experience hunger as a multispecies phenomenon, one distributed across humans, plants, and animals who once sustained each other through nourishing exchanges of flesh and fluids.

In contrast to the fleshy stories of sago palms and sago people that enliven the landscape, oil palm—the cash crop relentlessly taking over grove and forest—is considered a destructive, rapacious, and selfish plant-being by many Marind. Oil palm thrives in heavily guarded concessions that erode the dynamic topography of the forest and rupture the flowing paths of plants, animals, and humans. The plant's expansion fragments the mutual lifeworlds of human and other-than-human beings and dislocates them from their constitutive relations and environments. In the monocrop ecologies replacing the diversely populated forest realm, few species other than oil palm can survive. Oil palm, Yustina, a young woman from Mirav, told me, refuses to coexist with other lifeforms because it "does not like to live with others" and "prefers to be alone." Similarly, Selly, a middle-aged widow from Bayau, described oil palm as a selfish plant that "has few friends" and that "does not want to share space with others."

Oil palm's inexorable proliferation is also associated by some Marind with insatiable greed. "When oil palm is hungry," Selly continued, "it eats everything, just like the bulldozers and the state. It eats the land and it eats the water. It kills our plant and animal siblings and it kills Marind people. Oil palm eats everything. It leaves only scraps for the others." Under the regimented surveillance of the monocrop landscape, physical encounters with oil palm are rare and dangerous. Consequently, oil palm is devoid of the affectively charged fleshiness that enables organisms in the forest to respect and respond to each other in transformational interspecies encounters. Instead, the plant exists through the meaningful voids and obstructions it creates within the landscape—the vast swaths of razed vegetation, the oily waters of the Bian River, the poisoned fish strewn across the riverbanks, and the choking haze enshrouding the villages. The cash crop itself has yet to be planted in many concessions, but its presence is already violently tangible in the haunting rubble and ruination of the forest.

The opacity of oil palm's story is heightened by the fact that few community members know where oil palm seeds originate from, what trajectories they take to reach Merauke, and how they travel beyond West Papua. Throughout its serpentine journey from seed to frying pan, palm oil as a product flows through the palms of multiple actors across various sites. From biotechnology labs to nurseries, plantations, mills, and refineries, the oil travels to manufacturing plants across the globe, mixing with oils and ingredients from other sources, only to disperse and form new liquid mélanges as it is loaded onto ships, planes, and trucks for transport to warehouses and stores. Yet, for Indigenous Marind on the ground, the processes, labors, actors, institutions, and relations that coalesce and congeal in palm oil remain shrouded in mystery. Similarly, the consumers of palm oil produced on Marind soils live in distant places, and their identities are unknown. The plant's ambiguity is thus exacerbated by the invisibility of the human actors driving and benefiting from its expansion.

And what of hope in the midst of extinction? Kristofera, a middle-aged woman from Bayau village, once told me: "Marind do not know the story of oil palm. It comes from a foreign place and it kills the sago. But maybe one day, oil palm will come to understand us and we will come to understand oil palm. Then, there may be hope. Then, there may be new stories."

Many Marind resent oil palm for its devastating effects on the multispecies lives and futures enabled by sago palms. However, others like Kristofera express great curiosity toward the foreign plant taking over their lands. For instance, many among my interlocutors pondered at length over where palm's home is, who its kin are, and what relations it sustains with humans and other beings in its native soils. Speculation abounded over oil palm's multi-sited flows as plant, part, and product along dispersed channels of provision, distribution, and accumulation. Community members wondered how oil palm grows in the other places where it is cultivated industrially—for instance, Colombia, Nigeria, Ecuador, India, and Peru—and, more importantly, whether oil palm is as destructive in these distant countries as it is in Merauke. Others were curious as to how plantations in West Papua connected them to palm oil-consuming communities across the Indonesian archipelago and beyond vast oceans to the biofuel-hungry nations of Europe and the United States. Oil palm, too, I was often told, has a home, kin, and relations to humans and other organisms back in its native soils.

As such, Marind are not indifferent to the lifeworld of oil palm beyond what they themselves experience in its destructive presence. Their animosity toward this introduced and harmful plant-being goes hand in hand with a recognition that oil palm, too, has a storied existence—with other beings, in other places. As Kristofera suggests, finding hope in the rubble of capitalist expansion will require that Marind find ways to relate to, and better understand, the needs, growth, and stories of oil palm—a plant whose proliferation currently undermines the possibility of multispecies hope. Imagining what that storied existence might be constitutes a form of care in the absence of the encounters and knowledges that enable plants and persons to make stories together. Then, perhaps, unexpected collaborations across species lines may enable more livable shared futures. Budding organismic assemblages may work together to remake the sentient landscape of the Upper Bian (at least a little) differently and less violently. But whether and what the future can be will depend as much on Marinds' attempts to know the story of oil palm as on oil palm's own willingness to partake in the shared stories of the forest and its sentient beings.

CHAPTER 30

Samphire

Salicornia europaea

Harriet Tarlo with images by Judith Tucker

up to fuller creek, light growing golden

lavender over, inflorescences wash
into estuary to wash in, seed back in spring

samphire, samphire, pale pink
tips taking light samphire shadows
risen all over out of dark-mud flats

weed-draped samphire
scattered then dense wet-smoothed dried
skin over *cachrys*
between creeks, stirring pinkgreen, greenpink in low wind
tasting, scenting salt in samphire
shaped samphire

casting an eye for figures
metal detector, cockle-picker, dog-walker
human purposes here but the bigger place is sky, birds
and their purposes
more, so many flights and calls

over fallen wood, sand-filled bark striations, turning silver
sand gold layered over into each other

feels like morning   where beach meets marsh   mud-dapple-sand

creek narrows at curve, where the crossing place is, ripples under wind-line dynamic

crushing tread through   thick softness
yellow-ending marsh plants   no ground visible
samphire pink-tipped salt-made succulence plant tangles
through it all   small pipings fly up and   over warm narrow creeks
flowing their brown through green through orange gold
mud-waters   full life almost hidden in silty opaque
in shallows, a crab crosses into weed   then gone into camouflage complete

in places, at moments
still bubbles hold still
after everything

sometimes something flickers intermittent particles shifting surface
rise from below or fall from sky, catching light, seeming
to decide or drift, not one way, but stir
or rock, gentle, within
mud-bowl bank curves
a lapping line of translucent light … follow
and it enters shadow, paled edge, reflects marsh plants
somehow stilled, from their windblown life above, lying over a leaf,
a sycamore wing, a strand of weed   floating   through flickering water-life

long-curved-beaked call of grey plover   urgently over and back and over
marshes, searching mud channels run out now
their drying, cracking, slipped sides slow-subsiding
into heaped rich-sludge-thick once-was-water places

we couldn't know how it all works, so multitudinous a movement
of much mud, much sand, much water, many, many plants the same, their roots
merging under it all each and every[1]

Fig. 1: Judith Tucker, *Crushing Tread Through*, 2015, oil on canvas, 61 x 183 cm, collection N. Edwards.

In this poem, part of a long series, I walk the reader over a particular Northeast Lincolnshire beach in England and wonder about the many plants that grow around the creekside. The walk was not taken alone. Since 2011 I have been working with painter Judith Tucker, responding to the deeply entwined human and more-than-human elements of specific places in the British landscape. This could perhaps be said of most of our landscape in the UK, a small and all too lived-in nation. Since 2013, when this poem was written, we have responded to the beaches, marshes, agricultural fields, canal and locks, plants and birds, as well as the local environmental politics relating to water and energy in Lincolnshire. We stayed at the Humberston Fitties Plotland or Chalet Park near the seaside town of Cleethorpes, where Northern British working people have holidayed since the Industrial Revolution and made work about that too.[2]

At the beginning of 2019, we narrowed in on the saltmarsh and its plants to develop a series of texts under the name "Saltwort" and paintings under the name "Dark Marsh." These appeared together in a London exhibition, "Low Lying," and we are making more work for a further exhibition in Scunthorpe, entitled "Hideaway."[3] These titles are suggestive of the marginalized nature of these plants, the adjacent chalet park, and the whole area, which I have elsewhere called "behind land."[4] During the development of this work, the walk from our chalet lodging on the old plotland above, over the beach to the creekside marsh, became a sort of pilgrimage. Fieldwork is a particular kind of walking, sensing, and looking leading to drawing, painting, and writing—all slow, circling, embodied processes. Our poking about in small areas is closer to the behavior of scientists than one might suppose, and it often brings to mind the opening of Lorine Niedecker's poem "Darwin":

His holy
          slowly
                    mulled over
  matter

As the poem cited at the beginning shows, samphire is a dominant plant of this saltmarsh. Together with cordgrass (*Spartina anglica*) it is one of the "pioneer plants" (dubious as the human connotations of the term may be) that expands or re-establishes saltmarsh where it has been depleted.

Fig. 2: Judith Tucker, *Dark Marsh: Cord Grass*, oil on linen, 30 x 40 cm, 2019

When I first encountered samphire properly, you could almost say I fell in love with it—for its colors, its scent, and its taste. I repeat its name as a lover might in this poem, and its pinkness hung over the marsh paintings made by Judith at this time. Although other plants are important to the marsh, such as the ever-present sea blite (*sueda*) and purslane (*Halimione portulacoides*), and many grasses, reeds, rushes, and plantains, samphire is a constant at every level, ignoring ecologists' and botanists' attempts to zone the marsh into lower, middle, and upper levels, zones, and such like.

Only when we embarked on our current project into saltwort plants was I to learn to respect samphire's agential powers, for its pioneering behavior, the hermaphroditic abilities located in its tiny flowers, but most of all for its tenacity. I researched scientific "facts" in books about saltmarsh ecology to understand how halophytes survive high and varied levels of salination and exposure to river and rainwater via a series of processes called "plant-water relations."[5] The plants make rooted and cellular decisions, pumping ions back out of the cytoplasm, exercising mechanisms of "exclusion, shedding, and dilution," and other energetic actions necessary for their survival in relation to tide and weather.[6] I began to conceive of each cell as active and engaged as if there are not just one, but many brains at work in each plant and between plants. The "relations" element also seemed important in an understanding that multiple active agencies are at work here.

Fig. 3: Judith Tucker, *Dark Marsh: Samphire,* oil on linen, 30 x 40 cm 2019

It is a truism that we need to close—or inhabit—disciplinary gaps to understand our environment, especially those between arts and sciences. As Rachel Carson said in her acceptance speech for the National Book Award in Nonfiction in 1952: "It seems to me, then, that there can be no separate literature of science… If there is poetry in my book about the sea, it is not because I deliberately put it there, but because no one could write truthfully about the sea and leave out the poetry."[7] Equally important is the comment by Objectivist poet Lorine Niedecker (1903–70) made in a letter to Louis Zukofsky in 1958: "For me, when it comes to birds, animals, and plants, I'd like the facts because facts are wonderful in themselves."[8] It is in the meeting of those "facts" with the poetic that we might find mind-changing understanding.

Samphire has an extraordinary color range. The "pinkgreen greenpink" of the September plant celebrated in the poem above is but one stage. In my fieldwork notes from visits to this patch of saltmarsh from 2013 to 2020, I find many references to the fresh green brightness of the early tiny protuberances of the plant in late spring and growing shoots of early summer. As it grows into its prime, the pink creeps from tips to stem, and this is followed by the deeper reds, caught in the vermilion, magenta, and alizarin crimson of Judith's winter saltmarsh paintings. In an entangled piece of prose poetry, I explored the seasonal development of the samphire plants along with their companions:

Fig. 4: Judith Tucker, *Dark Marsh: Winter Samphire*, oil on linen, 30 x 40 cm, 2020

SALTWORT

Cord grass colonizing sand under water out of water setting roots setting mud flat wedges curling up to ever-present sea purslane (*Halimione portulacoides*) mycorrhizal roots spreading below, branches creeping sandpink edges above into **MAY** samphire (*Salicorna europea)* seedlings pushing up on open mud, pushing up globular not yet branching pinkgreen across mud flats salt pans shallow pools at the creek edges higher according to light, tide, strength, site, climbing tiny banks higher at bottom shorter struggling up   broad lush leaves of sea lavender (*Limonium vulgare*), occasional buds in tight turned swirl of energy, high over others, pioneering, pushing through just stalking not branching under cord grass flags (*Spartina anglica* and *S. maritima* long gone) green out of dry stalks slowing water down building mud build gutweed bladder-wrack crab corpses stranded over purslane sprawl surely more than one pattern strong or foolish ones/individuals in relation to light, sun, place, tide brave it out of seed, of roots seedings to tangle with pale early white-pink thrift flowers within flower out of bronze sheath under singing lark sky low and middle marsh zones will not separate at beach edges, even high marsh resists definition entering in marsh heart of golden creek & pool land, points of white English sea scurvygrass *Cochlearia anglica, one of the first flowers of saltmarsh* leaves storing up water anglica with a catch and tapering a single serration distinguishes separation from self yellow hearts eye in tiny white flower some already podding up rosettes flowing up from crimson stem through grey-green tangle mosaic purslane spreading rosettes purslane leaves elliptical seeming soft but sharp spreading covering salt glands sending salt out into leaves, dropping colour on mud-sand scurvy grass threads through marsh takes its space & time first sea arrowgrass *Triglochin maritima* slim half-cylindrical curving among early plantain leaves emerging higher by mud-rush clumps pools wet edges sheath-spiking out of curves just making early purples tiny separate globes holding seeds on inflorescent stalks annual seablite *Suaeda maritime* curling coming up quickly out of making sediment quirky swirling into stem, leaf thick with water, salts in near cylindrical stems red-greens streaks, red-flushed leaves **JUNE** they push up through sun & rain, hold against wind, bright against grey sea lavender's orangey roots washed over sand edge of salicorna flags establishing low tide at edges samphire rising forming side shoots not yet full so bright green near pale purpling tiny purples lavender some arrowgrass pale, some purple new bright red squiggles of seablite scurvy grass finished flowering green-seed podded purslane putting up higher shoots starting to form flowers - shoots getting higher silvery grey sea wormwood serrated fronding broken shell path edges **JULY** mauve-purples gradating lavender flowering swathing through thrift formed small pale pink grey green white seed pods within pods, colour sucked back purslane almost flowering beginnings of little yellow flower heads offsetting grey, goldy brown haze (lead tin yellow)   cord grass putting up flower stems begins with single white-light fringed edged stem each forming muddy bubbles as it breaks pool-surface   next to samphires spreading trees, glassworts once dashed & burnt for soap and glass, poor man's asparagus, pickle weed, succulent   shrubby seablite breaking out of last year's dry stems   wormwood pushing up to form flowerheads over long time curving round blank warning disk sign faded out but still standing, one among many wordless signs   seablite still rising, not flowering, tight-bobbling forming   Sea Plantain *Plantago maritima* growing yellow anthers purple petals up-stem up stigma shape to shaking wind fruit flicker lines out of damp land nurtured arrow grass sea arrowgrass rubbery succulence sheath us out leaf-curve into space through marsh thickening deepening colour, lengthening long semi-cylindrical spikes of ovaries   dark stemmed clumped sea rushes, their pointed round spiked stems, bees crickets winds maritima purling yellow through purple-green-grey marsh mosaic breathing salt in, out of I each we cell water hold behind color withered below, flowering mid-stem, moving up to form top fruit.

Fig. 5: Judith Tucker, *Dark Marsh: Roots*, oil on linen, 30 x 40 cm 2019

Seasonal changes are evident here, but also the environmental factors that affect this: the varying dominance of grass, mud, and sand, the relation to sea, creeks, saltpans, and pools; and the exposure to sun and shade (see lines 4–7). So, I experience and embody saltmarsh here more as a mosaic than a set of zones, a term some writers do use.[9] Molecular biologist and advocate of plant intelligence, Anthony Trewavas, considers how colonizing land leads to a distribution of essential resources in a "spatial and temporal mosaic."[10] Throughout his work, Trewavas de-turns language used about animals to plants, offering new ways of seeing them:

> Just as the roving animal locates potential food and *moves* towards it, growing plants have to identify the locations of richest support of resources in their surrounding space and *grow* towards and capture them. In this situation, growth acts like very slow movement.[11]

In noting that plant growth and turgor changes are "too slow and below our ability to easily see," Trewavas throws the emphasis back on our failure to perceive the otherness of plants in a subtle rhetorical maneuver. In this prose poem, I try to bring out the agency of the plants, the sense of embodied—yet thinking—processes that they engage in, including observations that bring out the commonalities and differences between saltmarsh plants. The title "Saltwort," in the singular, gestures toward the ecosystem as a singular being, not just a series of individuals. In all these ways, the emphasis is not purely on the aesthetic.

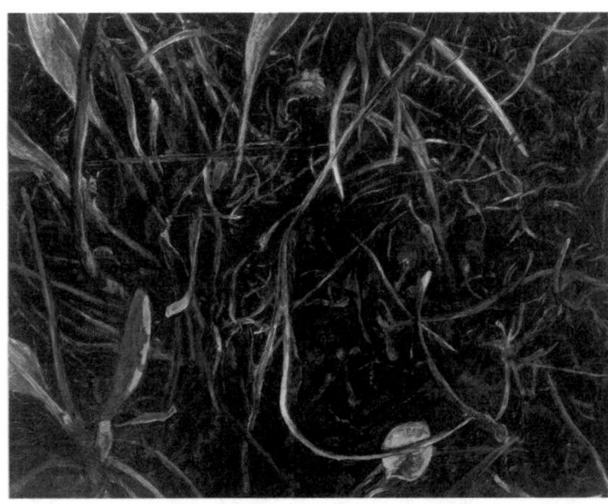

Fig. 6: Judith Tucker, *Dark marsh: winter tangle*, oil on linen, 30 x 40 cm 2020

It is, strangely, an effort of mind, body, and heart, a pushing against our conditioned senses, to think like this about plants, or to think with plants, or even to think about "Becoming Plant."[12] The visitor to the Humberston saltmarsh in mid-summer will find that their eye is drawn to the purples of the common sea lavender *(Limonium vulgare)* and, in the autumn, to the mauves of the sea aster (*Aster tripolium*). These are the stars of the saltmarsh show, the "charismatic species" of the coastal plant world. Our conventional aesthetic values trump other definitions of value that might exist, including the multiple ways of being of the plant itself. This can all too easily close off and objectify a plant, denying it its own senses, actions, and, ultimately, mind.

Our predecessors might have come to the marsh seeking food or medicine rather than aesthetic pleasure. Exploring the names of individual plants and genera, as I do in this work, reveals how humans, the Adamic labelers of nature, have extracted and manipulated the raw material of plants for our purposes. "Wort," from the old English "wyrt," is a common and ancient suffix referring to a plant's medicinal or culinary uses. In this, it is distinguished from plant names with the suffix "weed," which were (are still?) seen as less useful, and in danger of choking out the valuable worts—for example, knotweed, hawkweed, fireweed, and bindweed. So, lungwort, spleenwort, bladderwort, nipplewort, and liverwort all reference parts or ailments of the body that might be treated by the plant concerned. As "glasswort," samphire was commonly burnt between the sixteenth and nineteenth century in order to release sodium. The resulting soda ash was fused with sand to make glass, and this discovery is intimately connected

Fig.7: Judith Tucker, *Dark marsh: sea lavender,* oil on linen, 30 x 40 cm 2019

with a resurgence in English glass-making.[13] This was not the only halophyte to be used in this way, hence the generic name "saltwort." The current name, samphire, derives from the French, *herbe de Saint Pierre* via the intermediary term, *sampiere*.

Judith and I have written elsewhere about how working together as artist and poet help us try to combat these different anthropocentric perspectives by an open, exploratory approach full of repetitions and variations. Our texts and images appear together in different guises: concrete, discursive, online, and sonic. "Saltwort," for instance, was built up from smaller, more minimalist poems that relate to each other as individual plants relate to their ecosystem. Seen on the wall, alongside Judith's paintings, the viewer can perceive language spatially and "read" painting and poem together.

scurvy grass
podding up
storing water
anglica with
a catch single
serration distinguishes
separation
from self

Our two disciplines work together against the distancing and objectification that a single form can produce, complementing each other and attempting to offer space for the viewer to be in conversation with the work, to be the third component in the equation and thus to question, in this case, what a plant like samphire is and does.

glasswort greenpink globular
across pools, flats climbing under
tiny banks up to under tight turned buds
pale thrift green lavender
out rooting

Fig. 8: Judith Tucker, *Dark Marsh: Thrift,* oil on linen, 30 x 40 cm. 2019

The wall offers a ground for these plants and their organic forms, allowing us to imagine plant shapes and energies in self-propelled movement under and above earth. Lines stretch out, spaces allow words to interweave between lines, and space evokes but does not explicitly draw stalking, leafing, rooting dynamics.

pioneering   breaking saltpan   stalking then
branching cord grass flags
spartina green
bubbles
surface
slows
water
down building
sediment mud   land

Even the most sensitive embodied "lyric I" so easily, so quickly, takes over in the language of poetry—these short pieces allow that poet person to be suppressed, to attempt to allow the plant consciousness to surface in acts of radical imagining.

bees browse
plantago
up stem up

stigma to
wind quake
fruit flick
past dark
sea rush
points
breathe salt
in out each
cell hold
water
behind
yellow

Our paintings and poems play with scale, and hence value, in that plants are defamiliarized, seen very closely so that the human eye seems restricted and the plants the center of action and focus. No walker would see plants like this. You would have to be lying low in the marsh, as close as an insect to the flowerhead.

Fig. 9: Judith Tucker, *Dark Marsh: Evening Thrift*, oil on linen, 30 x 40 cm.

wetgold creekside arrowgrass inflorescent
spines early purples out curves
into thickening space
deepening colour time
lengthening *maritima*

The uncanniness of the paintings cannot be reduced to sublime, picturesque, or beautiful. The very juxtaposition of the two disciplines contributes to a shift in scale as macro plants loom over the micro-letters and lines of poems.

cochleria   white   flowing up
through   softgrey   purslane   rosettes   sharp
elliptical   leafed   yellow eyed tangle
crab corpse   strewn   bladderwrack
under   singing lark   skies

The closer in, the more micro we go, the deeper we get into the embedded broader, even global, issues and ideologies. Once again, the names give us the clue as to where samphire might go next. Its culinary uses are clearly discerned in its common names, reflecting its uses as a cooked, raw, or pickled vegetable rich in vitamin C and antioxidants. Like the aptly named scurvygrass, the first plant to flower on the saltmarsh every year, it was used as a preventative against scurvy, picked fresh by sailors or taken to sea pickled. The names also demonstrate its ubiquity along coasts all over the world, where it and its relative, rock samphire, are called sea bean, sea fennel, pickle weed, pickle grass, sea asparagus, crow's foot greens, *glasört* (Swedish), *toongtoongmadi* (Korean), *zeekraal* (Dutch), *almyrides* (Greek), and *yan jiao cao* and *hamcho* (Chinese).[14] It has been reclaimed as an element of gourmet cuisine, but also grown commercially in Kuwait, Mexico, California, and Europe for food, for oil, for its antioxidant, antimicrobial, anti-inflammatory, and anti-tumor medicinal properties, and for wastewater management. As this develops, there is the common temptation to increase intervention with the wild plant, as a recent study in developing samphire in Ireland suggests: "selective breeding and PGPB [plant-growth-promoting bacteria] work has not yet been conducted on *S. europaea*, however, this work could greatly improve its commercial development."[15] How will this be regulated, or will it?

All this seems a world away from our little patch of samphire at Humberston. Not all eating of wild plants has to be exploitative, of course. We can forage samphire carefully for domestic use by picking the tops and leaving the woody stems to re-grow. Whilst older people at the Fitties plotland talked to us about harvesting samphire and cockles from the beach, many younger inhabitants did not realize samphire was present, nor that it could so simply be picked and eaten. Yet, for us, to walk along in sunny weather, eating the crisp, salty, fresh, succulent stalks made us feel as if the sea was inside us, rather than alongside us. To take samphire back at the end of a fieldwork trip to our home ninety miles inland was to bring the sea with us in edible form.

Fig. 10: Judith Tucker *Dark Marsh: Winter Samphire,* large oil on linen, 60 x 80 cm, 2020

Samphire also helps us to think about conservation issues in the face of the climate crisis. Such bioregions have been under threat from as early as Roman times, when they first began to be "reclaimed" from the sea for agriculture and human settlements. Now, in our "Anthropocene" age, modern developments, climate change, sea-level rise, and hard sea defenses erode them even further, threatening this habitat. The original "soft defense," the sand dunes, are long gone, replaced by groynes and gabions, with stones most often imported from Norway. However, through their low-lying, low-layering land-building processes, "pioneer" samphire and cord-grass are capable of establishing sedimentation and new saltmarshes (to the tune of 200 meters of new marsh in twenty-five years just up the coast from Humberston).[16] They might prove saviors of the land on the eroded east coast of the UK if humans were to hold back from seeing the "dangerous creek" and muddy saltmarsh as threats to prized sandy beaches.

Let's fantasize that saltmarsh all along the east coast were left to its own devices. Would it build a new Planthropocene coastline, one from which humans might also benefit from if they were capable of doing so within sustainable limits, rather than building "Capitalocene" markets? Natasha Myers' playful speculative fabulations about a possible future Planthropocene in which humans cede control to plants and find new ways to live and make art has taken off on the web among plant-lovers.[17] This would, however, require a change in our thinking in which we no longer perceived plants as caught within anthropocentric, binary thinking as objects for exploitation or as passive victims of exploitation. We might then be able to perceive plants as knowing their own minds, and this might make all the difference.

POEM 9

Sandalwood

Santalum spicatum

Chelinay Gates (Malardy)

For as long as we the Sandalwood can remember,
You black fellas have always come on foot.
Walking this hot land in small family groups,
Respectfully you collect our wood, twigs, and leaf,
For special ceremonies and as medicine for devil's kidney and dysentery.
Our drupe is a tasty treat for the children, although it's not sweet.

Twigs and Branches,
Leaves and Roots.

Hey girl,
You're lookin' lost.
The sun is fierce, it's far too hot,
Come sit down beside me,
Lean in real close.
I'll protect you and give you insight into them worries you've got.
Take a couple of me blue leaves and chew 'em real good,
They'll wet your tongue and calm your heart.
And even put a smile on them dry lips.

Twigs and Branches,
Leaves and Roots.

When I was young,
Still growing on my host,

Huge humpbacked creatures with cloven hoof,
Lurched to a halt just over there.
They'd brought their tall-nosed masters here to pray.
The men didn't stay,
But their long-tongued, rubber-lipped creatures still devastate us today.

Twigs and Branches,
Leaves and Roots.

Soon white men poured in
On things called trucks.
The old were first,
Limbs and trunks were felled.
A sweetness rose up and filled the air.
It was grace that we offered,
To those men who didn't care.

Twigs and Branches,
Leaves and Roots.

I'm alone just like you.
My mother is dead.
But her heart is near you just off to your left.
Sweet girl, dig it up for me,
Her heart-wood is still good.
Please set her heart alight,
So that our souls may take flight.
And there from above we'll send out a prayer,
To bless this world, its people and all plants and creatures.
And the Sandalwood trees,
Growing everywhere.

CHAPTER 31

Silver Fir

Abies alba

Céline Cholewka and Giorgia Tresca

It was a sunny autumn afternoon, and I was sitting on a terrace in Abruzzo, Italy, gazing over five firs planted below me in a garden. The phone rang, and it was a woman I knew named Céline. She told me she wanted to share something with me, which until that moment had remained between her and some firs she knew. She began her tale, and I was immediately immersed in the events she described, many of which are a challenge to recount. Nevertheless, I am quite sure that once you have heard it, you will agree that my account is just an ordinary bit of communication in this quite extraordinary story.

I will start by setting the scene: a magical place in the countryside of the French region of Auvergne, called Pachamanta, which means "what comes from the earth" in the Quechua language. I had the chance to visit it in the summer of 2018, as I was conducting fieldwork on the development of Amazonian healing practices in Europe for my master's thesis. Pachamanta presented itself to me as a sun-kissed French farmhouse, with old, rustic flower pots and radiant, rambling roses growing up against the walls. Yet, from the main house, a path opened up and led down to the forest, dampened by an ice-cold river, embracing hectares of shade filled with moisture and fermented smells. And I consider it magical because it seems to, or perhaps now truly does, lie in another dimension. A world inhabited by beings allowed to freely wander the forest, beings who are visible only to some—a place where one discovers nature as soulful.

It is important to tell you how this place came to be. As a young French herbalist in her twenties, Céline set out to work in the herbal manufacturing laboratory of Takiwasi, found in the city of Tarapoto in the Peruvian Amazon. Both a research center for traditional Peruvian medicine and a therapeutic community, Takiwasi aims at combining the practices of

Amazonian herbalism with psychotherapy in order to treat addiction. As Céline became acquainted with the regional healing practices, she felt called to be initiated into the local herbalism and was apprenticed by a curandero or healer from the nearby village of Chazuta. As part of her initiation, she dieted with Amazonian plants for months. This refers to the practice of ingesting medicinal plant preparations in a state of seclusion, surrounded by nature, abiding to dietary and behavioral restrictions. Through this dieting, she would acquire knowledge of the plants' properties, tune her senses to their language and establish relations to their spirits for healing purposes.

One day, while resting in her diet hut in Peru, she received specific teachings on the use of European plants. In another instance, a dream revealed to her that she should return to diet the plants of her own native territory in France. Although this was unexpected, Céline followed the advice, moved back home, and embarked on a learning journey by choosing the plants she had grown up with to be her teachers. Dedicated to the task of developing this intimate form of herbalism, she bought land where she could have a safe space to engage with her teachers. In Pachamanta, she would not be distracted by what we tend to define as "life," even though she committed herself to researching life. With oaks, birches, firs, deer, and boars as her neighbors, she created a place of safety for plants and animals to be recognized as beings to interact with and learn from. She continued to diet plants, and in doing so, could feel their character, learned how to summon their power, and also allowed them to accompany her in her day-to-day life. As she walked this path, she was regularly called by the plants who wanted to teach her.

I remember when I first heard about Céline's work. I was volunteering for a project in Peru in February 2017 and had barely any knowledge of plant shamanism when someone introduced me to the concept of plant diets and how they may offer a connection to the plant spirit world. I have to admit it was one of the rare moments that I felt like a child again as if magic was brought back into my world. One of the first questions that popped into my mind was if I could diet the plants back home in Europe. I saw in dieting a tool that could offer a way for me to relate on a deeper level to the plants I knew already, the trees onto which I had climbed as a child, or the shrubs I observed on my daily walks. Reaching out to their knowledge and drawing closer to their mind felt both necessary and healing to me. I remember how, in that moment, I was told that a woman called Céline Cholewka worked with European plants in France. One year later, when I had to choose my research topic for my master's thesis, it did not take me long to find my way to Pachamanta and explore how diets were shaping people's relation to the environment in Europe.

It was through my fieldwork with her that I discovered how plants participated in Celine's personal development: her thoughts, emotions, and identity. I also discovered how they offered her a gateway into time and into their personal history. It was almost as if they were passing on their experience, gathered over centuries, through an environmental memory of what they had witnessed. So, by dieting trees, she was also dieting their surroundings—both learning them and becoming part of them. The ecosystem made its way inside of Céline; her mind and her thoughts are now shaped by the perspectives, knowledge, and chemistry of her land. One could say Céline no longer thinks alone; she thinks with her environment.

One day, as Céline was passing under a giant white fir, she was struck by something I could probably call a feeling, but that I will call knowledge instead. In that immediate moment, she knew the tree was very old, possibly much older than many others surrounding it. Céline perceived the tree's "mother" identity within that space, for it held a supporting role to smaller kin-related trees. She felt it calling her to diet it. Days later, she dwelled in the forest and, by ingesting it, allowed its presence to permeate her. She ascertained how, beyond simply opening up respiratory ways through its well-known expectorant properties, the fir freed up energetic passages in the body to dissolve those tensions and emotional blockages that hinder a smooth breath and keep us from breathing deeply. Thanks to fir, thoughts became more fluid and less of an obstacle to her sense of awareness and belonging to the environment. Céline described a feeling of having her feet grounded to the earth and her hair up in the stars.

As she was dieting fir, Céline also received an icaro or chant, from the plant itself, that can be used to summon fir's spirit and unleash its healing power. At one point, the chant goes like this: "Make sure I don't lose my colors, paint all my wounds and all my sorrows green." This is a call for strength and resilience in the face of pain, sorrow, and illness. Perhaps it is tied to fir's evergreen nature and to its ability to thrive in cold and shady environments. But, as Céline also reminded me, firs have powerful deep roots, which keep them anchored to the earth and allow them to safely grow in height. When the wind blows, they sing and dance together, their tips gently swaying. They are not threatened. By choosing to grow side-by-side, they can protect each other, as well as other species, from the wind. Therefore, their spirit of loyalty, resistance, and humility finds echoes in their ecological character.

During Céline's therapeutic practice—offering diets in Pachamanta—she does not reduce plants to therapeutic tools for personal growth, nor to dispensers of molecules that serve only to polish the lens on one's inner world. She recognizes them as subjects; she lives among them, studies their ecological and spiritual lives, and assimilates them through her senses. She affirms that healing requires developing one's knowledge of nature, learning to maintain harmony with it, and confronting one's interrelatedness to non-human others. Similar, in a way, to how one would heal by reconnecting with a family we never had the chance to get to know.

When people visit Pachamanta, they are, on some level, agreeing to be guided by Céline into a relationship with a plant and the surrounding space. They are offered a small wooden hut under the welcoming shade of trees. The hypnotic sounds of insects and the slow passing of time allow people to feel, see, and liberate pieces of inner worlds that have been neglected and that therefore have clogged their perception and blurred their clarity. A lean and saltless diet opens up pockets of space in one's self and increases the physical, emotional, and spiritual porosity, both to the surrounding environment and to the medicinal plant, allowing it to participate in their life and thoughts. When overseeing the diet process, Céline approaches the huts twice a day, bringing the plant medicine, but also food, water, and bed covers or hot water bottles, in case it is cold. She asks the dieters how they feel every day and what they have dreamt the night before. By monitoring their symptoms, she is able to watch over the relationship that is coming to life between the dieter and the plant and then mediates it through additional rituals or advice.

Through the diet, a person is given the chance to slow down and open up to the possibility of beginning a conversation with nature, where it is not only us humans who talk, interpret, and act over an inert "it." We sit still, isolated from people and distractions, and give the plants the chance to show themselves, the same way we would need to stop, sit down and drink a coffee with someone if we really want to see, feel, and get to know them. I remember my own experience when I started dieting birch at Céline's place during my fieldwork. I immediately had a strong feeling of vulnerability, one I did not have in the previous days while walking in similar forests. I felt that the diet invited me to give up a form of power and safety and no longer depend on my domination. As I was resting on my hammock, I could not do much else other than wait for the plant to visit me. I was surrendering to her and allowing her to show me the way. I could not control my emotions or my thoughts. I remember feeling anger I did not want to feel. The word "intention" became weak, and I slowly gave up on having one during this week. I understood the plant was actually pushing me into feeling anger and freeing me from it.

When the diet was over, I made my way back home, stopping at my mother's house in Switzerland. I was weak from the fasting and drained from the heat of the summer, the long train ride, and the swarms of people. I remember coming home through the front door and only a few minutes later having to walk straight out the back door to sit under the trees and find some relief. As I sat in the shade of a small Elder, I turned around and suddenly acknowledged the giant, possibly century-old fir at the end of our small garden. I cannot explain why, but it was the dieting that finally made me see the power of this tree—how it had stood by our family house, guarding and protecting it for so many years without me paying it any attention. I am not sure what my mother thought when I tried to explain to her the importance of this fir, and I am not sure how much of that understanding is still with me today, but for a few days, I recognized its age and its power. For weeks following the diet, it was only under the shade of a tree that I felt safe and joyful, perhaps a nurturing way of the plant I dieted to call me back to her and to her intention. I came to realize how dieting may open a window for plants to connect with our minds and show us a different world, gifting us with moments in which we realize they are far more present than we would think.

One of these moments of realization for Céline was when she was leading someone in a one-week-long fir diet in Pachamanta. Céline prepared the plant medicine with the firs growing in her land and, in order not to harm the firs, she collected small quantities of plant material from various trees on her land. Throughout the preparation of the brew, she chanted her icaro, invoking the spirit of fir, inviting it to be present and guide her work. Absorbed in the production of her remedy, Céline heard her golden retriever, Kuko, bark outside. This happens continuously because Pachamanta abounds with animals that attract his attention. Yet, in this instance, Céline felt driven to follow him. With no clue as to where this would take her or why she was even following him in the first place, she unquestionably walked behind him. Kuko led her five hundred meters downhill to a spot by the river, immersed in the forest of firs below her land.

When Céline arrived, she saw a man on the opposite shore, just outside the border of Pachamanta. Under the shade of those trees, with no hesitation, she warned him that he was walking on private land and asked him what he was doing there. He told her that he was a timber company employee and had been hired by the owner of the land he was standing on to chop down an acre of firs. He confirmed that he would come back tomorrow to start the job. Céline felt an authoritative voice break out of her, "No, this is not possible." To her stupor, he did not argue or leave. Instead, he looked straight at her as he handed her a card with the land owner's number. He suggested to her that she buy the land off the owner if she wanted to avoid the trees being felled. Why would he encourage her to buy this land and renounce his economic gain? In a state of confusion, Céline walked back home and hastily called the owner. Land is very difficult to purchase in that area, so once again, Céline felt disoriented by the owner's availability to negotiate a sale price.

The "council" of firs, as Céline refers to them now, consists of about forty individuals on the outer border of her land. They now provide a thick barrier of protection from the gazes of curious passers and perhaps had something to do with the course of events on that day. Their loyal character infected Pachamanta with a spirit of resistance and defiance in order to defend their land. One wonders who was overseeing the fir diet that day and whether it was their alert that spread out across land and air, all the way to Kuko at the top of the hill, to reach Céline, who discerned their message. It may be that by ingesting fir, Céline has amplified the perception of her surroundings or that, through dieting, she has developed the ability to perceive the signals of plants. Surely, by learning a new language to summon their spirits, she cannot avoid hearing them too. She knows that they warned her and kept her from finding it all out on the following day through the loud noise of machines. Perhaps on some level, the firs of Pachamanta and Céline cannot be understood as separate entities—they are, in fact, intertwined and interdependent.

Every time we breathe or eat, each one of us could, in theory, be aware of our interdependence with other organisms. Yet, most of us hardly think about it or have even learned to think about it. The edibility approach, proposed by Luci Attala[1] in the field of anthropology, provides a theoretical paradigm that may help us to unlearn the world as consisting of separate parts and instead understand it as one of networks whereby nobody can exist without blending with other bodies. Eating and ingesting plants are ways we "become with" the environment, engage with it consciously or start a chemical conversation between the eater and the one being eaten.[2] I think dieting provides us with an opportunity to re-imagine our world and our individual existence as one of interconnection. By stepping out of ordinary life and slowing down, we offer our attention to one place and one plant in particular, ritualizing and amplifying the process of "becoming with" another being. Getting to know Céline has given me hope that regularly practicing diets may be one way to facilitate our sense of belonging to our environment and to reflect upon a more responsible treatment of it.

Céline once told me she never takes a decision "alone." Visible and invisible beings draw her attention to problems that may arise on her land. Even cutting down a tree becomes a rather participatory decision-making process, as she may receive messages from a number of beings on her land giving her suggestions. In this way, she nourishes her relations of reciprocity with plants and animals by interacting with them daily, participating in their (well) being, and inviting them to participate in hers. Yet, what most stands out to me is that she is often not fully aware of why she is doing something or why she is called somewhere; she simply participates, lets herself be guided, trusting that she only plays her small part in a larger system, society, or perhaps "mind"—and in so doing she is constructing an alternative, magical reality in central France.

Listening to this story has reminded me to trust those small actions and rituals that weave plants into our daily lives, even when we are not too familiar with them—for these gestures nourish something much greater: the healing awareness that nature is inseparable from our very being and consciousness.

POEM 10

Spinach

Spinacia oleracea

Martín Espada

My mother and father met at Vera Scarves, the Brooklyn factory
in 1951. My mother was a receptionist, my father a shipping clerk.
She was twenty and would blush at pictures of Gregory Peck in
movie magazines; he was twenty-one and six foot four, one inch
taller than Gregory Peck. He asked her on a date to see *Captain
Horatio Hornblower*, starring Gregory Peck. They were standing at
the corner of 5th Avenue and 42nd Street in Times Square, waiting,
hand in hand, for the red light
to glow green, when a soggy ball of spinach fell from the sky, landing
on my mother's head. I would say only God knows why, but He
doesn't. Maybe Popeye staged a mutiny, pouring his can of spinach
overboard rather than punching Bluto in the face again for the sake
of Olive Oyl.
Maybe an eight-year-old boy who yearned to pitch for the Yankees
flipped a screwball of spinach out the window to shock his mother.

My mother's meticulously ironed curls wept green down her neck.
Her eyes wept too. My father was an airplane mechanic in the Air
Force. He knew what to do when something came plummeting
from the sky.
Go down to the subway toilet, he said, *and rinse your hair in the sink.
I'll wait for you up here.* And so my mother did. She returned from
the subway toilet with hair wet and spiky, standing up like the crest
of a startled cockatoo. They went to see *Captain Horatio Hornblower,*

sat in the balcony and kissed throughout the movie, missing every line
of dialogue from Gregory Peck wooing Virginia Mayo as Lady
Barbara.

Once, I heard a poet deaf with age declaim a poem about seeing
Halley's Comet as a boy in 1910. The ball of spinach was my
mother's comet.
Every day, my eyes scan the heavens, waiting for the soggy tarantula
of spinach to plummet from the sky and splatter my thinning hair.
This is my inheritance: not the spinach, but the certainty that spinach
is hurtling at my head, or maybe a baby grand piano spinning from
the clouds, and all I can do is wait. Only God knows why, but
He doesn't.

CHAPTER 32

Suicide Tree

Tachigalia versicolor

Afshin Akhtar-Khavari

I have labored immensely about how to write this, the first sentence and paragraph of this essay. I believe this to be because I am keen to do justice to the spectacular and unique *Tachigalia versicolor* tree that dies after fruiting and creates a hole in the forest canopy to allow light for its seedlings to grow. I first discovered this tree while reading the 2018 novel *Overstory*, written by Richard Powers. Powers writes of the character Patricia Westerford who toasts this tree for its life of sacrifice at the end of a powerful and thought-provoking speech. Despite the common name for *Tachigalia versicolor*, which is the "suicide tree," I recall feeling exhilarated by the sense of love and sacrifice that connects the various generations of this tree with one another.

Tachigalia versicolor is a socially embodied living thing, and by that, I mean that its physical life represents something much more meaningful than cellular growth. The tree was clearly more than just a trunk or seeds that it produced; it was more than an autonomous and individual material object in a forest. It appeared to live a meaningful life, but not for the sake of human beings. The tree was socially significant without human beings doing anything to it. Viewed across a longer timescale, *Tachigalia versicolor* seemed to sacrifice and love rather than just survive and prosper by competing for resources. Could it be that by reducing the timescale through which we view life, we also prioritize competition, autonomy, and individuality? This tree had captured my imagination and had provoked some really meaningful questions about fundamental building blocks of how we think about the world. Sacrifice was as meaningful a lens as competition for how I thought about the social life of trees and plants.

When I started sharing stories about the life of *Tachigalia versicolor*, I always managed to provoke a reaction. The "suicide tree" is a name that will augur a reaction in people. People's visceral reactions to the idea that a tree produces seeds once and kills itself for its offspring was instructive. I experienced a range of reactions when sharing facts about *Tachigalia versicolor*—from a sense of enthusiasm in discovering something so new and interesting to a feeling of excitement for me that I connected to something emotionally significant. Most interestingly, however, I was always left with a feeling that by sharing the story of the "suicide tree," and connecting people to its socially embodied life, I had provoked people to think differently about the life and significance of trees.

Tachigalia versicolor is monocarpic, which means that the tree flowers once when it has reached maturity and then dies within a year, releasing its seeds which disperse to around five hundred meters.[1] Though there are other monocarpic plant and tree species, tropical monocarpic species are rare. Yet the tropical *Tachigalia* can grow to around thirty meters tall and produce one of the densest and hardwoods in the old-growth forests between Costa Rica and Colombia. This means that when it dies, it creates a sizeable hole in the forest canopy bringing plenty of much-needed light for its seeds to grow and survive. The decaying timber, branches, and leaves also feed the soil, which provides the seedlings with nutrients to thrive. The *Tachigalia* trees reproduce in four-year cycles, although no one has found an explanation as to why this is the case. The timber of *Tachigalia* is increasingly heavily harvested because it grows faster relative to other hardwood trees.

Upon first reading about the suicide tree, I decided to research further to learn more about the fascinating species. In my research, I discovered a more commonly discussed "suicide tree," the *Cerbera odollam*. This tree, also known as pong pong, is native to India (in particular, the state of Kerala) but grows across other regions of Asia too. The *Cerbera odollam* tree produces a pod-shaped fruit called *othalanga,* which is often used to assist in death or committing suicide because of the potent poison that it contains. While I was impressed by the *othalanga*'s capacity to protect the *Cerbera odollam* from natural harms through use of this poison, I was also distressed by its potential for indiscretion in terms of who and what it killed. Human beings use the fruit to provide themselves with a service, even if it's not one we would sanction.

The two different species of the "suicide tree" seem to share very little in common and grow in almost opposite sides of the world from one another. Both trees, however, have the typical hard and material forms that we associate with trees. Also, more importantly, their lives are socially determined and constituted by their connections with other living things, their broader physical environment, and also the future generations of their own kind. Neither tree is simply a collection of cells nor living an individual life that can be controlled without intervention from known or unknown influences. I am not referring here to the tree's need for nutrients and minerals, but something more—a social reality and an interspecies intersubjectivity that subsumes them and is constitutive of their life in the world. The *Cerbera odollam* thrives because its pods are used by human beings and are now exported. On the other hand, to separate the *Tachigalia* from its social and intergenerational embodiment and constitution significantly narrows what it is, its identity, and its use in this world—not just for the tree and its seedlings, but also for the ecosystem within which it thrives and functions.

I am not suggesting that tree species have emotional experiences with which we can empathize and relate. But what if we adjusted our human understanding and frame of reference to appreciate that the lives of these trees are socially, and not just materially, constituted? Essentially, this means that the world is not just made up of materials that co-exist or individuals and living things that exist to maximize personal interests. Energy and information move around in the world through interactions and relationships and are stabilized and directed by being socially constituted and embodied.

To assist my explanation of this social reality, I take you back to the *Tachigalia versicolor* and present the tree's act of sacrifice to adjust our frame of reference about love. Through a broad range of acts and activities, trees and plants are far more socialized and deeply constituted than we commonly assume by simply studying their trunks, branches, roots, leaves, and flowers. First, the idea of individualized and personal love amongst human beings does not capture the essence or the extent of the experience of love, and that to empathize with the *Tachigalia versicolor*'s experiences, we need to move beyond commonly-held conceptions of human love. This is important because love is more than just an idea conceptualized through the human experience of it. It is also because the *Tachigalia versicolor* is not defined by the autonomy of its harvestable timber trunk but rather by its act of constituting itself through dying for its progeny after it has flowered and dropped its seeds to the ground. While the idea of the "wood wide web" suggests that trees are connected and act socially by using the mycorrhizal network to communicate, the *Tachigalia versicolor*'s autonomy and individuality is also ruptured and thrown into disarray by its deep and innate connection to its offspring. The emotional landscape created by love enables us to see this shift away from the timber and individuality of its life in the forest. The story we need to learn and appreciate is that love and self-sacrifice are necessary for this tree's life and define the tree as much as anything else.

This notion takes us in a different direction, to the idea that trees are interstitial beings,[2] or are able to embody their history.[3] Broader notions of love and social connection question our preconceptions of intelligence, independence, and choice, which seem to be more generally embroiled (and arguably, caught up in a fiction) in the idea of autonomy than in conceptions of life as deeply interdependent, symbiotic, and socially organized. Also, the temporal frames human beings use are shaped by concepts and ideas that define us. Prioritizing competition and individuality also shrinks the timeframes through which we view what is real and important. The tree has the capacity, through its socially embodied life, to remind us and help to illustrate how human beings have defined what is real, using liberal concepts and short timeframes.

This notion of autonomy, for instance, has sustained—and is critical to—the utility of law and legal institutions and the concepts and ideas that flow through the law and use it as a governance tool. The atypical metaphor of the law is the scales of justice balancing the autonomous identities, rights, and interests of human individuals. Western liberal democracies, in particular, rely upon concepts of rights to entrench the centrality of the notion of autonomy. That is, individuals, trees, animals, and everything in our lives exist independently of everything else. What we recognize as real is the autonomous, legal personality of the individual and the material form of living and inert things. We humans like boundaries and the central processing units that have to exist to sustain the idea that we are truly autonomous agents. This is what our data-driven world needs to process and administer systems and ideas. While our buildings, technologies, individuals, and generally hard things are omnipresent, they are shaped by, represent, and facilitate the flow of energy and information. While an individual person can do things on their own, it is the social institution of the law that helps construct so much of what they do in society.

LOVE AND WHY IT IS IMPORTANT FOR THIS STORY

The *Tachigalia versicolor*'s life is socially constituted by love and sacrifice, yet some of our human-held conceptions of love cannot relate to this reality because these conceptions also depend upon human notions of autonomy and agency. There is a larger, more abstract, universal, and yet grounded notion of love that is moving energy and information around. Individualized forms and expressions of love between humans are significant but do not go far enough to explain or enable an understanding of some of the deeper connections within our world. As such, we have to go beyond them to see how far love penetrates into material existence and how actions influence its force and power.

This broader notion of love is perfectly represented by something I have pondered on numerous occasions—why is it that electrons can circle endlessly around protons and neutrons to make up the atom? A satellite could not continue to circle the Earth without input or assistance, and neither could a merry-go-around continue to operate without intervention from external forces. How is this internal cohesion maintained within an atom when entropy would surely cause the electrons to collapse due to an eventual lack of energy? So, here is the crazy idea! Is it possible that love is the binding and cohesive power that holds together the atomic structure sustaining all life? This is clearly not the place to try and debate such a notion, and I am certainly not qualified to make this argument. However, the reason I propose this unconventional notion is because I have always been drawn to the idea that "love" is quite possibly the "*very cause of life*," the "*cause of the existence of all phenomena*."[4] Love is capable of explaining more of reality than what we have traditionally allowed ourselves to acknowledge because so much of our experience of what is true has to be bound to material, hard, and observable things.

Here, I continue in pursuit of evidence of this concept's emanation or instantiation. Martha Nussbaum, who is one of the most influential philosophers of the last two decades, has written that "all the core emotions that sustain a decent society have their roots in, or are forms of, love . . . If love is needed even in Rawls's well-ordered society—and I believe it is—it is needed all the more urgently in real, imperfect societies that aspire to justice."[5] Just as I used the atom to explain the potential significance of love for understanding life, Nussbaum also suggests that love prefigures all other emotions and justice itself. In Nussbaum's view, love is possibly the very foundation of the expression of the intelligence that we experience through emotions. Is it possible that love is also the glue that makes the atom a real thing? I will come back to this larger notion of love a little later. First, it is important to consider human love for one another.

In much of philosophical literature, the idea of love is described as an emotion or reasoned action. In a way, love is an attitude that living and oft sentient beings have toward one another, and as such, we can dwell upon it and analyze love. From this perspective, for instance, love is the union between two people which influences their sense of autonomy and individuality. Through loving interactions, these people have their identities dissolve into this union. Friendship, as a result, is different to love. Love goes beyond interdependence because the emotional nature and structure of a loving relationship creates a bond where we do not place a value on something or someone.

While this perception of love is attractive, it is not sufficiently informed by the complexity inherent in the nature of human emotions. Love is historically shaped and determined by how we respond emotionally to someone else—or a group—when we are interdependent with them. The dynamic nature of a loving relationship is informed and shaped by perceptions, feelings, and thought.[6] The point being that the historically informed nature of love ensures that it does not disappear or fade quickly but instead acts as a glue connecting people and communities with one another.

While love is historically informed and determined, it is also a dynamic influence on the social interactions between the people involved, making sense of their future. The sense that love is dynamic means that anyone experiencing it is changing and shifting by factors that are not always within their control. The loss of autonomy and individuality is, therefore, a combination of historicism and complex interactions that one cannot fully determine.

This makes love a social glue rather than an autonomous decision. Aristotle famously suggested that love is a mirror that helps us to better understand ourselves. Love is an inherently social act and process, while it is also an act of volition. It is the glue that can explain how, while we have lost our autonomy, we remain deeply connected to and shaped by others around us. It is a means for explaining how the social is central to connecting and defining us and everything we do. The social nature of love is epitomized by acts of sacrifice, which are often referred to as the essence of love. Central to the idea of sacrifice is the act of giving and at a substantial cost to the giver. The experience of pain, unease, discomfort, or a sense of loss is both an expression of love and an act that creates new potentials for the giver and the relationship. Sacrifice socially connects a giver through love to another person, cause, community, or group of people and can range from giving something small to a loss of identity. Sacrifice is, therefore, an act that embodies the connection or cohesion that is socially created and justified.

CONCLUSION

I started this essay by suggesting that competition and sacrifice seem to represent alternative views of social reality in a more-than-human-world. That the notions of autonomy and short timeframes get in the way of thinking more deeply about how everything is socially constituted and embodied. Sacrifice and love as social realities help us see how a tree, like *Tachigalia versicolor*, is socially embodied and constituted. I confess, right here at the end of this essay, that I have never seen this tree and have only read about it in books and journal articles. However, I have experienced joy, exhilaration, and happiness when I have shared stories about it with friends, colleagues, and strangers.

Tachigalia versicolor is unique in that it is a fast-growing and dense tree that can become very tall before it produces its seedlings and dies. However, my experience of *Tachigalia versicolor* is only in the sharing of its story of love and sacrifice. Sharing its story has connected me to the tree, but also to others with whom I have shared. Every time I have spoken about *Tachigalia versicolor* with someone or within a group, I have witnessed genuine smiles on people's faces, and on occasion, people get excited because they can relate to what the tree is doing and experiencing. I have witnessed people get goosebumps, shed tears, and make a personal connection with the story because they, too, have loved and sacrificed themselves. More interestingly, sacrifice is usually seen as a quality displayed by people and human beings. It's a sign and a symbol of what it is like to be virtuous. People may or may not act consciously when they sacrifice. *Tachigalia versicolor* not only provoked the people I spoke with to think differently about trees. It made them connect with and share stories about sacrifice and love in their own lives. The tree connected people to itself even though they had never heard of or seen it.

It seems befitting then to finish this essay by taking inspiration from Richard Powers, the author who introduced me to this tree, and toasting *Tachigalia versicolor* just as Patricia Westerford did in his award-winning novel. Thank you for your life of love and sacrifice for your next generation.

CHAPTER 33

Sunflower

Helianthus annuus

▪ **Megan Ljubotina and James Cahill Jr.**

Biologists are often compelled to learn all they can about some organism or group of organisms. Although professional biologists need to present their research in terms of its practical application, or at least its intellectual significance, often they are driven by simple questions that come from pure curiosity and love for the natural world. For example, *what* does a living organism do, and *why* might it to do what it does? For those of us interested in the fundamental questions of *what* plants do and *why* they might do what they do, we often realize that there already exists an excellent, if untraditional, framework for asking and answering these questions—the behavioral sciences. Here we define behavior broadly, but with some precedent, as what an organism does in response to environmental stimuli.[1]

Many plant biologists and behavioral scientists agree that there is nothing restricting plants from behaving in the same way that slime molds, paramecia, rats, dogs, and humans can behave. In this essay, we encourage the adoption of a behavioral approach to botanical understanding, one which complements more traditional approaches. We apply this approach to the annual common sunflower, a charismatic species instantly recognizable by many and a plant that has long been noticed and appreciated for its sun-tracking behavior. As one step toward blending botanical and behavioral traditions, we imagine the process of creating an ethogram (catalogue of behaviors) for the common sunflower and discuss some of the further behavioral questions we might explore in this species.

Traditionally, botanical understanding of plant species has been rooted in descriptions of their use to humans, evolutionary relationships with other organisms, physical traits, and life histories. For example, one approach to describing the sunflower might be to describe its significance to human beings. The common annual sunflower is harvested for its seeds and the oil produced from them, and it is commonly used in landscaping and flower arrangements. As such, it is an economically important plant. It has a long history of cultivation and domestication by human beings, stretching back to at least 2600 BC in Mexico.[2] Sunflowers, images of sunflowers, and reproductions of sunflowers are common in art and pop culture, often representing hope, happiness, or nature. Sunflowers are important to humanity and have left an impression on us for millennia—but can we describe them in terms of their lives, independently of our own?

Another approach to describing what a sunflower is might be to pinpoint its place in the tree of life. Like us, sunflowers are eukaryotes distinguished from non-eukaryotes such as bacteria by the membrane-enclosed nuclei in our cells. They are members of the kingdom Plantae, the plants. Within that kingdom, they are part of a group called angiosperms: plants that produce flowers. And within the angiosperms, they are part of a large family of plants called Asteraceae, which are united by the typical arrangement of many flowers into dense, flower-like heads (other members of this family include dandelions and daisies). They are members of the genus *Helianthus*, and the scientific name that distinguishes the sunflower from all other species is *Helianthus annuus*. This description helps us to understand the common sunflower's evolutionary relationships with other organisms and some of the broad characteristics that distinguish it but is lacking some detail for understanding what this plant is really like and how it lives its life.

A conventional description of the species, then, might read as follows: common sunflower is an annual plant, meaning that it completes its life cycle within a single growing season. It is herbaceous (producing no wood) with an upright stem and coarsely toothed, alternate leaves; belowground, it possesses a central taproot and branching lateral roots. Sunflower leaves and stems usually possess trichomes, hair-like structures thought to be important in defense from herbivores. When it reaches reproductive maturity, its flowering head resembles a single flower but is actually composed of many small flowers, called florets. Many individual flowers called disc florets make up the central "button" of the flower, while each "petal" is an individual flower called a ray floret. Each of the reproductive disc flowers is composed of five fused petals, five fused anthers (the male reproductive parts of the plant), and a single pistil (the female reproductive part of the plant). The individual flowers are hermaphroditic and typically protandrous, meaning that the flower is functionally male first (pollen exposed) and then female (stigmatic surface, where pollen is deposited, exposed).[3] When the disc florets are pollinated, they produce seeds surrounded by a kind of dry fruit called an achene (what we typically refer to as the shell of the seed). This description provides a fuller idea of what a sunflower is, and yet it is quite static, and for many readers, more than a little dull. It describes the plant dryly in terms of its anatomy and unchanging components of its life history.

All three of these coarsely sketched approaches—of the sunflower's relationship with human beings, of its place in the evolutionary tree of life, and of its anatomy and life history—are important components of understanding all living organisms. However, for any organism, the environment is full of dynamic challenges: scarce resources, competition, and attack by predators, among other things. These challenges change throughout the lifetime of each individual and preclude the use of a single pre-programmed way of life for any species, *Helianthus annuus* included. What do sunflowers *do* in the course of their lives: how do they respond to these complex and changing environments? In other words, how do sunflowers behave?

Of course, sunflowers demonstrate a conspicuous and famous behavior that has been noted by humans for centuries: the young flowering heads follow the sun through the day, exhibiting heliotropism.[4] Heliotropism in sunflowers may stand out to humans because it reminds us of how we mediate our relationship with the environment, largely through rapid and conspicuous movements. Modern research has demonstrated that the behavior also serves an intuitive function, allowing the plant to more efficiently gather food (light energy from the sun).[5] This example notwithstanding, sunflowers and other plants often respond to their environments in ways that are far more difficult for us to perceive or understand. However, the fundamental problems that sunflowers face, including finding food, defending themselves from enemies, and reproducing successfully, can be strikingly similar to the challenges that animals like ourselves must manage in their lives. Therefore, understanding these responses in plants can be essential not just to understanding plants but also to an integrated understanding of how living organisms in general deal with the challenges inherent to their environments.

If we were interested in describing sunflower behavior, how might it be done? A traditional approach to understanding behavior involves the creation of an ethogram for a species. An ethogram is simply a dictionary or catalog of behaviors observed in a type of animal, and in animals, they can be and often are produced through the careful observation of animal subjects. No special equipment is necessarily required, other than a pen and paper. An ethogram for a plant simply could not be produced in this way: in the course of their living, and doing, and behaving, plants do not provide much of the visual or auditory stimuli we are particularly attuned to as human beings. And yet, as scientists working in the field of plant behavior, there is something captivating about the idea of such a comprehensive list for a single species, something that emphasizes the diversity of behavior that can be found in just one of over a quarter of a million of species of plants that we share a planet with. It is appealing as plant behaviorists to imagine a world where one could sit and spend some time with a plant and be able to easily observe exactly what it did as the environment changed. In the course of watching, we would see sunflowers actively solve some of the fundamental problems in their lives.

Living organisms share a primary, common need that drives much of their behavior: to gather the necessary resources for survival, growth, and reproduction. Plants forage for their required resources of sunlight, water, and mineral nutrients using a variety of strategies. As mentioned earlier, young sunflower flower heads track the sun, maximizing the light energy they receive. Watching a sunflower subject, we would at least be able to observe this change with our eyes, although we likely could not detect the motion as it happened. Currently, there are many limitations to our ability to see what plants are doing below the soil, but if we could see through the opaque soil and appreciate the slower type of movement plants express through growth, we would likely be impressed by how responsive roots are in their search for mineral nutrition. Shortly (hours or days) after sunflower roots encounter a cluster of nutrients in the soil, they concentrate their roots in that area, equipped with many "mouths" that take up the food. They also have a variety of chemicals they can even more quickly release into the soil to help them take up the nutrients they need. If we could observe and understand these processes as they happened in response to the environment, we would likely appreciate how releasing chemicals can be an act that plants perform to accomplish their goals, rather than a passive or constant state of the organism.

Another behavioral domain of interest, fighting, focuses on how an organism deals with its enemies: other creatures that want to eat it, steal its food, or take its mates. Generally lacking teeth, claws, and the ability to move quickly, many plants resort to chemical weapons to deal with their antagonists. Following an attack by an herbivore, a sunflower might release toxic chemicals that deter further attack or produce a scent that attracts the parasites of plant-eaters to the plant, an enemy-of-my-enemy approach that can kill the animals that target plants.[6] They can also target their fellow plants, secreting toxic chemicals into the soil when resources are low and stopping the germination of seedlings that could one day grow into fierce competitors.[7] From our own research, we know that sunflowers tend to grow roots away from fellow sunflowers that are growing in the same space, avoiding competitive interactions. Sunflower roots also extend further down in the soil to escape competition for nutrients with fellow plants.[8] Of course, these interesting patterns raise far more questions than they answer. Do all sunflowers respond to each other in the same way? Could a given individual be more aggressive and another more conflict-averse? What about when it comes to other species of plants that may present more or less of a competitive threat? Again, the difficulties of observing the roots—and plant behavior in general—make these questions historically difficult to answer.

A comprehensive ethogram for the common sunflower would likely also focus on behaviors relating to reproduction: sex and child-rearing. Sunflowers, like most plants, are hermaphroditic, and so in reproduction, they face some very different issues than humans (or other mammals, which are often the subject of behavioral work). For example, when it comes to choosing a mate, sunflowers have the convenient option of mating with themselves. However, negative consequences often result for the offspring of plants that take this approach; any recessive gene copy (allele) with a negative effect on the organism's ability to survive will be more likely to be passed on to the offspring. In sunflowers, we find individuals hedging their bets. Sunflowers may wait for cross-pollination (pollen from another plant) to a certain point. If it has not happened, they can move the receptive female part of the flower to pick up pollen from the male part. That way, offspring can still be produced, even if they are potentially less viable than the cross-pollinated ones.

So far, in imagining aspects of an ethogram for the common sunflower, we have described some of its behavioral repertoire: how it actively responds to its environment and makes choices based on the information it perceives. These examples of behavior are drawn from the literature or from the authors' own work that took many months to compile. For example, when the authors of this piece collaborated on a study looking at how the common sunflower responds to nutrients and neighboring plants in the soil, data collection involved months of careful root-tracing using an image analysis software (understandably, by the researcher with less seniority). Certainly, any study of behavior, including of animals, can require painstaking data collection, but there are also far more examples of animal behaviors that are obvious enough to at least capture our imaginations immediately. Many television series and films that document animal behavior illustrate this point. It is far more difficult for us to try to understand what plants are *doing* and relate it to the causes of the behavior.

The known behaviors of the common sunflower must represent only a fraction of what it does in a continuous stream of behaviors throughout its life; there is still much to learn by carefully observing what individual sunflowers do. Furthermore, there is much potential for experimental approaches that attempt to tease apart whether these responses are stereotyped behaviors exhibited by all individuals of a given species or whether they are the result of learning by individuals throughout the course of their life. For example, sunflowers can turn to face the direction of the dawn at night, before the sun has risen. Is this a pre-determined response shown by all sunflowers (to face east at night), or is it the result of individual sunflowers learning to anticipate where the sun will rise? Further behavioral research is required to determine the answer to questions such as these.

The reason why it is useful, perhaps even essential, to consider these responses to be of the behavioral kind is because the plant often expresses choice through these changes: choice in where it lives, how it finds food, how it mates, and how it cares for its offspring. Approaches to botany that view plants as insensitive or unresponsive cannot allow us to fully understand a ubiquitous species like the common sunflower or any other plant.

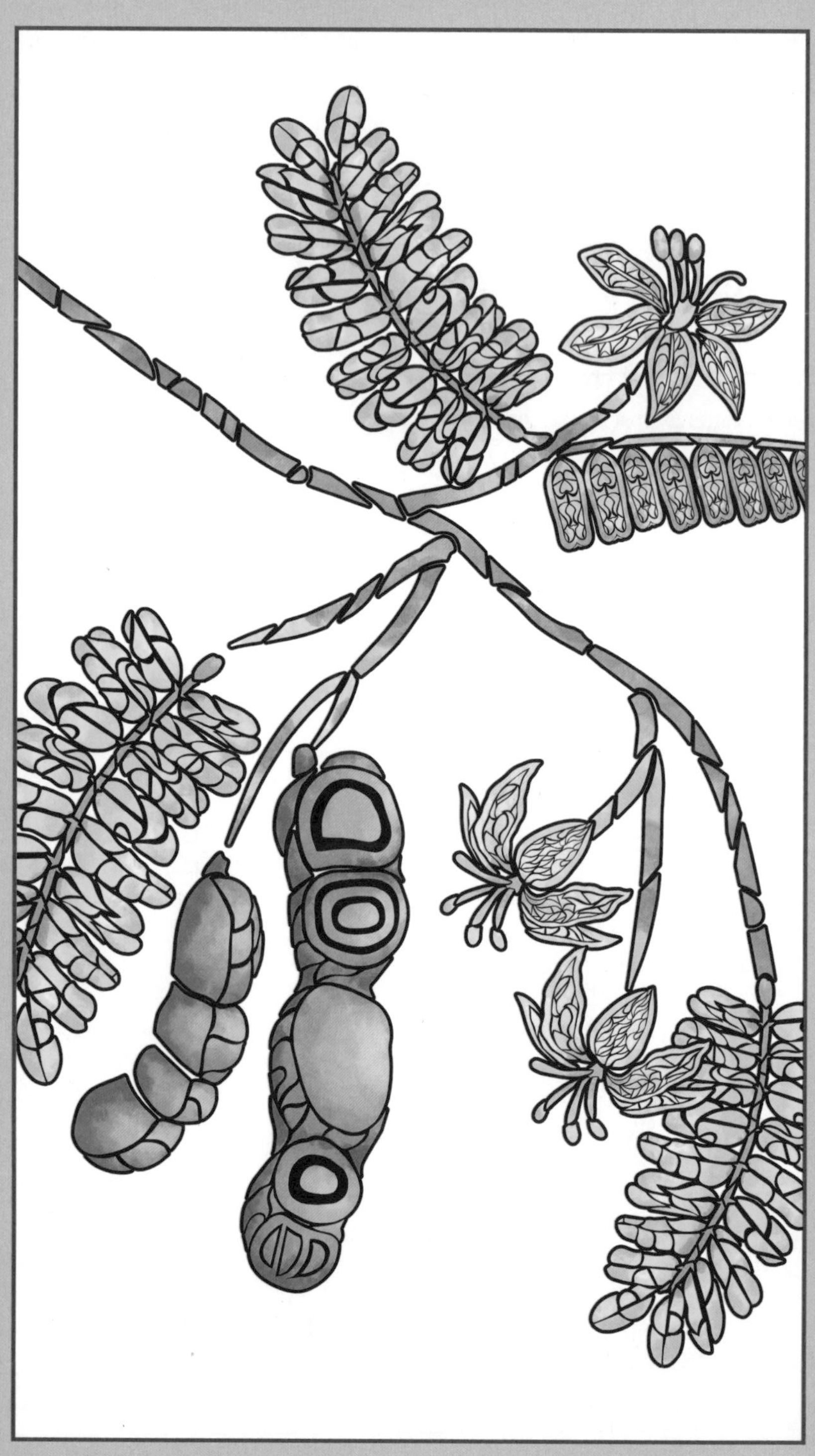

POEM 11

Tamarind

Tamarindus indica

John Charles Ryan

Lombok asam
prostrate seeming
slanted into
twilight saline
skewered up through
stony rupture
bonsaied mind of
algal sealine.

Thing squall-coppiced
splotched with lichen
camouflaged in
boulder breaches
pinnate-green pate
balding leeward
bluffs enclose us
lit in neon.

Among to sleep
scarce roots that clutch
harsh cleft between
that which was—will
make thought as sweet
as deep brown pulp
from sickled pod
of tamarind.

CHAPTER 34

Tea

Camellia sinensis

Janice Lee

I feel the rough edges of my ceramic cup as I bring it towards my lips—the small tendrils of steam emanating from the green, earthy liquid within. I breathe in, slowly, evenly, bringing my awareness back to my body, and for this moment in time, I am here, in the present moment of the tea and in the present moment of my own body. This is an open and intimate encounter with the tea—a moment I have the privilege of experiencing because of everything that went into the process of making this cup of matcha green tea a reality—and, as I breathe, I can expand that thought to myself and acknowledge that I also depend on infinite living beings in order to exist in this moment, just as the tea does.

There is a Japanese saying, "ichigo ichie" (一期一会), which roughly translates to "one time, one meeting," or, as I prefer, "a once in a lifetime encounter." The sentiment of "a once in a lifetime encounter" is the foundation of a traditional tea ceremony or tea meditation, the truth that every single encounter is a once in a lifetime encounter. Different ceremonies call for different teas and methods of preparation. A Japanese chanoyu (茶の湯) ceremony focuses on both the ceremonial preparation and presentation of matcha. In a Korean darye (다례) ceremony, it is typically a type of green tea. In a Chinese gongfu (工夫茶) ceremony, pu-erh tea. What unites these practices is the intention of mindfulness and presence, but also the source of the tea itself: *Camellia sinensis*.

Many are often surprised to find out that all varieties of tea (white, green, oolong, black, pu-erh) come from the same plant. What makes different types of tea distinct from each other is the variety of plant (though one can technically make any type of tea from the leaves of any *Camellia sinensis* plant) and how the leaves are processed.

Yunnan province in China is considered to be the original home of *Camellia sinensis*, and popular mythology tells of how Shennong, the mythical sage ruler of China, discovered tea when fresh tea leaves detached themselves from a nearby tree and landed into his cup of hot water. Others credit various Buddhist monks traveling between India and China, and green tea was later popularized in Japan around 1200 when a Zen Buddhist returned to Japan from China with tea plant seeds and bushes. Though Zen monks originally used the tea as a means of staying awake during meditation, the ceremony became the meditation itself and has turned into an important part of Buddhist meditation practice.

After repeated attempts throughout my youth to develop a meditation practice, it is only recently that I have been able to really understand its importance. Through ceremony, I am able to demarcate between ordinary and non-ordinary reality, and through prayerful and mindful actions, step into intention and articulate gratitude and appreciation. For me, the practice of a tea ceremony is about being in right relation with life and the world. In this meditative space, I can feel the joy of this once in a lifetime encounter. When I breathe with my tea, I bring my awareness back into my body. And in breathing with the tea plant, I share life and acknowledge the network that I am a part of. The tea encourages the modification of our conception of subjectivity in order to become open to a new way of being, existing, and *becoming* in relation to the whole living world.

In my current work as a healer, shaman, teacher, and writer, I think about how plants make it possible for us to consider other ways in which to narrate our trauma and our wounds, how we might be able to imagine ourselves outside of bodies and identities defined by the past. As a Korean-American, I think of trauma and its inheritance through the concept of han (한), which Suh Nam-dong describes as "a feeling of unresolved resentment against injustices suffered, a sense of helplessness because of the overwhelming odds against one, a feeling of acute pain in one's guts and bowels, making the whole body writhe and squirm, and an obstinate urge to take revenge and to right the wrong—all these combined."[1]

I think about the feeling of a mausoleum, the feeling of becoming a mausoleum, the skin of one's body thickening and hardening into concrete walls—this as a mechanism to keep others out in order to survive and to keep ourselves from being vulnerable, an attempt at safeguarding against permeability. I think about the unbalanced human belief in a singular self, while plants understand cycles of growing and dying inside the same body, inside multiple bodies, the reciprocity of bodies in the shimmering, undulating sea, so that the shuttered human idea of "identity" becomes impossible.

The tea I drink is possible because of an acceptance of the cycles of life and death. That is, the tea plant must grow and be harvested, in its death be consumed by me in the form of tea, and one day I too will return to the Earth to contribute to its great mulching process. The once in a lifetime encounter also refers to the openness and vulnerability that I inherit when I consume the tea. The Zen master Thich Nhat Hanh says, "How would we continue to live if we were changeless? To live we must die every instant. We must perish again and again in the storms that make life possible."[2] There is presence and death in each moment of life. This is vulnerability. This is healing. This is the gift of the tea: the preparation for a new death and new birth in every moment of our life. This is the process of opening your heart.

When I was a little girl, my mother taught me the Korean concept of *nunchi* (눈치). When I was older, I came across more official definitions of *nunchi* (a combination of the Korean words for "eye" and "measure/psychic energy") as an unspoken social intuition, an awareness of the feelings of those around you, or the ability to sense another person's mood. *It is about survival,* my mother would repeat to me. *That friend of yours,* 눈치 없다 *(She doesn't have nunchi).* As a child, the concept seemed to be linked to the necessity of tact and emotional intelligence to survive in a hostile world as a girl and as a person of color. I inherited a feeling of this concept and its importance through the way my mother would use it to describe other people and in the ways she forced me to pay attention to the invisible gestures, details, resonances, and feelings around me. Even of my dog, Benny, who is unusually intuitive and constantly watching his surroundings, she would say, 눈치를 보다 *(He's watching nunchi).* Essentially, she taught me to *feel* at a distance. This, of course, is the definition of telepathy. Coined by Frederick W. H. Myers in 1882, telepathy essentially means "feeling at a distance."

From the tea plant, we might learn to better feel at a distance, to invoke change from within, and to heal with a focus inwards. *Camellia sinensis* plants, like other plants, are sessile beings, meaning they aren't mobile. They are rooted in place so that any encounter with an other is never just a simple question of waiting or coincidence. Because no physical movement or action is possible, the plant's encounter with an other is made possible through metamorphoses of the self. That is, it is only by internal transformation that the immobile plant can encounter the world. This is an important lesson for those trying to heal. As a species, we tend to run away from our problems—both physically and figuratively—and it's important to remember that to truly encounter the world and to perceive it means to be touched and penetrated by it to the point of being changed and modified by it. What is interesting to me is that harvesting *Camellia sinensis* is always done by hand, as only the top leaves are plucked, so that a real physical encounter between human and plant needs to take place for the later encounter of a human consuming plant tea to be possible.

Plants, though, are not simply *of* the world, passively shaped by external forces. They produce the space in which they live rather than being forced to adapt to it. *Camellia sinensis*, an evergreen shrub, can reach tree-like heights in the wild if left undomesticated.

A meditative exercise I might embark on: What would it be like to view all of humanity and philosophy not through the lens of human history and accomplishment (which can only produce a very partial image of the cosmos and is constrained by the illusion of linear time), but through the lens of plants, plants as the real mediators, the gaze through which all gazes are first filtered, the world as interconnected and entwined and balanced? What would the world look like through the tea plant's eyes?

For plants, life is one of immersion. It is important to remember that the verb "to be" could be thought of as "to *make world*," that we cannot separate ourselves from the matter of the rest of the world. Worlding requires everyone's participation. That is, though it is true that we are water and stardust, we are also airplane fuel, dog shit, the plastic trash building up in the ocean, pollens, flattened bugs on the car windshield, a dead baby orca on its mother's back.

We might consider the tea leaf, that part of the plant from which tea is produced, the paradigmatic form of openness: it absorbs from the atmosphere around it and is permeable, constantly open to influence by the world without being overwhelmed or destroyed by it. For plants, to exist, to be in the world means to *make world*, every action within is also an action without, and without passivity, they exercise their will on the world.

In this dynamic, the world is not simply a geographical place. It is "a state of immersion of each thing in all other things… In order for immersion to be possible, *everything needs to be in everything*."[3] So that the inhalation that is my first breath in the morning is the habanero pepper I harvested and made into salsa for dinner last night, is the energy of the autumnal equinox and of the entire cosmos, is this sentence I formulate for this essay, is the first sip of hot tea in the morning, is the profound love I have for my aging dog Benny, is his peaceful snoring in the middle of the night, is his exhalation.

In the breath, there is the acknowledgment that we are all a part of the same sphere of life, not the division of natural and human or plant and animal, but that the breath itself can decategorize the arbitrary categories of living, because whether we ask them to or not, plants breathe for all of us, and don't ask of us anything in return.

Emanuele Coccia writes, "Everything in the realm of the living is the articulation of breath: from perception to digestion, from thought to pleasure, from speech to locomotion. Everything is a repetition, intensification, and variation of what takes place in breath." What we inhabit isn't simply the Earth, the ground, or a planetary body, but all of the air around us and the atmosphere, "atmosphere as the vital breath that animates the Earth in its totality."[4] Breath itself, like tea, is immersion, is articulation, is presence, is everything.

Every act of knowledge is an act of atmosphere and because everything is in everything: "To inhale is to allow the world to come into us—the world is in us—and to exhale is to project ourselves into the world that we are."[5]

Here is how the tea plant teaches us about intimacy, about closeness, about forgiveness, about empathy, about compassion, and about love.

Camellia sinensis shows us to recognize that the world as a space of immersion means that there are no real or stable borders. The world is the space that cannot be reduced to my house or your house, to property, to land, to what is owned, to what can only be defined in immediate and linear terms.

I think about how so much of my pain begins in the gut, *han* being defined as a pain that emanates from the bowels. But in many practices of self-healing, meditation, and breathing, we focus on this very center of ourselves, the focal point of breath, the *kath* point in Sufism, the *dantien* in Chinese medicine.

As I pick up my cup of tea, I breathe in and bring my awareness back to my belly.

The tea plant's leaves begin small, and the growth happens discreetly, but each individual plant becomes a little more each day—reciprocity and exchange being the primal and primary desire. This is a communion of sorts. The distance between bodies can't ever be measured effectively if "distance" is a word that remains as a vehicle for articulation, and in a place where the interplays between life and death are never forgotten, the persistence of darkness is not something to flee from. Rather, one might simply sit under a tree after it rains with a cup of hot tea, lingering with the petrichor, and try not to destroy too much.

Here, a world of relation, of breath, of atmosphere. In this world, the in-between liminal states of day and night, land and water, and life and death find concreteness in the pale colors of the sky. These are certainties rooted in transition, and the creatures here know to pay attention. "Think lightly of yourself, and deeply of the world," they repeat. Plants are beings that inhabit two different worlds simultaneously, immediately, and naturally. Everywhere, all of the plants and animals breathe together in an intimate cycle that is shared and, just like language, can only exist *because* it is shared, because of the *together*. Today the relational qualities of air are the relational qualities of words, and you may learn more from paying attention to what lies beneath your feet than what composes the sky above you.

The core of it all is the breath, the long and sustained breath that connects us all together.

I drink my tea slowly and reverently because it is here where everything dies, and it is here where everything begins. In this moment, drinking my tea is the most important thing in my life. In this moment, here is the origin of the entire world, the ancestral and ancient wisdom whispered through the tea leaves. In this moment, I have arrived, and I am home. This is a moment of complete vulnerability and of complete joy. This moment is unique, a once-in-a-lifetime encounter. And, it will happen again.

CHAPTER 35

Toad Lily

Tricyrtis imeldae

Kathleen Cruz Gutierrez[1]

My father named a lily after Imelda Marcos. That's right, you know the one. The legend with a shoe closet. The eccentric politician. The second half of the plundering pair, whose dictatorial government motivated my dad's relocation to the United States in 1985.

Imelda Marcos wasn't a familiar name for me when I was growing up in Los Angeles. But I knew how she looked. I remember a second-hand store using her likeness to encourage store-goers to sell their shoes. She appeared in newspapers that crossed our family's dining room table. She was the butt of jokes—jokes I couldn't fully yet comprehend. In truth, I thought Imelda was my aunt. My dad's sister-in-law styled her rich black hair like Imelda's. She, too, had a beehive with nary a bobby pin to be seen. My aunt also had a majesty about her gliding from one parlor to the next. I admit I had some measure of awe seeing her at weekend family parties, wondering what kind of political responsibilities she needed to address when she left the room.

It was sometime in high school, during one of our monthly dim sum dates in LA's Chinatown, when my dad disclosed his discovering and naming a lily after the former First Lady. She also happened to be former Governor of Metro Manila, former Member of the now-defunct Philippine Parliament, and former Congressional Representative of the first district of the island of Leyte—my paternal grandmother's island.

My dad was a botanist in Manila before he migrated to California. He was a specialist in the archipelago's Dipterocarpaceae, known more commonly as the Philippine mahogany. I knew almost nothing of his career when I was younger. He worked at a cargo truck terminal in south Los Angeles. He signed checks with "PhD" following his name, and I can only lightly comprehend now how the letters weighed on his mind as a reminder of a life past. It would take at least a decade of dim sum dates for me to have a steadier hold over what his previous botany career entailed.

As my dad told me then, he discovered a toad lily—distinguished by its spotted flowers and leaves and wart-like nectar glands—while on a botanical collecting mission to the island of Mindanao. He was living with the Tasaday, a cave-dwelling people in South Cotabato. While there, he found the peculiar lily. He returned to Manila with the specimen and identified it as a new species. He named the toad lily after Imelda Marcos. Because of the honor, the Marcos government issued a postage stamp featuring the new "Imelda lily." Over on my side of the table—spotted with chili sauce and rice grains—I nodded along, my mind's eye flickering between Imelda's image and Aunt Remy's.

A couple of years later, I sat in my first college class on the history of island Southeast Asia. Jeffrey Hadler taught the course. He was a specialist on the Minangkabau of Indonesia. For our unit on contemporary Philippine history, Professor Hadler spent a full 80-minute lecture on the Tasaday controversy. In his retelling of the history, the Tasaday were a made-up "cave-dwelling people" as part of a grander spectacle contrived by the Marcos regime in the early 1970s. He showed us clips of a documentary that deconstructed the "discovery" as one brilliant international ruse.

I stewed in class. I stewed at home. I stewed for days. A vigilance to correct a mistake finally overcame me. I went to Professor Hadler's office to speak with him. The matter drove me to do so. I explained that my father went on the same Tasaday expedition he discussed in lecture. *He collected their plants*, I insisted. Professor Hadler nodded. His eyebrows revealed a historian's doubt—perked high enough to show interest, slanted enough to show skepticism. I would become familiar with this look after entering my PhD program. Seven years after that first class in Southeast Asian history, Professor Hadler became Jeff, my PhD advisor. He became my most direct mentor, my advocate when my graduate education was so systematically difficult. Unfortunately, he passed before I could share just how much that meeting moved me—one of many that pushed me toward Philippine history.

I brought back this news of the controversy to my dad when I came home from college for the summer break. *They were made up! They had other names. There're, like, documentaries on their fakeness!* We argued bitterly. The volume of his voice increased with every reference I made to their being a hoax. *No, they are wrong!* could be heard across the rolling breakfast carts.

I have had to pare down my hubris. Despite the secondary literature on the topic, the documentaries that have debunked the Tasaday people, and even the list of the *real* names of the ostensible actors who played "gentle cave-dwellers," how can I undercut the experiences of another person? Of my own father? Those experiences are rightly his. His professional responsibility brought him to southern Mindanao. He deployed his skills as a collector and in plant identification. He gathered the plant material that, surely, could not have been as fake as the Marcosian fantasy of a new Philippine society.

Can a plant be a hoax?

I compose this piece not to continue to undermine my father's intellectual labors. Yet, I do not aspire to catalog another scientist-hero's tale. How does one, after all, write about her father's contribution to this humiliating time in modern Philippine history? Instead, I write to focus on the power of the political hoax and its entanglements with the *unminding* of plants. I weave my dad's recollections with accounts shared in Philippine newspapers about his discovery, his botany publications, tellings of the Tasaday controversy and of the Marcos regime, and media on the *Tricyrtis imeldae*—and on the toad lily herself, Imelda.

A DICTATORIAL FANTASIA

The Marcos era marked a considerable shift in how science was perceived, promoted, and practiced by the Philippine state. Ferdinand Marcos was an Ilokano politician and President of the Philippines from 1965 to 1986. Notorious for his declaration of martial law on September 21, 1972, Ferdinand attempted to usher in a "New Society" for the Philippines, one characterized by a dictatorial push for social and political modernity. Part of its mission was a "response to the rebellion of the poor."[2]

Science had a distinct role in Ferdinand's social project. "Science and its application of technology," Ferdinand wrote, "is at once the key to the willful transformation of society and the development of a kind of outlook that rejects despair, addresses itself to problems, and tries to find solutions. I am of course referring to a scientific outlook, which in developing societies—with their legacies of superstition, ignorance and fear—is often lacking among the majority of the people."[3] His administration can be credited for the establishment of the Balik Scientist Program (est. 1975), a "brain gain" initiative to repatriate and remunerate Filipino scientists; the promotion and expansion of Philippine Science High School (f. 1963), the premier government-funded STEM training system for young scholars; and the near-complete construction of the Bataan Nuclear Power Plant, which promised to divert the Philippines from reliance on foreign oil.

Concurrent with the administration's preoccupation with science was the Tasaday controversy. In 1971, at least two dozen cave-dwelling individuals were discovered by Manuel Elizalde, Jr., then head of PANAMIN (Presidential Assistance on National Minorities; f. 1968), an organization purportedly committed to the protection and interests of Philippine Indigenous communities. The event garnered international media attention since the individuals were touted as a unique tribe of the Stone Age that had been isolated from nearby Manobo and T'boli peoples in South Cotabato, Mindanao. Select anthropologists, journalists, celebrities, and scientists visited the Tasaday until 1976, at which point the government forbade any further visits. It was likely no coincidence that Ferdinand declared martial law in 1972 at the height of Tasaday popularity.

A BOTANICAL ROMANCE

On September 18, 1974, Philippine newspaper *Bulletin Today*, known currently as *Manila Bulletin*, published an article by Rodolfo Mallari entitled "New Philippine Lily named after First Lady." It announced that my father's plant discovery during "an ethno botanical expedition to the Tasaday's mountain forest lair" had been named after Imelda Marcos. It shared:

> [National Museum] Herbarium Curator Gutierrez, who has behind him a number of new records in Philippine flora and whose background includes studies at the Harvard University and a UNESCO Fellowship on Humid Tropic Vegetation, promptly christened the Philippine species **Tricyrtis Imeldae** after the President's Lady 'in

> recognition of her sincere concern for the plight of the country's cultural-linguistic communities and for her efforts to uplift their conditions and hasten their integration in the national political lifestream.'[4]

The article lauded the *Tricyrtis imeldae* as "a beautiful flower found among the wilds, something which would inspire any poet into making romantic allusions about the flower and the First Lady." In 1975, Philippine scholar E.P. Patanñe regaled the toad lily as "a rare flower," "the only one of its kind in the world."[5]

My father introduced his new species to the international botany community just ahead of the media's romance with the Imelda lily. In the September 1974 issue of the *Philippine Journal of Science*, he announced the *Tricyrtis imeldae* as a "new record for the Philippines and the Malaysian region."[6] This species was unusual: nearly all species of the *Tricyrtis* genus are distributed in East Asia. He described the species as having "greenish-white" and "rather large, showy" flowers flecked with purple, and as one that is "[a]ttractive as an ornamental plant." He, Ernesto J. Reynoso of the National Museum, and Douglas E. Yen of the Bishop Museum in Honolulu, Hawaii, collected the *Tricyrtis* specimen on August 2, 1972.

During my most recent chat with my father about their expedition, he narrated how Manuel Elizalde sent messengers to the National Museum to identify botanists ready to visit South Cotabato. My father and his colleagues took a plane to Mindanao in July of 1972. After several bus and *jeepney* trips and one ride in a helicopter, they arrived to a camp already set by Manuel's team. In Robin Hemley's nonfiction work *Invented Eden: The Elusive, Disputed History of the Tasaday*, my father was also joined by Richard Elkins, a specialist of Manobo languages and Protestant missionary with the Summer Institute of Linguistics, and Dad Tuan, a teenaged T'boli guide hired to assist with plant collection and identification.[7] Altogether, my father recalled about two weeks among the Tasaday, surviving on government-issued rations and locally gathered food and sleeping on beds of leaves, branches, and blankets. Approximately three days into the collecting trip, and accompanied by Douglas and a Tasaday guide, my father collected the toad lily along a stream.

The *amutmagiso*, the Tasaday name for the *Tricyrtis imeldae*, was reported to be useful locally. In the absence of hunting or trapping equipment, the Tasaday utilized the plant for barehanded animal capture. The plant's leaves and flowers would be crushed, and their sticky secretion would be rubbed on hands to prepare for catching evasive frogs.[8] The Tasaday also likened the plant's flowers—which are also edible—to a frog's tongue. My father didn't think much of the species' newness until he returned to Manila, where he began to identify the entirety of their botanical collection.

My father concluded his 1974 article in the *Philippine Journal of Science* by indicating that the species was "named in honor of Mrs. Imelda Romualdez Marcos in recognition of her continuing contributions to the upliftment of the Philippine cultural minorities including the Tasadays." This wasn't the only work of his he pledged to her either. In his 1980 volume, *An Illustrated Manual of the Philippine Materia Medica*, he credited "our First Lady" for articulating that "[t]he keen revival of interest on herbal medicine is a return to our roots."[9] As I see it, conflating local flora with Imelda Marcos was *the thing* to do during this time. When I've prodded my father about his naming choices (for both plants and the names of his children), he has confessed there wasn't always much personal attachment to the decisions. My oldest brother, Marlow, got his name from the imposition of *mar*tial *law* in 1972. In the case of the Imelda lily, how else was my father supposed to garner favorable attention for the research conducted by the Philippine National Herbarium of the National Museum?

UNMINDING THE TOAD LILY

Anthropologist David Hyndman has described the Tasaday hoax as exemplary of the "romantic palliative trope" that renders Indigenous communities as Other; he and political scientist Levita Duhaylungsod have traced the resource extraction in South Cotabato and the displacement of the T'boli people as conveniently veiled by the Tasaday masquerade.[10] Film scholar Talitha Espiritu has argued that the invention of the Tasaday reveals the "ideological pacts enmeshed" in the "touristic co-production between business savvy "primitives" and cannibalistic transnationals."[11] Their analyses are arresting.

With the toppling of Ferdinand Marcos in 1986, Swiss journalist Oswald Iten and Filipino activist–reporter Rizal Lozano cautiously snuck into the Tasaday reserve that had been cordoned off by the government. Iten and Lozano spoke with its residents, who revealed that they were pressured to act as a cave-dwelling tribe. They were local farmers, coaxed to use new names and to wear little to no clothing. As Hemley has recounted in *Invented Eden*, global reaction to Iten and Lozano's 1986 exposé was as fantastic as it had been after the initial discovery of the Tasaday. By 1989, scholars of the Tasaday controversy agreed that the band of individuals was not from the Stone Age. Given the data, however, the Tasaday were more likely to be a "genuine enthnolinguistic group" separate from nearby ethnolinguistic communities.[12]

The *Tricyrtis imeldae* had become subsumed in the hoax. My father confided that ahead of the big 1986 reveal, Filipino intellectuals turned toad lily against toad lily. They used the *Tricyrtis imeldae*'s frog-like appearance to demean Imelda. The flower's bewitching exterior concealed a gummy sap to capture unwary frogs. This sticky analogy was prescient. As of this writing, Imelda is a member of the Philippine House of Representatives for the second district of Ilocos Norte—my father's home province. The Marcoses have ascended politically once again. Like a rare lily's mesmerizing of curious taxonomists, Imelda's eccentricities have inspired documentarians and internationally known artists. It feels that over two decades after the release of British musician Fatboy Slim's "Praise You"—a song that blasted through LA's alternative rock station, 106.7 KROQ—I am transported to the radio of my childhood, prophesying the debut of his, and David Byrne's *Here Lies Love* (2010), and my telling of this history. An Imeldarrific concept album, *Here Lies Love* plumbs the First Lady's entrancing contradictions and her relationship to Estrella Cumpas, the First Lady's longtime housekeeper and caretaker of her youth.

I've sensed disappointment in my father when he has spoken of the *Tricyrtis imeldae*'s fall from intellectual repute. He was unsure of what became of his publication in the *Philippine Journal of Science*, of the "Imelda lily" postage stamp, of updated taxonomic studies on the *Tricyrtis* genus. He left that debacle, and his intellectual passions, when he moved to California in

1985. Botanical research under the Marcos government had been restrictive. After publishing two volumes on local medicinal plants, my father was questioned at Camp Crame, the headquarters of the Philippine National Police, for his alleged ties to the Communist Party of the Philippines (CPP). His books were found among cadres of the New People's Army, the armed wing of the CPP. The books were likely used as a field guide in the absence of medical resources. The research environment had also become stifling, and government funds that had been originally allotted to advance *materia medica* research inexplicably disappeared. He left with my mother, who was a journalist, to Los Angeles, where his youngest brother was dying. They chose not to return.

Following updates to the taxonomy conducted by Japanese and Filipino plant biologists, the *Tricyrtis imeldae* has been reduced to a synonym of *Tricyrtis formosana*, a native to Taiwan. How the *Tricyrtis formosana* landed in southern Mindanao remains unclear. Since the species is not in cultivation in the Philippines, the updates have worked from my father's 1974 description, available line drawings, and images of the type specimen held in the Philippine National Herbarium.[13] The reduction of a purportedly new species to a synonym of one that has been previously described is par for the course in botany. The news hasn't unmoored my father.

Others have written about the erroneous provenance of "toad lily," the common name for the *Tricyrtis* genus. They associate it with the Tasaday hoax, calling it a "more infamous and blatantly false story for the origin."[14] My father and Douglas Yen recorded their informants' knowledge of *amutmagiso* in 1974. Were its practical use and frog-like resemblance manufactured, too? I agree with Hemley when he writes, "To the scientific community of the seventies, the Tasaday were a question mark, not, by any means, a laughingstock." Douglas and my father methodically cataloged the useful plants of the Tasaday, but it seems that in the unminding of the *Tricyrtis* because of its ties to the hoax, the plant has become less reputable, less valid, less *real.*

Can a plant be a hoax? I muse. The Imelda lily's puzzling habitat in southern Mindanao, caught in the lights of the dictatorial spectacle of 1970s Philippines, makes me wonder how much, in actuality, the plant hoaxed us.

CHAPTER 36

Ushpawasha Sanango

Tabernaemontana undulata

■ **Matteo Politi**

"Interesting things happen in the Amazon," I am thinking while crouched on the rock in front of my *tambo*, a small bamboo and leaf hut deep within the tropical rainforest. Immersed in an expanded state of consciousness, my body almost immobile, my mind calm and silent, this sentence comes from nothing to give me new awareness.

I have a background in pharmaceutical chemistry, and I have been educated, or I would say indoctrinated, to see medicinal plants as simply insentient containers full of potentially useful molecules for human health. Instead, plants are complex living beings, and as such capable of acting, communicating, influencing, even teaching. In recent years, I have been finding this view of plants in many scientific and popular writings. Now I experience it directly, and for the first time, this awareness becomes part of my whole being. It is the middle of the night when this simple and clear thought emerges in my contemplating mind while a smile spreads on my lips. I am happy and at peace as I slowly become nature. I feel a part of me escaping out of my neck. I would say it is my consciousness, but I don't know, I have no idea—some call it soul or spirit or many other names. What is certain is that my physical body is there on that rock, serene and undisturbed. But a part of me is elsewhere, expanded in the forest and in the starry sky, and I don't feel at all alone in this dimension. It is as if I am fused with the whole but also taken by the hand and led by a subtle presence. I perceive it as the consciousness of that plant being, whose material body I continue to ingest with tenacity during these days, in the form of a difficult-to-swallow concentrated decoction.

This story describes my first experience of Amazonian medicinal plant diet, simply known as dieta,[1] performed at the botanical reserve of the Takiwasi Center in Peru.[2] This involved the ingestion of a plant decoction prepared from the root bark of Ushpawasha Sanango (*Tabernaemontana undulata* Vahl—Apocynaceae), considered at Takiwasi as a remedy for the "memory of the heart." The plant is often named simply ushpa by the locals in this territory of the high Peruvian Amazon. It is used to help metabolize relevant feelings and foster the reconnection and harmonization between one's emotional and mental world.[3] Several indole alkaloids are identified in this species,[4] and this class of compounds is typical of this botanical genus, where ibogaine represents probably the best-known example of such kind of compounds with potent activity on human neurobiology.[5]

It is a Thursday, the day dedicated to the planet Jupiter, the largest in our solar system. Jupiter is associated with Zeus, the King of the mythological Greek Olympus, and also an archetype of abundance and expansion. And who knows if this universal force has favored the expansion of my consciousness, bringing me to the peak of this herbal experience, embraced by the green arms of the mother forest.

My first diet with Amazonian medicinal plants began the previous Saturday when I started to write in my diary about this experience. This immediately triggered the playful game of linking each day of the week to the corresponding astrological planet, and quickly I had the feeling that this game was actually quite serious. Several years ago, I began to study astrology, driven above all by the frustration of not knowing anything about it. No one during the years of my education had told me about it, despite the fact that in the past there was neither a scientist nor a serious herbalist, at least in the Mediterranean area where I come from, who did not consider the disposition of the sky when formulating a plant remedy. I have always been interested in traditional medicines during my career as a researcher specializing in medicinal plants, and I learned little by little to be wary of my colleagues and of the academic environment in general—especially when they all too quickly dismissed certain axioms belonging to past cultures. I noticed that often this happens because of an extreme ignorance, in the true sense of the term. They set aside a topic so lightly, very often knowing nothing about it. Even with a university degree, a doctorate, and with many years as a scholar and researcher, it took me a whole year and a half to begin to understand something about astrology. Since then, I have never stopped taking it seriously, especially in relation to certain herbal practices. However, I am not sure why I started the association between the planets and the days of the week in my diary of the Amazon diet. I certainly did not plan it, but it simply happened. Nevertheless, it had a determining impact throughout the experience.

The diet began on Saturday, which is the day dedicated to Saturn, known in Greece as Cronus, god of time, and particularly dear to me as I was born under the Capricorn sign upon which he rules. When interpreting astrological birth charts and personal horoscopes, I consider it particularly important to evaluate Saturn's cycle, which moves by 90 degrees every seven years. This generates relevant astrological "aspects," especially in relation with one's date of birth, marking significant stages in someone's lifetime. It was 2017, I was forty-two years old, and by doing some quick calculations, I realized that in that period of the diet, Saturn was marking one of those relevant stages in my lifetime. I could not drop this thought, and so I started playing the game of going backward in time—where was I at in my life seven years ago? Was there a common thread that linked me to the present experience? And by moving further back by another quadrant, was there still assonance? By traveling further back into my past, I wanted to trace the path of this planet on my chart and evaluate a new possible perspective on my life path. And so began the journey within my memories, perhaps pushed by the subtle effects of drinking ushpa.

Exactly seven years before this diet experience, I bought my first distillation equipment and started to experiment with herbal medicine at home. At the time, I had been used to undertaking laboratory experiments with very advanced technologies, passing through important chemical-pharmaceutical research centers around Europe. I graduated in Italy, but quickly migrated to Switzerland, then Spain, England, and Portugal. I finally returned to Italy, this time as a senior scientist at the Joint Research Center of the European Commission, perhaps one of the most advanced research centers of the old continent. Yet, now the academic circles increasingly bored and disappointed me; there was too much bureaucracy and political-economic interests and very little desire for knowledge. It was as if the merchants had invaded the temples of knowledge, as seems to have happened in Palestine two thousand years ago. I never stopped studying medicinal plants from new perspectives, and at that stage, I decided to begin a three-year training course in naturopathy. For that purpose, I bought myself a small distiller found in a second-hand market to practice the art rather than the science of medicinal plants. In a tiny house in the old district of a small provincial town in Northern Italy, I imbued the walls of my kitchen with the most diverse aromas, the essences extracted from the wild flora collected in my surroundings. Saturn is known to love the essential, and recalling those days of artisan herbal medicine, I can only smile, feeling its presence. This line of activity then continued much over the years, and today aromatherapy is an integral part of my job as a researcher and naturopath. Swinging in the hammock of the *tambo*, smiling and satisfied with this first observation, I continue to travel backward—where was I fourteen years ago? Did I, by any chance, experience something connected with my being in the Amazon isolated in the wilderness? And it is at this point that I begin to understand that this game of remembering under the effects of the ushpa could be a revelation for me.

In 2003, I finished my doctorate and planned to start my first postdoctorate in five months' time. I celebrated with friends and then started backpacking, as I used to do when I traveled for pleasure. I had already explored distant lands like Africa and Central America, so this time I decided to go not too far away and instead travel to Greece near Mount Olympus, as I had heard that a hippie community was gathering to celebrate the Moon. As I reminisce in my *tambo* about that time, I get irritated with the mosquitoes and the *zancudos* of the Amazon jungle—painful gnats that force me to spend most of the time under the mosquito net of that small bamboo hut. Annoyed by this feeling of imprisonment, the memory of that wild month passed in Greece suddenly emerges. We lived in a dense mountain forest, far from any town comfort, with only stream water for drinking and washing, food cooked on the fire, and so much beautiful music and sociality. I remember my ankles devastated by the bites of gadflies, far more terrible than any other mosquito bite. Yet, at the time, the bites fell into the background, while joy and happiness prevailed. How I changed. What happened?

For a moment, I get lost in the melancholy of those thoughts; a pang in the heart pierces my emotions and opens a river full of memories and connections that overwhelm me. Is the ushpa really behind all this? It's Monday when that happens in my *tambo*, the day dedicated to the Moon: sensitive, intuitive, unpredictable. I spent all my five months of freedom with those neo-hippies, thousands of them coming from all over the world, in caravans from valley to valley, from one country to the next, chasing the lunar cycle and celebrating it around primitive fires. Food reduced to the essentials, we fed on other energies, on happiness and communion between us and creation. Immersed naked in the green for entire days, I took on the rhythm of nature, very different from the urban one. I became silent, as words were not needed anymore and I started speaking through the heart and the eyes, through smiles and through hugs. Disconnected from electricity and screens, far away from intellectual discussions, restaurants, and things of the everyday for five months, Saturn stripped me of everything superfluous and made my essence shine in communion with other beings of nature, human and otherwise. In my little hut in the Amazon, I pull up the mosquito net, heedless now of any angry *zancudo*. Astonished, almost ecstatic, I salute the sky and its stars through the branches of those giant trees in the mother forest as I realize the similarity between my diet in the Peruvian forest and those months of isolation in the wild mountain valleys of the Mediterranean. Yet, my intuition had already pushed itself beyond this consideration, nourishing that state of astonishment and ecstasy. Ushpa was truly doing its work in facilitating reconnection to my heart's memories.

I take good old Saturn on a full turn back in time, and I find myself at the core of my adolescence, drawn to books, particularly those on medicinal plants. I used to roam around second-hand stalls, loving to rummage through those old volumes—but even simple booklets on herbal teas captured my attention. It was at that young age that I began my dedicated collection of plant medicine books that is still in continuous evolution. I come from a family of intellectuals; the house I grew up in was full of books. One about drugs attracted my attention one day, even though drugs was a concept that I barely understood. I only read one random paragraph from this book about a certain Timothy Leary, followed by three capital letters that struck me for their beauty: DMT. I had no idea what they meant, but I liked them. I often scribbled them on my diaries and school notebooks during boring school hours. But teenagers grow rapidly, and only a short while later, I had the opportunity to ask an adult, who I knew to be an expert in this field, whether he knew anything about Timothy Leary and DMT—the first was one of the pioneers in looking at the therapeutic potentials of psychedelics, the latter is one of the most powerful alkaloids with these properties. He smiled and began to tell me a story that lasted a quarter of a century, and that has led me now to the Amazon. Only later did I realize he had been a mentor to me, opening up my path to the world of states of consciousness and traditional medicines.

My passion for these subjects grew every day. I read ravenously and experimented on both myself and my friends with the effects of psychoactive plant potions that I dared to prepare following instructions of experienced adults. With little success, I repeatedly endeavored to use plants from the Mediterranean area to reproduce the famous brew from the Amazon called ayahuasca, which I now finally have the honor of meeting in the jungle. Driven by the frustration of those initial failures but also by the curiosity to investigate them, I began my university career in pharmaceutical chemistry, hoping to find many colleagues and teachers with whom to share my passion. How naïve one is at that age! No one was inspired by the world of the unknown, mysteries, esotericism, alchemy, or shamanism. The pharmaceutical world is looking for cures for cancer and other organic popular diseases to alleviate pain and fight infections. No one was seeking to find the philosopher's stone that turns lead into gold, let alone medicinal plants that can open the doors to subtle, invisible, or spiritual worlds. Now they are barely recognized as useful to treat some psychopathologies, but I think this is not the same thing. Poor in poetry is science today, devoid of imagination. Yet my incurable thirst for knowledge pushed me to continue to study and stay afloat as a researcher in the scientific community, which I still thought was the only one that had the authority to establish whether a certain phenomenon is real or not. Inevitably, however, I had to adapt my research to limiting circumstances since the funding was directed only to certain areas. And slowly, shaped by those adaptations, I found myself at the age of forty, ever more distant from my original drive, and now almost in the arms of a system that channels talents by forcing them to express themselves only in certain selected contexts. At that time, I received a very important job offer from a relevant research institution in China—a beautiful setting inside a tropical garden. This was a great achievement for a small Italian researcher without connections. But, following a long-lasting inner struggle, I refused the offer, entering into the midst of my mid-life crisis. I slowly emerged from this crisis a couple of years later as I began my journey in the middle of the Peruvian Amazon, at the antipode of where I should have been, looking for help and knowledge through traditional plant medicine.

From my *tambo,* I realized with great clarity that this experience of traditional Amazonian medicine was inevitable. Dieting ushpa has revealed to me, through recollection of my earlier, pivotal memories, how along the way of life I got lost, forgetting not only about my passions but also about my friends and teachers: wise plants able to teach and take care of humans too. Perhaps they themselves wanted to push me onto one of those authoritative pedestals of science to spread the voice of a minority, the voice of a lover of herbalist traditions, who stands in contrast to the logic of mainstream pharmacy. Here I recognize a plant mind: patient and farsighted, capable of planning, interacting, and influencing the choices of all living beings, including those of humans. With its typical slowness, the entire plant kingdom has, over the years and all around the world, teased the curiosity of inquisitive learners so that one day they would be able to express themselves on their behalf. A coordinated and global work to give life to a new generation not only of frontier researchers but also of environmentalists in general, acting in the realms of politics, economy, education, and society, in order that they may fight in defense of the environment for the common good and against private interests. Of course, we are still a minority, but we are certainly on the rise, demonstrating the effectiveness of this plant strategy that I consider to be true and consistent, without having to wait anymore for scientific proof of the observed phenomenon. Dieting ushpa, I realized that plants hold specific qualities, but this is not a matter of "therapeutic potential." It's something much more related to "personality."

Thanks to their personalities and know-hows, plants can influence and direct life on Earth, including human dynamics. So, from this point of view, environmentalists of all sorts are recruited by the green world as helpers to save the planet. Such a beautiful vision: one that makes humans step down from the top of the pyramid of life. Thank you, ushpa, for letting me understand all of this! Allowing me to relocate humans to a much more serving position in nature. A right dose of humility is a good cure-all on both a personal and a planetary level.

Humans are only just starting to notice the potential of the "world wide web": a structure that may recall the dendrites and neuronal synapses of a human brain, usually associated to the word mind, but which perhaps resonates even more with the underworld of plants, something that is becoming known with the term of "wood wide web." Under the green surface, a swarm of interconnected roots spread in a hidden world known as the rhizosphere. The Earth is a planet dominated by green plants. One is therefore invited to imagine the deep, mind-like power of this neuro-vegetal tissue of our planet.

From these insights acquired in a widened state of consciousness, I had the feeling of being captured by something much larger than my little human body. My tiny individual mind opened up into the collective intelligence of the plant kingdom. Thus, plants teach just as the traditions in the Amazon claim, and if necessary, they also have the goodness to heal. In fact, in my hypothetical role within the scientific community as a spokesman for an ancient and often marginalized herbalist tradition, I have probably failed. And yet, the green kingdom has not abandoned me. In my *tambo,* plants relieve and heal the wounds of my soul. Ushpa reminded me of the essence of myself, of when I was a kid vehemently chasing my dreams. It made me understand that one should never abandon one's desires. Perhaps fooled by social roles and economic recognition, we risk dying while still alive. The plant taught me that there are moments to conquer our dreams and others to regain strength and soothe our wounds. In all of this, ushpa took care of me in the little hut made of simple bamboo and leaves, inspiring in me a profound sense of gratitude.

Interesting things happen in the Amazon.

POEM 12

Weeping Beech

Fagus sylvatica 'pendula'

Tamryn Bennett

"where does all the grieving go?"

when the world gets too heavy
go to ground, lay yourself down
be still a hundred years

let go of the paper lives,
what could you carry
all these seasons anyway

breath, rain, sun...
none are ours to keep
leaves are lessons of release

give yourself to dirt, birth
and birth again, umbilical limbs
lacery of thought

music of xylem
tears into cloud
branches knowing as stone

CHAPTER 37

Wheat

Triticum

Monica Gagliano

It was November 2015 and my academic career had come to a sudden and screeching halt. The situation had unleashed such an emotional turmoil that something needed to be done about it and needed to be done quickly. Despite the urgency, I had no idea what that *doing* was supposed to look like until January 2016 landed me in Cambodia for a few weeks. There, the knot of the anxious preoccupation that had materialized in my life was to become unfastened thanks to the care and guidance of a nagual—a Toltec name for *shaman*—and the combination of dynamic and meditative practices he instructed. Straight from the beginning of the encounter, our conversations were powerful and stormed across many different topics, including food and health, as well as the disturbing state of crisis on the planet. Little did I know that by the end of our first week together, one of the most surprising and profound revelations about both topics—and how closely they related to one another—would be delivered to my heart, and most unexpectedly (and certainly, less romantically), my guts.

The topic of food and healthy eating had come up several times over the course of that week. At that point in my life, I had been vegetarian for eight years and had been very healthy overall, consciously sourcing the best quality produce I could find. "You are a scientist, then do this as an experiment," the nagual had proposed while pointing out the need for me to consider removing some specific items from my diet. We were talking about milk and wheat products. Carefully, I listened to his suggestion and considered what that would entail. In my pondering, I realized that I had already drifted away from consuming most milk products because my stomach had never truly mastered digesting them. It then occurred to me that over the previous several months, my body had also, naturally, become disinterested in all those delicious breads and scrumptious pastas that, given my Italian upbringing, I had enthusiastically championed since childhood by consuming them religiously every day in vast quantities. Only a few years earlier, the thought of intentionally removing these two ingredients from my diet would have had me panicked and horror-stricken. In fact, I remember declaring with confidence that life without pizza—the most perfect marriage between dairy and wheat—would simply not be possible for me. And here I was, invited to abandon them both, invited to *choose* to relinquish them, and for good. "You are a scientist," he had said, "do this as an experiment." And so I did. It was no problem removing milk products from my diet because, as mentioned, they were already on their way out of my life.

Parting from wheat, however, was quite a different story. The idea alone provoked an immediate and unexpectedly exaggerated "state-of-emergency" reaction. As if this choice posed a real threat to my very existence and identity. My mind nose-dived into fight-flight mode, and the body faithfully followed the instructions by releasing adrenaline and cortisol, two adrenal hormones that fuel the body ready for action by spiking the blood sugar levels (among other things). As we already know, this powerful reaction happens automatically, courtesy of the sympathetic nervous system in collaboration with the adrenal glands, but it does not mean that it is always accurate or appropriate—for example, it is quite unbefitting when there is no real life-threatening peril in sight. When misreading occurs repeatedly, and the mind turns the state-of-emergency into an unreflecting habit, this reaction may become chronic and, like any chronic bad habit, it takes its toll on the body. Incredibly for me, after an initial moment of false alarms and panicked reactions, my mind seized something new about the wheat affair and responded by following the body and delivering one of its greatest acts of self-determination. To appreciate what I am trying to convey here, you need to know a little bit more about this plant and her role in our shared history.

Wheat is a plant like no other. By changing form and identity like a master shape-shifter, she has faithfully accompanied humanity for well over 10,000 years. Originally born in the Fertile Crescent region of the Middle East, she dispersed her own ripe seeds out of wild existence to re-sow them into domesticated patches in the Karacadağ mountains of south-eastern Turkey and elsewhere. During the process of domestication that spread across a wide area over several thousand years (a process an increasing number of scholars refer to as the "protracted" model),[1] we made her into the staple food—breads and pastas of all shapes—we are so familiar with. She, on the other hand, made us into the humanity that we have become. By drawing us together like the awns of her own spikelets, she has propelled us deep into the ground of our history. And like the hairs on her awns prevent the spikelets from reversing back out of the soil where they have dug themselves into, she has hooked us—firmly in place—via remarkable (and kind of creepy) mind-altering effects and intoxicating gastro-political maneuvers. Indeed, she filled our bellies with "our daily bread" and rewarded us for it with her drug-like addictive (opioid and dopaminergic) properties, which made her hard to give up. It is bewildering how she made herself palatable and rewarding to the point of comprehensively replacing our traditional (hunter-gatherer style) foods—primarily based on fruits, nuts, edible roots and tubers, and some meat—despite her being less nutritious and demanding far more of our labor. And it is equally extraordinary how this run-of-the-mill grass cultured our species through major behavioral changes that gave rise to agriculture and a "civilization" of social classes and inequalities, governments and armies. By securing the roots of imperialist ideals, fortifying their colonialist implementation, and, more recently, sprouting into invasive capitalist economies,[2] this plant has single-leafedly staged our journey toward industrialization and globalization, and a society—ours—that makes bitter violence palatable and distasteful horrors acceptable.[3] What would happen to our global affairs if we were to terminate our alliance with this mighty historical, cultural, and social agent? Well, like many relationships, it is complicated. My personal experiment in Cambodia effectively drove the point home, but I needed to understand how addiction works before being able to truly appreciate my relationship with this plant.

Like other addictive substances (legal and illegal), wheat targets the brain's reward system with the sweetness of her carbohydrates. As the sugars flood the bloodstream, they cause a huge spike in the production of a nifty little chemical—dopamine. Dopamine tells our brain that it is worth getting more of whatever feel-good thing we just experienced and rewards our behaviors by motivating us to repeat that which made us feel so good. Clearly, dopamine is essential for many of our daily behaviors and emotional experiences, including our ability to feel pleasure and pain. It keeps us healthy when released in moderation, and we know the devastating effects of Parkinson's disease, which is caused by its absence in nerve cells.[4] Wheat seizes this system with incredible physiological and psychological mastery by triggering huge but short-lived spikes in dopamine production that leave us wanting more and craving for the next hit. Through this reward-reinforcement system, she prompts us to seek her out, again and again, craving for another slice of pizza or one more cookie. Before we know it, she has us all hooked by the guts into an addictive dopamine cycle, fully compliant and unable to forego her even though we know she is harmful.[5] Yes, harmful... not only does her continuous activation of the dopamine reward pathway wear our neurons out, but to add insult to injury, she also interferes with our hormones, including insulin and cortisol. Of these hormones, the first helps move glucose out of the bloodstream and into the cells for energy, and it is essential for staying alive. The injection of high sugar levels delivered by constant consumption of wheat causes the pancreas to release chronically elevated amounts of insulin into the bloodstream, a situation that further amplifies the addictive effects of dopamine in regulating motivation and reward and, most infamously, cultivates diabetes. On the other hand, cortisol, which regulates normal carbohydrate metabolism and immune system function, when released in high levels, depletes dopamine by damaging the receptor sites of this neurotransmitter and ultimately contributes to depression; this leaves us feeling unmotivated, lethargic, and more inclined to reach for a sugar hit to get going. Then our minds and bodies are back in the vicious cycle all over again. And to complicate things even further, wheat releases her cargo of endorphin-like chemicals, which mimic our brain-relevant substances involved, for example, in the regulation of memory consolidation and several neurophysiological functions. These chemical look-alikes—wheat-derived exorphins—are able to bind to our opiate receptors and engage in actions much like those of our in-house endorphins.[6] In essence, they simulate a feel-good experience fortified with a pleasant (albeit fleeting) feeling of euphoria, stimulate our appetite for more of the same, and also sedate us through postprandial lethargy. This may explain the addictive feeling of happiness we experience as we enthusiastically tuck into that bowl of pasta or munch insatiably on that packet of biscuits and why we experience "brain fatigue" immediately after eating them. On that first day when I stopped eating wheat, all these feelings awakened, gravely amplified, before subsiding away.

On that day, a note in my travel diary read, "Today is a slow day." It was a forewarning of the profound effects that the dietary changes I was implementing would bring to my physical, mental, and emotional state. Because these changes were certainly not confined to the physical discomfort that such detoxification process might generate. My mental and emotional state had been tied up with wheat on a daily basis for decades since childhood, and the removal of this addictive physical presence from my diet was likely to challenge my mind and emotional body in new and unfamiliar ways. My personal identity had been profoundly conditioned by and attached to this plant, so her absence from my life was bound to cause some upheaval. Was I prepared for it? That morning I had completed the movement-based practice as instructed by the nagual and then eaten a whole half a watermelon, which I had bought at the local market in town the day before. In the clammy Cambodian heat, the distinctive red-fleshed fruit felt instantly refreshing and hydrating, as well as much more delicious and satisfying than a piece of toasted bread. That was until I decided to leave the sanctuary of my hotel and wander in the hustle-bustle of Siem Reap's Old Market area. The small Cambodian town was besieged by Western tourists who had come there primarily because of its proximity to the remains of the iconic Angkor Wat temple complex with its massive strangler fig trees, who lounged in the sun with their grey roots lazily melted like wax over the old ruins. The tourists were sitting around small tables, selecting familiar items out of a food menu that could have been at home in a Parisian café in the middle of Montmartre. In fact, many of the cafés in Siem Reap served traditional Cambodian Khmer dishes with a French twist... of wheat. Baguettes, croissants, fine pastries, pies, and several boulangerie and pâtisserie specialties featured on the various menus across town as a reminder that France had had a long intellectual and imperial relationship with this part of the world. Cambodia as a geo-political resource had been officially lost to France at the beginning of the 19th century. However, it was clear that the colonizing effect had not been lost at all but simply crumbled into pastries and kneaded into breads. It seemed that the imperialist gastro-political discourse that wheat had enabled (i.e., the superiority of wheat-eating Europe over rice-eating Asia) still persisted, covertly, in the social transactions around food.[7]

I picked my table at a cute vegetarian café in a quieter alleyway known as The Passage and joined the masses in the foraging liturgy we call lunch—even though I was not hungry. I reluctantly skirted around the beautiful baguettes and all the mouth-watering dishes containing wheat and settled instead for rice spring rolls and a salad. Leaving the café, I caught myself mindlessly lingering at the pâtisserie window. Glistening croissants were summoning me with their sleek half-mooned bodies—I craved them even though I was certainly not hungry. I walked on and a strange tiredness descended over me, a tiredness that felt new, emotional, and clearly different from the common postprandial stupor. In those brief but remarkable moments, I was met with the first of several realizations regarding the centrality of wheat as a *habitual* food in my diet. How strange that this plant would trigger the arising of seemingly concrete emotional needs (comfort) and physical cravings (hunger) according to this habituation. How unsettling to realize that I had been unaware of what I was really doing every time I reached out for something—a *wheat*-something—to eat. Then, how not to entertain the possibility that wheat might have entrained my mind to respond in what had become the only way I knew how? In other words, to what extent my thoughts and choices about food were my own, and to what degree, my actions—culinary and beyond—were manipulated by this vegetal mind? To even dare consider the idea sounded ridiculous at best, if not completely nonsensical. However, given her highly addictive properties, I could no longer exclude the possibility that this plant had successfully stretched herself beyond the confines of her slender grassy body and enacted herself through the cognitive faculties of my mind and that of many of us for millennia. So, I went cold turkey. And as my relationship with this plant came to an end, my wheat-induced stupor slowly lifted, and my relationships with people, places, and histories changed.

Truly, wheat is a plant like no other. The wheat plant has shallow roots, but her influence on the world as we know it today runs deep. She sprouted our civilization into being and grew vitally important to the stability of our societies (arguably, holding the power to fuel societal unrest and collapse, too). Indeed, she has built economic empires by incarnating the agricultural commodity markets worldwide. We so anxiously crave her and fear being left alone without her, that at the time of pandemics, we thoughtlessly rush out, stockpiling anything that bears her name. No other plant has had so hypnotizing an effect on our minds. No other plant has had so powerful a bearing on general economic and social conditions. And no other plant has had so devastating an impact on the environment. Wheat production and the monocultural practices that go with it are responsible for soil erosion, water runoff, and drought—all of which are being aggravated by rising global temperatures. And to satisfy the ever-increasing global demand, conventional agricultural wheat relies on our excessive and indiscriminate use of pesticides. Engineered to kill unwanted insects, weeds, fungi, and bacteria that may diminish yields, these chemicals are known pollutants, including organophosphates (e.g., chlorpyrifos diazinon and malathion), organochlorines (e.g., dioxin and DDT), herbicides (e.g., glyphosate and atrazine), and neonicotinoids (e.g., imidacloprid, clothianidin, and thiamethoxam) among many others. Because most of these chemicals do not break down easily but persist in the environment contaminating water systems, soil, air, and silently creeping up food chains, they cause serious harm to wildlife and human health.[8]

Wheat is a plant like no other—she is *the political plant*. Wheat is the most significant single crop in terms of human consumption and the most abundant and widely spread dietary component, particularly for people of European origin. Indeed, informed by European gastronomic history, the choice of eating wheat had been made for me by my socio-cultural familial background; I was a child then and lacked the cognitive competence to understand the real terms and conditions of the contract binding me to her. To start eating wheat might not have been my own conscious choice, but the decision to stop eating it was. I had to stop eating wheat to appreciate that such a simple culinary decision carried a power that moved far beyond the dinner table—the power to refuse my consent to the devastating destruction of life and our planet that the global techno-production of wheat embodies perfectly today.[9] What if the world stopped eating wheat? What if a simple culinary choice could turn out to be the most radical act of mindfulness on our part? For many of us, it is simply a matter of making up our minds to do this straightforward experiment. What if we did—and what if we discovered that this was the experiment that would change our lives by freeing our collective mind from the stupor of a millennia-deep intoxication,[10] and unleashing our creative ability towards reversing the current ecological crisis and powering the process of regeneration of this planet?

CHAPTER 38

White Pine

Pinus strobus

Robin Wall Kimmerer

When I come beneath the pines, into that particular dappled light, time slows, and I fall under their spell. My science brain and my intuitive brain are both alight with knowing. Is it the spaciousness of the leafy vaulted ceiling? Maybe the terpenoids in pine vapors exert a psychological influence, producing an altered state of tranquil alertness. Perhaps it's the quivering energy of electrical micro-discharge from the needles. Maybe we are humbled simply by their size. Is it the sound of boughs rising and falling, like slow breathing? There's something there we sense, but cannot name, a feeling akin to sitting quietly in the presence of an elder. So it is, with pines. You want to slip into their circle and listen.

My favorite place to read on a summer day is leaning against the bole of a big old white pine. There's almost always a hollow there, upholstered in a coppery brocade of pine needles with comfy armrests of the buttressed roots which hold up the pillar of pine rising two hundred feet above me. These piney points above the lake's water are beloved in the north woods, for the sand and granite below, sun and wind above, and a view across the lake, which at this moment is dancing up white caps in the breeze. In this woodland library, I have one book on my lap and the other against my back. One written on cellulose, one written in cellulose. When I sit with white pines, I wordlessly come to know things that I didn't know before.

White pine is revered across Indigenous cultures as a symbol of wisdom, longevity, and of peace. They are thanked for their material gifts of medicine, materials, fuel, and food and for their spiritual gifts. Pines are understood as among our oldest teachers; in fact, they are of an ancient lineage in the tree world and have seen much change across the earth. Among some people, white pine is regarded as the "*ogema*" of the forest, the seat of leadership. The pine, like all trees, is spoken of in my Anishinaabe language, not as an object, an "it" but as a "who," a person of some standing, whose name is *Zhingwak*. Charismatic white pines are honored as elders. They are the esteemed companions of the visionary eagle who uses their emergent canopy as nest and watchtower. *Zhingwak* plays many roles in the canon of Native stories, as a protector of human people and the embodiment of highest virtues. Known as the Tree of Peace, white pine is the iconic symbol of the Five Nations of the Haudenosaunee (Iroquois) Confederacy, who taught the people peace through unity, by its five soft needles, bound together as one. The tallest, strongest, most enduring being in the forest is the botanical representation of the oldest democracy on the planet.

Traditional cultures who sit beneath the white pines recognize that human people are only one manifestation of intelligence in the living world. Other beings, from Otters to Ash trees, are understood as persons, possessed of their own gifts, responsibilities, and intentions. This is not some kind of mistaken anthropomorphism. Trees are not misconstrued as leaf-wearing humans but respected as unique, sovereign beings equal to or exceeding the power of humans. Seneca scholar John Mohawk wrote that according to his culture, "an individual is not smart [...] but merely lucky to be part of a system that has intelligence. Be humble about this. The real intelligence isn't the property of an individual; the real intelligence is the property of the universe itself."

The Indigenous story tradition speaks of a past in which all beings spoke the same language and life lessons flowed among species. But we have forgotten—or been made to forget—how to listen so that all we hear is sound, emptied of its meaning. The soft sibilance of pine needles in the wind is an acoustic signature of pines. But this well-known "whispering of pines" is just a sound, it is not their voice.

What if you were a great teacher, a holder of knowledge and vessel of stories, but had no audible voice with which to speak? What if your listeners presumed you to be mute, save for the passive whispering of your needles? How would you bring your truth into the world? Wouldn't you dance your story in branch and root? Wouldn't you write it in the eloquence of cellulose? In the lasting archive of wood? Plants tell their stories not by what they say but by what they do. They tell their story in their bodies, in an alphabet once as familiar as the song of every bird, which we have also forgotten, as we became afflicted not only with plant blindness but plant deafness as well.

If you know how to see, their storytelling goes deeper than the curve of a windward branch. Everything that affects the pine is expressed in its body. The tree is an integrator of all its experience and that of the surrounding community. When you have learned its lexicon, the story of the weevils, the drought, the fire, the blister rust, the wind, the canoe makers, and the maples are all plainly written. And more.

The book I brought in my backpack is an honest account of the life of a woman known for her intelligence and generosity. It chronicles her growth from an uncertain child to an advocate for justice whose voice resonates around the world. Her path of becoming was marked by times of poverty and of abundance. She tells the story of a house fire that took everything, raising children, losing her parents, finding her place in the world, growing into a strong protector of her community; it is the story of a life.

One thing I find curious in this book, although scarcely unusual, is that in a world filled to bursting with two hundred million species, this book only mentions one, *Homo sapiens.* It is a hallmark of our time in human history, that we think we are alone, perched at the top of the pyramid of life, in charge of it all. She writes of her girlhood in the church. Aided by religion that made God in the image of man, humans alone were perceived to have the capacity for reason, for sentience, for choice, for language. But long before that error was promulgated, people knew the trees were storytellers. But then we forgot. Or were made to forget by the ones who chased divinity out of the forest and forced it into the sky. The stories of trees were erased from our knowing. I doubt she ever imagined that her words would end up on a page, read by me, with *Pinus strobus* looking over my shoulder.

How remarkable, really, is this phenomenon of reading and writing. We literate folks take for granted that abstract little marks, in repeated patterns on a sheet of cellulose paper, a tree body, can be decoded to make meaning. Even if those black marks are arrayed in a form we don't understand like Chinese characters, Anishinaabe pictographs, or cuneiform marks on a clay tablet, nonetheless we still recognize them as writing. The very fact of the patterned marks on the page, the systematic recording and interpretation of lived experience, is evidence of intelligence, whether we can read them or not. We don't dismiss them as meaningless just because we don't understand; we go looking for the Rosetta stone. Unless of course, those texts are written by a tree.

The story of intelligences other than our own is one of continual expansion. I am not aware of a single research study that demonstrates that other beings are dumber than we think. Octopi solve puzzles, chickadees create language, crows make tools, rats feel anxiety, elephants mourn, parrots do calculus, apes read symbols, nematodes navigate, and honeybees dance the results of cost-benefit analysis of sucrose rewards like an economic ballet. Even the slime mold can learn a maze, enduring toxic obstacles to obtain the richest reward. The blinders are coming off, and the definition of intelligence expands every time we ask the question.

The ability to efficiently sense, identify, locate, and capture resources needed in a complex and variable environment requires sophisticated information processing and decision making. Intelligence is today thought of as "adaptively variable behavior," which changes in response to signals coming from the environment.

Where is intelligence situated? Our conceptions of intelligence are based on animal models and a kind of "brain chauvinism." Every animal, from the flatworm to the black bear, has a brain, central meeting place of sensation, and coordinated response. Because animals are mobile autonomous beings who must pursue their food, the brain must itself be compact and portable.

But a centralized brain is not needed for plant intelligence. Rapid movement is not necessary when the food comes to you. For an autotrophic, sessile being, bathed in the needed resources, networked in intimate relationships with myriad others above and below ground, a very different system of sensation and response might well evolve, which looks nothing like the animal model.

If food becomes abundant, no animal can grow more legs to chase after it or a new mouth to eat more. In times of shortage, most cannot cast off a limb that it has no energy to sustain. The whole organism is static in form and flourishes or suffers within those constraints. Not so for plants, who can adaptively alter their circumstances by growing additional parts or losing unneeded ones. Decision-making at tree pace looks like passivity to us herky-jerky animals, accustomed to our own short lifespan. But pine behavior is a slow-motion pursuit of adaptive solutions. Plant intelligence or "adaptively flexible behavior" may be manifest in their extraordinary capacity to change form in real time by altering their allocation of carbon to different functions in response to changing needs.

This slow dance of parts emerging and disappearing is the tree-paced equivalent of movement. Branches expand into light-filled gaps and retreat from dense shade, adjusting their architecture to optimize light capture. Roots are deployed in new directions to follow changing gradients of water and minerals, not randomly but with purpose. They are hunting light and grazing for phosphorous by differential deployment of apical meristems.

Plasticity is possible because trees have myriad growing points, or meristems, a reservoir of adaptation poised to respond to changed circumstances. Tissues that animals never dreamed of, meristems—like totipotent stem cells—can be modified into the new tissues that best suit the conditions. Trees like white pine also have a lateral meristem, the vascular cambium, which gives rise to the cells that increase the diameter of the stem. It is an entire body stocking of meristematic tissue, perpetually embryonic. This nexus of nutrients and hormones and sensory chemicals, and creative cell making, is perhaps a fertile location to search for the decentralized seat of pine intelligence. It is the cambium, starting and stopping on an annual cycle that writes in the language of cellulose, of tree rings. Let us consider for the moment that the cambium is the author, that it is the pen that writes its own history.

There are so many stories here. I'm distracted from the human-telling on the page by the pine-telling on the land. Once you become attuned to the body language of pines, much is revealed. Far from being just a fixed expression of genetic inheritance, individual pines record their journey through life in the form of their body, sketching their autobiography. Gazing out at the pines around my reading nook, I see what their childhoods must have been like, in the stature and density of the stand. I see the age and health of their children and grandchildren. I see the way their neighborhoods changed with immigration, their annoyance with balsam, and their camaraderie with blueberries. These stories remind us, though, that we can't always judge a book by its cover; to know the real story, we need to open the book. My favorite place to read those chapters is in my lab, sitting at my microscope with a cookie.

The circular disk sliced from the trunk, or what dendroecologists fondly call "tree cookies," has remnants of bark on the outside and still carries the scent of pine pitch. To the untrained eye, the cookie is inscribed with what every schoolchild recognizes as annual rings in a tree stump. One ring is laid down for every year of growth, each one outside of the next so that the sapling years are in the center and recent history just under the bark. You can count them up to know how old the tree was when its life was interrupted by someone with a saw.

To read that story, I slide the cookie under my stereomicroscope at low magnification. What seemed uniform is anything but. Some rings are clear and even like pine floorboards, others wavy and dark. Some as wide as a pencil eraser lie next to a series each year as narrow as a thread. Like the human autobiography, there are good times and bad, years when the rains did not come, but the caterpillars did, and spans when all she had to do was stand in the sun and grow like the sky was calling.

I zoom in further and catch my breath at the beauty of the cells, lined up in continuous files linking young ones to their ancestors in an unbroken lineage. It is strangely moving, an intimate privilege to read a private diary after the death of the writer. This very cell is a word, a day in the life. Unlike the book I am reading, this story is not made of marks on a page which represent a life; the tree has written its story in the life of its own body.

Ring width is highly correlated with the favorability of the growth conditions, of course, and dendrochronologists have been able to reconstruct long-term records of climatic variation that range centuries. Those tight dark rings correspond to a historic drought, the broad ones to years of wet summers. Just reading ring width is like skimming a chapter for the main idea but missing the rich detail. Life is not lived in years, but in moments, I zoom my microscope on a single ring to share that moment.

The story is written with a rich vocabulary, from the pale honeycomb of springwood to the varnished amber of cells laid down in fall. In spring, the script is loopy and wide, effusive with energy of long bright days. In fall, it narrows with concentration. The ratio of early wood to late wood tells the length of the growing season and the timing of rains. How the snow melted early, and it rained all the way to July when the midsummer drought arrived but yielded to October rains. Several of the rings are pocked with resin canals, like potholes in the smooth surface of the wood. The formation of traumatic resin ducts speaks of beetles and wounds. An individual ring might read like a sentence, but a sequence of rings becomes a page that tells how a windstorm tore a hole in the canopy and released a young pine from the suppression of shade. Sentence, paragraph, chapter over the lifespan of a tree, an entire book is written. Every single thing that affects the physiology of the tree is written in these rings. Dendrochronologists can read the stories of distant volcanos, air pollution, landslides, nuclear testing, and climate change.

Like the human biography in my backpack, I read in these rings of a life unfolding, the hungry times, years when illness or weevils put life on hold, days of raising a family of seedlings, of release from poverty when suddenly light streamed in, of injury and healing, and the effects of losing a parent. It is all written here in tracheids, parenchyma, and resin ducts. And the house fire, where the orderly rings are interrupted by a swath that glitters like coal, a fissure filled with the black lava of fire-boiled resin. The stories are similar, yet we call the human writer a brilliant author, while we call the pine writer timber.

The entry for each pine year is written in just four kinds of cells: thin-walled parenchyma, thick-walled tracheids, sugary ray cells, and resin ducts. They line up in orderly files from inside to outside. Punctuation isn't necessary in pine time since everything flows into everything else, and commas have little meaning for a being who can live for centuries. The only punctuation comes with winter when the pen is laid down.

Dashes and dots seem to mean nothing until you know Morse code. The open apertures of cells look like strings of zeroes and ones, themselves empty of meaning, that encode every digital document ever written. If just four chemical bases of DNA can write the script for life's being, why not arboreal literature in cellulose? Denying the possibility of writing to trees is simply a failure of imagination.

If you had a sheet of paper made of cellulose cell walls, with abstract little black marks laid down in lines across its surface, if those black marks made a coherent pattern that could be decoded to yield information, if that information changed in response to changing conditions, if it conveyed meaning about natural phenomena such as climate and disease if that information correlated with the known history of the world...wouldn't you call it writing? But we don't—in trees, we only call it growth as if the cells, each distinctive as handwriting, were only made for one function, as if the human throat were made only for respiration and not for singing.

All of these cells have internal functions for the tree: they conduct water, provide rigidity, transport resin, and store starch. They connect every cell to the next from deep in the soil to the atmosphere; they are conduits for resources at the same time that they serve as support. Why not information storage as well?

The notion of rediscovering tree language reminds me of the reports of Native observers paddling the Salish Sea who told their stories of orca families, how they lived in complex clans, spoke their own distinct languages, and called one another by name. Western science, still mired in self-absorbed human exceptionalism, dismissed such claims as supernatural nonsense. Secure in the arrogance of expertise masquerading as scientific certainty, they pronounced that only humans were capable of language. They called their own story "fact" and Native facts "stories"—until marine biologists dropped hydrophones below the waves to eavesdrop on orcas, decoded what they recorded, and, like Columbus, discovered a New World. A new world in which humans are not alone in animal intelligence. Just like the Salish fisher folk had told them, in the sophisticated Indigenous science they dismissed as "stories."

Had we not questioned our assumptions of human exceptionalism, had we gone on believing that humans alone were capable of problem-solving, think of the insights we would have missed, the music of whales, the emotions of dolphins, the wit of squid, and the droll storytelling of parrots. I hope that we are today on the cusp of an expanded vision, unconstrained by plant blindness. Might we attend to Indigenous knowledge and to tree knowledge to find ourselves in a world full of thinking, feeling, green beings—and fall from our lonely perch at the top of the hierarchy in a landslide of wonder?

What are we missing because of a failure of imagination, caught in the narrow western materialist thinking? What if we proceeded from the notion of the intelligence of all beings? What might we learn if we took off the lenses of human exceptionalism and saw beyond ourselves into a world of beings possessed of their own gifts and responsibilities? What happens if we examine the dendrochronological record with the humility to explore the literature of trees?

My mind explodes to dream of what pines might write out of their stillness and arboreal perceptions, from a consciousness that transcends underground and sky, intimate with birds and snails and ancient lichens, the mysteries of water, the stories of lightning, the gossip of mycorrhizae, and the poetry of light. You know they tell jokes—haven't you heard the chuckle of nuthatches? Do they remember the weight of passenger pigeons, the breath of glaciers, the taste of strontium in the rain? Could they tell us what it is to stand in the sun and fulfill your destiny without chasing it? How to create lasting relationships when you can't run away? Could they guide us through the narrows of climate catastrophe toward a new way to live? No—not unless we're willing to imagine the mind of the pine who writes its own story and ours.

POEM 13

Wild Piper

Piper guamensis

Craig Santos Perez

the first eåmtis[1] who found me
                    in the deep jungle
bowed to my branches—
                    called me saina—
        & shared stories of her sick village—

i pitied them—no roots—
        fragile bark—prone to illness
                    & pain—they weep
        like no other wounded
animal on this island—

so i gifted her
        my leaves
to soothe her people—

when the time came
        i granted her permission
to teach her daughter
        the places i grow
abundant—what illnesses i treat—
                    when to harvest—& this
        was how we grafted
i taotao to i tano—

until
doctors arrived & hospitals erected—
until bulldozers uprooted our home—
until militaries & toxins
infected the soil—
until barbed wire fences separated
us—until i taotao tano
died from cancer & diabetes—

after so much loss
the descendants of eåmtis
are now returning
to relearn my names
& plant the sacred language
of åmot
back into their bodies—
so that we may grow perennially—
so that we may once again blossom
& heal—

CHAPTER 39

Xiang Si

Acacia confusa

- **Alex K. Gearin**

If plants were faculties of the mind, *Acacia* would be a versatile and global apparatus. The genus spans the Earth as a titan of the plant world with a very large diversity of species. Beyond providing the environment with oxygen, shade, and other basic elements of living, *Acacia* plants have also entered the pragmatic realm of the human species as medicines, aromatics, tannins, and building materials. Humans, also known as the reckless sorcerers of the Anthropocene, have developed contradictory relations with Acacia as both allies and enemies. The genus has penetrated the human soul through different channels of spiritual consciousness and artistic appreciation, with its species personified across the world as sentient creatures, powerful gods, and trickster spirits. The making of *Acacia* into persons offers us important clues for thinking about the mind of plants. By juxtaposing the significance of *Acacia confusa* in Chinese folklore, literature, and medicine with its recent use among psychedelic enthusiasts in Western societies, we can appreciate two key ways humans have projected or summoned plant sentience, which I will discuss as the symbolic and the relational plant mind. In both these traditions, the plant is described as embodying a certain kind of mind. But the differences in how the plant mind of *Acacia confusa* is defined can point to profoundly different ways in how humans relate to the plant itself.

Let's begin with an overview of human engagements with the plant. *Acacia confusa* is a perennial tree native to Southeast Asia and is particularly abundant in Taiwan, south mainland China, and the Philippines. In recent decades, it has been thriving in Hawaii as an invasive species. With a solid constitution that reaches firmly into the ground, *Acacia confusa* has grown strong against the fierce typhoon winds of the Pacific Ocean. The firm grip of its roots prevents landslides, and therefore, it has been intentionally planted on hills in parts of Taiwan and South China. Its dense body and attractive texture have made it a popular source of hardwood flooring known as Asian Walnut. The plant appears with a very minor status in traditional medicine in China, particularly as a substance that can help heal wounds and skin disorders. As outlined in some Taiwanese traditional medical texts, doctors would pulverize forty grams of fresh branches and leaves, mix it with wine, and administer the elixir to aid against digestive problems or to assist a patient in awakening from a coma. It is still occasionally used today for its medicinal properties in some parts of rural Taiwan.

But perhaps the plant's most impactful or longest resonance with humans has come through literature with classic Chinese writers and poets featuring the sturdy tropical tree in their works. In Mandarin, *Acacia confusa* has a very romantic name 相思树 or Xiang Si tree (literally "mutual, miss, tree"). It shares the same pronunciation as 像丝, ("[the love is] like a thread"). Xiang Si (相思) therefore implies notions of loving, missing, and yearning for someone. The shape of *Acacia confusa* stems are partially needle-like and give the impression of a thin thread being tied together. This morphology resonates with the etymology of the popular English word for Acacia, "wattle," and its original Old Teutonic meaning, "to weave."

Acacia confusa is woven into Chinese literary classics as an agent of love, yearning, and grief that often includes stories of family and political warring and turmoil. The collection of legends and short stories entitled *In Search of the Supernatural,* compiled in 350 AD by author Gan Bao, includes a popular narrative about an emperor who meets a very beautiful woman who is married to a low-ranking officer. The powerful emperor tries to force the woman to marry him, but in response, she and her husband tragically commit suicide. Although they requested in their wills to be buried together, the emperor is furious and orders the two coffins to be buried separately. Then overnight, during a wild storm, something supernatural happens. Two giant Xiang Si trees spring from the coffins. The two trees' branches and roots entwine and interweave, mysteriously uniting the dead couple's spirits. Perching on the tree branches are two love birds that sing mournful songs day and night. Against the seemingly omnipotent powers of the emperor, the Xiang Si tree appears as an intentional and ethical presence whose characteristically strong roots support true love and solidarity.

The tree also became firmly rooted in the human heart in Fujian, a province in southeast China, during the mid-20th century. Tragic stories of love and death traveled with *Acacia confusa* across a warring straight between Taiwan and mainland China. In one origin myth, a husband goes to Taiwan to make money while his pregnant wife waits at home in south Fujian. The wife dies of loneliness and grief, and the husband then attempts to overcome his loss by consulting with the spirit of *Acacia confusa*. When he finally returns to Fujian, he takes a seed with him and plants it where his wife died. The story concludes that, from then on, *Acacia confusa* starts to grow in Southern Fujian, and it is called Xiang Si tree. This myth is part of a larger regional complex of stories in which hundreds or thousands of *Acacia confusa* seeds were actually sent from Taiwan to Fujian mainland China during the war period as sorrowful gifts for widows to plant among tombstones in the mountains. As Chinese scholar Su Zurong notes, the flourishing and dense populations of Xiang Si trees in Fujian have grown from a strong and complicated cross-strait relationship.

For the last two years, I have been working in Fujian as an anthropologist and living among hills populated by *Acacia confusa* on the tropical island of Xiamen. Outside my kitchen window is a sturdy crowd of melancholic Xiang Si trees that bloom with spectacular golden flowers only for a short period during the early weeks of spring. The city of Xiamen is currently idealized in China as a beautiful holiday destination with clean air and fecund natural environments where new lovers flock from across the country to take wedding photos and romance. Visitors can stay at the Xiang Si Tree Seaview Hotel, which is good "for couples who want to spend their honeymoon next to the mountain and facing the ocean [...] awaken listening to birds chirping and the smell of beautiful flowers." The evergreen tree spans the tropical island and silhouettes a sweat sadness that is romanticized in local art, crafts, and music traditions. It surrounds and blends with hipster youth cultures in Xiamen—such as the *fo xi* (佛系) with its escapist idealism that draws inspiration from the minimalist aesthetics of Buddhism, or *sang* (丧) with its ironic tones that reject "modern progress" for insulated moments of joy or sadness. In the contemporary moment, *Acacia confusa* continues to germinate sentiments of love in the

Chinese heart with poetic expressions that entwine lovers, trees, and the wider non-human environment.

Gan Boa's supernatural story of true love and solidarity, the sorrowful Xiang Si tree of Fujian mythology, and the plant's association with romantic tourism in Xiamen are prime examples of the symbolic plant mind. In each of these cases, the plant is a mysterious figure—or spirit—whose personal agency and mentality are expressed in ways limited by what they offer to human predicaments and desires. In other words, the plant gives expression to human social affairs. Its supernatural or figurative existence is an extension of the human world.

The academic question of why people view human qualities in plants has generated a massive anthropological discussion under the banner of animism research, and it finds a diverse array of possible answers when considering *Acacia confusa*. The classic explanation is that people animate plants (or any non-human entity) with human characteristics and temperaments in order to express and organize the emotional, social, and political lives of humans. As anthropologist Claude Levi-Strauss said in his *Myth and Meaning* lectures, animism is "good to think with" for animistic societies and communities. This seems fitting when considering the significance of the Xiang Si tree in Chinese literary history and its romantic tourism, where the plant provides emotional refuge in tragic stories of lovers caught in political and historical tensions or prompts and guides romantic currents of the heart.

Yet, this explanation is only one side of the story, and it fails to cover an important alternate context of animistic thinking that surrounds *Acacia confusa*. The other side of the story is, in fact, less about story and more about a direct embodied or relational experience. During the last decade, *Acacia confusa* has pierced the human cranium and sensory faculties in a dramatic fashion among a newly formed subculture of Western societies. Beyond the awareness of the melancholic lovers of Chinese literature, members of an underground psychedelic culture have discovered that the plant embodies potent psychoactive alkaloids that can blast human consciousness into radically different states of perception when the plant is prepared and consumed appropriately.

Acacia confusa contains high concentrations of tryptamine alkaloids in its bark, including the powerful molecule *n,n-dimethyltryptamine* (DMT), which is famous for giving the classic Amazonian brew ayahuasca its reputation of being a vision-inducing potion. When bark from the roots of *Acacia confusa* are boiled with another plant—such as *Banisteriopsis caapi* or *Pegenum harmala*—the brewer is left with a mind-altering concoction. Among Indigenous Amazonian societies, plants that share a chemical affinity with *Acacia confusa* are described as sentient plant teachers or plant helpers that can assist shamans, healers, and sorcerers in various ways.[1] In North America, Europe, Australia, and elsewhere, urbanized explorers of the deep mind smoke *Acacia confusa* extracts and personify the plant not simply because it's "good to think with" in the classic Levi-Straussian sense—although this is probably partly true—but because it's "good to relate with." The peculiar states of consciousness that psychedelic substances inspire seem to respond better to an active and personal relationship between the inebriated human and the extraordinary figures, agents, or spirits of visions. This seems to be a kind of theme of the experiences.

Before moving to China, I spent ten or so years exploring or formally researching ayahuasca drinking communities in Australia. In this context, "Aussie-huasca" is often brewed using *Acacia* species and the ayahuasca vine or other plants. Despite brewing new plants, Australia drinkers still refer to the *Acacia* brews as "ayahuasca," too. Among the hundreds of stories that I listened to about people drinking Acacia ayahuasca brews, around fifty percent described seeing in their visions real and independent persons, spirits, or entities. The other approximate half described them as symbols of their psyche or personal unconscious. Interestingly, people who described ayahuasca as a person—and therefore as having intentions, thoughts, feelings, memories, etc.—tended to describe more elaborate narratives compared to those who described their ayahuasca visions as symbols of their own personal psyche. "Imagine seeing and talking with your own mother as a facet of yourself," one Australian ayahuasca drinker explained to me. "It could be insightful, although mum would think you are acting weird, and she would treat you as weird. It's kind of the same with ayahuasca." By relating to ayahuasca as an independent person, the visionary "journeys" seem to open with more social and mental depth. Treating plants as persons with minds and intentions changes how they appear and behave in altered states of consciousness. This is a prime example of a relational plant mind. When the plant is related to as having a complexity of mind that is comparable to, if not greater than, humans, then more elaborate descriptions of plant mind begin to flourish in human consciousness. Perceiving the plant in this way can evoke higher and richer qualities in the social relationship between human and plant.

During my research in Australia, I also came across the rich cultural undergrowth of experimental "psychonauts"—which is kind of like an "astronaut" of spiritual geography—who grow or acquire plants such as *Acacia confusa* for consciousness-altering properties. Reports of *Acacia confusa* inebriation often involve descriptions of seeing and interacting with spiritual entities or figures of mind. I became particularly interested in how the agents or spirits of *Acacia* visions—which often include wildly phantasmagoric motifs—were described as appearing unusually familiar, even to first-time users. For instance, in the mid-2000s, I witnessed a literary studies student in Melbourne smoke *Acacia* extracts and dissolve into a fifteen-minute ecstatic experience. She described being taken to marvelous inner temples and shown technological jewels by a wise woman made of light. The woman appeared to her like an auntie she hadn't seen for many years but who knew so much about her. Similar descriptions of an uncanny familiarity span tales of visionary experiences across ayahuasca drinking communities in Australia. They are part of larger sentiments of longing, mutuality, and spiritual affinity expressed about such sacred plants. There is a popular materialistic explanation that circulates among psychonauts and ayahuasca drinkers in Australia to account for this mutuality and familiarity. Because the powerful molecule—DMT—that is principally responsible for the altered state of consciousness is naturally occurring in all human bodies, some people argue that's why the altered experience may feel sharply familiar, natural, or "realer than real." Some people add that the disenchanted mentality and habits of modern, urbanized life have estranged them from a true spiritual nature and ecological consciousness that special *Acacia* species and ayahuasca inspire in humans.

I had the fortune of spending time with a spiritual disciple of *Acacia confusa* in urban Melbourne during the mid-2010s. Greg is tall with dark brown hair, twenty-five years old, and grew up in the outer suburbs of Melbourne. He speaks with a gentle nature and, commonly, a pensive-looking face. He was introduced to *Acacia* extracts six years prior as "spiritual sacraments" from a friend. Greg explained to me that he had smoked DMT from *Acacia confusa* four years earlier and realized that he did not want to work in society but, rather, was "destined to follow a spiritual path of sacred plants." Greg's desire to abandon ordinary paths of employment was matched by his desire to commune with nature. He described urban life as an obstacle on the journey toward a spiritual affinity with plants and nature, wherein *Acacia* extracts are placed at mythic heights. The visionary states of *Acacia*, he tells me, open the mind to a profound intelligence that is responsible for nature and the ecosystems and that which exists within and beyond time. Out the back of his house, I entered, on a hot day, what he calls The Chamber—a cool meditation, music, and recording space. Large and uncluttered, the space is where he spends most of his time playing and recording music, reading, drawing, meditating, and spiritual journeying with *Acacia* extracts. The room is windowless and relatively dark. The ground is covered with light blue and brown Indian rugs. The walls are also light blue and neatly lined with colorful psychedelic geometric art. In the corner rests a small shrine dedicated to Horus (the ancient Egyptian god of kingship and sky), dried *Acacia* leaves, and several small sigils. Outside of The Chamber is a garden area with entheogenic cactuses and plants growing.

The special connection that Greg feels with *Acacia confusa* and the natural world is shared by many other psychonauts and ayahuasca drinkers I met in Australia and abroad. The connection is invariably described as being forged out of the mercurial states of consciousness caused by taking the substances. Although the chemical name DMT has become the label most people use to describe *Acacia* extracts, the substances may contain a range of unique molecules depending on the species of origin. This has led some psychonauts in Australia to describe different *Acacia* species as having different personalities and temperaments. For instance, *Acacia obtusifolia*—which contains a range of tryptamine alkaloids and bufotenine—has a stronger kind of effect, lending it the status of trickster spirit. *Acacia confusa* also contains a range of tryptamine molecules that give it a unique psychoactive reaction with the human central nervous system. Yet across much of the talk of different molecules and neurological cascades are reports of people taking the substances and relating with an intelligence of nature. I'd like to finish by sharing a long quote by a person who goes by the alias of Kerelsk on the wildly popular Internet forum DMT Nexus. He described in 2014 what happened when he consumed five grams of *Acacia confusa* root bark and three grams of *Peganum harmala* as tea. The description tells the story of a plant spirit whose mind and intentions cannot be removed from its biological existence. Here we see the relational plant mind expressed in dazzling color:

> First the Acacia spirit showed me a vision of a Bengal tiger, ferocious, heavy, sharp claws and teeth. It put a 'thought-bubble' in my head that every member of an ecology knows everybody else [...] The tree spirit was very willing to talk about itself, and give personal insight into my life. First, it complimented me for being tree-like myself. It seemed as though it could read my thoughts and direct them to one thing or another. It gave me feelings about my recent fresh-growth [...] It showed a panorama of *Acacia confusa* growing wild in somewhere like Hawaii or Southeast Asia [...] tropical anyway, usually on hillsides. It showed me how it sees the sun, a strobing energy furnace, which it absolutely loves. It also showed me the moon. From my perspective the tree lives sacredly, that is, it lives by rhythms of the earth. It also mentioned how it loves having sex and trading genes and that it's nice to have a lot of members of the same species around. It showed a picture of a butterfly or moth, which I thought was a pollinator. It also gave botanical features of leguminous trees [...] I asked what I could do for it, and it replied that I should just continue doing what I'm doing. I asked what it could do for me, and it said that if I ever had a question I could address my little living sapling, where it would then transmit this idea to hyperspace and if an answer was found the idea would flip

> back to the tree like an enzyme and the tree would deliver it to me through 'thought-bubbling.' That is, I would just receive an answer without consciously thinking.

Intimately shaped by the material existence of the plant, the psychonautic example expresses a type of mentality that is closer to an embodied plant life. It's difficult to read the visionary report above as simply symbolic of the human. If we must draw symbolic significance from the report, then it would be the profound opening of a relation between human and plant. Whether we rationalize this opening as chemical, environmental, or spiritual, we still need to reckon with the fact that psychoactive *Acacia* experiences appear to become deeper when the plant is treated as a person. This points to a fascinating theme in which the mind of psychoactive plants may be ignorant toward those who ignore it. There is a kind of mirror philosophy at the core of psychedelic states of consciousness where the individual's immediate thoughts, feelings, and intuitions can profoundly shape the visionary environment. By approaching the plant mind as simply symbolic of the psyche or human world, we risk being thrown into an echo chamber of ourselves that gives little room for anything else to appear or be expressed. This can easily become a sad place, and not just for the Xiang Si tree, but for the broader kinship of life on Earth.

But my own experience among these two approaches to the mind of *Acacia confusa* leaves me feeling less polarized and absolute. Although the profound experience of smoking *Acacia* extracts can throw consciousness into a relational plant mind equipped with dazzling color and surreal apparitions, the cultural technologies of Xiang Si literature, folklore, and tourist packages also wedge open consciousness in the direction of plant mentality. In trying to think from the perspectives of Acacia confusa, I imagine the plant would evaluate the human's cultural or ritual technologies for encountering it by the human's ability to channel its actual existence in the web of life.

CHAPTER 40

Yoco

Paullinia yoco

Iván Darío Vargas Roncancio

The concept of plants as teachers is a well-established trope in Amazonian ethnology, and my first encounter with the yoco (*Paullinia yoco)* was in Bajo Putumayo, Southern Colombian Amazon, about ten years ago. I had the privilege of spending a short time with Indigenous Cofán and the vegetal beings with whom they live and work in this region.[1] While I didn't know it at the time, the purpose of this trip was to start learning about what I now conceptualize as a "vegetal protocol," namely the local ways of dealing with the entangled political, legal, and cosmological worlds of the *Bajo* with the special guidance of plants like the yoco, yagé (*Banisteriopsis caapi*), and tobacco (*Nicotiana rustica)*, among others.

A creeping vine often referred to as the forest's sap, yoco is both diet and ritual for several Amazonian communities today. The plant is normally used as a stimulating beverage early in the morning to sow, harvest, and hunt, among other activities in the forest, and also as a purgative before the ritual ingestion of *yagé* at night. For the Airo-pai (Secoya), for example, the yoco has the capacity to "*dar consejo*" (give advice), and in this sense, the plant is deemed a knowledge-holding self. However, yoco intake seems to be decreasing in this region. This is possibly due to the accelerated deforestation of Amazonian forests for cattle, monoculture, and other forms of extraction.

According to Balaunde and Echeverry,[2] the *cuacuiyó* bird (*Lipaugus vociferans)* propagates the yoco, and therefore this bird is considered the yoco's *ëjaë (owner),* or "the one who cultivates the yoco in the forest." The *cuacuiyó* feeds her offspring with yoco's *guayo* (the fruit) by swallowing the fruit and then throwing the kernel while retaining the pulp. Thus, the breeding habits of the *cuacuiyó* reflect the use of the yoco to *dar consejo*—nurture and educate the children.

I clearly remember the smile of *abuelo O* saying how the *yoquito,* as he fondly referred to the plant, "is like the morning coffee for us." You drink it fresh and cold very early in the morning before you work, and it'll give you *fuerza* (strength).[3] Given its concentration of caffeine and theobromine, a single cup is good as a stimulant to endure long working hours in the forest. Besides these tonic effects, the yoco, in larger dosages, is an anti-malarial febrifuge useful for the treatment of bilious disease, which is frequent in the region of Putumayo.[4]

To prepare the *yoco* infusion, you carefully rasp the phloem layer of the plant with a knife and then dissolve the resulting sawdust, or bran, in cold water. After drinking two full gourds of the local infusion, this vegetal protocol involves—I began to learn then—a very important skill: the patient cultivation of what Indigenous practitioners across Putumayo often describe as *pensar bonito* (good and beautiful thinking).

I first heard this idea of *pensar bonito* from Indigenous Inga artist Benjamin Jacanamijoy as he recalled how his father, a reputed yagé practitioner from Putumayo, shared this teaching during a ceremony with this plant. For Benjamin, *pensar bonito* is about "*(...) caminar con el corazón contento,*" walking with a full and happy heart. In my mind, *pensar bonito* refers to local ways of thinking with the forest[5] to orient good action in the world, while cultivating relations of care between humans, other-than-humans, and the territories they all help to co-create:

> *Bonito debes pensar [...] luego, bonito debes hablar.*
>
> *Ahora, ya mismo, bonito empieza a hacer.*[6]
>
> Do beautiful thinking [...] and then, do beautiful talking.
>
> And now go, right away, and begin to do beautifully in the world.[7]

Pensar bonito also comes with hard work and years of training with several plants. And the yoco helps to train this skill by showing humans how "to get rid of laziness (to work and think) and purge anger"[8] in their relationships with others—human and not.

In my experience, yoco ingestion sets in motion a reverberating sensation of warmth rising from the stomach up to the limbs and head, and then the expulsion of what the body does not need. Purging the body thus becomes an essential part of a learning protocol with the plant.

With the yoco helping to cleanse what impedes this distinct form of thought—good and beautiful thinking leading to good and beautiful action—the body starts learning something about the efficacious workings of this vegetal teacher's mind:

> Wandering through tobacco plants,
>
> listening to *moriche* palms (*Mauritia flexuosa*),
>
> grateful and bewildered,
>
> the body learns to learn;
>
> traveling far, inwardly, crossing the lakes of lucid moments,
>
> and the feverish fields of dreaming,
>
> the body learns to listen, carefully.

Discussing what it means to learn with Amazonian plants is, decidedly, a thorny task. And this is not only because one is unable to fully grasp personal experiences with them, but also because learning and knowledge can't always be accounted for through propositional language. There is always the chance of saying too much or saying too little.

As perfectly put by Indigenous political leader *H* during a plenary meeting about intercultural knowledge in Mocoa, Putumayo in 2019, "We have our own routes to access knowledge, but we ought to revitalize them." This teaching is common currency in Amazonian epistemologies today. To be sure, plants like the yoco teach a method to re-center corporeal experience back to the heart of knowledge-making in this region. As *abuelo O* said with clarity and precision, "to learn anything at all one needs a clear head." However, this "head," or better yet, mind, is emergent, delocalized, and distributed throughout the body.[9] The plant then helps to situate personal experience at the core of knowledge creation while decentering the mind from a head considered as the central locus of thinking, decision-making, and communication, among other skills.

Not long ago, I was seated next to a *tulpa*—a place of thought with three central stones for cooking, heating, and learning—to exchange ideas about what knowledge and learning could mean for Indigenous folk in the department of Putumayo, Colombian Amazon. Coming from various places, Indigenous practitioners, artists, academics, and former state officers were all invited to participate in a *minga de pensamiento*—a collaborative work centered on thinking together. The purpose of this *minga* was to share ideas about knowledge creation from an intercultural perspective in this region.

"To start learning anything," *abuelo O* continued as he carefully chewed on his thoughts, "one needs the clear head" one gets with plants like the yoco. In my mind, he was referring to a generic learning about the world that involves conversing with vegetal beings both in ritual and in everyday life—which are, of course, not separate domains in Amazonia. Yet, the *abuelo* was neither talking about the particularities of local botanical knowledge, nor about the cultural uses and social values associated with different plants of the forest. More crucially, he was addressing certain plants as knowledge givers, learning partners, and mind-bearing persons in their own right—that is, regardless of the human attribution of meaning. Yet, *abuelo O* probably would not use these notions at all.

While drawing an invisible semicircle with his hand in the air, pointing in the direction of the canopy, he said almost providentially: "we have our ways of learning about this infinite library out there [. . .] Our learning has always been [...] with the guidance of the mayores (elders) and the plants of the forest." It seemed to me that "clearing the head" was, after all, learning to *learn* otherwise and with plants.[10]

Having "a clear head," the *abuelo* may agree, involves a particular way to hold space open for vegetal others through the momentary suspension of a university-trained preference for description, taxonomy, and ultimately, academic certainty. Engaging with plants as teachers, then, requires a particular disposition of one's body, the attunement of the senses, and the intentional defamiliarization of entrenched habits of thought.

Underpinning disciplinary practices in "Western" academia, as suggested above, is the premise of the mind as an enclosed space where our human thoughts, decisions, and dreams reside. Fuzzy and erratic, when not forthright and focused, this mind would be, reaching for a metaphor, an active repository of an all-too-human brain. In fact, the *abuelo's* invitation was thinking about *mind* and *learning* in a completely different way, and with the help of the yoco, and other plants. A condition of possibility for learning, for having a clear head, is a stage in a larger process that he poetically called a "*mente fresca*" (acquiring a fresh or cool-mind). To be sure, a *mente fresca* often implies the purge of the body as its condition of emergence.

This is a method. In other words, the freshness of the mind that enables learning is something akin to cultivating a disposition to learn with the body. And such a disposition is a particular quality of (human and other-than-human) bodies that have been trained with mind-full plants, or plants full of mind. Thus, decidedly and quite formally, expelling what the body does not need is part and parcel of a vegetal protocol designed to endure the task of learning about/with the "infinite library" the *abuelo* referred to as the forest. An invitation to think otherwise, the *abuelo* was also conceptualizing learning as a process of cooling down one's body.[11] The body is, in a sense, a mind taking a cold shower early in the morning, a *mente fresca* with the strength to do the work of learning with the help of yoco. To put it differently, *abuelo O* was disrupting the famous modern division between mind and body by inviting the people at the *minga de pensamiento* to cool-down their minds-as-heads through their bodies-as-minds. I believe the *abuelo* was hinting at this the very first day of our encounter.

Indigenous artist and ethno-educator *Mama U* would further highlight what the *abuelo* was getting at when she shared this powerful statement: "my idea of a university is where people can also throw up and sweat as part of the process of learning." Based on my direct experience with the yoco, that statement clearly captured the workings of the plant:

> The bitter and earthy taste of the yoco infusion sparks an instant sensation of
>
> warmth through my limbs and head, to then ignite a mild *chuma (dizziness)* as my
>
> body quivers in slow motion. The *chuma* grows stronger and my stomach folds over
>
> onto itself, while the bile and the plant are both expelled with the urgency of a

powerful relief. Bewildered and grateful, I imagine the vibrant
presence of a gentle

song sprouting from the surrounding trees...

Fundamentally, both this learning process and the place to learn involves a fresh body-mind assembled in connection to other body-minds through countless vegetal bridges in Amazonia. If the first step in learning to learn required cleansing the body, then to have a clear mind is essential to know something about this "infinite library" and its spirit masters.

In addition, it is crucial to suspend the way we, humans, think about the plants involved in the task of clearing the head. We need to suspend the common sense that considers plants as mind-*less* and sessile objects to be able to encounter plants-as-people—namely plants full of minds rather than things for disciplinary description and market use.

Thus, learning to *learn* from the vantage point of the plant requires a particular form of training or corporeal discipline involving the incorporation of the plant as *gente* (as people). Or, in other words, making the plant part of the human, while making the human part of the plant through care and radical listening. Indeed, the *minga de pensamiento* about intercultural knowledge in this region was an opportunity to weave a vegetal protocol specific to the experience of knowledge-making, namely a collective reflection about the limits and possibilities of an interspecies protocol in Amazonia. Learning to learn this protocol is much more than the liberal deference towards the Indigenous (and vegetal) *other*. It is about learning to learn how to seriously and carefully engage with the yoco's perspective or point of view.[12]

In a way, the mind of the plant and the mind of the human co-emerge via ingestion rather than language—or even ingestion taken as a form of language and communication. More than the representation of an external reality, this learning process requires the ingestion of the plant as a some*body* rather than a some*thing*, so the initial learning outcomes of vomiting, defecating, and sweating are all essential to the task at hand, as well as forms of communication in their own right. Plants such as the yoco vine are capable of sensing the elements of their surrounding world and acting accordingly. Indeed, plants perceive us—humans—as part of the "environment" we help to co-create with them. And, in this sense, we humans co-emerge with the plant insofar as both "specify each other" by co-*laboring* and exchanging positions or perspectives. Like a dance that only exists in the relation between the two dancers. In my head, that is, in my stomach, engaging with this co-created world from a mind that supposedly resides in clusters of neurons is a limited way to imagine the task of orienting action in today's world. Plants like yoco help to put the mind back into the body, back into the heart, and back into the stomach, while removing whatever interrupts the *mente fresca,* or ability to *pensar bonito*—or, "*mirar bien bonito,*" (to gaze very beautifully) as *abuelo O* would also say.

Mind-*full* plants teach that humans are not all-too-rational agents garnering knowledge from an external world, but rather mind-full beings that relentlessly co-create it with plants and non-plants full of mind. Can we imagine social institutions from the vantage point of plant-human relationships? What might happen if economic and legal systems learn to learn a vegetal protocol? In my experience, learning to learn with the *yoco* is quite explicitly a form of ethical training to become better partners for our wounded and flourishing Earth—an "ethical know-how" to start learning good and beautiful thinking to orient good action in the world.

Indigenous practitioners and their vegetal partners in Amazonia are teachers in delinking from the entangled realities of colonialism, extractivism, and violence in this region. "Get(ting) rid of laziness and purg(ing) anger" with some yoco may indeed teach us a way to cool down the mind to learn how to care for the forest and its mind-full inhabitants.

Yopo

Anadenanthera Peregrina

▪ **Juan Carlos Galeano** (translated by James Kimbrell)

...when I was looking for the stories
of fishermen, *Anadenanthera Peregrina*
introduced me to the land.

1

I felt the colors coming towards me like waves the size of mountains. With more explosions of powder in my head, yellow and black serpentine lines grew bigger. The blue glass boa had been in my dreams. She was the river on whose shore sat fishermen's huts. I had arrived there the night before after the hustle in the jeeps and my canoe trip.

2

I saw three huge boas. The one that came from the mountains had been decapitated and was running through the jungles hoping to find her head. Another lived its life as a river complaining about the clouds who didn't give him enough water or the clouds who had gone to another side of the planet in love with other rivers. Then the one that descended from the heavens turned into a canoe and traveled down river dropping off animals, trees and people along the banks.

3

As the air and the water had become singular, I could, without getting wet, get in and out of the Mawari cities. Mawaris are children of those pink dolphins who fall in love with people and take them to live in the rivers. I was admiring their houses with their transparent walls on the riverbed. I saw how the people used tiny boas as belts and women frolicked with their babies in black and yellow boas that served as hammocks.

4

While I was trying to identify the many faces that appeared and disappeared with the insistent colors going up my nostrils, there appeared in a flash the morichales groves that I had seen before along the way. The youngest palm trees, to prevent being cut by people or slashed by the noise of planes, would change places in the lakes and shout at their boa mothers for help. Their mothers would answer them from the skies with their storm cannons.

5

In one of the rivers (and before they were rivers they were boas) there were ships that whipped and left marks on the backs of the rivers as they traveled. On the decks, the indigenous people and far away travelers who partied with their loud music, did not let the trees sleep. Those who had red faces as devils drank the finest liquors, made great noise and vomited their red bile into the river.

6

After the swells of colors and great emptiness, my eyes were overwhelmed with so many faces. Their voices thrummed in my ears. I was trying to figure out who was who, then the noises quieted, and I felt a sense of familiarity. I was reassured to know that so much of what I was hearing was from the green-eyed brook that I had not seen since my childhood. She passed by the side of my house and had the habit of talking all night while I stayed awake wanting to understand what she said.

ENDNOTES

Introduction

[1] Rabindranath Tagore, "The Palm Tree," *Poem Hunter*, https://www.poemhunter.com/poem/palm-tree-5/.

[2] Cfr. Monica Gagliano, "The Mind of Plants: Thinking the Unthinkable," *Communicative and Integrative Biology*, e1288333 (2017), doi: 10.1080/19420889.2017.1288333.

[3] Cfr. Mary Siisip Geniusz, Wendy Makoons Geniusz, and Annmarie Geniusz, *Plants Have So Much to Give Us, All We Have to Do Is Ask: Anishinaabe Botanical Teachings* (Minneapolis, MN: University of Minnesota Press, 2015).

[4] Cfr. John C. Ryan, "Writing the Lives of Plants: Phytography and the Botanical Imagination," *a/b: Auto/Biography Studies* 25, no. 1 (2020): 97–122.

[5] The expression "meeting the plant universe halfway" is adapted from Karen Barad's *Meeting the Universe Halfway: Quantum Physics and the Entanglement of Matter and Meaning* (Durham, NC: Duke University Press, 2007).

[6] Cfr. Tony Trewavas, "Plant Intelligence: An Overview," *BioScience* 66, no. 7 (2016): 542–551, doi: 10.1093/biosci/biw048.

[7] Cfr. Akira Azuma and Yoshinori Okuno, "Flight of a Samara, *Alsomitra macrocarpa*," *Journal of Theoretical Biology*, 129 (1987): 263-74; and Julian Vincent, et al., "Biomimetics: Its Practice and Theory," *Journal of the Royal Society Interface*, 3 (2006): 471–482, doi: 10.1098/rsif.2006.0127

[8] This is a reference to Charles Darwin who famously ended his seminal book *On the Origin of Species* (London, UK: John Murray, 1859) with an extremely poetic paragraph—the "entangled bank"–on the variety of life forms and the rich complexity of interactions between them, and the conclusion, "There is grandeur in this view of life."

[9] Cfr. Megan Craig, "Narrative Threads: Philosophy as Storytelling," *The Journal of Speculative Philosophy*, 28, no. 4 (2014): 438-453, doi: 10.5325/jspecphil.28.4.0438.

Chapter 1

[1] Paul Valery, *Collected Works of Paul Valery, Volume 1.* trans. David Paul (Princeton, New Jersey: Princeton University Press, 2016).

[2] Gregory Bateson, *Mind and Nature: A Necessary Unity* (New York: Bantam Books, 1979).

[3] Poem by Sarah Laborde, 2019.

[4] Bruno Latour, *Où atterrir?: comment s'orienter en politique* (Paris: La découverte, 2017)

[5] Thich Nhat Hahn, *Interbeing: Fourteen Guidelines for Engaged Buddhism* (Berkeley, CA: Parallex Press, 1987).

[6] Mary Oliver, *Wild Geese: Selected Poems* (Hexham, UK: Bloodaxe Books, 2004)

[7] Francisco J. Varela, *Ethical Know-How: Action, Wisdom, and Cognition* (Palo Alto, CA: Stanford University Press, 1999).

Poem 3

1 *Crotalaria cunninghamii,* also known as green birdflower or regal birdflower, is a plant of the legume family Fabaceae. It is native to, and widespread in, inland northern Australia. It is named after early-19th-century botanist Allan Cunningham.

Chapter 5

1 Cfr. Rob Nixon, *Slow Violence and the Environmentalism of the Poor* (Cambridge, MA: Harvard University Press, 2011), 17.

2 Cfr. Marcel Barbéro, et al., "Pines of the Mediterranean Basin," in *Ecology and Biogeography of Pinus*, ed. D. M. Richardson (Cambridge, UK: Cambridge University Press, 1998), 157–158.

3 Marco Armiero and Wilko Graf von Hardenberg, "Green Rhetoric in Blackshirts: Italian Fascism and the Environment," *Environment and History* 19, no. 3 (2013): 284.

4 Marco Armiero and Wilko Graf von Hardenberg, "Into the Fascist Forest–A Real Italian Controversy," *The Conversation*, October 9, 2017, https://theconversation.com/into-the-fascist-forest-a-real-italian-controversy-84656.

5 Piermario Corona, et al., "Surveying Black Pine Plantations in the Province of Rieti (Italy)," *Rivista italiana di Telerilevamento* 40, no. 1 (2008): 40.

6 Roberto Mercurio and Bartolomeo Schirone, "Black Pine Afforestations in Abruzzo (Central Italy): Perspectives and Management," *Journal of Environmental Science and Engineering* A, no. 4 (2015): 494.

7 Nigel Thrift, "Summoning Life," in *Envisioning Human Geographies*, eds. P. Cloke, P. Crang, and M. Goodwin (London: Arnold, 2004), 83.

8 Christopher Tilley, *A Phenomenology of Landscape: Places, Paths, and Monuments* (Oxford, UK; Providence, RI: Berg, 1994), 29–30.

9 Steven Feld, "Waterfall of Song. An Acoustemology of Place Resounding in Bosavi, Papua New Guinea," in *Senses of Place,* eds. S. Feld and K. Basso (Santa Fe, NM: School of American Research Press, 1996), 94.

Chapter 6

1 For more in-depth discussion of my approach, see, Craig Holdrege, "Doing Goethean Science," *Janus Head* 8, no. 1 (2005): 27–52, http://www.janushead.org/8-1/holdrege.pdf; Craig Holdrege, *Thinking Like a Plant* (Great Barrington, MA: Lindisfarne Books, 2013).

2 Johann Wolfgang von Goethe, *Scientific Studies* (Princeton, NJ: Princeton University Press, 1995), 46.

3 Andrew Beattie, *The Evolutionary Ecology of Ant-Plant Mutualisms* (New York: Cambridge University Press, 1985), 3.

4 Craig Holdrege, "Where Do Organisms End?" *In Context* 3 (Spring 2000): 14–16, http://natureinstitute.org/pub/ic/ic3/org_and_env.htm.

5 Roswell H. Johnson, "Aberrant Societies of *Sanguinaria* and *Trillium*," *Torreya* 9, no.1 (1909): 5–6; Warren P. Spencer, "Variation in Petal Number in the Bloodroot, *Sanguinaria canadensis*," *The American Naturalist* 78, no. 774 (1944): 85–89.

[6] Susanne Langer, *Mind: An Essay on Human Feeling*, Vol. 1 (Baltimore, MD: The Johns Hopkins Press, 1967), 378.

Chapter 7

[1] Rachel S. Jabaily, et al., "Historical Biogeography of the Predominantly Australian Plant Family Goodeniaceae," *Journal of Biogeography* 41 (2014): 2062.
[2] South West Aboriginal Land and Sea Council, "Connection to Country: Kaartdijin Noongar–Noongar Knowledge," www.noongarculture.org.au/connection-to-country.
[3] Philip A. Clarke, *Aboriginal People and Their Plants* (Kenthurst, NSW: Rosenberg Publishing, 2011), 11–17.
[4] South West Aboriginal Land and Sea Council, "Food: Kaartdijin Noongar–Noongar Knowledge," www.noongarculture.org.au/food.
[5] K.W. Dixon, et al., "The Promotive Effect of Smoke Derived From Burnt Native Vegetation on Seed Germination of Western Australian Plants," *Oecologia* 2 (1995): 185–192.
[6] John C. Ryan, "'Plants That Perform For You?' From Floral Aesthetics to Floraesthesis in the Southwest of Western Australia," *Australian Humanities Review* 47 (2009): 127.
[7] Georgiana Molloy to James Mangles, March 21, 1837, Unpublished Letterbooks of James Mangles, ACC479, Battye Library. All further quotations from Molloy refer to this source.
[8] D.A. Morrison, "Taxonomic and Nomenclatural Notes on *Lechenaultia* R. Br. (Goodeniaceae)," *Brunonia* 9, no. 1 (1987): 1–28.
[9] F. Tatsuzawa, et al., "Flower Colors and Anthocyanin Pigments in the Cultivars of *Leschenaultia biloba*, *L. formosa* and Their Hybrids," *Engeigaku Kenkyu* 12, no. 1 (2013): 23–28.
[10] John C. Ryan, "Sifting Horticulture from Botany: John Lindley's 'A Sketch of the Vegetation of the Swan River Colony' (1840)," *Australian Garden History* 23, no. 1 (2011): 10.
[11] James Veitch to William Hooker, cited in S. Heriz-Smith, "The Veitch Nurseries of Killerton and Exeter c. 1780 to 1863: Part I," *Garden History* 16, no 1 (1988): 41–57.
[12] J. Paxton, *Paxton's Magazine of Botany and Register of Flowering Plants* 8 (1841): 152
[13] James Drummond, "To the Editor, Letter XI," *Inquirer*, March 1, 1843, 3.

Chapter 10

[1] Part of the "Microcosms" collection can be found here: https://library.artstor.org/#/collection/100089947.
[2] In Asia, this tree is known by many names: boichu, bombax, booruga, boorunga, bouro, bula, buroh, edelsong, illavam, kaanti-senbal, kantakadruma, kantesavar, katesawar, kempu-booruga, leptan, malabulak, mu mian, mulilavu, mullelava, mullila-pula, mullilavau, mullilavu, mullubooruga, neibie, nglo, nuoliu, pagun, pan-ya, panchu, phakong, pula-maram, pulai, rakta-pushpa, red silk cotton tree, roktosimul, salmali, samar, sanar, saur, savar, savri, sawar, senur, shembal, shemolo,

shevari, shevri, shimla, shimul cotton, simal, simalo, simalu, simla, simlo, simolu, and sin.

3 "Gusanos en acción (chichi caste) atrapados," *YouTube*, www.youtube.com/watch?v=iR1YkVza0Fo&feature=youtu.be&fbclid=IwAR2TPrM4smCypYKi_rcu3r5x-uHk1HJuq7HTSTq-rFztbkbywebwO8s7BFHs.

Chapter 11

1 R. Allers and E. Freund cited in Heinrich Eduard Jacob, *Coffee: The Epic of a Commodity* (New York: Skyhorse Publishing, 2015), originally published 1935

2 Heinrich Eduard Jacob, *Coffee: The Epic of a Commodity* (New York: Skyhorse Publishing, 2015), originally published 1935.

3 Brian William Cowan, *The Social Life of Coffee: The Emergence of the British Coffeehouse* (New Haven, CT: Yale University Press, 2005), 52.

4 Jospeh Dumit, *Drugs for Life: How Pharmaceutical Companies Define Our Health* (Durham, NC: Duke University Press, 2012).

5 Harvard Health Publishing, "Can Coffee Help You Live Longer?" *Harvard Health Letter*, September 2012.

6 Ibid., emphasis added. Note that Michael Pollan's audiobook, *Caffeine: How Caffeine Created the Modern World* (2020), ignores this study and conflates coffee with caffeine.

7 Agricultural Research Service, *Scientific Report of the 2015 Dietary Guidelines Advisory Committee: Advisory Report to the Secretary of Health and Human Services and the Secretary of Agriculture* (Washington, DC: USDA, 2015).

Chapter 12

1 A striking example for the persistence of human plant bias is the historian Alexander Demandt's cultural history of "the tree" *Der Baum. Eine Kulturgeschichte* (2014) which claims that "the tree" is a site for all sorts of things but, in his effort to align humans and trees in as many ways as possible, loses sight of the distinctly vegetal and arboreal qualities of trees, which he constantly fails to address as beings in their own right.

2 Caspar David Friedrich, *Der einsame Baum* (Nationalgalerie; Staatliche Museen zu Berlin, 1822).

3 In numerous publications and a documentary which features both. See *Intelligent Trees* (2016) dir.: Julia Dordel.

4 See Stefano, Mancuso, *Brilliant Green. The Surprising History and Science of Plant Intelligence* (Washington D.C.: Island Press, 2018).

5 My translation.

Chapter 13

1 The term *thallus* refers to the vegetative growth and "tissue" components of a number of biological groups, including algae.

Chapter 15

1 Francis Bacon and William Rawley, *Sylva sylvarum: Or A Natural History in Ten Centuries. Whereunto Is Newly Added the History Natural and Experimental of Life*

and Death, Or of the Prolongation of Life (London: Printed by J.R. for W. Lee, 1670), 103. First edition published 1627.

2 John Ray, Vol. 1, *Historia Plantarum, vol 1* (London: Typis Mariæ Clark, prostant apud Henricum Faithorne [etc.], 1686), 1. Translated from the Latin.

3 Andrew S. Reynolds, *The Third Lens: Metaphor and the Creation of Modern Cell Biology* (Chicago: The University of Chicago Press, 2018), 10.

Chapter 17

1 Based on the work of the German philosopher Edmund Husserl, phenomenology is concerned with consciousness and our subjective experience. A phenomenological structure, in our case, refers to the artwork, which might be the trigger of a subjective experience.

2 Entheogens are psychoactive substances, naturally found in plants, capable of produce a non-ordinary state of consciousness. These substances are commonly used in spiritual and religious rituals.

Chapter 18

1 I would like to express my thanks to the editors, to the anonymous readers who critiqued an initial draft of this essay, and to the University of New England for providing me with the time and resources necessary for its completion. Most of all I am grateful to my older sister for her love, teaching, and guidance, and to the Ancestors for stepping in and leading the way.

2 There may be other reasons why *Hakea lorea* is overlooked, therapeutically speaking. At one stage during these years, I consulted a herbalist about my health. A couple of sessions in, the herbalist informed me that she had just begun to experiment with concocting bush-flower remedies. "Oh," said I, "which flowers are you trying out?" "Only two species so far," she said, "something something and the long-leafed corkwood!" Why this little-known species? Because it happened to be flowering abundantly when the herbalist ventured into that corner of the game. Fascinated, I bought a bottle of the tincture from her. I took the tonic regularly, but can't remember now whether it exerted any influence; if so, the effect was mild. Soon afterwards a mate came to stay with me; one night he said he was feeling a cold coming on, so naturally I gave him some of the corkwood tonic—five drops in a glass of water, the same dose I'd been having. Within minutes my friend began vomiting, really violently. He kept on spewing; nothing we tried would make it stop. I had to pull to the side of the road several times on the fifteen-kilometer drive to the hospital, where he was given a quelling injection. Once calmed, my mate slept a double shift and rose well again the next day.

3 Basil Sansom, "Irruptions of the Dreamings in Post-Colonial Australia," *Oceania* 72, no. 1 (2001): 23.

4 My sister and I wondered at the time whether rogue corkwoods might have sown themselves on other blocks along the valley. I was given the chance to check this a few months later when the senior tree put on a show of flowers. As it was likely that all individuals in the area would be in bloom, there should be no difficulty in spotting any from the road. So one morning I jumped in the car and went touring.

First I confirmed that the trees at the Ancestor site were in flower, then drove up and down the road dividing our valley; I noticed no *Hakea lorea* growing there.

5 Margaret Kemarre Turner, *Iwenhe Tyerrtye—What It Means To Be an Aboriginal Person* (Alice Springs, NT: IAD Press, 2010), 154.

6 Carl Gustav Jung, *Jung's Seminar on Nietzsche's* Zarathustra, ed. James Jarrett (Princeton, NJ: Princeton University Press, 1998), 231, 232.

7 By equating Dreaming with mythology here I am in no way demeaning the integrity or local sovereignty of the Dreaming; mythology is a serious concern, engaging with no less weighty a matter than existential meaning. Probably all cultures have interpreted and celebrated the living, ongoing Creation of the world with their own ways of Storying. These ways are understood, by those who think about them, to constitute the collective mythologizing of humanity. The equation of Dreaming with mythology is valid, however, only if mythology is seen to comprise the narrative raiment of living spiritual energies.

8 Carl Gustav Jung, *Memories, Dreams, Reflections* (Lond: Fontana, 1995), 373.

9 Yvonne Smith Klitsner, "Synchronicity, Intentionality, and Archetypal Meaning in Therapy," *Jung Journal* 9, no. 4 (2015): 27.

10 James Hillman, *Re-Visioning Psychology* (Oxford: Harper & Row, 1975).

Chapter 19

1 Michael Marder and Luce Irigaray, *Through Vegetal Being* (New York: Columbia University Press, 2016).

2 Newton, Isaac. *Two Incomplete Treatises on Prophecy,* Keynes Ms.5, King's College, Cambridge UK, accessed August 10, 2013, www.newtonproject.sussex.ac.uk/view/texts/diplomatic/THEM00005.

3 Jamie James, "W.B.Yeats: Magus," *Lapham's Quarterly,* Summer (2012). Accessed August 12, 2013, http://www.laphamsquarterly.org/essays/wb-yeats-magus

4 Marco Pasi, "Varieties of Magical Experience: Aleister Crowley's Views on Occult Practice," *Magic, Ritual, and Witchcraft* 6, no. 2 (2011): 123-62.

5 Isabelle Stengers and Phillipe Pignarre, *Capitalist Sorcery: Breaking the Spell* (New York: Palgrave Macmillan, 2011).

6 R. Spjut , M. Suffness , G. Cragg and D. Norris. "Mosses, Liverworts, and Hornworts Screened for Antitumor Agents," *Economic Botany* 40, no. 3 (1986): 310-38.

Chapter 20

1 Luke Fischer, *Paths of Flight* (Melbourne: Black Pepper, 2013), 16.

2 W.B. Yeats, *The Collected Poems of W. B. Yeats* (New York: Scribner Paperback Poetry, 1996), 217.

3 Johann Wolfgang von Goethe, *The Metamorphosis of Plants* (Cambridge, MA: MIT Press, 2009), 13–14.

4 Fischer, *Paths of Flight,* 19.

5 "Seminal" derives from the Latin *semen*, meaning "seed"; "disseminating" derives from the Latin *sēmināre,* meaning "to sow"; "germinal" derives from the Latin *germen,* meaning "sprout"; "burgeoning" derives from the Middle English *burjon* ("shoot") and *burion* ("bud") and earlier the Late Latin *burra,* meaning "wool" and

"fluff" and possibly referring to the down that covers certain buds; in Late Middle English "culture" means "tilling" or "place tilled".

[6] "Megan Blake reviews *Paths of Flight* by Luke Fischer," *Plumwood Mountain* 6, no. 1 (2014),

[7] Fischer, *Paths of Flight*, 10.

[8] Luke Fischer, *A Personal History of Vision* (Crawley, WA: University of Western Australia Publishing, 2017), 94.

[9] Fischer, *A Personal History of Vision*, 83.

[10] Fischer, *Paths of Flight*, 72.

[11] Ibid., 21.

[12] Fischer, *A Personal History of Vision*, 74.

Chapter 21

[1] *Macropus rufogriseus*

[2] *Acacia mearnsii*

[3] https://www.anbg.gov.au/gnp/interns-2002/brachychiton-populneus.html

[4] https://www.lushplants.com.au/blog/entry/ornamental-trees-shrubs/native-australian-Kurrajong-tree-bottle-tree-brachychiton-populneus-edible-useful-hardy-versatile.

[5] https://www.anbg.gov.au/gnp/interns-2002/brachychiton-populneus.html

[6] *Olea paniculata*

[7] *Petrogale penicillata*

[8] J.R.R. Tolkien, *The Lord of the Rings Trilogy* (London: Allen and Unwin, 1954).

[9] *Menura novaehollandiae*

[10] *Canis lupus dingo*

[11] *Macropus robustus*

[12] M. McKemey and H. White, *Bush Tucker, Boomerangs and Bandages: Traditional Aboriginal Plant Use in the Border Rivers and Gwydir Catchments* (Inverell: Border Rivers-Gwydir Catchment Management Authority, NSW, 2011)., 71

[13] Ibid., 71.

[14] Ibid., 71.

[15] Ibid., 71.

[16] Ibid., 71.

[17] Ibid., 71.

[18] A.B. & J.W. Cribb, *Wild Food in Australia* (Sydney: William Collins Publishers, 1975), 169.

[19] Ibid., 173-4.

[20] "The Kurrajong... trees are exempted from the operation of all timber licenses or permits, and cutting them down is prohibited; but in time of drought, if the leaves of the Kurrajong-tree are required for feed for stock, the lighter branches may be lopped" (Department of Mines and Agriculture, Sydney, 22nd March, 1895. "Timber and Quarry Regulations," *New South Wales Government Gazette* [Sydney, NSW: 1832–1900], Monday 25 March 1895 [No. 206 Supplement]).

Chapter 22

1 Renata Buziak. *Biochromes: Perceptions of Australian Medicinal Plants Through Experimental Photography,* Unpublished doctoral dissertation (Queensland College of Art, Griffith University, Brisbane, 2015).
2 Mike Vanderkelen and Brad Saunders. *Under the Linden Trees* (Highton, Victoria: Mike Vanderkelen, 2016).
3 Ibid., 48.
4 Ibid., 49.
5 Ibid., 63.
6 Ibid., 71, 73.

Chapter 23

1 See S.L. Prescott and A.C. Logan AC, *The Secret Life of your Microbiome. Why Nature and Biodoversity are Essential to Health and Happiness* (Gabriola Island, British Columbia: New Society Publishers, 2017).
2 See Ibid.
3 S.L. Prescott SL, G. Wegienka, A.C. Logan, and D.L. Katz, "Dysbiotic Drift and Biopsychosocial Medicine: How the Microbiome Links Personal, Public and Planetary Health," *BioPsychoSocial Medicine* 12 (2018): 7.
4 S.L. Prescott, A.C. Logan, "Down to Earth: Planetary Health and Biophilosophy in the Symbiocene Epoch," *Challenges* 8 (2017): 19.
5 Ibid.
6 A.C. Logan, "Dysbiotic Drift: Mental Health, Environmental Grey Space, and Microbiota," *Journal of Physiological Anthropology* 34 (2015): 23.
7 See S.L. Prescott, A.C. Logan, R.A. Millstein, and M.A. Katszman, "Biodiversity, the Human Microbiome and Mental Health: Moving Toward a New Clinical Ecology for the 21st Century?" *International Journal of Biodiversity* 2016 (2016): 1-18.
8 S.L. Prescott and A.C. Logan, "Transforming Life: A Broad View of the Developmental Origins of Health and Disease Concept from an Ecological Justice Perspective," *International Journal of Environmental Research and Public Health* 13:11 (2016): 1075-1119.
9 A.C. Logan, "Dysbiotic Drift."
10 See Ibid.
11 See S.L. Prescott and A.C. Logan, "Transforming Life."
12 A.C. Logan, F.N. Jacka, and S.L. Prescott, "Immune-Microbiota Interactions: Dysbiosis as a Global Health Issue," Current Allergy and Asthma Reports 16 (2016): 13.
13 See S.L. Prescott and A.C. Logan, "Transforming Life."
14 See E.M. Selhub and A.C. Logan, *Your Brain on Nature: The Science of Nature's Influence on Your Health, Happiness and Vitality* (Mississauga, Canada: Wiley; 2012).
15 See S.L. Prescott and A.C. Logan, "Transforming Life."
16 See Ibid.
17 See S.L. Prescott, *Origins: Early-Life Solutions to the Modern Health Crisis* (Perth: UWA Publishing, 2015).
18 See S.L. Prescott and A.C. Logan, "Transforming Life."
19 See Ibid.

[20] See R. Dubos, "The Spaceship Earth," *Journal of Allergy and Clinical Immunology* 44 (1969): 1-9.

[21] See S.L. Prescott and A.C. Logan, "Transforming Life."

[22] S.L. Prescott, A.L. Kozyrskyj, A.C. Logan, and D.E. Campbell. "Seventh Annual Conference of inVIVO Planetary Health on Transforming Life: Unify Personal, Public, and Planetary Health," *Challenges* 9 (2018): 36.

[23] See J. Salk and J.D. Salk, *A New Reality: Human Evolution for a Sustainable Future* (Stratford, CT, USA: City Point Press, 2018).

Chapter 24

[1] The research for this article was funded by a Grant from the Portuguese Foundation for Science and Technology (FCT), Project IF/00606/2015. I would like to thank the Olive Oil Museum at Bobadela and the Esporão Estate, in particular its olive oil production and sales manager Ana Carrilho, for their assistance in my research for this article.

Chapter 25

[1] *Passiflora incarnata* is the Linnaean classification that evolved from the Italian translation "fiore delle passione" after being gifted to Pope Paul V by missionaries in the 16th century (see S. Parlasca, *Il Fiore della Granadiglia, overo della Passione di nostro Signore Giesù Christo.* [Bologna, Italy: Bartolomeo Cocchi, 1609]; and V. Battisti Delia, Battisti Delia, "The Doctrine of Juli: Foundation, Development, and the New Identity in a Shared Space" in *Manufacturing Otherness: Missions and Indigenous Cultures in Latin America,* Ed. Sergio Botti [Cambridge UK: Cambridge University Press, 2014]).

[2] W.H. Felter and J.U. Lloyd, *King's American Dispensatory*, in two volumes. (Portland, OR: Eclectic Medical Publications, 1985), 1st. edition 1898.

[3] K.J. Gremillion, "The Development of a Mutualistic Relationship between Humans and Maypops (*Passiflora incarnata* L.) in the Southeastern United States," *Journal of Ethnobiology* 9:2 (1989): 135-155; J. Vanderplank, *Passionflowers* (Boston, MA: MIT Press, 1996).

[4] G. Wehtje. et al. "Reproductive Biology and Herbicidal Sensitivity of Maypop Passionflower (*Passiflora Incarnata*)," *Weed Science* 33:4 (1985): 484–490; C. McGuire, "*Passiflora incarnata* (Passifloraceae): A New Fruit Crop," *Economic Botany* 53:2 (1999): 161–176.

[5] D.B. Gaspar and D.C. Hine, *More Than Chattel: Black Women and Slavery in the Americas*. (Bloomington: Indiana University Press, 1996).

[6] This borrowing of terms arises more from histories in which biomedical explanations are given explanatory authority over "traditional" or "folk" remedies than from actual medical studies of passionflower, which are few and mostly informed by mice and rats (see K. Dhawan et al. (2003). "Evaluation of Central Nervous System Effects of *Passiflora incarnata* in Experimental Animals," *Pharmaceutical Biology* 41:2 [2003]: 87-91.).

[7] L.E. Luna, "The concept of Plants as Teachers among Four Mestizo Shamans of Iquitos, Northeastern Perú." *Journal of Ethnopharmacology* 11 (1984): 135-136.

Chapter 26

[1] Most *Wixarika* or Huichol People inhabit the Sierra Madre range in Western Mexico.

[2] It is unkown why peyote (*Lophophora Williamsii*) has the same name for both the Ralámuli and the Wixáritari, who are not neighboring Peoples but do belong to the same linguistic family. However, in the anthropological literature, it is written differently.

[3] Some examples are those cactuses classified as *Ariocarpus fissuratus*, *Mammilaria* and *Echinocereus* (for more detailed data see possibly the only ethnobotanical work available: Robert Bye, *Hallucinogenic Plants of the Tarahumara*, *Journal of Ethnopharmacology*, 1, 1979: 23-48.).

Chapter 27

[1] M.R. Jacobs, *Growth Habits of the Eucalypts.* (Canberra: Forestry and Timber Bureau, 1955).

[2] For example, see: Monica Gagliano, *Thus Spoke the Plant: A Remarkable Journey of Groundbreaking Scientific Discoveries and Personal Encounters with Plants* (Berkeley: North Atlantic Books, 2018).

[3] E.L. Westerhuis, C.A. Schlesinger, C.E.M. Nano, S.R. Morton, and K.A. Christian, "Characteristics of Hollows and Hollow-Bearing Trees in Semi-Arid River Red Gum Woodland and Potential Limitations for Hollow-Dependent Wildlife," *Austral ecology* 44 (2019): 995-1004; MacKenzie F Patton et al, "Transcriptome and Defence Response in Eucalyptus Camaldulensis Leaves to Feeding by *Glycaspis brimblecombei* Moore (Hemiptera: Aphalaridae): A Stealthy Psyllid Does Not Go Unnoticed," *Austral Entomology* 57 (2018): 247–54.

[4] See: Verica Aleksic Sabo, Petar Knezevic. *Antimicrobial Activity of Eucalyptus Camaldulensis Dehn. Plant Extracts and Essential Oils: A Review.* (Industrial Crops and Products 132, 2019): 1; Felter, Harvey Wickes, John Uri Lloyd. King's *American Dispensatory*. (Cincinnati, Ohio Valley Company, 1898); Locher, C. and Currie, L., "Revisiting Kinos—An Australian Perspective." *Journal of Ethnopharmacology*, 128, no. 2 (2010): 259-67.

[5] Roger McDonald, *The Tree in Changing Light*. (Sydney: Random House, 2001).

[6] Dexter, B. D. *Flooding and Regeneration of River Red Gum* (Eucalyptus Camaldulensis Dehnh). Melbourne: Forests Commission, 1967.; and Hulme, Karen Angela. Eucalyptus Camaldulensis (River Red Gum) "Biogeochemistry: An Innovative Tool for Mineral Exploration in the Curnamona Province and Adjacent Regions," 2008.

[7] See: Matthew J. Colloff, *Flooded Forest and Desert Creek: Ecology and History of the River Red Gum*. (Melbourne: CSIRO Publishing, 2014), 74; and K.A. Slessor, *One Hundred Poems 1919–1939*. (Sydney: Angus and Robertson, 1944), 110.

[8] Myburg et al, "The Genome of *Eucalyptus grandis*." *Nature* 510, no. 7505 (2014): 356-62.

[9] Media, Change. Moogy's Yuki. Vimeo, 2021. https://vimeo.com/44838721.

Chapter 28

[1] Horwood, Catherine. Rose. London, UK: Reaktion Books Ltd, 2018. For much of the cultural and historical knowledge in this contribution, I consulted Catherine Horwood.

[2] See Amy Stewart. *Flower Confidential: The Good, the Bad, and the Beautiful* (Chapel Hill: Algonquin Books, 2007).

[3] See Invasive Species Specialist Group. *Global Invasive Species Database*. http://www.iucngisd.org/gisd/.

[4] Urs Nanjaraj, Ankanahalli N., Yiling Hu, Pengwei Li, Zhiguang Yuchi, Yihua Chen, Yan Zhang. "Cloning and Expression of a Nonribosomal Peptide Synthetase to Generate Blue Rose." *ACS Synthetic Biology* 8, no. 8 (2018): 1698-1704. DOI: 10.1021/acssynbio.8b00187.

[5] Isabel Kranz. "The Language of Flowers in Popular Culture and Botany." *The Language of Plants: Science, Philosophy, Literature*. Edited by Monica Gagliano, John C. Ryan, and Patrícia Vieira (Minneapolis: University of Minnesota Press, 2017), 193-214.

[6] Gertrude Stein. "Sacred Emily." *Geography and Plays* (Boston: Four Seas Co., 1922), 178-188.

[7] Johann Wolfgang von Goethe. "The Little Rose on the Heath." Translated by Edgar Allan Bowring in 1853. Cited in Lucretia van Tuyl Simmons. *Goethe's Lyric Poems in English Translation Prior to 1860* (Madison: University of Wisconsin, 1919), 62.

[8] See exemplarily Michael Pollan. "The Intelligent Plant." *New Yorker*. December 15, 2013. https://www.newyorker.com/magazine/2013/12/23/the-intelligent-plant; Stephano Mancuso and Alessandra Viola. *Brilliant Green: The Surprising History and Science of Plant Intelligence* (Washington, D.C.: Island Press, 2015); and the work of Monica Gagliano at https://www.monicagagliano.com/.

[9] See Antony Funnell. "The Underestimated Power of Plants." *ABC RN*. March 8, 2016. https://www.abc.net.au/radionational/programs/futuretense/the-underestimated-power-of-plants/7227008 and Eleni Stavrinidou, Roger Gabrielsson, Eliot Gomez, Xavier Crispin, Ove Nilsson, Daniel T. Simon, Magnus Berggren. "Electronic Plants." *Science Advances* 1, no. 10 (2015). DOI: 10.1126/sciadv.1501136.

[10] See part XV, paragraphs 103 and 104 in any edition of Goethe's *Metamorphosis*.

[11] In the original, Goethe's diary entry reads "eine schöne und seltene Doppelrose" (translation mine) and can be found on July 1, 1817 in any edition.

[12] Goethe jotted down the note "Hypothese: Alles ist Blatt" during his Italian journey, but did not phrase this (inaccurate) idea as pointedly when he published the *Metamorphosis* a few years later.

[13] Joela Jacobs. "Phytopoetics: Upending the Passive Paradigm with Vegetal Violence and Eroticism." *Catalyst: Feminism, Theory, Technoscience* 5, no. 2 (2019): 1-18. DOI: https://doi.org/10.28968/cftt.v5i2.30027.

[14] See Michael Pollan. *The Botany of Desire: A Plant's-Eye View of the World* (New York: Random House, 2001).

Chapter 29

Sections of this chapter were previously published in Chao, S. (2018) "In the Shadow of the Palm: Dispersed Ontologies Among Marind, West Papua," Cultural Anthropology, 33(4), pp. 621–649.

Chapter 30

1 Extract from "Humberston Beach and Creek, 26 September 2013," in Harriet Tarlo, *Gathering Grounds 2011-2019* (Swindon, UK: Shearsman, 2019), 69-71.

2 For discussion of these projects, see Harriet Tarlo and Judith Tucker, "'Off Path, Counter Path:' Contemporary Collaborations in Landscape, Art and Poetry," *Critical Survey* 29:1 (2017): 105-132; "'Drawing Closer:' An Ecocritical Consideration of Collaborative, Cross-Disciplinary Practices of Walking, Writing, Drawing and Exhibiting" in *Extending Ecocriticism: Crisis, Collaboration and Challendes in the Environmental Humanities,* Ed. Peter Barry and William Welstead (Manchester University Press, 2017), 47-69; and "Poetry, Painting and Change on the Edge of England," Sociologia Ruralis 59: 4 (2019): 636-660.

3 Harriet Tarlo and Judith Tucker, *Low Lying: Painting and Poetry from the Saltmarsh,* Westminster Art Library, London (Nov.-Dec. 2019) and *Hideaway: Painting and Poetry* from the Saltmarsh, VisualArts2021, Scunthorpe (forthcoming April-July 2022).

4 "behind land" was used as an exhibition title for several group shows in the "Excavations and Estuaries" project and for an artists' book with Judith Tucker, *Behind Land: Poems and Paintings* (Leeds: Wild Pansy Press, 2015).

5 Steven P. Long and Christopher F. Mason, *Saltmarsh Ecology* (Glasgow and London: Blackie, 1983), 51.

6 J.R.L. Allen and K. Pye, *Saltmarshes: Morphodynamics, Conservation and Engineering Significance* (Cambridge: Cambridge University Press, 1992) and Long and Mason, *Saltmarsh Ecology*. 51-3.

7 Rachel Carson quoted in Judith Madera, "The Birth of an Island: Rachel Carson's The Sea Around Us," *Women's Studies Quarterly* 45:1/2 (2017): 294.

8 Lorine Niedecker in Jenny Penberthy, *Niedecker and the Correspondence with Zukofsky, 1931–1970* (Cambridge: Cambridge University Press, 1993), 243.

9 N.V. Jones, *A Dynamic Estuary: Man, Nature and the Humber* (Hull, UK: Hull University Press, 1988), 47.

10 Anthony Trewavas, "Mindless Mastery," *Nature* 415 (21 February 2002): 841.

11 Anthony Trewavas, "The Foundations of Plant Intelligence," *Interface Focus* 7 (2017): 2.

12 See recording of this piece on Camilla Nelson's "Becoming Plant" radio essay, Soundart Radio 2020 https://www.singingapplepress.com/becoming

13 S. Kurinsky, *The Glassmakers: An Odyssey of the Jews, the First Three Thousand Years* (New York: Hippocrene Books, 1991).

14 Names sourced from L.L. Price, "From Pedestrian Fare to Gourmet Trend: the Case of Salicornia europaea L., a traditional gathered wild sea shore vegetable" in *Changing Families and their lifestyles,* vol 2. Ed. H.H.S. Moerbeek and A. Niehof (Wageningen: Wageningen Academic Publishers), 201-211.

15 Daryl Gunning, "Cultivating Salicornia europaea (Marsh Samphire)," Irish Sea

Fisheries Board (August 2016). http://www.bim.ie/media/bim/content/news, and,events/BIM,Cultivating,Salicornia,europaea,-,Marsh,Samphire.pdf

[16] Jones, *Dynamic Estuary,* 48.

[17] Natasha Myers, "How to Grow Livable Worlds: Ten Not-so-Easy Steps" in *The World to Come, Harn Museum Catalogue,* 2018. https://www.academia.edu/37764209/How_to_grow_livable_worlds_Ten_not-so-easy_steps_extended_lecture_version.

Chapter 31

[1] L. Attala, "The 'Edibility Approach': Using Edibility to Explore Relationships, Plant Agency and the Porosity of Species' Boundaries," *Advances in Anthropology* 7, no. 3 (2017): 125-45.

[2] L. Attala, "I am Apple," in *Body Matters: Exploring the Materiality of the Human Body,* eds. L. Attala and L. Steel (Cardiff: University of Wales Press, 2019).

Chapter 32

[1] Robin Foster, "*Tachigalia versicolor* is a suicidal neotropical tree" *Nature* 268, no. 5621 (1977): 624–626.

[2] Lynda Mapes, *Witness Tree. Seasons of Change with a Century-Old Oak* (New York, NY: Bloomsbury, 2017).

[3] Dalia Nassar and Margaret M. Barbour, *Rooted* (https://aeon.co/essays/what-can-an-embodied-history-of-trees-teach-us-about-life).

[4] Abdulbaha Abbas, *The Promulgation of Universal Peace* (US Bahai Publishing Trust, 1982 2nd edition), 255.

[5] Martha Nussbaum, *Political Emotions: Why Love Matters for Justice* (Cambridge, MA: Belknap/Harvard University Press, 2013), 15.

[6] Amelie. O. Rorty "The Historicity of Psychological Attitudes: Love is Not Love Which Alters Not When It Alteration Finds," in *Friendship: A Philosophical Reader,* ed. N.K. Badhwar (Ithaca, NY: Cornell University Press, 1993), 73–88.

Chapter 33

[1] For examples, see Jonathan Silvertown and Deborah M Gordon, "A Framework for Plant Behavior," *Annual Review of Ecology and Systematics* 20, (November 1989): 349–66; and Daniel A. Levitis, William Z. Lidicker, and Glenn Freund, "Behavioral Biologists Do Not Agree on What Constitutes Behavior," *Animal Behavior* 78, no. 1 (July 2009): 103–10, https://doi.org/10.1016/j.anbehav .2009.03.018.

[2] D.L. Lentz et al., "Sunflower (*Helianthus annuus* L.) as a Pre-Columbian Domesticate in Mexico," *Proceedings of the National Academy of Sciences* 105, no. 17 (April 29, 2008): 6232–37, https://doi.org/10.1073/pnas.0711760105.

[3] John Brand Free, *Insect Pollination of Crops,* 2nd Revised edition (London: Academic Press, 1993).

[4] Ulrich Kutschera and Winslow R. Briggs, "Phototropic Solar Tracking in Sunflower Plants: An Integrative Perspective," *Annals of Botany* 117, no. 1 (January 2016): 1–8, https://doi.org/10.1093/aob/mcv141.

[5] Hagop S. Atamian et al., "Circadian Regulation of Sunflower Heliotropism,

Floral Orientation, and Pollinator Visits," *Science* 353, no. 6299 (August 5, 2016): 587–90, https://doi.org/10.1126/science.aaf9793.

6 For examples, see Craig R. Roseland and Teryl J. Grosz, "Induced Responses of Common Annual Sunflower *Helianthus annuus* L. from Geographically Diverse Populations and Deterrence to Feeding by Sunflower Beetle," *Journal of Chemical Ecology* 23, no. 2 (1997): 517–42, https://doi.org/10.1023/B:JOEC.0000006375.40885.24; and Aline Moreira Dias et al., "Attraction of *Telenomus podisi* to Volatiles Induced by *Euschistus heros* in Three Different Plant Species," *Arthropod-Plant Interactions* 10, no. 5 (October 1, 2016): 419–28, https://doi.org/10.1007/s11829-016-9453-9.

7 For examples, see Anthony B. Hall, Udo Blum, and Roger C. Fites, "Stress Modification of Allelopathy of *Helianthus Annuus* L. Debris on Seed Germination," *American Journal of Botany* 69, no. 5 (1982): 776–83, https://doi.org/10.2307/2442968.

8 V.O. Sadras et al., "Dynamics of Rooting and Root-Length: Leaf-Area Relationships as Affected by Plant Population in Sunflower Crops," *Field Crops Research* 22, no. 1 (August 1989): 45–57, https://doi.org/10.1016/0378-4290(89)90088-9.

Chapter 34

1 "Han (cultural)," *Wikipedia* (accessed September 9, 2019).

2 Quote by Thich Nhat Hanh, narrated by Benedict Cumberbatch, in film *Walk With Me* (Dir. Marc James Francis, Max Pugh, 2017), derived from *Fragrant Palm Leaves,* a journal of Thich Nhat Hanh from 1962 to 1964.

3 Emanuele Coccia. *The Life of Plants: A Metaphysics of Mixture* (Cambridge, UK and Medford, USA: Polity Press, 2019), 67.

4 Ibid. 55, 57.

5 Ibid. 66.

Chapter 35

1 I dedicate this piece to the memory of Carlos Celdran (1972–2019), cultural activist and Manila's modern paramour. His artwork, *Living La Vida Imelda,* inspired my reflections on the Marcos era. I thank the editors of this for the opportunity to share this botanical romance. David K.E. Cleary provided editorial insight during the cobbling of this piece. To Hermes G. Gutierrez I deliver this writing—one of several, I hope, to preserve your stories.

2 Ferdinand Marcos, "The Revolution from the Center: The Ideological Base of the New Republic," in *The New Philippine Republic: A Third World Approach to Democracy,* 239–266 (Manila: Marcos Foundation, 1982).

3 Ferdinand Marcos, "Science and Technology: Towards Modernization," in *The New Philippine Republic: A Third World Approach to Democracy,* 163–178 (Manila: Marcos Foundation, 1982).

4 Rodolfo Mallari, "New Philippine lily named after First Lady," *Bulletin Today,* September 18, 1974.

5 E.P. Patanñe, "One of its kind: Mysterious Imelda Lily," June 22, 1975.

6 Hermes G. Gutierrez, "*Tricyrtis imeldae,* a new Philippine lily," *Philippine Journal*

of Science 103, no. 3 (September 1974): 171–73.

[7] Robin Hemley, *Invented Eden: The Elusive, Disputed History of the Tasaday* (New York: Farrar, Straus and Giroux: 2003), 74–76.

[8] Douglas E. Yen and Hermes G. Gutierrez, "The Ethnobotany of the Tasaday: The Useful Plants," *Philippine Journal of Science* 103, no. 2 (June 1974): 97–139.

[9] Hermes G. Gutierrez, *An Illustrated Manual of the Philippine Materia Medica,* Volume I (Manila: National Research Council of the Philippines, 1980), iii. I grapple with how medicinal Philippine plants have been deployed for political and nationalist aims in the twentieth century, not only by my father but by other plant scientists as well. For further reading, see Kathleen Cruz Gutierrez, "Rehabilitating Botany in the Postwar Moment: National Promise and the Encyclopedism of Eduardo Quisumbing's *Medicinal Plants of the Philippines* (1951)," *Asian Review of World Histories* 6, no.1 (2018): 33–67.

[10] David Hyndman, "Indigenous Representation of the T'boli and the Tasaday Lost Tribe Controversy in Postcolonial Philippines: Interpreting the Eroticised, Effeminising Gaze in *National Geographic,*" *Social Identities* 8, no. 1 (2002): 45–66; Levita Duhaylungsod and David Hyndman, *Where T'Boli Bells Toll: Political Ecology Voices behind the Tasaday Hoax* (Copenhagen: International Work Group for Indigenous Affairs, 1993).

[11] Talitha Espiritu, "Native subjects on display: reviving the colonial exposition in Marcos' Philippines," *Social Identities* 18, no. 6 (2012): 743.

[12] Thomas N. Headland, "What are Plant Specifics?–A Critique of Olofson's Search for the Tasaday," *Philippine Quarterly of Culture and Society* 18, no.1 (1990): 28

[13] Ching-I Peng, Choon-Lin Tiang, and Tsai-Wen Hsu, "*Tricyrtis ravenii* (Liliaceae), a new species from Taiwan," *Botanical Studies* 48 (2007): 357-64.

[14] Dennis Carey and Tony Avent, "Tricyrtis–Perennial Toad Lilies for the Woodland Garden," *Plant Delights Nursery, Inc.,* https://www.plantdelights.com/blogs/articles/tricyrtis-toad-lily-bulbs-hirta, published March 2010. Accessed October 10, 2019.

Chapter 36

[1] Politi, M., G. Saucedo Rojas, T. Rumlerova, O. Marcus, J. Torres Romero, and J. Mabit, "Medicinal plants diet as emerging complementary therapy from the Amazonian tradition. Data from Centro Takiwasi, a Peruvian therapeutic community." *Journal of Medicinal Herbs and Ethnomedicine* 5, (2019): 23-28.

[2] Friso, F. and M. Politi, "Biodiversity conservation in a wild therapeutic garden; the case of Takiwasi center botanical reserve in the peruvian high-amazon." *Horticulture International Journal* 3, no. 2 (2019): 41-44.

[3] Politi, M., F. Friso, and J. Mabit, "Plant based assisted therapy for the treatment of substance use disorders - part 1. The case of Takiwasi Center and other similar experiences." *Revista Cultura y Droga* 23, no. 26 (2018): 99-126.

[4] Van Beek, T. and R. Verpoorte, "Phytochemical investigation of tabernaemontana undulata." *Fitoterapia* 56, no. 5 (1985): 304-07.

[5] Lavaud, C. and G. Massiot, "The Iboga Alkaloids." *Progress in the Chemistry of Organic Natural Products* 105, (2017): 89-136.

Chapter 37

[1] Terence Brown, et al., "The complex origins of domesticated crops in the Fertile Crescent," *Trends in Ecology & Evolution* 24, no. 2 (2009): 103-9, https://doi.org/10.1016/j.tree.2008.09.008.

[2] For discussion on this vast topic, see for examples: Greg Wadley, and Brian Hayden, "Pharmacological Influences on the Neolithic Transition," *Journal of Ethnobiology* 35, no. 3 (2015): 566-84, https://doi.org/10.2993/etbi-35-03-566-584.1; Greg Wadley, "How psychoactive drugs shape human culture: A multidisciplinary perspective," *Brain Research Bulletin* 126, no.1 (2016): 138–51, http://dx.doi.org/10.1016/j.brainresbull.2016.04.008; Paola Bressan, and Peter Kramer, "Bread and Other Edible Agents of Mental Disease," *Frontiers in Human Neuroscience* 10, (2016): 130, https://doi.org/10.3389/fnhum.2016.00130.

[3] Although now obsolete, in 1704 the word civilization referred to a law, which made a criminal process, civil. Also, see Glenn Davis Stone, "Commentary: New histories of the Indian Green Revolution," *The Geographical Journal* 185, (2019): 243–50, https://doi.org/10.1111/geoj.12297.

[4] Gerard Emilien, et al., "Dopamine receptors—physiological understanding to therapeutic intervention potential," *Pharmacology & Therapeutics* 84, no. 2 (1999): 133–56, https://doi.org/10.1016/S0163-7258(99)00029-7; Lazaros C Triarhou, "Dopamine and Parkinson's Disease," in *Madame Curie Bioscience Database [Internet],* (Landes Bioscience, 2000-2013), www.ncbi.nlm.nih.gov/books/NBK6271/

[5] Anna Sapone, et al., "Spectrum of gluten-related disorders: consensus on new nomenclature and classification," *BMC Medicine* 10, (2012): 13, https://doi.org/10.1186/1741-7015-10-13; see also, Elena Lionetti, et al., "Gluten Psychosis: Confirmation of a New Clinical Entity," *Nutrients* 7, no. 7 (2015): 5532–39, https://doi.org/10.3390/nu7075235.

[6] Both endorphins and exorphins are opioid peptides. Endorphins are "naturally released in the brain to reduce pain, and in large amounts can make you feel relaxed or full of energy." (according to Cambridge Dictionary). Exorphins are food-derived and capable of interacting with our opiate receptors.

[7] Lauren Janes, "Selling rice to wheat-eaters: the colonial lobby and the promotion of pain de riz during and after the First World War," *Contemporary French Civilization* 38, no. 2 (2013): 179–200, https://doi.org/10.3828/cfc.2013.9; and also, Blake Smith, "Starch wars: Rice, bread and South Asian difference in the French Enlightenment," *French Cultural Studies* 26, no. 2 (2015): 130–39, https://doi.org/10.1177/0957155815571521.

[8] For a review of the topic, see Muhammad Atif Randhawa, Anwaar Ahmed, and Muhammad Sameem Javed, "Wheat Contaminants (Pesticides) and their Dissipation during Processing," in *Wheat and Rice in Disease Prevention and Health: Benefits, Risks and Mechanisms of Whole Grains in Health Promotion,* eds. Ronald R. Watson, et al., (Elsevier Science & Technology, 2014), 263-77. On neonicotinoid insecticides specifically, see Wenchao Han, et al., "Human exposure to neonicotinoid insecticides and the evaluation of their potential toxicity: An overview," *Chemosphere* 192 (2018): 59-65, https://doi.org/10.1016/j.chemosphere.2017.10.149; Andria Cimino, et al., "Effects of Neonicotinoid Pesticide Exposure on Human

Health: A Systematic Review," *Environmental Health Perspectives* 125, no. 2 (2017): 155-62, http://dx.doi.org/10.1289/EHP515; Margaret R. Douglas, and John F. Tooker, "Large-Scale Deployment of Seed Treatments Has Driven Rapid Increase in Use of Neonicotinoid Insecticides and Preemptive Pest Management in US Field Crops," *Environmental Science & Technology* 49, no. 8 (2015): 5088-97, https://doi.org/10.1021/es506141g; Erik Stokstad, "Pesticides Under Fire for Risks to Pollinators?" Science 340, no. 6133 (2013): 674-76, https://doi.org/10.1126/science.340.6133.674.

[9] While global agro-industrial politics is also well-embodied by other grains, wheat remains a "special" case. The global production of corn, for example, dwarfs the production of wheat. However, only a small proportion of corn goes to human consumption worldwide, with the rest being used for animal feed and industrial purposes. On the other hand, 80% of the over 700 million metric tons of wheat produced yearly goes to human consumption. Stopping consuming wheat means putting a stick on the wheel of an agro-industrial complex designed by private interests and propagated through genetic patenting and the necessary application of toxic chemicals with little or no regard to the effect on human health and the planet.

[10] It is a loss of reverence and ceremony in our relationship with plants that turns them into poison. Like with many others including tobacco and corn, the toxicity of wheat speaks volumes of our abusive role within the human relationship with the vegetal. Their toxicity reveals what we have turned these plants into; highly addictive and harmful "commodities", objects which have little to do with the plants themselves, who can no longer nurture us. Then, the poisonous element here is not (only) the plant itself but the feedback between our consumption of these plants and the growth and demands of the agroindustry.

Poem 13

1 "Eåmtis" is the Chamoru word for a traditional healer who gathered and prepared native plants as "åmot," or medicine. Chamorus are the indigenous peoples of the Marianas archipelago, where I am originally from. Chamorus are also referred to as i taotao tano, the people of the land ("i taotao" translates as "the people" and "i tano" as "the land"). In Chamoru epistemology, plants are considered our ancestors, and are sometimes referred to as "saina," which means "parent" and "elder." Colonial western medicine and hospitals displaced the eåmtis tradition, US militarization polluted our lands and waters, fragmented the jungle, and endangered native medicinal plants. Today, Chamoru people suffer from high rates of cancer and diabetes. In response, a new generation of eåmtis are relearning the practice of åmot to heal our people and advocate for the protection of the environment.

Chapter 39

[1] See Luis Eduardo Luna's entry in this book under "Ayahuasca" (Chapter 2).

Chapter 40

[1] The text is based on personal experience, and the quotes do not represent the

position of any particular Indigenous group. These quotes are translations from Spanish of selected excerpts of my field notes in the Putumayo region, Colombian Amazon (2011-2019).

2 Belaunde, L.E. and Echeverri, J.A. "El yoco del cielo es cultivado: perspectivas sobre *Paullinia yoco* en el chamanismo airo-pai (secoya-tucano occidental)." *Anthropologica*, 26, no. 26 (2008): 87-111

3 I will use the Spanish "*abuelo*" throughout the text instead of the English term "elder" in order to acknowledge the local dignity of this position of moral, political, and shamanic authority.

4 Weiss, L. and Kearns, J. "Caffeine and theobromine analysis of *Paullinia yoco*, a vine harvested by Indigenous peoples of the upper Amazon." *Tropical Resources*, 34 (2015). In https://tri.yale.edu/publications/tropical-resources-bulletin/tri-bulletin-archive/tropical-resources-vol-34/caffeine-and (Dec. 24, 2019); see also R.E. Shultes and Killip, "Paullinia yoco." In https://pfaf.org/user/Plant.aspx?Latin-Name=Paullinia+yoco (Dec. 22, 2019).

5 On thinking forests, see Eduardo Kohn, *How Forests Think* (Berkeley: University of California Press, 2013)

6 By *Hugo Jamioy Juagibioy* Indigenous Kamentza poet, weaver, and practitioner from upper Putumayo, Colombian Amazon. *In Jamioy H. and Apushana V., (2013) Bonito debes pensar: luego bonito debes hablar.* Sudamericana, Bogota.

7 My translation

8 My translation from the Spanish expression "*para [botar] la pereza y [purgar] la rabia*" in Belaunde and Echeverry 2008, p 107

9 For discussion on the topic, see Varela, F.; Thompson, E., and Rosch, E. *The Embodied Mind. Cognitive Science and Human Experience.* (Cambridge, Mass: MIT, 1992); and Francisco Varela, *Ethical know-how: Action, Wisdom, and Cognition.* (Stanford: Stanford University Press, 1999)

10 The idea of *learning to learn* can be found, for example, in the work of Anishinaabe legal scholar Aaron Mills. See Mills, A. (2019). *Miinigowiziwin: All That Has Been Given for Living Well Together One Vision of Anishinaabe Constitutionalis.* PhD dissertation, University of Victoria.

11 On the Amerindian notion of "cooling down" (*enfriar*) with the help of plants like tobacco, see Echeverry, J.A., and "Kinerai" Candre, H. *Tabacoo Frio. Coca Dulce.* (Leticia: Universidad Nacional-Sede Amazonos, 2008)

12 On the notion of *perspectivism* see the work of Vivieros de Castro. *For example,* Vivieros de Castro, E. *"Cosmological Diexis and Amerindian Perspectivism," in Journal of the Royal Anthropological Institute,* 4 no. 3 (1998):469-489.

Special thanks to the Inga and Cofán peoples of Colombia. Also, to COLCIENCIAS and the Leadership for the Ecozoic program for their support. Special thanks to Monica Gagliano and John Ryan for their insightful comments.

Sabina Aguilera is a Mexican ethnologist who has been working for more than twenty years among the Ralámuli people living in northern Mexico. She obtained her academic degrees in Mexico, Holland, and Germany. Currently she is an independent researcher living in Berlin, but still working and learning among the Ralámuli. Her main research topics are textiles, iconography, worldview, stories, and landscape perceptions. Most recently, she has focused on Indigenous plant knowledge. Given the environmental crisis and the fragmented Western perception and relationship with the world, her intention is to contribute to alternative ways of being and thinking that, together with other leading researchers' work, might open pathways that can generate radical mind shifts.

Afshin Akhtar-Khavari is an international law scholar who studies and writes about the ontologies of environmental law, and is interested in legal responses to damage, destruction, and extinction. He uses a range of disciplines and approaches to explore how the natural world is socially, culturally, and politically significant for the way that environmental law functions and prioritizes itself. His more recent work has been shaped by thinking about recovery and restoration of ecosystems as techniques for dealing with damage and helping human beings to develop and train themselves to establish more cooperative relationships with the natural world. He is currently working on a book studying the potential role for the law in helping socio-ecological landscape to flourish.

Khairani Barokka is a Minang-Javanese writer and artist from Jakarta, Indonesia, whose work has been presented in sixteen countries. Her work focuses on disability justice as anti-colonial praxis. She is currently Research Fellow at UAL's (University of the Arts London) Decolonising Arts Institute, UK Associate Artist at Delfina Foundation, and Associate Artist at the National Center for Writing (UK). Among her honors, she has been *Modern Poetry in Translation*'s Inaugural Poet-in- Residence, a UNFPA Indonesian Young Leader Driving Social Change, an *Artforum* Must-See for work in her *Annah, Infinite* series, and a New York University Tisch Departmental Fellow. She is co-editor of two anthologies, most recently Stairs and Whispers: D/deaf and Disabled Poets Write Back (Nine Arches), and her books are *Indigenous Species* (Tilted Axis), *Rope* (Nine Arches) and her latest, poetry collection *Ultimatum Orangutan* (Nine Arches, 2021).

Tamryn Bennett is a poet and Artistic Director of Red Room Poetry. Her bilingual poetry collection phosphene is published by Rabbit Poet Series. A second collection icaros is forthcoming. She is the editor of *Líneas en Tierra/Lines in Land,* a collection of Mexican poems in translation. Tamryn is co-creator of the "plant symphony" and has exhibited work in Australia and internationally with residences in the Royal Botanic Gardens, Kew, Bundanon Trust, Royal Botanic

Garden Sydney, and El Centro de Cultura, Mexico. For more information: https://tamrynbennett.com.

Damiano Benvegnù is an environmental humanities scholar who teaches at Dartmouth College, USA. He is also an Associate Fellow of the Oxford Center for Animal Ethics and the Creative Writing and Visual Art Editor for *Ecozon@: European Journal for Literature, Culture, and the Environment*. Author of *Animals and Animality in Primo Levi's Work* (Palgrave Macmillan, 2018) and of several articles ranging from minority languages to soundscape ecology, Damiano's research focuses on the interaction between the arts, the environmental humanities, and the digital humanities. He is currently developing an augmented reality thick-map for a forest in Enfield, New Hampshire.

Renata Buziak is an ECO Harmony Guide, biochrome artist, researcher, and educator working at the nexus of art and science in close relationship with nature. Her research is based in plant life, and photography, which she learned and taught at Griffith University and other institutions in Queensland Australia. By bending the rules of traditional photography where she let the photographic materials interact with organic matter Renata developed her process of creating art, which she calls the biochrome, that helps her, and others connect with nature. Renata's biochromes have been displayed in solo and group exhibitions, nationally and internationally. She has received a number of awards for her work, and it is featured in private and public collections. Renata's innovative process led her to work with homeowners, business owners and leaders to help enhance the experience of their spaces in Harmony with the natural world. Currently, as the ECO Harmony Guide, she takes her clients on a journey of becoming ECO Harmony Leaders. For more information: https://renatabuziak.com/.

James Cahill Jr is a professor of ecology at the University of Alberta, Canada. His work attempts to integrate how plant decision-making alters species coexistence and patterns in biodiversity. This line of research has highlighted how behavioral ecological theory, developed primarily for mobile animals, is a very good starting point for understanding the social lives of plants. Over the last twenty plus years, he has trained numerous graduate and undergraduate students in experimental plant ecology, and offered a different perspective than expressed by the common ecological paradigms. He is also actively engaged in science communication, with a focus on using a data-driven approach to enhance public understanding. He may be most well-known for his work as the lead scientist on a widely viewed documentary about plant behavior, *What Plants Talk About* (PBS Nature and Smarty Plants, CBC Nature of Things). To date, those films have been viewed in excess of 2,000,000 times, indicating a public fascination with the biology of plants. For more information: https://grad.biology.ualberta.ca/cahill.

Esthela Calderón was born in Telica, Nicaragua. She is a poet and visual artist whose most recent books include the bilingual anthology of her selected poetry

The Bones of My Grandfather (2018) and *Paper Beehive* (2021), both published by Amargord Ediciones in Madrid. Her poetry has been anthologized in *El consumo de lo que somos: muestra de poesía ecológica hispánica contemporánea*, *Ghost Fishing: An Eco-Justice Poetry Anthology* and *The Latin American Eco-Cultural Reader*. She has published in the journals *World Literature Today* (University of Oklahoma) and *ISLE*. Her work as an artist was featured at the gallery in the Municipal Building of St. Lawrence County in Potsdam, New York, as well as the Brush Art Gallery. She has worked as an Adjunct Instructor in the Department of Modern Languages, St. Lawrence University.

María Luisa Chacarito was born in Ojachichi (*ojachi* is the name of a mushroom), a small ranch in southwestern Ralámuli territory. At a young age, she began seasonal movement with her parents between their ranch and different urban areas. At some point, she established herself in Chihuahua City, where she was for nine years the main authority of a Ralámuli settlement. Today she works independently together with other Ralámuli women selling their crafts.

Sophie Chao is an environmental anthropologist and multispecies ethnographer whose research explores the intersections of Indigeneity, ecology, and capitalism in the Pacific. She is currently a Postdoctoral Research Associate at the University of Sydney's School of Philosophical and Historical Inquiry. Sophie has carried out long-term ethnographic fieldwork among Marind in Indonesian West Papua and examined how the destruction of biodiverse forests radically undermines the moral, emotional, material, and cultural ties between sago palms and Indigenous communities. Prior to her academic career, Sophie worked for human rights organization Forest Peoples Programme, supporting Indigenous communities in defending their rights to land in the face of state and corporate interests. Outside of work, Sophie enjoys listening to the voices of the forest and making friends with trees—just as Marind taught her to. For more information: www.morethanhumanworlds.com.

Stuart Cooke is a poet, scholar, and translator. His books include the poetry collections *Lyre* (2019), *Opera* (2016), and *Edge Music* (2011), as well as the critical monograph, *Speaking the Earth's Languages: A Theory for Australian-Chilean Postcolonial Poetics* (2013). He has also translated Gianni Siccardi's *The Blackbird* (2018) and *George Dyungayan's Bulu Line* (2014), and he is the co-editor of *Transcultural Ecocriticism: Global, Romantic, and Decolonial Perspectives* (2021). Stuart is the recipient of numerous awards and grants, and has been a fellow at the Atlantic Center for the Arts (under Joy Harjo), Djerassi Resident Artists Program, and Omi International Arts Center, among others. In 2020, he was a BR Whiting Fellow in Rome, Italy. His current projects include the exploration of ethological poetics (or, practices of articulation, composition, and/or expression in a variety of plant and animal species), and the development of a transcultural poetics in southern Chile with leading Huilliche-Mapuche poet Juan Paulo Huirimilla. He is a Senior Lecturer in Creative Writing and Literary Studies at Griffith University in Brisbane, Australia.

Joseph Dumit is an anthropologist of passions, improvisation, brains, games, bodies, drugs, and facts. His research and teaching ask how exactly we came to think, do, and speak the way we do about ourselves and our world. He asks, what are the actual material ways in which we come to encounter facts, conspiracies, and things and take them to be relevant to our lives and our futures? He serves as Chair of Performance Studies, and is Professor of Science and Technology Studies, and of Anthropology at the University of California, Davis. He is the author of *Picturing Personhood: Brain Scans and Biomedical America* (Princeton 2004), *Drugs for Life: How Pharmaceutical Companies Define Our Health* (Duke 2012), and co-editor of *Cyborgs and Citadels; Cyborg Babies; and Biomedicine as Culture*. He drinks a lot of coffee. For more information: http://dumit.net.

Anne Elvey lives on Boonwurrung Country in Seaford, Victoria, Australia. Author of *Obligations of Voice* (2021), *On arrivals of breath* (2019), *White on White* (2018), *Kin* (2014), and co-author of *Intatto/Intact* (with Massimo D'Arcangelo and Helen Moore, 2017), she is managing editor of *Plumwood Mountain: An Australian Journal of Ecopoetry and Ecopoetics*. She also curated the ebook *hope for whole: Poets Speak up to Adani* (2018). Anne is an Adjunct Research Fellow, School of Languages, Literatures, Cultures, and Linguistics, Monash University, and Honorary Research Associate, Trinity College Theological School, University of Divinity, Melbourne. Author of *The Matter of the Text: Material Engagements between Luke and the Five Senses* (2011), she is coeditor, with Keith Dyer and Deborah Guess, of *Ecological Aspects of War: Engagements with Biblical Texts* (2017). Anne's most recent scholarly book is *Reading the Magnificat in Australia: Unsettling Engagements* (2020).

Martín Espada was born in Brooklyn, New York in 1957. He has published more than twenty books as a poet, editor, essayist, and translator. His new book of poems from Norton is called *Floaters*. Other books of poems include *Vivas to Those Who Have Failed* (2016), *The Trouble Ball* (2011), *The Republic of Poetry* (2006), *Alabanza* (2003), *A Mayan Astronomer in Hell's Kitchen* (2000), *Imagine the Angels of Bread* (1996), *City of Coughing and Dead Radiators* (1993), and *Rebellion is the Circle of a Lover's Hands* (1990). He is the editor of *What Saves Us: Poems of Empathy and Outrage in the Age of Trump* (2019). His many honors include the Ruth Lilly Poetry Prize, the Shelley Memorial Award, the Robert Creeley Award, the National Hispanic Cultural Center Literary Award, an American Book Award, an Academy of American Poets Fellowship, the PEN/Revson Fellowship, and a Guggenheim Fellowship. *The Republic of Poetry* was a finalist for the Pulitzer Prize. His book of essays and poems, *Zapata's Disciple* (1998), was banned in Tucson as part of the Mexican-American Studies Program outlawed by the state of Arizona, and reissued by Northwestern University Press. A former tenant lawyer, Espada is a Professor of English at the University of Massachusetts-Amherst.

Luke Fischer is a poet and philosopher. He is the author of the poetry collections *A Personal History of Vision* (UWA Publishing, 2017) and *Paths of Flight* (Black

Pepper, 2013), the monograph *The Poet as Phenomenologist: Rilke and the New Poems* (Bloomsbury, 2015), and the children's book *The Blue Forest* (Lindisfarne Books, 2015). He is a co-editor of *Rilke's Sonnets to Orpheus: Philosophical and Critical Perspectives* (Oxford University Press, 2019), *The Seasons: Philosophical, Literary and Environmental Perspectives* (State University of New York Press, forthcoming), and a special issue of the *Goethe Yearbook* (2015) on "Goethe and Environmentalism." He frequently collaborates in events with other writers, musicians, and artists, and is an Honorary Associate of the Philosophy Department at the University of Sydney. For more information: www.lukefischerauthor.com.

Rachel Gagen is a Western herbal medicine therapist, facilitator of rites of passage, forager, medicine maker, traditional body worker, and musician. Co-founder of Mulai Lagi Iboga, an addiction interruption and psychospiritual retreat service in Indonesia, she works with matters of healing and sickness, utilizing relationship, and herbal medicine as a mechanism of reconnection with the Self. She has been initiated into the Bwiti sect Mabanji, a living and growing feminine Gabonese tradition that utilizes Iboga as a sacrament of transition and embodiment teacher. Her interest in ethnobotany has led her to pockets of Indigenous cultures across the globe to learn from their relationships with plants, including their use of specific styles of music for enhanced communication and integration while in shamanic spaces. She works from the Sunshine Coast, Australia, as a health practitioner, teacher, and musician. For more information: www.entheobotanica.org.

Monica Gagliano is a Research Associate Professor in Evolutionary Ecology and former Fellow of the Australian Research Council. Monica is also a Research Affiliate at the Sydney Environment Institute at the University of Sydney and an Adjunct Associate Professor at the University of Western Australia. She is currently based at Southern Cross University, Australia, where she directs the Biological Intelligence (BI) Lab funded by the Templeton World Charity Foundation. She has pioneered the brand-new research field of plant bioacoustics, for the first time experimentally demonstrating that plants emit their own "voices" and detect and respond to the sounds of their environments. Her work has extended the concept of cognition, including perception, to learning processes and memory in plants. Her latest book is *Thus Spoke the Plant* (North Atlantic Books, 2018). For more information: www.monicagagliano.com

Juan Carlos Galeano is a poet and environmentalist born in the Amazon region of Colombia. He has published several books of poetry and has translated North American poets into Spanish. Over a decade of fieldwork on symbolic narratives of riverine and forest people in the Amazon basin resulted in his production of a comprehensive collection of storytelling *Folktales of the Amazon* (ABC-CLIO, 2008) and the documentary films *The Trees Have a Mother* (Films for the Humanities and Sciences, 2008), and *El Río* (2019, Gaia Award, USA). His poetry inspired by Amazonian cosmologies and the modern world (*Amazonia*, 2003, 2011, and *Yakumama and Other Mythical Beings*, 2014), has been anthologized and published in international journals such as *Casa de las Américas* (Cuba), *Poesia* (Italy/Europe), *The Atlantic Monthly*, and *Ploughshares* (USA). He continues to lead field work and service learning journeys to the Amazon Basin with scholars and students from several universities in the States. He lives in Tallahassee, Florida, where he teaches at Florida State University Latin American poetry and cultures of Amazonia. For more information: myweb.fsu.edu/jgaleano.

Chelinay Gates (Malardy) is a Doctor of Traditional Chinese Medicine, a practitioner of Hypnosis and Esoteric Acupuncture, as well as a professional artist and Aboriginal author. Known for her light-filled, impressionist works, Chelinay has won numerous prizes and was awarded "Female Artist of the Year" in Australia in 1990. She writes for film, television, and theater, and her latest book, *Lucky-Child: The Secret* (Tellwell Talent, 2019), was winner of the prestigious 2020 Next Generation Indie Book Award (for fiction and best first novel). Inspired by her father and other Indigenous elders, she has also been involved in issues of social justice, community services, and protection of sacred sites. For more information: www. lucky-child.com.au.

Alex K. Gearin is an anthropologist from Australia who spends most of his time researching the Amazonian shamanic brew ayahuasca. He has conducted research in Peru, Australia, and China on the use of ayahuasca by Indigenous and Western cultures and is the co-editor of the book *The World Ayahuasca Diaspora*. He is the founder of the online ayahuasca learning hub Kahpi.net, which teaches courses by ayahuasca scholars, scientists, and therapists. He is an Assistant Professor of anthropology at Xiamen University, China.

Prudence Gibson is author of the Critical Plant Studies series book *The Plant Contract* (Brill Rudopi, 2018) and lead investigator of a major environmental aesthetics grant project 2020–23, in partnership with the Sydney Botanic Gardens Herbarium. She is Postdoctoral Research Fellow at the University of New South Wales, Sydney. Her particular field of study interrogates the crossover of plant life and art/narrative, and how this energetic interaction can improve human perception of vegetal life. She is author of several other monographs such as *The Rapture of Death* (2010) and *Janet Laurence: The Pharmacy of Plants* (New South Publishing, 2015). She co-edited *Aesthetics After Finitude* (Re.press, 2016) and *Covert Plants* (Punctum Books, 2018). She has also published over three-hundred-and-fifty essays and articles for *Art & Australia*, *The Conversation*, *Art Monthly*, etc., and has written many essays for art catalogues.

Kathleen Cruz Gutierrez is Assistant Professor in the Department of History at the University of California, Santa Cruz, where she teaches courses on the Philippines and modern Southeast Asia. She obtained a PhD in Southeast Asian Studies with a Designated Emphasis in Science and Technology Studies at the University of California, Berkeley. Her writing and research have contributed to the history of modern Philippine botany, scholarship on Itneg textile production, Philippine STS, and the environmental humanities of the Asia-Pacific region.

Joela Jacobs is Assistant Professor of German Studies at the University of Arizona and founded the Literary and Cultural Plant Studies Network (https://plants.arizona.edu/). Her research focuses on 19th–21st century German literature and film, animal studies, environmental humanities, Jewish studies, the history of sexuality, and the history of science. She is currently working on a monograph entitled *Animal, Vegetal, Marginal: Being (Non)Human in German Modernist Grotesques*, in which plants are agents in the creation and disruption of human identity re-production. She has published articles on monstrosity, multilingualism, literary censorship, biopolitics, animal epistemology, zoopoetics, phytopoetics, cultural environmentalism, and contemporary German Jewish identity.

Megan Kaminski a poet and essayist—and the author of three books of poetry, most recently *Gentlewomen* (Noemi Press, 2020). By exploring ideas of indeterminacy, rootedness, and resilience, her current book project *Withness* uses plant-thinking as a model for response to our current moment and toward the future. Her public-facing work, in the form of the Prairie Divination Deck (with L. Ann Wheeler) and the Ad Astra Writing Project, helps people connect to their own ecosystems for strategies to live in their world, to grieve and heal after loss, and to re-align thinking toward kinship, community, and sustainability. She is an Associate Professor at the University of Kansas specializing in poetry and poetics, ecosomatics, queer ecology, plant studies, nonfiction, and the environmental humanities. Her work is informed by collaborative and interdisciplinary research in social welfare, evolutionary biology, the visual arts, and philosophy, as well as previous work in the healing arts and at non-profit environmental organizations.

Robin Wall Kimmerer is a mother, scientist, Botany professor, and enrolled member of the Citizen Potawatomi Nation. She is the author of *Braiding Sweetgrass: Indigenous Wisdom, Scientific Knowledge, and the Teaching of Plants*, which has earned Kimmerer wide acclaim. Her first book, *Gathering Moss: A Natural and Cultural History of Mosses*, was awarded the John Burroughs Medal for outstanding nature writing, and her other work has appeared in *Orion*, *Whole Terrain*, and numerous scientific journals. She is a SUNY Distinguished Teaching Professor of Environmental Biology, and the founder and director of the Center for Native Peoples and the Environment, whose mission is to create programs that draw on the wisdom of both Indigenous and scientific knowledge for our shared goals of sustainability. As a writer and a scientist, her interests in restoration include not only restoration of ecological communities, but restoration of our relationships to land. She holds a BS in Botany from SUNY College of Environmental Science and Forestry, an MS and PhD in Botany from the University of Wisconsin, and is the author of numerous scientific papers on plant ecology, bryophyte ecology, traditional knowledge, and restoration ecology. She lives on an old farm in upstate New York, tending gardens both cultivated and wild. For more information: www.robinwallkimmerer.com.

John Kinsella is a Fellow of Churchill College, Cambridge University, and Professor Emeritus at Curtin University, but most relevantly he is an anarchist vegan pacifist and environmental activist of over thirty-five years. He often works in collaboration with other poets, writers, artists, musicians, and activists. His most recent volumes of poetry include *Insomnia* (Picador, 2019; WW Norton, 2020), and *Brimstone: Villanelles* (Arc, 2020). His volumes of criticism include *Activist Poetics: Anarchy in the Avon Valley* (Liverpool University Press, 2010) and *Polysituatedness* (Manchester University Press, 2017). He has also written many volumes of fiction and memoir. John Kinsella lives in the Western Australian wheatbelt on Ballardong Noongar land.

Craig Holdrege is co-founder and director of The Nature Institute in Ghent, NY (natureinstitute.org), an organization dedicated to research and educational activities applying phenomenological, contextual methods. He is deeply interested in the interconnected nature of things and how we can understand life in truly living ways as a basis for responsible human action. His studies of plants and animals, as well as his commentaries on scientific thinking and new developments in the biological sciences, aim to stimulate a transformation in human thinking and perception. Craig is the author of many articles, monographs, and books, including *Thinking Like a Plant: A Living Science for Life* and *Do Frogs Come From Tadpoles? Rethinking Origins in Development and Evolution*. He gives talks, workshops, and courses nationally and internationally.

Sarah Laborde is a Research Fellow at the Australian Rivers Institute, Griffith University, Australia. She is a student of the connections between people and water. She has a background in the hydrological sciences as well as the social sciences, and completed a PhD at the University of Western Australia in 2012 with joint affiliations in water resources engineering and environmental anthropology. Her current research projects relate to the notion of "flow" and to the links between water and well-being. Some of her teachers are Nyikina and Gooniyandi custodians of the Warlibiddi and Mardoowarra (Margaret and Fitzroy Rivers, named in Gooniyandi and Nyikina languages respectively) in Northwest Australia.

Janice Lee is a Korean-American writer, editor, and shamanic healer. She is the author of seven books of fiction, nonfiction, and poetry, most recently, *The Sky Isn't Blue* (Civil Coping Mechanisms, 2016), *Imagine a Death* (Texas Review Press, 2021), and *Separation Anxiety* (CLASH Books, 2022). She writes about interspecies communication, plants and personhood, the filmic long take, slowness, the apocalypse, inherited trauma, and the concept of han in Korean culture, and asks the question, "How do we hold space open while maintaining intimacy?" She is Founder and Executive Editor of *Entropy* and Co-Founder of The Accomplices LLC. She currently lives in Portland, Oregon, where she is an Assistant Professor of Creative Writing at Portland State University.

Megan Ljubotina is a plant biologist and horticulturalist who has frequently worked with *Helianthus annuus*, the common sunflower, using it as a model organism to ask questions about how plants seek out nutrients, respond to stress, and interact with other plants belowground. Her work with James F. Cahill Jr. on sunflower root foraging and social behavior has recently been published in an article in *Proceedings of the Royal Society B* (2019).

Luis Eduardo Luna was born in Florencia, Colombia, in 1947. He conducted research on shamanism and the use of sacred plants among the Indigenous and mestizo population of the Peruvian and Colombian. He has a BA from Madrid University (1972), an interdisciplinary Master's degree from Oslo University (1980), and a PhD from the Department of Comparative Religion, Stockholm University (1989). He is a Guggenheim Fellow (1986), a Fellow of the Linnaean Society of London (1989), and is a Doctor Honoris Causa, from St. Lawrence, Canton, New York (2002). Luna is the author of *Vegetalismo: Shamanism among the Mestizo Population of the Peruvian Amazon* (1986), a co-author with Pablo Amaringo of *Ayahuasca Visions: The Religious Iconography of a Peruvian Shaman* (1991), and co-author with Rick Strassman, Slawek Wojtowicsz, and Ede Frecska of *Inner Paths to Outer Space: Journeys Through Psychedelics and Other Spiritual Technologies* (2008). He is co-editor with Steven White of *Ayahuasca Reader: Encounters with the Amazon's Sacred Vine* (2000, 2016). He is director of Wasiwaska, Research Center for the Study of Psychointegrator Plants, Visionary Art, and Consciousness, Florianópolis, Brazil. For more information: www.wasiwaska.org.

Barry MacDonald lives in rural Australia. He envisions his life in terms of relationship rather than achievement, of deep engagement with Land, Ancestors, family, and Story. Barry continues to explore, in writings across a variety of media—poetry, creative non-fiction, and song—the expanding dimensions of his relational experience.

Sally Birch is a freelance writer with a Bachelor of Arts in Russian language and literature and Spanish language, including Latin American history and literature. Her recent work was published in the Australian quarterly cultural periodical *Dumbo Feather*. She is currently a research assistant at the Biological Intelligence (BI) Lab at the School of Environment, Science and Engineering at Southern Cross University, Australia. For more information: sallybirchwriter.com.

Jeremy Narby studied history at the University of Kent at Canterbury, and received a doctorate in anthropology from Stanford University. For the last thirty years, he has coordinated projects in favor of Amazonian people for Swiss NGO Nouvelle Planète, involving land titles, bilingual education, and sustainable forestry. He has written several books including *The Cosmic Serpent, DNA and the Origins of Knowledge* (New York, Penguin Putnam/Tarcher, 1998), and *Intelligence in Nature: An Inquiry into Knowledge* (New York, Penguin Putnam/Tarcher, 2005), and co-edited with Francis Huxley, *Shamans Through Time: 500 Years on the Path to Knowledge* (New York, Penguin Putnam/Tarcher, 2001). He recently co-signed with Rafael Chanchari Pizuri, *Plant Teachers: Ayahuasca, Tobacco, and the Pursuit of Knowledge* (Novato, CA, New World Library, 2021).

Solvejg Nitzke leads the research project "Making Kin with Trees. A Cultural Poetics" (Fremde Verwandtschaft. Eine Kulturpoetik der Bäume) at Technische Universität Dresden in Germany. She was part of the DFG-funded project "Climate's Time" at the University of Vienna and earned her doctorate at Ruhr-University Bochum in 2015 with a thesis on the Tunguska-Event ("Die Produktion der Katastrophe. Das Tunguska-Ereignis und die Programme der Moderne" 2017). She works on proto-ecological knowledge in nineteenth-century countryside-literatures (Precarious Nature); disaster and science fiction; the intersection of story-telling and knowledge production; and ecological thought. Her work on plants focuses on trees and their relationship with and agency in story-telling. The collection *Baum und Text* (in German) was published in 2020.

Guto Nóbrega is an artist and Associate Professor in Art at the School of Fine Arts of the Federal University of Rio the Janeiro, Brazil. He is a Research Fellow in Art and Technology in the postgraduate program in Visual Arts/UnB and PhD (2009) in Interactive Arts by the postgraduate program Planetary Collegium (former CAiiA-STAR), the University of Plymouth, UK. He founded and acts as one of the coordinators of NANO–Núcleo de Arte e Novos Organismos, an academic research lab for investigation and artistic creation on the intercrossing of the domains of art, science, technology, nature, and spirituality. He was the coordinator of the postgraduate program in Visual Arts/EBA/UFRJ (2015–2017) and currently holds a Research Productivity Fellowship CNPq–Level 2.

Kristi Onzik is a doctoral candidate in the University of California Davis program in sociocultural anthropology. Her dissertation research studies a small but growing community of scientists experimenting with the boundaries of the scientifically (un)thinkable: plant thought. Building upon conversations in feminist science studies and a "more-than-human" anthropology, she asks how concepts such as plant cognition, neurobiology, and behavior are being assembled from within the experimental practices of a variety of plant scientists—many of whom are risking their careers on not simply the possibility that plants think, but working from an inner feeling, a "tacit" knowing, that plants have always already been making sense of us; we just need to learn how to listen. She has been a visiting researcher at LINV in Florence, Italy, the MINT lab in Murcia, Spain, the Plant Growth Lab in Seattle, Washington, and is an ongoing collaborator with the Biological Intelligence Lab in New South Wales, Australia, and the Plant Studies Collaboratory.

André G. Parise holds a bachelor's degree in biological sciences from the Federal University of Santa Catarina, in the southern Brazilian city of Florianópolis, and has recently completed his master's degree in plant physiology at the Federal University of Pelotas, in the more-southern-still Pelotas, also in Brazil. In the last years, he has been studying plant cognition, intelligence, and communication, which is a new and fascinating topic of research. He is very fond of science communication and, as much as possible, he is always trying to make science understandable to a general audience.

Craig Santos Perez is an Indigenous Chamoru poet from the Pacific island of Guåhan (Guam). He is the author of five books of poetry and the co-editor of five anthologies. He is a Professor in the English department at the University of Hawai'i, Mānoa.

Matteo Politi has a PhD in natural product chemistry and a specialization in naturopathy. He has more than twenty years of multidisciplinary experience related to herbal medicine, working for several university centers, not-for-profit organizations, and private companies. He is currently a research collaborator at the Takiwasi Center in Peru and at the University of Chieti in Italy. He has a deep passion for all sorts of traditional medicines, especially those orally transmitted from biodiverse cultural contexts. He likes to travel to remote and wild environments, constantly looking for new insights from people and nature. He supports the vitalistic approach to health and the animistic vision of nature. He practices with pleasure herbal medicine as a form of care and learning.

Susan Prescott is a pediatrician, immunologist, and internationally acclaimed physician scientist, well known for her cutting-edge research into the early environmental determinants of health and disease. At the global level, as the Founding President of inVIVO Planetary Health, her work focuses on the interconnections between human health and planetary health, promoting holistic value systems for both ecological and social justice. Locally in Western Australia, she is Director of The ORIGINS Project, which examines how the environment influences all aspects of physical and mental health throughout life. She was also the founding President of the DOHaD Society (Developmental Origins of Health and Disease) of Australia and New Zealand, and previously served as a Director of the World Allergy Organization. Susan has over three-hundred scientific publications. She is also an artist and award-winning author of several books including *The Allergy Epidemic*, *The Calling*, *Origins*, and gold medal-winning book *The Secret Life of Your Microbiome*. Her inspiration to study medicine came from her grandmother, one of the few women to study medicine in the 1930s. For more information: www.drsusanprescott.com; @susanprescott88.

Laura Ruggles is a postgraduate researcher at the University of Adelaide in philosophy of biology and cognitive science, and an avid gardener and macrofungal enthusiast. Informed by psychology and cognitive neuroscience, her research explores the emerging use of plants as model organisms in the cognitive sciences. She looks at how plant research is offering novel insights into the diversity of cognition and how cognitive frameworks offer insights into understanding plant mechanisms. She is interested in how our ways of framing plants and the metaphors that we use as thinking tools constrain the questions we ask about them and the research we do, and how plant theorizing and plant-human relations have changed over time.

John Charles Ryan is an Adjunct Associate Professor at Southern Cross University and an Adjunct Senior Research Fellow at the Nulungu Research Institute, Notre Dame University, Australia. His research interests include contemporary poetry, Southeast Asian literature, ecocriticism, critical plant studies, and the environmental humanities. His latest co-edited book is titled *Australian Wetland Cultures: Swamps and the Environmental Crisis* (2019, Lexington Books, with Li Chen). His textbook *Introduction to the Environmental Humanities* (with J. Andrew Hubbell) is forthcoming with Routledge in 2021. The botanical poetry collection *Seeing Trees: A Poetic Arboretum*, with Western Australian poet Glen Phillips, was published in 2020 by Pinyon Publishing in Colorado. In 2020, he served as Visiting Scholar at the University of 17 August 1945, Surabaya, and Visiting Professor at Brawijaya University, Malang, Indonesia, as well as Writer-in-Residence at Oak Spring Garden Foundation in Virginia.

Kirli Saunders is a proud Gunai Woman and award-winning international writer of poetry, plays, and picture books. She is a teacher, cultural consultant, and artist. In 2020, Kirli was named the New South Wales Aboriginal Woman of the Year. Her books include celebrated *The Incredible Freedom Machines*, *Kindred*, and *Bindi*.

Harriet Tarlo's single author poetry publications are with Shearsman Press and Etruscan books and her artists' books with Judith Tucker are with Wild Pansy Press. Her first volume of the *Cut Flowers* series is out with Guillemot Press in 2021. She is editor of *The Ground Aslant: An Anthology of Radical Landscape Poetry* (2011) and special features on ecopoetics for *How2* and *Plumwood Mountain* and on cross-disciplinary environmental art in *Green Letters*. She is the author of numerous academic essays on poetics, place, and environment, including recent joint essays with Judith Tucker on walking, landscape, and collaboration in special features of *Sociologia Ruralis* and *Critical Survey*. She is Professor of ecopoetry and poetics at Sheffield Hallam University.

Gabriel R. A. de Toledo was born in the west of São Paulo state, Brazil, and always was troubled with the destruction that the region's environment suffered through the years because of greed and ignorance. Willing to learn more about life and its links with human behavior, he started his bachelor's degree in Biological Sciences at the State University of Maringá. However, he completed it at the University of Western São Paulo. Later on, he did his master's degree in Environmental and Regional Development, also in the University of Western São Paulo. He received his PhD at the Federal University of Pelotas, in Rio Grande do Sul state. He has worked with topics related to plant cognition, such as plant behavior, communication, and intelligence. For ecological, educational, and conservation purposes, he always tries to show the importance of considering plants as intelligent beings.

Mauricio Tolosa is an independent writer and photographer. For the last few years, he has been working on arborecer, a multimedia project depicting the interaction and possible communication between plants and human beings. He feels honored to have the chance to get a glance at what could be in the future a shared world, where all life will be respected and cherished. He has worked as a communication expert and international consultant for governments and organizations in different cultures. He has also developed teaching programs for universities and foundations. As a writer, he has published books on communication and science, a novel and two books of poetry. He creates and directs writing workshops, the latest ones being "The Voices of Plants" and "Flourish," which explore new ways of thinking about and expressing our relationship with plants. For more information: www.mauriciotolosa.com.

Giorgia Tresca studied social anthropology and recently completed a master's in environmental anthropology at the University of Kent. Her thesis addressed Amazonian plant healing diets and how they are adopted into European natural and cultural environments. Currently she lives in Italy, takes people on wine and forest tours, and, through her writing, continues to explore how developing a relation to plants may challenge our understanding and stimulate our experience of what it means to be human.

Judith Tucker's work explores the meeting of social history, personal memory, and geography; it investigates their relationship through drawing, painting, and writing. The paintings in this volume are from her ongoing series Dark Marsh, exploring the pioneering salt marsh plants of the Humberston Fitties, Tetney Marsh area, considering plants that are both vulnerable to sea level rise, but that also help to protect the land from flooding. In 2018 and 2019, she was a finalist in the Jackson's Open Painting Prize, third time lucky, in 2020 she won a category prize. In 2020, she was shortlisted for the New Light Art Prize and in 2019 she was shortlisted for the Westmorland Landscape Prize. Other exhibition venues include Arthouse1 and Collyer Bristow, London, and regional galleries throughout the UK, and further afield in Lasi, Romania, Gdansk, Poland, Brno, Czech Republic, Vienna, Austria, Minneapolis, and Virginia, USA, and Yantai, Nanjing and Tianjin in China. She is an invited artist in Contemporary British Painting, a platform for contemporary painting in the UK. She is currently vice-chair of the organization. She co-convenes the networks Land2 and Mapping Spectral Traces. She also writes academic essays, which can be found in academic journals and in books. When she is not in her studio, she is Senior Lecturer in the School of Design at the University of Leeds. She has a long-term collaboration with the poet Harriet Tarlo. For more information: www.judithtuckerartist.com

Iván Darío Vargas Roncancio is a PhD in natural resource sciences at McGill University, and a postdoctoral researcher in the Leadership for the Ecozoic program. He is a lawyer with master's degrees in Bioscience and Law (National University of Colombia, 2012), and Latin American Studies (Duke University, 2016); Junior Specialist (CPPR-UC Davis), and ethnographer (Everyday Peace Indicators-George Mason) and has been a Colciencias scholar (Colombia, 2013), and a FLAS fellow (Foreign Language and Area Studies-PUC São Paulo, 2016).

His research ethnographically follows Indigenous practitioners, scientists, legal scholars, and ritual plants across territories, documents, and courts of justice to contribute to a larger paradigm shift: from reductionist environmental law and governance models to ecological, systems-based, and other-than-human jurisprudence in post-conflict Colombia. Iván asks how forests become legal agents through different sets of practices; how human and other-than-human beings such as Amazonian plants co-produce protocols for forest governance, and how a law that comes from the territory challenges concepts of justice, agency, and value in times of socio-ecological transitions. His interests include Earth Law, Indigenous Law and Cosmologies, Ethnography, and Amazonia.

Patrícia Vieira is Senior Researcher at the Center for Social Studies (CES) of the University of Coimbra, Portugal, and Professor of Spanish and Portuguese at Georgetown University, USA. Her fields of expertise are Latin American and Iberian Literature and Cinema, Utopian Studies and the Environmental Humanities. Her most recent book is *States of Grace: Utopia in Brazilian Culture* (State University of New York Press, 2018). She is currently working on a project on Amazonian animals and plants as co-creators of human cultural productions. For more information: www.patriciavieira.net.

Jonathon Miller Weisberger is an ethnobotanist who has spent the past thirty years studying rainforest plant medicine traditions. Since 1994, he has organized biannual "Rainforest Medicine Councils," experiential workshops and journeys promoting personal, community, and planetary renewal. Participants immerse themselves in an intimate first-hand experiences, meeting and learning from Indigenous elders, cultural adepts, the majesty of the wilderness, and the omnipotent plant teachers themselves. He has collaborated on historic rainforest conservation and cultural heritage revalidation initiatives in the Ecuadorian Amazon, such as the demarcation of the Waorani peoples' ancestral homelands and the demarcation and protection of the isolated limestone massif of Napo-Galeras in the upper Amazon. His passion is plants, and to share them with others! He is the author of *Rainforest Medicine: Preserving Indigenous Science and Biodiversity in the Upper Amazon* and the steward of Ocean Forest Ecolodge in Costa Rica where he lives most of the year.

Steve Whalan is an Associate Professor at Southern Cross University, Australia, with two decades of experience researching life in marine ecosystems. He has published over fifty scientific articles on the ecology of marine invertebrates, with a focus on the behavior of their larvae. He spends his time piecing together the puzzle of marine population maintenance, particularly for sponges and corals—both groups have remarkable biologies, but it is how their motile larvae disperse, and choose their homes, that intrigues him most. As an animal ecologist it is perhaps wacky to write about connections to the "mind of plants," but it is the connection among us all that provides fodder for interesting stories. Here, sponges and corals are intricately entwined with their coralline algae neighbors.

Jessica White is the author of the award-winning *A Curious Intimacy* (Penguin 2007) and *Entitlement* (Penguin 2012), and a hybrid memoir about deafness, *Hearing Maud* (UWA Publishing, 2019). Her short stories, essays, and poems have appeared widely in Australian and international literary journals and have been shortlisted or longlisted for major prizes. Jessica is the recipient of funding from Arts Queensland and the Australia Council for the Arts and has undertaken residencies in Hobart, Rome, and Munich. She is currently working on an ecobiography of Western Australia's first non-Indigenous female scientist, nineteenth-century botanist Georgiana Molloy, as well as a scholarly monograph on the genre of ecobiography.

Steven F. White was guest editor of a special issue on ecology and Latin American literature of *Review: Latin American Literature and the Arts*. He did the bilingual ecocritical study *Seven Trees Against the Dying Light* by Nicaraguan poet Pablo Antonio Cuadra (Northwestern University Press). A second edition for Synergetic Press of his coedited work (with Luis Eduardo Luna) *Ayahuasca Reader: Encounters with the Amazon's Sacred Vine* won an Independent Publishers Book Award. His current research with microscopy specialist Jill Pflugheber is called "Microcosms: A Homage to Sacred Plants of the Americas" and can be viewed here: <https://library.artstor.org/#/collection/100089947;colId=100089947;size=72>. He recently retired from St. Lawrence University after teaching Latin American literature and film as well as Spanish and Portuguese language classes for more than thirty years.

Catherine Wright grew up on a cattle station in northern New South Wales, Australia. She first received a Bachelor of Economics before completing a Bachelor of Arts in Performance and then worked as an actress. Since turning to writing, her poems and creative non-fiction have won or been shortlisted for a number of awards, a Varuna residential fellowship, and been published in literary journals and anthologies in Australia and overseas. She is finishing her first collection *The Consolation of Birds*, and continues to find inspiration especially in the natural world and its power over us. After many years of travel, Catherine has returned to live close to her childhood home in Anaiwan country outside Armidale, NSW.

INDEX

D

T